Clinical Sociolinguistics

Language in Society

GENERAL EDITOR
Peter Trudgill, Chair of English
Linguistics, University of Fribourg

ADVISORY EDITORS
J. K. Chambers, Professor of Linguistics,
University of Toronto

Ralph Fasold, Professor of Linguistics,
Georgetown University

William Labov, Professor of Linguistics,
University of Pennsylvania

Lesley Milroy, Professor of Linguistics,
University of Michigan, Ann Arbor

Clinical Sociolinguistics

Edited by Martin J. Ball

Blackwell Publishing

BLACKWELL PUBLISHING
350 Main Street, Malden, MA 02148-5020, USA
9600 Garsington Road, Oxford OX4 2DQ, UK
550 Swanston Street, Carlton, Victoria 3053, Australia

First published 2005 by Blackwell Publishing Ltd

1   2005

Library of Congress Cataloging-in-Publication Data

Clinical sociolinguistics / edited by Martin J. Ball.
p. cm. — (Language in society ; 36)
Includes bibliographical references and index.
ISBN-13: 978-1-4051-1249-9 (hard cover : alk. paper)
ISBN-10: 1-4051-1249-2 (hard cover : alk. paper)
ISBN-13: 978-1-4051-1250-5 (pbk. : alk. paper)
ISBN-10: 1-4051-1250-6 (pbk. : alk. paper)
1. Sociolinguistics.   2. Speech disorders.   I. Ball, Martin J.
(Martin John)   II. Series: Language in society (Oxford, England)

P40.C547 2005
306.44—dc22
2005004135

A catalogue record for this title is available from the British Library.

Set in 10.5/12.5pt Ehrhardt
by Graphicraft Limited, Hong Kong
Printed and bound in India
by Replika Press

The publisher's policy is to use permanent paper from mills that operate a sustainable forestry
policy, and which has been manufactured from pulp processed using acid-free and elementary
chlorine-free practices. Furthermore, the publisher ensures that the text paper and cover board
used have met acceptable environmental accreditation standards.

For further information on
Blackwell Publishing, visit our website:
www.blackwellpublishing.com

Contents

Notes on Contributors

Martin J. Ball is Hawthorne-BoRSF Endowed Professor, Head of the Department of Communicative Disorders, and Director of the Doris B. Hawthorne Center for Special Education and Communication Disorders at the University of Louisiana at Lafayette. Dr Ball has authored and edited 20 books, 30 contributions to collections and over 60 refereed articles in academic journals. He is co-editor of the journal *Clinical Linguistics and Phonetics*, and associate editor of the *Journal of Multilingual Communication Disorders*. His main research interests include clinical phonetics and phonology, and the linguistics of Welsh. He is currently President of the International Clinical Phonetics and Linguistics Association. His most recent book is *Vowel Disorders* (co-edited with Fiona Gibbon, 2002).

Robert Bayley is Professor of Sociolinguistics in the Division of Bicultural-Bilingual Studies at the University of Texas at San Antonio, where he has taught since 1991. In addition to work on American Sign Language, his publications include *Language as Cultural Practice: Mexicanos en el Norte* (with Sandra Schecter, 2002), *Language Socialization in Bilingual and Multilingual Societies* (ed. with Sandra Schecter, 2003) and *Second Language Acquisition and Linguistic Variation* (ed. with Dennis Preston, 1996).

David Britain is Senior Lecturer in Linguistics at Essex University, UK. His research has mainly focused on the linguistic consequences of dialect contact, much of it examining the new dialect that emerged in the British Fens following seventeenth-century reclamation. He is currently working both on geographical aspects of sociolinguistics (such as the inadequacy of innovation diffusion models in accounting for the spatial spread of linguistic changes), as well as on a project led by Kazuko Matsumoto investigating the birth and death of a colonial dialect of Japanese spoken on Palau in the Western Pacific.

Linda Bryan is Assistant Professor of Communicative Sciences and Disorders at the University of Louisiana at Monroe. She earned a Master's degree in Communicative Sciences and Disorders from Northeastern Louisiana University and a doctorate in Applied Language and Speech Sciences from the University of Louisiana at Lafayette. She has worked as a school-based clinician and as a clinical instructor where she conducted an extensive literacy project. Her research interests include language and literacy, clinical interventions with dyslexic children, and childhood language disorders.

Cynthia G. Clopper received a PhD in Linguistics and Cognitive Science in 2004 from Indiana University. She received a BA in Linguistics and Russian from Duke University in 1999 and a MA in Linguistics from Indiana University in 2001. She is currently a post-doctoral fellow at Indiana University, working under the direction of David Pisoni.

Jack S. Damico is the Doris B. Hawthorne Eminent Scholar in Communication Disorders and Special Education at the University of Louisiana at Lafayette. He earned a Master's degree in Communicative Disorders at the University of Oklahoma Health Sciences Center in 1976 and a doctorate in Linguistics at the University of New Mexico in 1985. His research interests include language as a synergistic phenomenon and language as social action. His primary research focus involves applications of various qualitative research methodologies in communicative sciences and disorders including language and literacy, clinical aphasiology, language disorders in children, attention deficit hyperactivity disorder, and service delivery to multicultural populations.

Barbara Dodd is Professor of Speech and Language Pathology in the School of Education, Communication and Language Sciences, University of Newcastle, UK. Her research interests cover a wide range of topics in speech and language disorder in children. She is author and editor of numerous books and papers, including *Hearing by Eye: The Psychology of Lip-reading* (with Ruth Campbell, 1987), *The Differential Diagnosis and Treatment of Children with Speech Disorder* (1995), *Evaluating Theories of Language* (with Ruth Campbell and Linda Worrall, 1996), and *Hearing by Eye II: Advances in the Psychology of Speech-reading and Auditory-visual Speech* (with Ruth Campbell and Denis Burnham, 1998) and *DEAP: Differential Evaluation of Articulation and Phonology* (with Zhu Hua et al., 2002).

John Edwards received his PhD from McGill University in 1974. After working as a Research Fellow at St Patrick's College, Dublin, he moved to Nova Scotia, where he is now Professor of Psychology at St Francis Xavier University. His research interests are in language and identity. Professor Edwards is on the editorial boards of ten language journals, and is the editor of the *Journal of Multilingual and Multicultural Development*. He also edits a companion series of books. Professor Edwards's own books include *Language in Canada* (1998), *Multilingualism* (1995), *Language, Society and Identity* (1985) and *The Irish Language* (1983). He is also the author of about 200 articles, chapters and reviews.

Martin R. Gitterman is Executive Officer of the PhD Program in Speech and Hearing Sciences at the Graduate Center, City University of New York and a member of the faculty of the Department of Speech-Language-Hearing Sciences at Lehman College. His areas of specialization are second language acquisition and neurolinguistics. His work has appeared in *Brain and Language*, *Aphasiology*, the *Journal of Neurolinguistics*, and the *TESOL Quarterly*. He has been a frequent presenter at local, national, and international conferences.

Jackie Guendouzi is currently Associate Professor of Clinical Linguistics in the Speech Pathology and Audiology Department at the University of South Alabama. She did her doctoral work at the University of Cardiff, Wales, and worked as a senior lecturer in the Speech Pathology Departments at the University of Central England and as Assistant Professor at Southeastern Louisiana University. She has published work on discourse and gender and is currently investigating communication within the context of Alzheimer's disease.

Holly Hawley is a doctoral student in Applied Language and Speech Sciences at the University of Louisiana at Lafayette. She earned a Master's degree in Communicative Sciences and Disorders from Our Lady of the Lake University in San Antonio, Texas. She has worked in various clinical settings and has an interest in language and literacy, therapeutic discourse, and interactional power in intervention settings.

Kim M. Isaac is a speech pathologist who has completed a doctoral dissertation on the interaction between speech–language pathologists and interpreters in clinical practice at the University of Newcastle (Australia). She currently works at the University of Newcastle, Australia, as a clinical supervisor for speech pathology students and as coordinator of the university's speech pathology clinical services.

Arlene Blumenthal Kelly was born deaf to deaf parents, and was raised in Baltimore, Maryland. After graduating from Gallaudet College in 1977, she was a librarian in Tucson, Arizona. She obtained her MA in linguistics from Gallaudet University, Washington, DC, in 1992 while employed as a researcher in the Gallaudet Research Institute. Since 1995, she has been a Deaf Studies Professor at Gallaudet. Her dissertation, completed in 2001 for American Studies at the University of Maryland, is entitled "How Deaf Women Construct Teaching, Language and Culture, and Gender: An Ethnographic Study of ASL Teachers."

Li Wei is Professor of Applied Linguistics and Head of School of Education, Communication and Language Sciences, University of Newcastle, UK. He is author and editor of numerous books and papers on bilingualism, including *Three Generations, Two Language, One Family* (1994), *The Bilingualism Reader* (2000), *Opportunities and Challenges of Bilingualism* (with Jean-Marc Dewaele and Alex House, 2003) and *Bilingualism: Beyond Basic Principles* (with Jean-Marc Dewaele and Alex House, 2003). He is editor of the *Child Language and Child Development* book series for Multilingual Matters and co-editor of the *International Journal of Bilingualism*.

Ceil Lucas is Professor of Linguistics in the Department of Linguistics and Interpretation at Gallaudet University, Washington, DC, where she has taught since 1982. Her publications include *The Linguistics of American Sign Language*, 4th edn (with Clayton Valli and Kristin Mulrooney, 2005), *Language Contact in the American Deaf Community* (with Clayton Valli, 1992), *Sociolinguistic Variation in American Sign Language* (with Robert Bayley and Clayton Valli, 2001), and *What's Your Sign for PIZZA? An Introduction to Variation in American Sign Language* (also with Robert Bayley and Clayton Valli, 2003). She is also the editor of the Gallaudet University Press series, *Sociolinguistics in Deaf Communities*.

Margaret Maclagan specializes in sociolinguistic variation. Her main area of interest is the origins and evolution of New Zealand English, including sound changes in progress. She is a Senior Lecturer in the Department of Communication Disorders, at the University of Canterbury, New Zealand.

Kazuko Matsumoto is Associate Professor of Sociolinguistics at the University of Tokyo, Japan. Her academic interests are on language contact and change. Having completed an ethnographic survey on multilingualism and a social network analysis of language maintenance and shift and an investigation of linguistic hegemony in Micronesia, she is currently researching Japanese dialect contact and obsolescence in Palau and Palauan English, along with David Britain.

Norma Mendoza-Denton is Assistant Professor of Anthropology at the University of Arizona-Tucson. She has variously investigated Latina girls' linguistic and semiotic practices; language, politics, and gesture; and quantitative sociolinguistic variation in varieties of English. She is the author of the book *Homegirls: Symbolic Practices in the Making of Latina Youth Styles*, forthcoming.

Nick Miller is Senior Lecturer in Speech and Language Pathology in the School of Education, Communication and Language Sciences, University of Newcastle, UK. His research interests include speech and language disorders in the multilingual population and acquired neurogenic speech disorders. He is the editor of *Bilingualism and Language Disability* (1984) and author of *Dyspraxia and its Management* (1986). He is co-editor of the *International Journal of Bilingualism*.

Nicole Müller is Associate Professor in Communicative Disorders at the University of Louisiana at Lafayette, and holds a Hawthorne/LEQSF-Regents Endowed Professorship. A native of Germany, she gained an MA from Bonn University, and a DPhil from Oxford University, specializing in Celtic languages. Among her current research interests are bi- and multilingualism, and the communicative effects of dementing conditions, such as Alzheimer's disease, on both patients and their environments. She edits the *Journal of Multilingual Communication Disorders*.

Ryan L. Nelson is Assistant Professor of Communicative Sciences and Disorders at the University of Texas at El Paso. He holds a Master's degree in Communicative Sciences and Disorders from Northern Arizona University and a doctorate in Applied Language and Speech Sciences from the University of Louisiana at Lafayette. He has worked as a school-based clinician and his research interests include childhood language disorders, language and literacy, and phonological impairments. His recent dissertation focused on the natural progression of literacy skills and the affective reactions of language-impaired children as they progressed in reading proficiency as a result of meaning-based literacy instruction.

Janna B. Oetting is Associate Professor in the Department of Communication Sciences and Disorders at Louisiana State University. Her research interests focus on the semantic and morphosyntactic abilities of normally developing children and those with specific language impairment. Since moving to Louisiana in 1992, her research interests have expanded to include children's acquisition of nonmainstream dialects of English and the study of nonbiased assessment tools that speech language clinicians can use to identify children with language impairments.

Janet L. Patterson is Associate Professor of Speech and Hearing Sciences at the University of New Mexico and has a Master's degree in Speech-Language Pathology and a PhD in Educational Linguistics. She has extensive teaching and clinical experience in child language assessment. She has published research on lexical development among Spanish-English bilingual toddlers. Her current research focuses on parent and teacher perceptions of bilingual preschool children's communication.

David B. Pisoni is one of the leading figures in the field of speech perception and spoken language processing. He received a PhD from the University of Michigan in 1971 and did post-doctoral work at MIT under the direction of Kenneth Stevens. He joined the faculty at Indiana University in 1971 and was promoted to Professor of Psychology in 1977 and Chancellors' Professor in 1996. He has been Program Director of the NIH-sponsored training program in Speech, Hearing and Sensory Communication at Indiana University since 1978.

Dennis R. Preston is University Distinguished Professor of Linguistics at Michigan State University. He is a past President of the American Dialect Society and was Director of the 2003 Linguistic Society of America Institute. His most recent work focuses on what real people (i.e., nonlinguists) believe about language and how they respond to it ("folk linguistics" and "language attitudes," respectively) and how minority, second language, and rural groups accommodate to new dialects, particularly the Northern Cities Chain Shift.

Julie Roberts is Associate Professor of Communication Sciences at the University of Vermont. She has published articles in the areas of child language variation, language impairment in children, and New England dialects. She is currently working on a project on Vermont speech and endangered rural dialects and presents frequently on the topics of dialect diversity and multiculturalism and the practice of speech-language pathology.

Gregory C. Robinson is a speech-language pathologist and a doctoral student at Michigan State University focusing on multicultural issues in communication sciences and disorders with a minor in sociolinguistics. He has practiced as a speech-language pathologist in skilled nursing facilities, public schools, and university clinical education programs. He is currently investigating the attitudes and perceptions that practicing speech-language pathologists wittingly or unwittingly carry with them when evaluating children with stigmatized dialects.

Barbara L. Rodríguez is on the faculty of the Speech and Hearing Sciences Department at the University of New Mexico. She has a PhD in Speech-Language Pathology from the University of Washington. Barbara has extensive clinical experience working with bilingual populations. Her research interests include bilingual language development, literacy development, and Hispanic parents' literacy beliefs and practices.

Nina Simmons-Mackie is Professor of Communicative Sciences and Disorders at Southeastern Louisiana University in Hammond Louisiana. She holds a Master's degree in Communicative Sciences and Disorders from Tulane University and a doctorate in Communicative Sciences and Disorders from Louisiana State University. Her research interests include clinical aphasiology, language as discourse, therapeutic discourse, and the social implications of competence and incompetence judgments. Her research activities include experimental, quasi-experimental, and qualitative research applications.

Jennifer Smith is lecturer in language variation and change at the University of York, UK. Her research concerns the morphosyntactic features of non-standard dialects, focusing particularly on Scottish dialects and their relationship to Englishes worldwide. She is currently also investigating the acquisition of linguistic variation among preschool children.

Nicole Taylor is a doctoral candidate in the Department of Anthropology at the University of Arizona. Her dissertation is a qualitative study examining differences among Hispanic and Caucasian adolescent males and females of varying body sizes regarding perceptions of body images, norms, and ideals within the larger context of weight/size-related stigma, attitudes toward physical activity, and attitudes toward food environments in a local high school. Her research interests include linguistic anthropology, medical anthropology, cultural constructions of the body, body image and obesity, adolescent identity construction, and communicative practices within the public school environment.

Humphrey Tonkin edits the journal *Language Problems and Language Planning* and chairs the Center for Research and Documentation on World Language Problems. He is University Professor of Humanities and President Emeritus at the University of Hartford. His recent publications include *Language in the Twenty-first Century* (ed., with Timothy Reagan, 2003) and *Service-Learning Across Cultures* (2004).

Dominic Watt teaches phonetics and sociolinguistics at the University of Aberdeen, Scotland, and his research interests are phonological variation and change, phonological acquisition, and topics in language and identity. He is currently working on a project investigating patterns of phonological variation in north-eastern England. He is the author (with Arthur Hughes and Peter Trudgill) of the fourth edition of *English Accents and Dialects: an Introduction to Social and Regional Varieties of English in the British Isles* (2005).

Walt Wolfram is William C. Friday Distinguished Professor of Linguistics at North Carolina State University. He has authored or co-authored 16 books and more than 250 articles on vernacular varieties of English, including one of the earliest books on African American English; his most recent book (with Erik Thomas) on this variety is *The Development of African American English* (2002).

Zhu Hua is Lecturer in Language and Communication in the School of Education, Communication and Language Sciences, University of Newcastle, UK. Her research interests are in cross-linguistic studies of language acquisition and disorder, and cross-cultural communication. She has published widely in journals such as the *Journal of Child Language*, *Clinical Linguistics and Phonetics*, the *International Journal of Language and Communication Disorder*, the *Journal of Pragmatics*, and *Multilingua*. She is author of *Phonological Development in Specific Contexts* (2002) and *DEAP: Differential Evaluation of Articulation and Phonology* (with Barbara Dodd et al., 2002).

Foreword

The world is so full of a number of things,
I'm sure we should all be as happy as kings.
                    Robert Louis Stevenson, "Happy Thoughts,"
                    A Child's Garden of Verses, *1885*

The natural world is rife with variation, and the human brain is able to both observe and ignore it. We observe variation when we note that one clover in a patch has four instead of three leaves, that a typed page has a typographical error, that this navy-blue item is different in color from that one, that certain speakers sound like they are not from where we are. We ignore variation when we treat a set of different individuals or things as a group: when we include family members who have been adopted into or have married into our family as family, when we overlook typographical errors or speech errors, when we hear allomorphic variants and phonetic variants as instances of the same phoneme. In the first year of life, Werker and Tees (1984) have demonstrated, infants develop from being able to distinguish among all the sounds of the world to being able to ignore those differences that are not meaningful in the language (or, presumably, languages) to which they are exposed.

Although all of us can view the world in both ways, some are more disposed to pull out/abstract patterns from variation, others to note differences. In neuropsychological terms the former are considered holists with, simplistically put, good "right-hemisphere" skills, the latter analytic, with good "left-hemisphere" ones. When asked to identify the letter they see in a pattern like that in Figure 1, the holists are more likely to say "A," the analytic "B."

In science, as in life, both approaches are necessary. One must abstract patterns out of apparent chaos (e.g. in learning a new language, or in analyzing it as a linguist), and one must observe when two things that appear to be similar are in fact different in meaningful ways (e.g. when

Figure 1   An ambiguous image

cognate words in two languages in fact have markedly different meanings, as with Spanish "embarasada" (pregnant) and English "embarrassed"). Over the course of development of a science, one can see periods or schools of thought where the focus is on elucidating patterns and others where the focus is on appreciating individual differences. In neurolinguistics, the late nineteenth century serves as an example of the former, as neurologists observed first what has come to be called "Broca's aphasia," then Wernicke identified a contrasting fluent aphasia that would later bear his name and predicted the existence of conduction aphasia, and so labeling the aphasia syndromes evolved. A century later, another school of thought took the pendulum to its opposite extreme with the argument that any two Broca's aphasics are so different from each other that research must be conducted on individual cases only, or on aphasics chosen for their performance on specific tasks, rather than on groups or subgroups of aphasics. For such researchers, for example, agrammatism is not a syndrome.

When clinicians consider "individual differences," they are generally focusing on the need to treat each client as an individual, with differing language histories and social conditions, and different brain organization that will require individualized therapy. When scientists turn from broad classifications to study "individual differences," however, they are usually looking for sub-categories of prior groups, rather than truly *individual* differences. Thus, they may be looking for gender differences, e.g. in brain organization, expecting that male and female brains may have different, if overlapping, ways of organizing and/or processing cognitive abilities. Groups of different handedness, likewise, may be seen to manifest so-called individual differences, with left-handers, e.g., processing language somewhat differently from right-handers.

For the clinical speech-language pathologist confronted with a client seeking services, what is crucial is the difficult task of observing both how this client shares similarities with the syndrome groups of other patients, and how this client differs from them. Finding the similarities with syndrome groups will lead the clinician to select among appropriate therapeutic approaches those most likely to be effective. At the same time, focusing on the individual permits the clinician to observe what interventions are working and which must be modified in order to be most useful. Taking such a stance is not easy, as our experience with such visual illusions as the Necker cube suggests; it is easy enough to "see" either the one side or the opposite one as the front side, but it is virtually impossible to "see" both at the same time. Perhaps with experience such double vision can be mastered; many of us have mastered bifocals, or even graduated lenses; a few choose to have one eyeglass-lens adjusted for distance viewing and the other for near vision. The newly manifest field of clinical sociolinguistics can provide us with new lenses to refine our vision as both clinicians and researchers.

Loraine K. Obler
Milton, Massachusetts

Preface

The study of the interaction of language and society – sociolinguistics – has had a major impact on linguistics for the past half-century. However, with a few exceptions, this major branch of the language sciences has had little impact on the field of communication disorders. It is the purpose of this collection to go some way toward addressing this lacuna.

There are two possible approaches to making the insights of sociolinguistics available to a speech-language pathology audience: first, through an exposition of the main concerns of the subject; and second, through examples of the application of sociolinguistics to assessment, diagnosis, and intervention. I have followed this bipartite division in constructing this collection of articles by leading experts in the field. The chapters in Part I introduce the primary trends within sociolinguistics since the early studies of the 1950s and the 1960s. To understand the concerns of sociolinguistics, therefore, a reader needs to know about the debates surrounding what a speech community is, before going on to study how such communities structure their linguistic variation (Chapter 1). This initial discussion is followed by a consideration of many of the main social variables determined in sociolinguistic investigations as important correlations to patterns of linguistic variation: regional and social divisions (Chapter 2); gender (Chapter 3); power relations (Chapter 6); and cultural differences (Chapter 7). We also look in detail at bi- and multilingualism (Chapter 4) and the related phenomena of code-switching (switching between language codes) and diglossia (status and usage patterns in multilingual situations) (Chapter 5). An area of study which brings together much of the preceding work is African American English and this topic is given a chapter to itself (Chapter 8); reflecting also the importance of knowledge of this variety for speech-language pathologists.

The remaining chapters in Part I look at broader sociolinguistic interests: language change over time (Chapter 9) and the forces promoting and restraining such change; and language planning (for example, in regard to the maintenance of minority languages) (Chapter 10). The final chapter of Part I deals with the study of the perception of linguistic variation, and the attitudes that members of a speech community have towards the different varieties available to speakers.

Whereas Part I of this collection introduces sociolinguistic research to the speech-language pathology audience, Part II explicitly demonstrates how these research paradigms can be applied to the clinical situation. The chapters here start with those that deal with language acquisition; first, with how linguistic variation is acquired (Chapter 12), and then with language acquisition in bi- and multilingual populations (Chapter 13). These two topics are then followed by two chapters that look explicitly at the challenges to assessment with speakers of non-standard varieties of a language, and with multilingual populations (Chapters 14, 15). The following chapter focuses on the perception and processing of talker-specific features such as identity, gender, and dialect. These issues are described in normal-hearing populations, and then recent findings on hearing-impaired populations are introduced (Chapter 16).

The next two chapters deal specifically with multicultural and multilingual populations, covering characteristics of aphasia in multilinguals (Chapter 17); and the design of assessment materials for multilingual clinical populations (with specific reference here to Hispanic clients) (Chapter 18). The final three chapters deal with specific clinical applications of the insights derived from sociolinguistic research. The area of literacy research is a controversial one, and it is argued here that clinical sociolinguistics is a powerful tool for the remediation of literacy difficulties (Chapter 19). The field of sign language studies is a vast one, and we have space in this collection only to look briefly at the large amount of sociolinguistic work that has been undertaken on American Sign Language (Chapter 20). The final chapter looks in some detail at the practical problems often encountered in the clinic with a linguistically diverse client base. The use of interpreters may throw up problems related to linguistic and cultural differences, and Chapter 21 describes insights into ways to ensure communication and session success.

My hope in putting together this collection is that it will inspire readers to explore the sociolinguistic literature further, to appreciate how much the field has to offer speech-language pathology, and to promote the application of the research paradigms and concerns of sociolinguistics to the fascinating area of communication disorders.

Finally, I would like to thank Brent Wilson for his help with the references, and Mary Lobdell for compiling the indexes.

Martin J. Ball
Lafayette, Louisiana

Part I
Sociolinguistic Research

1

Language, Communities, Networks and Practices

David Britain and Kazuko Matsumoto

Introduction

It is a fundamental tenet of sociolinguistic theory that language structure, in its most consistent and rule-governed state, resides not in the speech of the individual but in the speech of the "community" that binds those individuals together. The view of William Labov – the pioneer of sociolinguistic ap-proaches to language variation – is that the overall patterns of language used by individuals in a community, seen together, show a remarkable clustering around a set of (often variable) language norms – a "grammar" – and that these norms can only be accessed and explored (i.e., the wood can only be seen from the trees) by looking at the community as a whole, rather than looking in turn at each of its (highly heterogeneous) component parts – the speech of individuals (e.g., Labov, 2001: 34). It was his conviction in the community as the locale of grammar that led Labov to explore, in his research on Martha's Vineyard, New York, and subsequently (e.g., Labov, 1963, 1966, 2001), the patterns of language variation and change as they are embedded within class, ethnic, gender and age groups rather than tracing the effects of change among (dislocated) individual speakers.

One question that arises here, however, is "what is a community?" We present here a brief tour of three models of "community" that have been influential in the sociolinguistic literature: (1) "speech communities;" (2) "social networks;" and (3) "communities of practice." Here, we explore the applicability of each model, focusing, in particular, on how two particular studies of the intersection of language with social group formation – one monolingual, one multilingual – could be considered using each of the three approaches.

The monolingual case study will be Labov's research on the accent of the Lower East Side of New York (Labov, 1966) in which a random sample of speakers of different backgrounds were recorded in structured interviews which incorporated techniques attempting to elicit both informal speech as well as styles where more attention is paid to speech production, such as the reading both of word lists and of stories. It was on the basis of this study that Labov demonstrated that, using certain sociolinguistic techniques, it is possible to infer language change in progress, by comparing the variable uses of different accent forms across different subsections of the city's population. The study has been extremely influential and has promoted a vibrant sub-field of sociolinguistics known as "variationism."

The multilingual case study comes from South-West Germany which, like other parts of the country in the past 40 years, has seen widespread immigration from southern Europe and beyond. Gal (1987) reports socio-linguistic research on a group of adolescents – the children of Italian migrants to the city of Konstanz – and demonstrates their problematic status in a community where they are perceived as foreigners not only by the local population but also by residents of their "home" towns back in Italy who refer to them as "I germani" – "the Germans." She discusses how code-switching is used fluidly and dynamically in the adolescent group for a range of both identity-marking and role- and turn-management functions. Code-switching is so highly valued in the adolescent group that those members who command an equal mastery of the two languages "win leader-ship positions in peer networks" (Gal, 1987: 641), despite the fact that both German and Italian schools regard it as an impediment for them. How do the different types of "community" proposed in the literature deal with these and other similar examples?

The speech community

Of the three types of "community" outlined here, the "speech community" (henceforth "SC") has the longest history within the sociolinguistic enter-prise, and, despite the fact that its original sociolinguistic theorists formu-lated clear views about what such a community comprises, the term has often been used in a fairly unconscious way to refer to "the group being sociolinguistically researched" – the semantic bleaching of the term reflect-ing the extent to which it has become embedded in the sociolinguistic psyche.

Labov's definition of "speech community" is probably the most often cited and critiqued:

The speech community is not defined by any marked agreement in the use of language elements, so much as by participation in a set of shared norms; these norms may be observed in overt types of evaluative behaviour, and by the uniformity of abstract patterns of variation which are invariant in respect to particular levels of usage. (Labov, 1972b: 120–1)

Important here is the idea that members of an SC do not *necessarily* have to speak the same way – they must simply share a set of evaluations about the speech of that community. We can exemplify this, from a monolingual perspective, by taking a look at one accent variable from Labov's aforementioned study of New York which, he claims, "is a speech community, *united* by a common evaluation of the same variables which *differentiate* the speakers" (Labov, 1966: 125; our emphasis) (see Figure 1.1).

Figure 1.1 examines the use of non-standard variants of (th), as in "think" and "thumb." Alongside the standard variant [θ], New Yorkers also have at

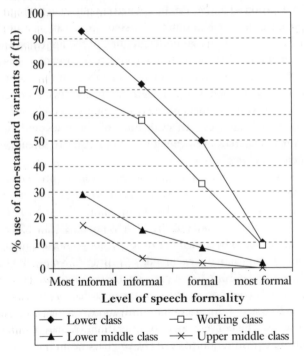

Figure 1.1 The use of non-standard variants of (th) in New York City (Labov, 1968: 243)

Source: Reproduced by permission of Mouton de Gruyter.

their disposal a wide range of other pronunciations, including the alveolar stop [t]. The graph along the *y* axis shows the percentage use of this and other non-standard forms. The data for each speaker are grouped into distinct social class categories as well as different "styles," from least formal (casual conversation) to most formal (the reading of lists of words). It was examples such as this which motivated Labov to propose his definition of the SC. Although some speakers in the community use non-standard forms of (th) in over 90% of possible instances (the "lower class" in the most informal style) and some in less than 15% of instances, Labov claims they are united in the same SC because they all style-shift towards a greater use of standard forms in more formal styles (indeed, those who used over 90% non-standard forms in the most informal style do so on only 10% of possible occasions in the most formal style), *thereby demonstrating a shared evaluation of the social prestige of the standard form.* In short, New Yorkers may not speak the same way, but they think the same way about the way they speak.

Labov's definition of the SC can be applied equally to multilingual settings. The adolescent group in Konstanz discussed above can also be seen as an SC in that its members share an understanding of the linguistic and discursive norms, including the (sometimes conflictual) use of code-switching, despite the fact that some younger or new members of the group feel more competent in Italian than German and are hence less "proficient" than those central statusful members of the peer group who code-switch fluently between the two languages. An evaluation of the roles and functions of code-switching is shared, even though the actual ability to engage competently in such switching is not.

Some cases, both mono- and multilingual, appear problematic for the proposed definition of "SC," however. Paul Kerswill, famous for his research on the dialectology of mobility, questions the role of community "nativeness" in Labov's model of the SC (Kerswill, 1993). Must a speaker be a native of an SC to be a member of it? Although not explicitly stated in his definition, Labov actually excluded, according to Kerswill, over 50% of New York residents from his survey on the grounds of non-nativeness. This was, indeed, common practice in social dialectological studies for at least the first 20 years of the discipline – only more recently have variationists begun to examine the consequences of migration, of dialect mixing, and of second dialect acquisition on patterns of language use.

The nativeness issue raises two fundamental questions: first, given the levels of mobility in society today, how valid can dialect descriptions be which exclude non-natives (often defined as those who entered the community at a very early age)? Early work in second dialect acquisition has shown us that migrants are variably able to acquire lexical items and simple (but not complex) phonological rules of their new home (Chambers, 1992), suggesting partial but not complete membership of the community. In situations where new communities are being created from scratch, e.g., new towns (Kerswill and Williams, 2000)), is a community not formed until shared evaluations of its patterns of usage emerge?

Second, and perhaps more fundamentally, excluding non-natives can mask the very origins of some linguistic changes that are underway in the community. Horvath (1985), for instance, who did *not* exclude Italians and Greeks from her study of the English of Sydney, Australia, found that it was indeed these groups that were leading certain linguistic changes affecting the whole city. Furthermore, Fox (2005), studying the dialect of adolescents in Tower Hamlets, an "East End" suburb of London and supposedly the home of its "Cockney" dialect, has found that a number of the linguistic changes underway there are led by the now numerically superior Bangladeshi immigrant population and are spreading to the speech of white (especially) male adolescents there. Failing to include the relatively recently arrived Bangladeshi group and concentrating solely on white adolescents would have led to almost unexplainable patterns of variation which represent a very clear and quite sudden break from the "Cockney" dialect which preceded in this part of London.

Another criticism of Labov's SC definition comes from those who believe that it buys in to a consensual model of society where those without power somehow "share" (rather than have imposed upon them) the values of the socially dominant group. Is the use of standard forms of (th) by the lower working classes in New York City a sign that they share an evaluation of the prestige of the [θ] variant – the one native to the upper middle classes? Or is it because they have been indoctrinated with a standard ideology that tells them that the standard form is correct, proper and acceptable and that the non-standard form is bad, lazy and inadequate and hence can legitimately be discriminated against in the workplace, at school and beyond? The sanctions imposed on those who do not "share" these norms can be great. As J. Milroy (1992: 209) states: "in Labov's analysis . . . speakers are said to agree on the evaluation of the very linguistic norms that actually symbolize the divisions between them . . . the reality and persistence of non-standard vernacular communities uncovered by many researchers constitute evidence not primarily of consensus, but of conflict and sharp divisions in society."

Social networks

Social network (SN) approaches are based not on shared language use or shared evaluations but on the social ties people engage in, such as with kin, close friends, colleagues and neighbors. An SN measures *actual* connections in a "community" whose members know each other, and assesses the extent to which those members are differentially grounded in that community. SC approaches, however, do not insist that members actually know each other or interact regularly and make few claims (beyond nativeness) about the extent to which members are integrated socially into communal life.

The term SN has been used in two different ways. The first is rather metaphorical, referring to groups that are most likely to have common social ties (such as "peer network;" e.g., Gal, 1987). The second is more methodological, focusing on ways of defining and measuring the structure of the "community;" the strength or centrality of relevant types of network is quantified and used to account for language behavior in the community (e.g., Milroy, 1980; Li Wei, 1994).

James and Lesley Milroy – who pioneered sociolinguistic research using SN models in a ground-breaking study of the English of Belfast, Northern Ireland – suggested that the *strength* of our social networks in our local communities was closely related to our *maintenance* of local dialect norms. In the sociological literature, the strength of social networks has been determined broadly by "a combination of the amount of time, the emotional intensity, the intimacy (mutual confiding) and the reciprocal services which characterize a tie" (Granovetter, 1973: 1361). In sociolinguistic research, these factors have often been distilled down to two key measures of network strength, namely:

1   Multiplexity (e.g., a link with someone who is a neighbor, a workmate and a friend represents a multiplex social network tie as opposed to with someone who is only tied in a network through one type of social connection – a uniplex network link).
2   Density (if the close ties in your network are also ties of each other, the network is considered to be denser than if your ties do not know each other).

It is hypothesized in the SN literature that people engaged in very strong social networks together are able, through the close and intimate ties they share, to effect a certain control over each other's behavior, leading to the enforcement of group behavioral norms, including linguistic norms. Consequently, strong SNs help maintain and enforce local dialect forms, while weaker networks, with less internal pressure to conform, are much less likely to resist external linguistic influences including diffusing linguistic changes. Milroy and Milroy (1985: 375) therefore claim that "linguistic change is slow to the extent that the relevant populations are well established and bound by strong ties, whereas it is rapid to the extent that weak ties exist in populations."

The bilingual Italian-German community in Konstanz, as discussed by Gal, is one which lends itself rather well to SN interpretations of language use. Linguistically resisting both repatriation to Italy and integration into mainstream German culture, balanced bilingualism – and the resulting ability to code-switch fluently – are mastered and valued by the most central core network members among the Italian adolescent group, while those toward the margins of the group, with weaker ties (because of lack of integration, recent arrival from Italy, younger age, etc.), tend towards greater use of Italian than German. An SN analysis, probing the key characteristics of core group membership and the extent to which individuals in the adolescent group possess them could shed important light not only on how both languages are negotiated and enmeshed, but could also provide an inclusive analysis incorporating those with weaker ties as well as those at the center of the group. The SN model, thus, can cope with mobile societies, such as societies with substantial immigrant populations, which the SC cannot.

Labov's (1972b) New York study would not be easily interpretable from an SN perspective. We do not know whether individuals in this study know or engage with each other on a regular basis, nor, if they do, the extent to which the individuals concerned possess strong or weak networks. This could be seen as a *strength* of the SC model – *despite* the lack of obvious connections between the speakers, there still exists a common core of evaluations among members of the community, suggesting perhaps that dense strong multiplex networks are not a prerequisite for a community to "share" this common core. On the other hand, the SN approach has consistently shown in a number of studies the fundamental relationship between a person's network strength and adherence to the local dialect, suggesting that a random selection of informants from the SC does not adequately demonstrate how speakers are socially and therefore linguistically embedded in the locale.

Communities of practice

Of the three types of "community" outlined in this chapter, the "community of practice" (hereafter CofP) is the most recent notion, introduced and applied to sociolinguistic investigations by Eckert (Eckert and McConnell-Ginet, 1992a, 1992b, 1999; Eckert, 2000). Eckert and McConnell-Ginet (1999: 185) define CofPs as being: "groups whose *joint engagement* in some activity or *enterprise* is sufficiently intensive to give rise over time to *repertoires of shared practices*." "Joint engagement" indicates that members of a CofP "*must be engaged with one another and not simply share a certain characteristic*" (Moore, 2003: 19; our emphasis). This sets a CofP apart from both an SC and an SN. As mentioned earlier, members of an SC do not necessarily know each other. Members of an SN certainly do know each other – some (closer, denser, more multiplex) network links have regular and intimate interaction, while (weaker, sparser and more uniplex) others exchange goods, advice and services. However, simply knowing each other and regularly interacting with one another is not sufficient for CofP membership. The key is whether members are jointly engaged with one another. As Moore explains, SNs highlight "what people are," CofPs highlight "what people do" (Moore, 2003: 22). For example, the salesperson at a corner shop near your home with whom you have a brief conversation almost every day when you buy the newspaper can be considered to be a loosely tied member of your SN, but you cannot be regarded as members of the same CofP. It is true that members of a close-knit network could well be classified as members of a CofP together, so there are some areas of overlap. However, the subtle difference between an SN and a CofP lies in members' consciousness. As Meyerhoff (2002: 531) explains, "one can be a member of a social network by chance or circumstance, while membership in a CofP is conscious." A CofP appears, therefore, to be a "smaller" and more focused group than those in the SC and SN models (Meyerhoff, 2002: 526).

Can Labov's study of New York – a study which helped define the SC – meet this first CofP criterion of joint engagement? The random sampling method that he adopted was criticized for being a "top-down" analysis, starting with predetermined social categories and allocating individuals (who may not have much in common with each other) to one of those categories, such as "lower middle class" or "young." This contrasts with both CofP and SN approaches which both demand a "bottom-up" analysis, starting with the individual as the basic unit of the group, with the membership and boundaries of a CofP/SN being defined on the basis of members' *subjective* perceptions (e.g., whether an individual is a central or marginal member) (Meyerhoff, 2002: 533).

The second criterion of a CofP, "enterprise" refers to "the *purpose* around which mutual engagement is structured" (Moore, 2003: 19; our emphasis). This factor helps differentiate CofPs from both SC and SN analyses. As explained above, within the SC model, neither mutual engagement nor purpose is a requirement of membership. Some SNs, on the other hand, may have such purpose, but as Milroy (2002: 552) claims, "network analysis typically does not attend to the identification of . . . the enterprises undertaken by members." Thus, among the three types of "community," this is the criterion that only the CofP requires the "community" to meet. Sociolinguists who hope to conduct a CofP analysis, therefore, have to bear in mind that the community in which a shared enterprise is substantially lacking should not be treated as a CofP (Meyerhoff, 2002: 528).

Penelope Eckert's (e.g., 2000) investigations of Belten High School in Detroit – one of the earliest and best-known studies adopting a CofP analysis – highlight how the "enterprise" engaged in by members of a CofP can lead to the deployment of a repertoire of shared linguistic resources. Employing ethnographic research methods, Eckert identified two oppositional CofPs among the adolescents in the school, the "Jocks" and the "Burnouts" (as well as a third larger group, the "in-betweens"), each of which came together around common goals, dreams and desires, both for the present and for the future, within the context of the school. The ultimate goal of the Jocks is sufficient academic success to enable them to enter a good university, while that of the Burnouts is to secure a skilled job in the locality. For the university-bound Jocks, the legitimacy of the school that prepares them for college is unquestionable, and they actively engage in institutionally-oriented CofPs (e.g., extra-curricular activities, such as clubs, sport and the school newspaper). As a result, the Jocks are given "special freedom, recognition, and visibility – they attain institutional status, and gain control of many aspects of the daily life of the school" (Eckert, 2000: 48). The workforce-bound Burnouts, on the other hand, reject the legitimacy of the school that does not prepare them for the local job market, minimize their engagement with the school and resent any role that the school plays in restricting their personal freedom. Their CofP is more locally and personally oriented (e.g., hanging-out in the neighborhood). Eckert demonstrates that the Jocks' and Burnouts' differing enterprises result not only in different social and cultural behavior, but also different linguistic behavior: Burnouts, regardless of gender, were more advanced in the backing of (e) to [ʌ], the backing of (ʌ) to [ɔ] and the raising of the nucleus of (ay) to, for example, [əɪ] (Eckert, 2000: 118).

The third criterion of a CofP, "repertoires of shared practices" refers to a set of resources that "are a *cumulative result of internal negotiations*" (Meyerhoff, 2002: 528, our emphasis). Such a shared collection of resources may include the way members dress, move and behave, as well as the way they talk. The key here is that such repertoires are *not static, but dynamic, continuing to be negotiated and constructed through mutual engagement*. This also distinguishes a CofP from both SC and SN, although, in one rather simple sense, the other two types of "community" may both meet this criterion: members of a SC share a similar evaluation of the way people talk, and those of a strong SN tend to share norm-enforced linguistic strategies. However, the important difference is that neither explicitly addresses how community members *come to share* a set of evaluations about linguistic features, nor how those features come to gain their social meaning and evaluation in the first place. A CofP is said to provide the solution for this, as it reveals the detailed negotiation process through which social meaning and evaluation are being constructed.

Gal's study of an adolescent group in Konstanz provides a multilingual example of a CofP that well captures the dynamic nature of such repertoires of shared practices. Its members share "distinct cultural practices" (Gal, 1987: 643) as part of which

> . . . choice of language is constantly being negotiated, because every codeswitching puts into question the previously negotiated language of inter- action. The negotiations are implicit as turns at talk are exchanged. Often, each speaker responds in his/her "preferred" language, until one capitulates and the language of the conversation is set, at least until the next codeswitch. (p. 641)

She is careful to show here the *interconnection* between linguistic practice and the creation and negotiation of a CofP which incorporates the members' perception of group boundaries and the emergence of a new and distinctly in-group linguistic code as well as marking resistance to external pressures:

> The Italian young people . . . use their bilingual repertoire to create a syncretic form of conversation that continually includes the stream of newcomers, but symbolically rejects both alternatives offered to them by the state: integration into German society and repatriation to Italy. This genuinely novel form is not only symbolic of a newly forming social entity; it is instrumental in creating it. (p. 650)

Conclusion

As we have seen, the time-honored tension in the social scientific literature between structure and agency is apparent when we compare the three models with more recent approaches giving significantly more weight to individual agency than was earlier accepted. The top-down approach of the SC – where structure reigns over the contribution of individuals – is replaced in more recent models, such as the CofP, by groups of individuals developing shared linguistic practices through their conscious coming together in a joint endeavor. But how far can the individual go in deciding his/her own linguistic destiny? Some recent sociolinguistic research has focussed on specific individuals – often performers or people in public life – and the way they "draw on a wide range of linguistic resources . . . negotiate identities, relationships, contexts moment by moment" (Swann, 1996: 324). This individual identity-oriented approach has developed from work by Le Page and Tabouret-Keller, who stated that: "the individual creates for himself the patterns of his linguistic behaviour so as to resemble those of the group or groups with which from time to time he wishes to be identified, or so as to be unlike those from whom he wishes to be distinguished" (1985: 181). It should not be read from this, however, that the individual is without constraint in this identity marking. Although the sociolinguistic literature provides ample evidence of the role of identity in understanding linguistic variation, it has also been established that there are limits on the extent to which we can massage and change our vernacular accents. Indeed, Le Page and Tabouret-Keller themselves note that the ability to linguistically adapt, noted in the quotation above, is constrained among other things by our "ability to modify our behaviour" (1985: 181). Evidence of the nature of these constraints comes from research on the acquisition of a second dialect (Chambers, 1992), mentioned earlier, and evidence that *linguistic* factors shape our accent and dialect variability *more* than social factors (see Preston, 1991). Eckert (2000), in her CofP research, for example, finds that many of the linguistic variables that distinguish Jocks from Burnouts are strongly constrained by *linguistic* factors above all else. Even in signaling locally highly important social identities, the adolescents shape their dialects within a set of structural linguistic confines.

Over the past 40 years in the sociolinguistic literature there has been a gradual shift from a top-down to a bottom-up model of language community. Today, "community" involves a group of individuals coming together to perform shared practices in a shared endeavor. Before, members of the

SC taking part in sociolinguistic research were not necessarily aware that others even existed. Today, in many ways, therefore, and although much more importance is placed on the role of the individual, the "community" is a more "concrete" entity (albeit one that is constantly evolving and renegotiating itself) containing real people actually interacting with one another and with purpose. But language is *not*, however, an identity "free-for-all," a dressing-up box from which we can freely pick whatever suits us at that moment. The internal structures of the language impose quite considerable constraints on the linguistic scope for marking social allegiances and social distinctions, constraints which sociolinguistic research has shown are consistently adhered to by the community.

Further reading

Chambers, J., Trudgill, P., and Schilling-Estes, N. (eds) (2002) *The Handbook of Language Variation and Change*. Oxford: Blackwell. This includes chapters on speech communities, social networks and communities of practice.

Eckert, P. (2000) *Linguistic Variation as Social Practice*. Oxford: Blackwell. The model is here applied to sociolinguistic concerns.

Milroy, L. and Gordon, M. (2003) *Sociolinguistics: Method and Interpretation*. Oxford: Blackwell. This provides methodological and theoretical detail about social networks in sociolinguistics.

Wenger, E. (1998) *Communities of Practice: Learning, Meaning and Identity*. Cambridge: Cambridge University Press. This offers an in-depth account of CofPs.

2

Regional and Social Variation

Margaret Maclagan

Whenever speech-language pathologists move to different countries, or even different regions within the same country, they will potentially encounter regional or social variation in language. Forms that are unacceptable in one region or social class may be usual in another. Because speech is so much a part of a person's identity, it is essential that speech-language pathologists are aware of the regional and social variation that is present in the speech community in which they are working, before they undertake any treatment.

In the past linguists tried to ignore language variation. It was seen as a nuisance, as something which got in the way of their work in describing language. Chomsky wrote: "Linguistic theory is concerned primarily with an ideal speaker-listener, in a completely homogeneous speech-community" (1965: 3). Traditional school grammarians, in their pursuit of the one true standard of correctness, saw variation as some kind of corruption of the language. Today, in sociolinguistics, variation is central. It is seen as an integral and essential part of language. To a sociolinguist a completely homogeneous speech community would be most peculiar, if not pathological. In the 1960s sociolinguists led by William Labov developed methods of studying language variation and their work has produced something of a revolution in the study of language.

One of the early descriptions of language variation divided it into two categories: variation according to the user and variation according to use (Halliday, McIntosh, and Strevens, 1964: 87). This is still a useful distinction. Variation according to the user involves aspects of language which a person always carries around with him or herself – language which reveals that speaker's place of origin, gender, age, social class, ethnicity, education. Together these make up part of that individual person's identity and reveal his or her group membership. Any attempt to change a person's language is a serious matter. It will send messages to other members of the group that this person no longer wishes to be part of their group. Language variation according to use is variation which can occur in anyone's speech as they move from one situation to another. Let us say Professor Smith is the mother of two small children. In the course of her day, Professor Smith's use of language will vary as she moves from talking to her children, to giving a university lecture, to talking to her colleagues over morning tea, to ringing the electrician to fix the lights, to doing the shopping, and so on. In all these situations her speech will still reveal her Australian accent, her sex, and social class which are with her all the time – language variation according to the user – but she will also make changes and adjustments according to the situation she is in and those she is talking to – language variation according to use.

In this chapter, regional and social variation will be considered. Regional variation occurs because people often speak differently in different places. Social variation involves non-regional differences – the result of such things as social class, gender, ethnic background and education; it also includes variation according to changes in a speaker's situation.

All areas of language – phonology, morphology, syntax and lexis – can potentially show regional and social variation. However, there is an interesting question about whether all areas of language are subject to variation in the same way. Pronunciation seems to be more sensitive to regional and social class variation than grammar and vocabulary. Hudson (1996: 43) suggests that pronunciation is less liable to standardization, whereas grammar and vocabulary are more likely to be standardized because of their connection with writing. He puts forward the idea that pronunciation identifies our origins, whereas our grammar and vocabulary identify our current status in society, such as the amount of education we have had. This difference could explain why even a huge amount of exposure to, say, American English through TV and films will not bring about a change in a person's pronunciation, though it might result in changes to vocabulary. New Zealand English, for example, has a steadily increasing amount of American vocabulary, but no American influence on pronunciation.

In this chapter, KEY WORDS (Wells, 1982) will be used to indicate both the vowel phoneme being referred to and the set of words containing this phoneme. KEY WORDS have each phoneme surrounded by unique consonants, so that each vowel is immediately identifiable. FLEECE can thus refer to the phoneme /i/ and also to the lexical set of words containing the phoneme /i/. TRAP similarly refers to the phoneme /æ/ and to the lexical set of words containing this phoneme.

Regional variation

When we travel overseas, even to another country where people speak the same language, we are usually aware of lots of language differences. Differences in pronunciation or vocabulary can make it extremely difficult to understand what others are saying, and there are many stories of unsuspecting people, such as New Zealanders in Britain, being offered a *pin* in a shop when they had asked for a *pen*. In the past, regional dialects arose wherever there were barriers to communication. These barriers could be physical – mountain ranges, or rivers, both of which were difficult to cross – or political, with borders between countries or even villages proving effective in hampering communication. In such cases the change of dialect can be abrupt. However, dialect differences can also occur very gradually. In dialect continua, very small differences between individual villages can become cumulative in a dialect chain so that small individual differences become incremental and produce large differences between more distantly separated villages (see Chambers and Trudgill, 1998: 5, 6).

As communication became easier with telephones, radios and televisions, many people expected that regional dialects would slowly disappear. It was even suggested that the differences between the Received Pronunciation (RP) of Great Britain and General American English would be ironed out in favor of some mid-Atlantic dialect. However, many years after the advent of television, with material freely available in many different accents, no one now expects a single mid-Atlantic dialect to develop. In fact, in some places, the opposite of convergence is occurring. In the United States, for example, the results of current sound changes are leading to greater differences between the pronunciations of the northern and southern regions (see, e.g., Wolfram, 1997).

The study of regional varieties of language has been going on for a long time. Dialectologists have produced dialect maps showing different usages in different areas. For example, in England, a map could show different terms for "cross-eyed:" *cock-eyed* in Northumberland, Westmoreland and parts of the Midlands, *boss-eyed* in South-East England and East Anglia, *squint-eyed* in Devon and parts of Somerset, and *cross-eyed* in Cheshire, Derbyshire and the Isle of Man (Upton and Widdowson, 1996: 102).

Regional variation is greater in countries that have been settled for longer periods. In England there is a rich variety of dialects which have formed over the 1,500 years in which English has been spoken there. In America, where English has been used for around 400 years, there is far less regional variation, though there is relatively more variation in the Eastern USA, New England, New York City and the South East which have been settled the longest. In countries like Australia, South Africa and New Zealand, where English has been spoken for 200 years or less, there is relatively little regional variation.

People often consider that the difference between *languages* and *dialects* is that dialects of the same language are mutually intelligible where two different languages are not. While this distinction often holds, in real life the situation is less clear-cut because languages are often defined partly on political grounds. Swedish and Norwegian or Spanish and Portuguese are different languages, and yet there is a degree of mutual intelligibility between the pairs, especially for speakers who live close to the country borders. By contrast, speakers of rural dialects in Britain and the United States may find it very difficult to understand each other even though they all speak English.

At a different level, it is also useful to make a distinction between *dialect* and *accent*. Accent is concerned with pronunciation (see Wells, 1982). Each distinct style of pronunciation is called an accent and every single person has an accent. In common use, only "other people" are regarded as having an accent, and many people are insulted if you point out that they too speak with one. Accents can be regional (a "Canadian accent") or social (a "posh accent" or a "vulgar accent"). In Britain the most prestigious accent is RP which seems to have developed in the public schools in the nineteenth century. It is not associated with any specific region, though in some respects it is most similar to accents of South-East England. Most linguists agree that *accent* refers to pronunciation, but they differ on whether or not to include pronunciation features in their definitions of dialect.

We can also identify a *standard* form of most languages. In England, the dialect of the south-eastern region has become the standard. Historically it was associated with the capital, and hence with political and economic power. There are two distinct ways of seeing the relationship between the standard language and dialects. In the first perspective, everyone speaks a dialect, one of which is the standard. In Britain, for example, Standard English, is a dialect just like other dialects. It differs from other dialects because it has prestige, but it is only an accident of history that this particular variety has been so promoted. In the second perspective there is a distinction between the standard language and dialects so that speakers who use a dialect are regarded as speaking a non-standard form of the language. Whether or not the standard form of a language is regarded as one dialect among many, it can be controlled in two different ways: explicitly by a body such as the Académie française, or implicitly by people such as broadcasters ("BBC English").

We turn now to the specific areas of language where regional variation can be found. As well as pronunciation differences, variation can also occur in the phonological inventory, in grammar or in vocabulary (lexis). When people are recognized as speaking different regional dialects, there are usually differences in several of these areas.

Regional differences in *phonology* occur when speakers from different regions make a different number of phonemic contrasts. Speakers from the north of England use the same vowel in the words *cup* and *look*, where speakers from the south use different vowels. Speakers from the south of England have six short vowels (KIT, DRESS, TRAP, LOT, FOOT and STRUT) whereas those from the north have five (KIT, DRESS, TRAP, LOT, FOOT) with those in the north using the FOOT vowel for both the FOOT and STRUT sets of words. As in this example, phonological differences may involve all occurrences of the relevant phoneme. In other cases, phonemes can be merged in some contexts only. Many American speakers do not make a distinction between the vowels in the words *merry, marry, Mary* and sometimes also *Murray*. In other contexts, the DRESS, TRAP, SQUARE and STRUT vowels are distinguished, but not before intervocalic /r/.

Grammatical differences include both morphological and syntactic differences. Regional differences in *morphology* often involve regularization or simplification of inflectional paradigms so that the number of forms for irregular verbs like *do* is reduced. Instead of the standard *do, did, done* for base, past tense and past participle a simpler paradigm of *do, done, done* is used. *Come* becomes *come, come, come* instead of *come, came, come*. Most New Zealand speakers use the standard forms for *come* and *do*, but on the west coast of the South Island and in the far north of the North Island there are communities where the simplified paradigms are the most common. The same pattern holds for many other English-speaking regions.

Regional differences in *syntax* result in different structures being used in similar contexts. The verb *need* is usually followed by a present participle in constructions like *the cat needs feeding* or by a passive, as in *the cat needs to be fed*. However, in parts of America (especially Western Pennsylvania or Eastern Ohio) or Scotland or in the south of New Zealand, the structure is used with the past participle: *the cat needs fed*. Similarly, Americans usually *write someone* whereas British speakers *write to someone*. People tend to be very critical of regional differences in both morphology and syntax criticizing the form that they do not use themselves as wrong or clumsy. However, all the different regional forms convey the relevant meaning within their appropriate context and none of the forms is intrinsically better or worse than any other.

Regional differences in *vocabulary* (lexis) are often obvious to a new-comer. Lexical differences can be simple substitutions of one word for another, as with *hood/bonnet*, *trunk/boot* and *gas/petrol* as one drives in America or England. A different sort of lexical variation occurs when the same word is used in slightly different senses in different regions. A *bush* is a medium-sized plant (as in *rose bush*) in both England and the southern hemisphere. But in the southern hemisphere, *bush* has the added meaning of areas of native vegetation, including sizeable trees. Colonists often took words like this from Britain but gave them new meanings in the new countries. An Australian *hawk* is not the same as an English hawk, nor are NZ *magpies, robins, cuckoos* or *beech trees* the same as their British namesakes.

A different sort of lexical variation occurs in regions that have been colonies. Southern Hemisphere Englishes, i.e., Australian, South African and New Zealand English, have all been affected by indigenous languages. Loan words are often familiar to people who live in the area but do not move into the mainstream lexicon of English. Exceptions to this are *kangaroo*, *boomerang*, and *koala* (from Aboriginal languages into Australian English), *kiwi, haka* and *moa* (from Maori into New Zealand English) and *donga* from Xhosa into South African English, all of which are now familiar to people outside their original regions (see Gordon and Sudbury, 2002: 84).

Regional variation in language can easily be eroded. Britain (2002) de-scribes how several regionally different paradigms for the past tense of the verb *be* are being simplified in the Fens region of England so that *was* is used in all positive contexts (*the farms was . . .*) and *weren't* is used in all negative contexts (*the farm weren't . . .*). In this particular case, several local regional forms have been levelled out partly under the influence of forms used in surrounding districts. There are many similar stories about the gradual loss of distinctive regional forms of language. However, not all distinctly regional forms are disappearing. One of the most famous cases of strengthening regional patterns is Labov's (1963) study of Martha's Vineyard, an isolated rural island off the coast of Massachusetts. During the twentieth century, Vineyarders seemed to be gradually adopting more general American speech patterns, but 30–40-year-olds in rural areas showed a strong pattern of centralization for the PRICE and MOUTH diphthongs (as [ɐɪ] and [ɐʊ] respectively), a pattern that was at variance with the general move-ment of these diphthongs elsewhere. Labov found that these were old-fashioned pronunciations which would have been heard on the mainland of

America in the eighteenth and nineteenth centuries. Fishermen from Chilmark, who had the highest percentage of such traditional forms, were very strongly identified with the island and its traditional way of life, and opposed to the tourists who were vital for the economy. Younger speakers who identified with the island used higher percentages of the centralized diphthongs than those who wanted to move elsewhere. Wolfram found similar results for the isolated community of Ocracoke, where the members of the "Poker Game network," who were most strongly identified with the island, had the greatest usage of the [ɔi] form of PRICE and were known as the "hoi toiders" (for *high tiders*) (see Wolfram and Schilling-Estes, 1998: 116).

Social variation

To reiterate, social variation involves non-regional differences – the result of such things as social class, gender, ethnic background and education; it also includes variation according changes in a speaker's situation. Social variation is highly correlated with gender, and this is discussed in Chapter 3.

In most communities we can find differences in the *social status* of people. Social classes can be ordered from those with the highest prestige to those with the lowest. It has long been recognized that there are differences in the speech of people of different social classes, but it was only in the 1960s that this began to be studied systematically, in America by William Labov and in Britain by Peter Trudgill.

For example, Peter Trudgill analyzed the speech of 60 informants in Norwich in 1967 and classified his sample into five groups according to social class. The classification was done according to their occupation, income, education, father's occupation, housing and locality. Among other variables, Trudgill investigated the presence or absence of (h) in words like *hammer* and *heart*. Trudgill's Norwich study can be compared with research into h-dropping in Bradford. There was a close and similar relationship between h-dropping and social class in both places in that the lower working class showed most h-dropping. But the percentage use was different. Lower working class speakers h-dropped almost all the time in Bradford, but only 60 percent of the time in Norwich (see Table 2.1).

This raised the question of why there was more h-dropping in Bradford than in Norwich. Chambers and Trudgill suggest this could have come about because the h-dropping was relatively new in Norwich but was a long-standing feature of English in Bradford (1998: 59).

Table 2.1 Incidence of h-dropping (%)

Class	Bradford	Norwich
Middle middle class	12	6
Lower middle class	28	14
Upper working class	67	40
Middle working class	89	60
Lower working class	93	60

Social class is notoriously difficult to define, and categories which work well in one place might not work in another. (For example Trudgill's housing index for Norwich would not suit New Zealand circumstances where people do not live in semi-detached or terraced houses.) One common method for social class determination is through a social class index whereby people's occupations are given a rating with, for example, a rating of 1 for professional occupations and 6 for menial occupations. Another way is to combine an occupational rating with an educational rating.

In some countries regional and social variation is closely inter-related. For England, Wells (1982: 14) pictures the relationship as a pyramid with regional variation on the horizontal dimension and social variation on the vertical (see Figure 2.1). The wide base indicates that working-class accents show a great deal of regional variation. The higher up the social class scale one goes, the less regional variation there is, until at the top there is RP which does not show any regional variation. In England, a regional accent always indicates that the speaker is from one of the lower social classes.

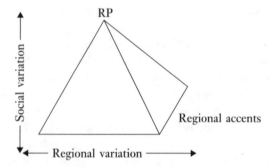

Figure 2.1 The relationship between social and regional variation in England (adapted from Wells, 1982: 14)

Wells notes that this image does not work for other countries. In America, for example, higher class accents are very different in different regions – there is no single accent like RP at the top of the pyramid. In countries like Australia and New Zealand where regional variation is minimal, the pyramid becomes a column. Within New Zealand, where non-standard forms such as past tense *come* are becoming increasingly common in certain regions, speakers from these regions may automatically be regarded as lower class even if this is not accurate.

As with regional variation, social variation can occur in phonological, morphological, syntactic or lexical areas of language. Non-standard features of phonology (such as "broad" pronunciations of the MOUTH and PRICE diphthongs or h-dropping) and syntax (such as double negatives, *I haven't done nothing*) are usually avoided by higher social class speakers and may become social stereotypes.

In England in the mid-twentieth century, the terms "U" and "non-U" (for upper class and non-upper class) were coined by the linguist Alan Ross and publicized in the book *Noblesse Oblige* (edited by Ross and Mitford, 1989) as a light-hearted way to describe social differences in vocabulary use. *Serviette* and *mirror*, for example, were non-U while *napkin* and *looking glass* were U. Words which were non-U in England at the time could often be the most common and non-stigmatized terms in other varieties of English. Over time, the social connotations of many of the listed words have changed but vocabulary is still an indicator of social class.

There are two different sorts of variation associated with *age*. The most common age-related variation occurs as languages change. Younger speakers usually lead in language changes, and they end up using newer forms than older speakers. This is most obvious in slang which, by its very nature, must continuously change. Slang terms serve to mark speakers who are part of a particular group. As soon as other speakers start to use a particular term, such as *cool*, or *choice* or *sweet as*, it no longer functions as a way of identifying the inner members of the group and a new term is coined. If terms are sufficiently well known to be referred to in linguistic text books, they have probably ceased to function as slang words for the group that originally coined them!

All areas of language are constantly changing, not just slang. Linguists have identified historical sound changes such as Grimm's Law that changed Latin /p/ (as in *pes, pedis*, 'foot') to /f/ in Germanic languages (*foot* in English and *Fuss* in German) many centuries ago or the Great Vowel Shift that changed Chaucer's relatively phonetic spelling into the pronunciation used by Shakespeare (so that *fine*, for example, changed from /finə/ to

/fain/). Similar sound changes continue to take place in languages all over the world. The Northern Cities shift is changing American pronunciation from Rochester (New York) to Chicago, especially in urban areas, so that, among other changes, the short front vowels (KIT and DRESS) are becoming more open. The Southern Shift is simultaneously changing the same vowels so that they become higher in pronunciation in southern areas of the United States (see Labov, 1994; Wolfram and Schilling-Estes, 1998, for details). These changes are most noticeable in the speech of younger speakers. Similar sound changes, again led by younger speakers, can be heard in many other parts of the world. Over time, sound changes can gradually move through the whole speech community so that all speakers eventually use the newer form.

One question that is currently exercising sociolinguists is how much adults change their speech over their lifetime. It is usually assumed that a person's pronunciation and grammar are more or less fixed by early adult-hood although people continue to learn new vocabulary throughout their life. However, recent research has shown that even people's pronunciation changes over time, with adults accommodating somewhat to the sound changes that are happening around them (see, e.g., Harrington, Palethorpe, and Watson's 2000 study of the way Queen Elizabeth II has changed her pronunciation).

The second type of language variation related to age is called *age-grading*. Age-grading occurs when younger and older speakers have different ver-sions of a particular language feature, and a first impression could indicate that a change is in progress. However, over time, the proportion of speakers who use the newer form of language never changes: younger speakers con-tinue to use the apparently newer form and older speakers the traditional form. Young children in Canada, for example, call the last letter of the alphabet *zee*, presumably under the influence of American children's televi-sion programs. However, after they start school, this changes and they start to use *zed*. So far, this change continues to take place as new cohorts of children grow up: the name for the last letter of the alphabet is thus subject to age grading in Canada.

The best documented variation associated with *ethnicity* is what is now known as African American Vernacular English (AAVE) which is discussed in Chapter 8. A problem with identifying language variation due to ethnic-ity is that all the members of a given ethnic group may not use the ethnic variety (there are many African Americans who use a General American English pronunciation), and speakers from different ethnic groups may adopt ethnically marked features to show solidarity with the group in question. In

New Zealand, for instance, there is an ethnic variety of New Zealand English known as Maori English. Not all Maori use this variety, and non-Maori, especially men who live or work in close association with Maori, may adopt it.

So far we have considered social variation that is correlated with the user. We turn briefly to social variation according to use. Speakers speak in different *styles* depending on the formality of the context. Reading is more formal than speaking and word lists or sets of minimal pairs (such as *beer*, *bear*, or *duel, jewel*) elicit the most formal speech of all. Choice of vocabulary will be affected by formality with words such as *bloke* or *chook* ("hen") appearing in informal speech and *erudition* and similar words appearing in much more formal contexts. As the formality increases, speakers use greater percentages of both standard forms (like *running* rather than *runnin'*) and higher-class pronunciations (with [pɹɔis] being avoided for PRICE). Many specialized areas of language have their own vocabulary and syntax and can be called *registers. And they're off* or *coming down the inside* are from the register of horse racing whereas *cold fronts* and *wind chill* are from weather forecasting. There is an interaction between style and social class and also between style and gender, with speakers from higher social classes and also women usually producing more standard pronunciations and standard syntax in all contexts than do lower-class speakers or men.

Further reading

Coulmas, F. (ed.) (1997) *The Handbook of Sociolinguistics*. Oxford: Blackwell. This provides an excellent introduction to social factors that affect language.

Labov, W. (1994) *Principles of Linguistic Change*, Vol. 1: *Internal Factors*. Oxford: Blackwell.

Labov, W. (2001) *Principles of Linguistic Change*, Vol. 2: *Social Factors*. Malden, MA: Blackwell. These two volumes focus on language change, and cover in depth the factors that lead to regional and social variation in language.

Trudgill, P. (2000) *Sociolinguistics: An Introduction to Language and Society*, 4th edn. Harmondsworth: Penguin. This is a good, readable introduction to the field of sociolinguistics.

3

Language and Gender

Jacqueline Guendouzi

> The potential ambiguity of linguistic strategies to mark both power and solidarity in face-to-face interaction has made mischief in language and gender research, wherein it is tempting to assume that whatever women do results from, or creates, their powerlessness and whatever men do results from, or creates, their dominance.
>
> *Tannen (1993: 173)*

The above quote is an important starting point for anyone unfamiliar with the literature on language and gender, and, indeed, it is a remark that the reader should bear in mind when reading this chapter. Much of the research into language and gender has focused on how the dynamics of power and solidarity are played out within our daily interactions. The "difference" versus "dominance" gender debate has long held sway in sociolinguistics and it is evident from the mass popularity of books such as *Men Are from Mars, Women Are from Venus* (Gray, 1992) and *You Just Don't Understand* (Tannen, 1991) that this notion has struck a chord within western society. It is easy when reviewing the literature on language and gender to fall into the trap of extending the results of studies, which were often based on small samples of discourse, to entire populations. Tannen reminds us that "an instance of discourse" should not be "taken to represent how discourse works for all people" and that the ambiguity and polysemy inherent in language make interpretation of "true intention or motive" something that "cannot be determined from linguistic form alone" (1993: 165–6). Conversational interactions are joint productions that rely on both the speaker's illocutionary force (intention) and the perlocutionary uptake (interpretation or outcome) of the interactional partners. Meaning can be seen as an emergent property resulting from the interplay of individual variables present in any given interaction at a particular moment in time (Müller and Guendouzi, 2003). Therefore, when considering the issue of gender, it is important to avoid suggesting that specific discourse features are "natural" markers of power or gender.

Much of the research into language and gender falls within the following three main frameworks: traditional sociolinguistic studies of variation and dialectology (Labov, 1966; Trudgill, 1974), discourse and interactional studies (Coates, 1986; Tannen, 1994; Holmes, 1995) and polemic works that address the broader political and social implications of language and gender identity (Spender, 1980; Cameron, 1992). This chapter will focus on research that has had the most impact within the gender debate and then consider the implications of this debate for clinical professionals.

Language, gender and society

Any discussion of language and gender inevitably becomes an account of women's speech, it is hard to discuss gender in any field and avoid feminist theory. Accounts (Coates, 1986) of folklinguistic views surrounding women's talk have noted that the negative associations attached to "women's language" may have marginalized women's position in society. Early linguistic research, for example, assumed men's talk as the "norm" against which women's "deficits" were measured (Jespersen, 1922). This trend began to change in the 1960s when sociolinguists working in the Variationist Paradigm commented on the gender-specific use of dialectal variants. Labov's work in New York (1966) reported that female shop assistants were more likely to use the more prestigious post-vocalic [r] variant in their working environment, while Trudgill's work (1974) showed that female respondents in the United Kingdom reported a higher use of the Standard forms of a dialect when asked to self-evaluate their language usage. Contrary to earlier beliefs, that males were more likely to be agents of change in dialect variation, work focusing on social networks has identified women as instigators of dialectal change within their communities (see, for example, Thomas, 1989; L. Milroy, 1992). Research by Cheshire (1982) and Eisikovits (1981), looking at the use of vernacular language forms in adolescent groups, echoed the findings of Trudgill and Labov. Drawing on network theory, Cheshire's work showed that adolescent social groups tend to be organized in terms of gender, the boys hang out with boys, the girls with girls, therefore, their speech patterns tend to be reflective of their own same-sex groupings. Eisikovits's study, examining vernacular use in two different age groups, showed that while 16-year-old girls conformed to the expected pattern, the 13-year-old girls showed a higher usage of non-standard vernacular forms. Eisikovits's work suggests that socialized patterns of language use maybe both age- and gender-related. Work by Eckert (1989) has also considered the issue of social groups and their effect on linguistic choice, and her work concludes that for adolescent high school students, the influence of group membership and identity may have a bigger impact on vernacular language use than gender alone.

Various reasons have been put forward to account for gender-specific patterns of language use, including, women's position in society, the need for women to work harder to prove themselves in the marketplace and the issue of covert prestige among males in using vernacular slang. However, although these trends in language use have been well documented, we should always remember that as Eisikovits and Eckert show, a choice to use vernacular forms may be affected by numerous variables such as group identity, class, age, culture and even affective mood.

Gender and social interaction: difference and dominance

Studies within the *dominance* approach have often centered on specific discourse features such as turn-taking (Lakoff, 1975). It has been suggested, for example, that men are more likely to interrupt women (Fishman, 1978; Sattel, 1983) and control the conversational floor (Edelsky, 1981). However, other research has questioned whether we can identify such differences as being gender-specific. O'Barr and Atkins (1980) have suggested that power is a variable affected by status rather than gender. Leet-Pellegrini (1980) also takes this line but suggests that the issue is more complex. Leet-Pellegrini's research examined conversations in mixed gender dyads, when one member of the dyad was given knowledge that conferred upon them "expert status" in relation to a topic. Her conclusion was that women, as well as men, talked significantly more when adopting the role of "expert," suggesting that power dynamics and dominance within a conversation emerge from the interaction of both status and gender. Research by Woods (1989) supported Leet-Pellegrini's viewpoint but also suggested that, while the interactions examined showed an interplay between gender and status, gender was the most salient variable invoked.

The *difference* approach (Maltz and Borker, 1982; Tannen, 1993) suggests men and women are socialized within "different" cultures and it is this socialization process that accounts for the variations in their talk. As with the dominance approach, much of the research in this paradigm has involved examining conversational patterns within cross-sex interactions (Zimmerman and West, 1975; Aries, 1976; Dubois and Crouch, 1977;

Tannen, 1994) and a considerable body of research into the use of interruptions, turn-taking, topic management and use of tag questions within cross-sex interactions has emerged. Many of these studies concluded that men were more likely to interrupt, topic switch and take longer turns, features "typically" seen as evidence that men dominate conversations. Women, on the other hand, were more tentative in their use of discourse strategies, showing a higher use of forms such as tag questions. However, contrary to these claims, a critical review of over 40 studies (James and Clark, 1993: 268) found no significant differences between the sexes in the respect of both interruptions and the amount of talk of either sex.

Women's talk and cooperativity

Cooperativity is a common theme within gender research (Kalcik, 1975; Coates, 1986, 1991, 1996). It has been argued that women are more co-operative and supportive both within cross-sex and single-sex conversations. Coates (1989), in particular, has argued that women's use of tentative linguistic features such as epistemic modality and back-channeling led to its being wrongly labeled as "powerless." Such features, Coates suggests, function to reinforce solidarity and promote cooperativity. For women, the group voice dominates the voice of the individual, resulting in an "end product that is cooperative talk" (Coates, 1991: 301). Certainly, research has established that "talk plays a very important role in the maintenance of egalitarian relationships between female friends" (Atkinson, 1993).

Self-disclosure and gender

Matching or "mirroring" (Coates, 1996) of stories within talk involving painful self-disclosure (PSD) suggests that women actively seek solidarity within all-female interactions. While PSD has often been "labeled as characteristic of all-female talk" (Atkinson, 1993: 39), there have been few studies closely examining PSD in men's talk and, therefore, such generalizations may not be a true representation of reality. Askew and Ross (1988), for example suggested that self-disclosure, particularly the telling of sensitive information, may be seen as a sign of vulnerability. Boys, they claim, are conditioned not to express weakness whereas girls are socialized to express their feelings. Just as it is socially more acceptable for women to cry, so it is apparently perceived as less face-threatening for women to self-disclose, in both same-sex and cross-sex interactions. Askew and Ross conclude that the gender bias inherent in the use of PSD is due to socialization.

Coates (1996) has suggested that the intimate and personal nature of PSD relies upon cooperative talk. Features such as hedging, back-channeling, simultaneous speech and topic matching are more likely to occur in PSD. Coates argues that, as men do not typically disclose intimate topics in all-male groups, they have less need to use these forms of linguistic strategies. Tannen, however, suggests that men respond to self-disclosure with advice rather than "matching" stories (1991: 49). Thus, it may be that it is the choice of discursive strategies that reflects the real difference between men's and women's approaches to PSD, women tending to cooperate by offering evidence of similar troubles while men, rather than avoiding PSD encounters, attempt to offer solutions. However, women's PSD talk does not always orient towards cooperativity or a collaborative floor. For example, Guendouzi (1998) found that in her data-set, women "mirror" PSD accounts in a way that was competitive rather than cooperative.

Gender and social capital

Historically society has come to value talk that is instrumental, or task-oriented, talk that is concerned with "important" issues such as culture, business or politics, and typically this is talk that is seen as functioning within the male domain. On the other hand, talk that reflects the interpersonal dimension of society, such as gossip or small talk, has been associated predominantly with women. Ethnographic studies examining language use within specific communities show that gossip is a discourse practice that is socially marked for gender (Haviland, 1977; Yerkovich, 1977; Bok, 1983; Bergman, 1993). It has been suggested that, for example, women may self-regulate their own behaviors for fear of becoming the targets of gossip and losing social status (Rysman, 1977). Eckert (1993) described gossip as an element of "girl talk" that allowed females to keep track of an individual's behavior in relation to "acceptable" norms.

Eckert argues that women had to sell their moral worth within the social marketplace in order to obtain "domestic status" (1993: 34). The "better" woman got the "better" domestic situation. Women, therefore, have a vested interest in maintaining a "good" reputation. Eckert points to a competitive element in all-female conversations that is embedded within the dimensions of historical tradition and everyday social interaction. The notion of competing within a social market where the commodity is "women" themselves suggests that women may discursively use cooperative strategies in order to maintain social status by competing for social capital.

It is because sociolinguistics has focused on identifying the features of women's speech, rather than on the ways in which women's talk functions within individual social contexts, that overgeneralizations, particularly in relation to cooperativity have been made. Ochs has suggested "the relation between language and gender is not a simple straightforward mapping of linguistic form to social meaning of gender" (1992: 336) and as Guendouzi's work on gossip (2001) suggests, we cannot simply assume a positive function for all instances of "women's talk."

Gender, language and socialization

A further area that needs mention in any review of language and gender is the research relating to gender socialization in pre-adult contexts (e.g., Goodwin-Harness, 1980; Sheldon, 1990; Eckert, 1993; Eder, 1993), particularly those studies that involve educational settings. Schools and other institutional settings "develop and reinforce sex segregations, stereotypes and discriminations" (Delamont, 1990: 2). Certainly many of the claims of the adult literature relating to gender-specific language use have been reported in educational settings. Boys have been reported to adopt more dominant roles within the classroom, while girls, it is claimed, are more cooperative. However, this may be due to teacher expectations and/or socialization rather than simply biological difference. As Swann and Graddol (1995: 135) note, educators "routinely differentiate between girls and boys." A large body of literature (e.g., Spender, 1982; Clarricoates, 1983; French and French, 1984; Sadker and Sadker, 1985; Swann and Graddol, 1988, 1995; Delamont, 1990) has backed the claims that certain forms of verbal behaviors, for example "calling out," are more acceptable from boys. In her study considering the issue of gender difference in the classroom, Altani (1995) has reiterated the viewpoint that gender-specific behaviors may be reinforced by teacher expectations.

Lee, Hewlett and Nairn (1995) have investigated the question of whether children's gender can be identified from speech alone. As they have noted in their review of the literature, it is a "foregone conclusion" that gender is identifiable in adult studies of speech (1995: 194). In their own study they found that overall the judges correctly identified the gender of the speakers, despite the fact that the statistical evidence showed no significant difference in fundamental frequency (fundamental frequency is often seen as one the most obvious markers for gender in adults). While their research was primarily concerned with acoustic measurement of speech, the results suggest that beyond fundamental frequency, language use, in children, is marked for gender.

Accounts of both the dominance and difference approaches have focused on the discussion of gender socialization and women's historical social roles. While these theories may differ in many respects, one aspect of the debate that most researchers appear to agree upon is the fact that, based upon the evidence in the data examined, women's and men's talk often reveals different discourse features. As noted above, the features associated with men's talk were traditionally seen to be more powerful – men's talk is talk that gets things done! Women's talk, on the other hand, has been seen as functioning within the interpersonal domain and has been associated with domesticity and relationship building. Given these factors, it is easy to see why, in terms of what was historically valued in western society, women's talk was devalued.

However, despite a call for a "re-thinking" (Bergvall, Bing, and Freed, 1992) of the gender debate and research suggesting that speaker styles may be context-bound (Leet-Pellegrini, 1980; O'Barr and Atkins, 1980), not enough attention has been paid to the complex variables involved in interactions when discussing language and gender. It is understandable that feminists have felt a need to challenge those aspects of language that they felt helped to support a patriarchal society. The devaluation of women's language styles was a hegemonic issue that needed addressing; yet, in the debate that followed we may have marginalized both women and men and more particularly our children. We seem to be left with a legacy that assumes women are always from "Venus" and men from "Mars." Perhaps it is now time to move on and refrain from defining these forms of talk as gender-specific and view communication practices as products of both their function and context.

Speech pathology and the gender debate

In relation to clinical contexts there are two major areas where the gender debate is highly important; first, the question of whether individual language ability is a learned or biologically based behavior and, second, the issue of how "expert" clinicians interact with their clients. The first issue is probably the most controversial – are the differences that have been noted in the language abilities and behaviors of girls and boys a result of gender socialization or biological difference? It will not have escaped the attention of anyone who has worked in a pediatric speech pathology clinic that the majority of the clients receiving therapy are male. The numbers of boys who are diagnosed as having dyslexia, as being PDD or autistic are noticeably greater than for girls. Further, child language studies have shown a difference in the rate of phonological development in boys and girls (Berko-Gleason, 2001). This also applies to children diagnosed with ADD/ADHD, although recent revisions in the DSM-IV (2000) diagnosis for Attention Deficit Disorders, to include individuals who do not have the "hyperactive" component has resulted in many more girls being diagnosed with ADD (Ratey, 2002). Very few clinicians, if any, would deny the likelihood of some biological basis for the differences in boys' and girls' language abilities, the sheer number of boys coming into clinics stands testament to this fact, but we also need to be aware that gender stereotyping may account for some of these trends.

The issue of ADD/ADHD and dyslexia provides a good example of a potentially socialized gender behavior masking a real learning difficulty. Girls have often fallen through the educational net when it comes to diagnosis of ADD/ADHD and dyslexia simply because they are quieter and less likely to disrupt the class. Girls have historically been brought up to be quieter and "more ladylike" so therefore language problems are often missed until later or may be overlooked completely. Conversely, it is often the case that, as boys are expected to be louder and more aggressive, people will talk to them in louder voices which results in the boys reproducing more aggressive verbal behaviors. Women have been socialized to be more cooperative and less dominating in their talk and it is interesting to note that former British Prime Minister, Margaret Thatcher, whose "dominant" style of leadership and talk proved highly successful in the political arena, was often described by the media as an honorary "man."

Cognitive scientists and behaviorists have long argued the issue of whether language behaviors are socially learned or genetically hard-wired. Recent research in the neurosciences and improved imaging technology have given us greater insight into the ways in which language is processed in the brain, and it is now the case that many disorders that may have previously been attributed to bad parenting, for example, ADHD/ADD or autism, have been shown to have biological bases. While we do not yet fully understand the implications of these biological differences, we now know that we cannot simply attribute speech or behavioral disorders to socialization alone. Ironically our increased knowledge about the brain's plasticity has also shown just how important a role "input" plays when wiring the brain. So, while we have learnt that there are real biological differences within individual brains, we are also more aware that social and environmental input plays a major role in "wiring" the brain. We do have biological differences but these, like gender traits, are not always "hard-wired" and immutable (Ratey, 2002).

So where does this leave us in relation to the question of language, gender and the clinician? The gender debate has implications within client–clinician interactions, particularly in relation to the issue of power dynamics. As Leet-Pellegrini (1980) has shown, individuals tend to adopt a "powerful" style of talking when they have "expert" status conferred on them. It is likely that a female clinician may verbally index her identity through her social role of "expert" rather than the variable of gender. It is not necessarily the case that because she is a women, she will adopt a different style to her male colleagues, although it could be claimed that a lifetime of gender socialization may lead to a higher percentage of female clinicians being less dominating and more supportive of interlocutor needs within their conversational interactions.

We should also consider whether or not "female" styles should be actively encouraged, or even taught within the clinical professions. While clinical contexts, whether therapeutic or diagnostic, often call for the professional to adopt the "expert role," it may ultimately prove more useful to use conversational styles that are more cooperative and less "dominating." There is of course a converse side to this viewpoint; there are always contexts where the immediate circumstances demand a more aggressive or decisive approach. For example, military contexts, 911 calls and medical emergency situations may call for instantaneous expert input, with one participant, regardless of gender, taking control of the interaction. Furthermore, "appropriateness" of style may also be related to the expectations of the participants. "Some clients/patients may want the clinician to play the expert role, at least initially and with regard to diagnosis; after all, they are the specialists" (Müller, personal communication, 2003).

In reviewing the literature, it is clear that interpretation of much of the research has resulted in a viewpoint that sees the verbal behaviors of both men and women in terms of polar opposites. While early gender studies interpreted women's speech styles as powerless, later work sought to reinterpret this research in positive ways (Coates, 1996). However, we should

remember that much of the work within sociolinguistics has focused primarily on men's and women's talk from the critical ideology of feminism and,
while there have been some exceptions (e.g., Johnson and Meinhof, 1997;
Shockey and Coates, 2003), little has been done to thoroughly examine the
features of men's talk. Interactions are complex manifestations of human
behavior and in seeking to explain certain styles of talk we need to look at
communication from a functional perspective, considering all aspects of the
interaction. Linguistic behaviors are dependent on many variables, for example, affective mood, biological ability, knowledge of a subject, degree of
social distance, environment and speaker goals. Our choice of linguistic
strategies will ultimately be the result of many things, the way we have been
socialized, the context we are in, our immediate needs or perhaps our long-
term goals, therefore, we cannot attribute features of communication to
gender alone. Although socialization is a major influence on behavior, we
cannot assume that all men are naturally aggressive and competitive, or
that all women are naturally cooperative and supportive – boys can be cooperative clients and girls may have aggressive behaviors. The good clinician should be "critically" aware of the findings and limitations of gender
research and recognize that speech styles may arise through the functional
or social needs of the individual rather than simply their biological gender.

Further reading

Eckert, P. and McConnell-Ginet, S. (2003) *Language and Gender*. Cambridge:
  Cambridge University Press.
Hall, K. and Bucholz, M. (1995) *Gender Articulated: Language and the Social Con-
  struction of Self.* London: Routledge.
Holmes, J. and Meyerhoff, M. (2002) *The Handbook of Language and Gender*.
  Oxford: Blackwell.
Talbot, M. (1999) *Language and Gender: An Introduction*. Cambridge: Polity Press.

4

Bilingualism and Multilingualism

John Edwards

Competence in more than one language can be approached either at an individual or a social level and, depending upon the perspective, different dimensions must be emphasized. A discussion of individual bilingualism, for instance, may involve linguistic and psycholinguistic matters which figure much less prominently, if at all, at the social level – where historical, educational, sociological and political aspects are often the most salient. Nonetheless, we are not dealing with watertight compartments here and so – while they provide convenient categories for discussion – it is always salutary to remember the connections between the two. Since other chapters in this collection focus upon second-language acquisition and its ramifications, I shall highlight some of the broader factors. It is important, however, to begin with some basics although, even here, I shall stress the social aspects of individual bilingualism, if I may put it that way.

Definitional matters

Who does not know at least a few words in languages other than the maternal variety? If, as an English speaker, you can say, or at least understand, *c'est la vie* or *gracias* or *guten Tag* or *tovarisch*, you clearly have some "command" of a foreign tongue. Such competence, of course, does not lead many to think of bilingualism. If, on the other hand, you are conversationally fluent in more than one language, then bilingualism may be an apt designation. And if, like the Steiners, Stoppards, Kunderas and Nabokovs of the world – and millions more like them – your linguistic competences are highly developed, perhaps to the extent that abilities are balanced, then the bilingual (or multilingual) label seems apter still. The question here, of course, is one of degree. Beyond the informal interest attaching to degrees and abilities – who is Guinness book material in the language category? – the assessment of linguistic competence has considerable scholarly importance.

It is easy to find definitions of bilingualism that reflect widely divergent responses to the question of degree. Bloomfield (1933) once observed that bilingualism resulted from the addition of a perfectly learned foreign language to one's own, undiminished native tongue, but he confused the issue by admitting that the definition of "perfection" was relative. With this acknowledgement, Bloomfield did not remove the question of degree, but he implied that any division between monolingualism and bilingualism should occur nearer to the Steiner/Nabokov end of the continuum than to the *gracias* one. Others have been purposely vaguer: Weinreich (1953), for instance, was content to define bilingualism simply as the alternate use of two languages. At about the same time, Haugen (1953) suggested that bilingualism began with the ability to produce complete and meaningful utterances in the second language. While "complete" and "meaningful" are, once again, hardly transparent concepts, the suggestion here is that even members of the *gracias* camp might be deemed bilingual. Generally speaking, earlier definitions tended to restrict bilingualism to equal mastery of two languages, while later ones have allowed much greater variation in competence. But since this relaxation proves in practice to be as imprecise as an argument from perfection, most modern treatments acknowledge that any useful discussion must be attempted within a specific context, and for specific purposes.

Further complicating this matter of degree, on this question of where bilingualism starts, is the fact that any line drawn must cross not just one general language dimension, but many specific threads of ability. Consider, first, that there are four basic language skills: listening, speaking, reading and writing. Consider further the possible subdivisions: speaking skill, for example, includes what may be quite divergent levels of expression in vocabulary, grammar and accent. In fact, there are about 20 elements here, all of which figure in the assessment of bilingualism; and – as any cursory regard to "bilingual" speech quickly demonstrates – it does not follow that strength in one means strength in another.

A number of tests are commonly employed to measure bilingualism: rating scales of various sorts, and fluency, flexibility and dominance tests. The first of these can involve interviews, usage measures and self-assessment procedures. In some ways, relying upon self-ratings has a lot to recommend it, but the strengths here rest upon the capacity of an individual to be able to self-report accurately, a roughly equivalent sense across individuals of what competence means, and a disinterested and unbiased willingness to communicate proficiency levels. None of these can be taken for granted and, indeed, some of the problems here can also affect the apparently more objective tests of fluency and flexibility. Beyond such difficulties, it can easily be understood that factors such as attitude, age, sex, intelligence, memory, linguistic distance between the two languages, and context of testing are all potentially confounding. Furthermore, even if we were able to gauge bilingual competence with some accuracy, there would remain problems of adequate labeling; after all, it is hardly to be expected that measured individuals would neatly fall into one, or two, or four neat categories of ability, or degrees of bilingualism. There even remains confusion as to what term ought to be applied to those intriguing individuals whose bilingual capacities are large: "balanced bilinguals," "ambilinguals" and "equilinguals" have all been suggested – and used. Baetens Beardsmore (1986) described the ambilingual as a person who, in all contexts, can function equally well in either language, and who shows no trace of language A when using B, and vice versa. But, given that such individuals constitute a "rare if not non-existent species" (p. 7), the terms "balanced bilingual" or "equilingual" are reserved for those whose mastery of both varieties is more roughly equivalent. While none of this is very clear, it is certainly the case that the vast number of those to whom the term "bilingual" can be at all reasonably applied fall into the category of "non-fluent" bilingualism.

There are some other matters too, which must be briefly mentioned here, and which cut across the larger topic of degree of fluency. For instance, a useful distinction can be made between receptive (or passive) bilingualism, and productive (or active) competence; the difference here is between those who understand a language but cannot produce it themselves, and those who can do both. A receptive competence only has been referred to as "semibilingualism" – which is not to be confused with another, "semilingualism," a term referring to a lack of full fluency in either language. In 1927, Bloomfield famously characterized this in his description of a North American Indian: "White Thunder . . . speaks less English than Menomini, and that is a strong indictment, for his Menomini is atrocious . . . he may be said to speak no language tolerably" (p. 437). More recently, the idea of knowing neither of two languages well has been advanced in connection with ethnic minority-group speakers, and this has meant that "semilingualism" has become extended from a solely linguistic description to a catchword with political and ideological overtones relating to majorities and minorities, domination and subordination, oppression and victimization. We see here a return to the confusion surrounding "balanced bilingualism," where complete monolingualism anchors the argument at one end, and "full competence" in two (or more, of course) languages is at the other. Thus, for example, one could imagine a person who was both a semilingual and a balanced bilingual, if one allowed that two *incomplete* fluencies were matched. Added to all this is the common metaphor of some finite language capacity, which has bedeviled the literature for some time: at its simplest, the suggestion is that what you gain on the swings of one language you lose on the roundabouts of the other. But using such a container metaphor for language acquisition and skills may be quite mistaken or, at least, vastly oversimplified, for even if we were to admit some finite-capacity model, all that we know of intellectual structures and functions would indicate that that capacity is quite large enough that we need not worry about exceeding our limits.

Another important distinction is that between "additive" and "subtractive" bilingualism. In some circumstances the learning of another language represents an expansion of the linguistic repertoire; in others, it may lead to a replacement of the first. The different outcomes reflect different social pressures and needs, and here we can only note that additive bilingualism occurs principally where both languages continue to be useful and valued; a classic example is found in the bilingualism of aristocracies and social elites in systems in which it was considered natural and proper that every educated person know more than one variety. Subtractive bilingualism, on the other hand, often reflects a social context in which one language is valued more than the other, where one dominates the other, where one is on the ascendant and the other is waning.

Yet another common distinction is between "primary" and "secondary" bilingualism, between a dual competence acquired naturally through contextual demands, and one where systematic and formal instruction has occurred. These are not mutually exclusive, of course – it is not uncommon to attain a conversational grasp of a language in a relatively informal way, and then feel the need to add some skills (in reading and writing, say) in a more rigorous fashion. Still, there are some interesting and broadly-based differences between primary and secondary bilingualism, some of which lead us towards the wider social level: compare, for example, those English–Gaelic bilinguals, in the west of Ireland or in the Highlands and islands of Scotland, whose fluencies result from growing up in a particular location, with those who, in Dublin, Glasgow or Edinburgh, have more self-consciously set themselves to become bilingual. Consider further the ways in which lumping these two groups together, under a single "bilingual" rubric, might muddy several waters.

Aspects of bilingual behavior

The fact that a majority of the global population has at least some level of multilingual competence surely indicates that adding a second language need not be some superhuman or unnatural feat. And yet, especially within powerful linguistic groups, it is common to find references to the difficulties involved or to the peculiar lack of language talents supposedly possessed. English and American monolinguals, for example, often complain that they have no aptitude for foreign-language learning, a lament often accompanied by expressions of envy for those multilingual Europeans or Asians, and sometimes (more subtly) by a linguistic smugness reflecting a deeply held conviction that, after all, those clever "others" who don't already know English will have to accommodate in a world made increasingly safe for anglophones. In fact – as I am sure those chapters focusing upon bilingual acquisition in theory and practice will show – the contexts for successful language learning, and the factors involved it, are quite well understood and are not theoretically inaccessible to speakers of "big" varieties.

Among the social elite for whom an additional language or two was always an integral part of civilized life, it has always been understood that one's personality broadens with the expansion of the linguistic repertoire Yet, if there have been many who have seen bilinguals as having an extra arrow in the quiver, there have also been those who demurred. Some of the most famous of linguists, in fact, expressed reservations; for example, here is Firth's opinion:

> The average bilingual speaker, it is true, has two strings to his bow – one rather slacker than the other . . . every cultured man needs a second and perhaps a third foreign language – but he need not be bilingual. The unilingual have the advantage, and the bigger the cultural community in that language the bigger the advantage. (1970: 211)

From the current standpoint, Firth's view looks quite misinformed, even if his second sentence does encourage a capacity which most would now admit as bilingual – although his concluding note surely has a contemporary resonance. Weinreich (1953), too, was able to quote many expressions of the problems allegedly faced by bilinguals; these included split national loyalties and problems of "marginalization" (or *anomie* – to use Durkheim's famous term), emotional difficulties, moral depravity (through receiving inadequate religious instruction in their mother tongue), stuttering, left-handedness, excessive materialism, laziness, and detrimental consequences for intelligence. These bizarre ideas are very dated, to say the least, and Weinreich himself was generally dismissive, preferring experimental evidence – which is always in shorter supply than the speculation underpinning most assertions. He cites with approval, for example, a study done in the 1940s which demonstrated that the problems of bilinguals are much more likely to stem from social factors in bilingual households than from linguistically-driven "mental conflict." This is much more in line with modern thinking, although if it were true that bilingual families have a heightened level of social tension this could be taken as an indirect discouragement of bilingualism. No such evidence is available.

There are some less contentious concomitants of bilingualism and among the most obvious – and most immediately socially relevant – are the phenomena of borrowing, interference and code-switching. For, while outright language choice is obviously available to bilingual speakers, less clear-cut accommodations are often made. Thus, it is common to find linguistic alteration occurring within one unit of speech directed to one listener, alteration deriving from contact among different varieties. In his classic volume on the subject, Weinreich (1953: 1) referred to all such "deviation from the norms of either language" as interference. It seems evident, however, that not every switch from one language to another results from the unwelcome intrusion which "interference" suggests; speakers may often switch for emphasis, because they feel that the *mot juste* is found more readily in one of their languages than in another, or because of their perceptions of the speech situation, changes in content, the linguistic skills of their interlocutors, degrees of intimacy, and so on. Some writers have thus opted for the more neutral term "transference," which implies *inter alia* a greater element of volition. An example of this "code-switching" is shown in Poplack's title: "Sometimes I'll start a sentence in English *y terminó en español*" (1980).

A considerable amount of research has been devoted to the understanding of the linguistic factors which may account for various types of transference, the constraints which make one form more likely or common than another, and so on; obviously this has a great deal to do with the grammar and syntax of each of the languages involved. Different *types* of language transfer can be easily understood. For example, if a Brussels French speaker uses the Dutch *vogelpik* for a game of darts, rather than the standard French *fléchettes*, this is an example of lexical transfer. Further, *vogelpik* in this context constitutes a "loanword" since it is an "intrusion" regularly used in unchanged form. (Sometimes, indeed, loanwords become very widely used and, if we go far enough, we reach the level of permanent inter-language borrowing: think of all the foreign words adopted in English.) It may, however, be given a French pronunciation, which indicates another type of alteration, an attempt to bring the foreign element into the maternal fold (think of the French adoption of *pullover* as "poolovaire"). Another variety of lexical transfer occurs when loan translation occurs: for example, the adoption of the English *skyscraper* into Dutch (as *wolkenkrabber*), German (*Wolkenkratzer*), French (*gratte-ciel*) and Spanish (*rascacielos*). Morphological transfers occur when a word in language A is more fully embraced by language B: the Dutch *kluts* (dollop) becomes, in Brussels French, *une clouche*, and *heilbot* (halibut) becomes *un elbot*. Syntactic transfer occurs in such examples as "*Tu prends ton plus haut chiffre*" ("You take your highest figure") – said by a native Dutch speaker, who makes the adjectives precede the noun, as they would in Dutch but not as they would in French. Phonological transfer is very common, of course, and is a most difficult area in which to avoid interference (think of fluent adult speakers with "horrible" accents); equally, prosodic transfer – subtle differences in stress and intonation between languages, such that one's dominant variety influences the other – is also difficult to avoid (see Edwards, 1994).

However we divide the subject up, and whatever labels we apply – interference, code-switching, mixing, transference – it is clear that in all cases something is "borrowed" from another language. Further, while the degree to which the borrowed element is integrated (or can be integrated) into its new linguistic home is of considerable interest in studies of the individual bilingual, it can be more useful still in illuminating aspects of group contact, of relative linguistic prestige, of the perceived or actual ease with which different languages deal with given topics, and so on. Borrowing also elicits attitudes, and these have often been negative, particularly on the part of monolinguals who may dismiss it as gibberish. Terms like "Tex-Mex," "Franglais," "Japlish" (and many others) are often meant pejoratively. But bilinguals themselves are sometimes wont to see their behavior here as "embarrassing," "impure," "lazy," even "dangerous," although the reasons they give for switching – fitting the word to the topic, finding a word with a nuance unavailable in the other variety, helping out a listener, strengthening intimacy, and so on – make a great deal of sense. If you have two languages to draw upon, why not maximize this happy circumstance as appropriate? The chimeras of impurity and laziness are exposed when we realize that, very often, switching involves the repetition – for emphasis, for intimacy – of the same idea in both languages.

Stable bilingualism

If we recognize that bilingualism, switching and other dual-language phenomena are still seen as suspicious by some and arcane marks of erudition by others, we should also recall their global nature. Expanded linguistic competence is usually driven by necessity but it has also historically reflected and supported upper-class boundaries. There is a distinction, in other words, between "elite" and "folk" bilingualism. In different ages, not to have known Latin or Greek or French in addition to one's mother tongue would have been unthinkable for educated people. At other levels and for other reasons more humble citizens have also been bilingual from earliest times: we know it was necessary under the Ptolemies to acquire Greek, even for quite minor posts, and Athenian slaves – representatives of the lowest class of all – were often bilingual as they were pressed into domestic service and teaching.

Collective bilingualism in many settings, ancient and modern, is an enduring quantity, unlike the impermanent, transitional variety common in many immigrant contexts – where, in fact, bilingualism is often a generational way-station on the road between two unilingualisms. Thus, the classic pattern for newcomers to the United States has been bilingualism (mother tongue and English) by the second generation and English monolingualism by the third. More permanent collective bilingualism remains, of course, largely because of a continuing necessity which is absent among most immigrant populations, and this necessity usually rests upon different social functions and different domains of use for each language. This situation is now commonly referred to as *diglossia*. This word is simply the Greek version of *bilingualism* and it does not logically encompass the social, collective aspect that, in practice, it refers to. However, "*la logique n'est pas maître de la terminologie*" (Mackey, 1989: 11). While diglossia was initially meant to signify the coexistence of dialects within the same language – typically "high" and "low" variants – it has been commonly extended to involve separate languages altogether. And, while diglossia is generally seen as the stable end of a dual-language continuum, it must be remembered that even

stability is relative. The French–English diglossia that prevailed in England
after the Norman conquest eventually broke down and the "low" variety
(English) achieved dominance.

Multilingual possibilities

While bilingualism (and multilingualism) at a personal level always imply
some degree of fluency in more than one variety, diglossia and societal
multilingualism may or may not involve more than monolingual individual
abilities. Some societies are made up largely of people who are multilingual,
and some are (explicit or implicit) federal arrangements that politically unite
different "monolingual" speech communities – I put the word in inverted
commas here, because there are surely very few groups so homogeneous
that no whisper of multiplicity can be heard. Similarly, some societies are
multilingual *de jure*, while others extract a single official variety from a *de
facto* multilingualism. Official stances on language matters are always important, for they build upon historical and traditional patterns of power and
tolerance – suggesting, for instance, underlying conceptions of diversity and
pluralism, illuminating the treatment of minority groups, and revealing
attitudes about linguistic usage and aspirations.

Multilingualism is clearly a more prevalent global condition than
monolingualism – a fact easily forgotten by those who speak a "big" language. A simple indication here is that something like 5,000 languages exist
in a world divided into only 200 states: the *de facto* situation is clear. At
official levels, however, we find that only about a quarter of those states
recognize more than one language and, even where this sort of multilingualism
has legal standing, one language is often found to be more equal than the
other(s), or varieties hold sway only in particular regions, or socio–economic
power adheres more closely to some forms than to others, and so on. The
relationship between policy and usage is not always clear. Multilingual
encounters may be *less* frequent in countries recognizing more than one
language (if, for example, the recognition is territorially limited) than in
officially monolingual states: Nigeria formally sanctions only English, but
its 80 million people speak some 400 languages. Much, of course, has to do
with individual and group needs and desires. In India, where 15 languages
have legal status, one could certainly live out one's days monolingually – but
there are multilingual potentials which cannot exist in more homogeneous
surroundings:

A Bombay spice merchant has, as his maternal variety, a Kathiawari dialect of Gujerati, but at work he most often uses Kacchi. In the marketplace he speaks Marathi and, at the railway station, Hindustani. On internal air flights English is used, and he may watch English-language films at the cinema. He reads a Gujerati newspaper written in a dialect more standard than his own. (Edwards, 1994: 2)

Simple mobility in a multilingual environment necessitates this sort of linguistic flexibility. Less immediately obvious, perhaps, is that multiple fluencies are rarely (if ever) equally developed (or fully "balanced"). It would be uneconomic, in the broadest sense, to "overdevelop" them beyond the needs associated with each: you may know just enough Marathi to buy rice, but your Gujerati is more fully-fleshed.

The development of multilingualism

The underlying dynamic behind multilingualism is that of mobility and contact. Immigrants bring their varieties together, and into contact with those of the "receiving" society. Other sorts of expansion – territorial, colonial, imperialist, mercantile – may produce similar effects, even though it is not always necessary for great numbers of people to physically move: military and economic pressures, for instance, involving only a handful of soldiers, bureaucrats and traders, can create cultural and linguistic contacts which give rise to multilingual adaptations. India is an apposite example once again, one that also illustrates how original exigencies can fade away without necessarily taking such adaptations with them. A foreign and intrusive language may leave various residues – of status, of culture, of international access – which continue to support multilingualism long after the imperial armies have gone home.

Another common scenario that leads to multilingualism is political union among speech communities: Belgium, Canada and Switzerland are examples here. Such unions need not involve, of course, partners equal in numbers or power and, even within the three democracies I have just listed, real or perceived imbalances find their linguistic expression; there are, of course, other much more pointed examples of asymmetrical unions. Federations may be built upon arbitrary and often involuntary amalgamations – the Canada which unites the two "charter" groups, the two "founding peoples," is *also* the Canada which incorporates a million members of the aboriginal "first nations." Welsh- and Gaelic-speaking parts of the United Kingdom remind us of another sort of incorporation. Colonial boundary-marking and state-creation – as carried out in Africa, Asia and South America – provide even more egregious examples of imposed associations that have linguistic consequences (see Edwards, 2003).

The consequences of multilingualism

There is a finite number of responses to the communicative problems created by multilingualism, and one of these is multilingualism itself. That is, faced with a diversity of languages, one could argue for the expansion of individual repertoires: if there are a dozen varieties spoken in your region, and if everyone knows each of them, then there is no problem. But this, of course, ignores the facts that not everyone might need to know all 12 languages, that some will be restricted in scope (by their speakers' status, or by accepted domain limitations), that it would probably be unproductive to aim for native-like fluency in all cases, and so on. There are other problems, too. Where does "your" region end? Why stop at the border within which these dozen languages are found? Won't you ever need to deal with the state next door, the state where there are another dozen varieties? We have every reason to believe that, given sufficient cause and motivation – and time – individual multilingual capabilities could be greatly increased; at the same time we realize that, however proficient we were to become, communicative difficulties would remain. Responses to multilingualism other than personal repertoire expansion are required. Beyond just expansion, there are two basic ways to cross the barriers created by a multilingual world: they involve either some sort of lingua franca, or translation.

If we look first at link languages, we find three categories. First there are powerful "natural" languages which have, in one way or another, risen to prominence (these are sometimes referred to as "languages of wider communication"); second, there are restricted or simplified forms of languages, whose limited scope is easy to master but yet sufficient for most communicative purposes (these include *pidgin* and *creole* varieties); third, there are constructed varieties (sometimes – but never by their adherents – called "artificial" languages). Dominant varieties have historically served as bridges between language communities, and Greek and Latin are perhaps the prime examples. Today English is clearly *the* global lingua franca; indeed, its ubiquity and penetration make it by far the most powerful lingua franca ever seen. Whereas earlier link languages tended to co-exist with more local varieties, English seems – to some, at least – poised to push the others off the stage altogether. The second category of link languages comprises pidgins and creoles. The former involves some sort of mixture between varieties: indigenous languages and colonial ones, for instance, in contacts occasioned by mercantile expansion and exploration. The resulting vocabularies and grammars are usually very restricted, intended only to allow simple communication. It is easy to see that some pidgins would have a relatively short existence, while others might be required for a long time. Indeed, pidgin may evolve into creole: this occurs when those born in pidgin-speaking communities begin to find their medium insufficiently nuanced. Creolization implies the greater linguistic richness and expression required in a mother tongue. Finally here, constructed languages can also act as lingua francas; Esperanto is the best-known example, but hundreds of varieties have been built. In most instances, the initial desire has been to produce some sort of neutral auxiliary that everyone could agree to learn as a second (or subsequent) language. The general failure of constructed-language efforts arises chiefly because they are always up against powerful natural varieties.

The other broad approach to multilingual matters is translation. There are, of course, many technical matters here but the basic idea is simplicity itself: selected individuals who have a foot in two (or more) linguistic camps can be bridges between them, relieving most members of each community of the need to expand their own repertoires. It is, admittedly, an unwieldy process, and works best when relatively infrequent contact is involved – or, of course, when the translation can achieve permanence through print or other stable record.

It is easy to understand that the forms and the consequences of multilingual contact assume special importance among groups of unequal status. Where minority-language populations are involved, for instance, concerns about linguistic (and cultural) survival are intimately entwined with the use of a lingua franca or the scope of translation. In fact, since minority status implies limited power, the agendas for cross-group communication are usually set by others. Lingua francas, as we have seen, are usually the languages of powerful communities, and they may elbow other varieties out of their indigenous niches altogether. This, at least, is the more or less constant worry among minority-group members. Similarly, translations involving "small" languages will inevitably decrease in quantity – and in appeal – as the languages themselves retreat before powerful neighbors. The overall danger is an accelerating downward spiral, the logical conclusion of which is one ultimate answer to multilingualism: monolingualism. If everyone speaks the lingua franca, then outright replacement of smaller varieties becomes a very real possibility. This is an unacceptable solution to many people, particularly (of course) those whose languages are threatened. It is beyond the scope and purpose of this chapter to investigate the linguistic impulses created by group interaction: language maintenance, shift and revival. They are among the most dramatic consequences of multilingual contact, reminding us of the formidable power of language as a marker of group identity. Why would people struggle so long and so passionately for a purely instrumental medium? The symbolic aspects of language, its role as mediator of cultures and civilizations, its literary expression, its central position in nationalist politics – these, too, are part of the larger story of multilingualism.

Further reading

Baker, C. and Jones, S. (1998) *Encyclopedia of Bilingualism and Bilingual Education*. Clevedon: Multilingual Matters.

Grosjean, F. (1982) *Life with Two Languages: An Introduction to Bilingualism*. Cambridge, MA: Harvard University Press.

Hamers, J. and Blanc, M. (2000) *Bilinguality and Bilingualism*, 2nd edn. Cambridge: Cambridge University Press.

Li Wei (ed.) (2000) *The Bilingualism Reader*. London: Routledge.

5

Code-Switching and Diglossia

Nicole Müller and Martin J. Ball

This chapter introduces two separate, but often related areas of interaction, or contact, of two languages or language varieties: code-switching (CS) and diglossia. We do not intend here to give a systematic overview of all the relevant literature in the field; this would far exceed the limits of this chapter. Instead, we wish to offer our readers some handholds, both classificatory and conceptual, that will enable them to further explore these fascinating fields.

Code-switching

Terminologies

The literature on code-switching is large and varied, originating in multiple traditions of scholarship and investigation: sociology, sociolinguistics, psycho- and neurolinguistics, applied linguistics and language teaching, first and second language acquisition, and clinical linguistics, to name only a few. Different traditions bring with them different terminologies, and the scholarship on code-switching is no exception. Thus, one finds the terms code-switching and code-mixing, as well as (apparently) more straightforward terms such as borrowing, or loan-word. Terminologies always include underlying assumptions about the phenomena thus labeled or described, and our definitions will be no different in this matter. In our discussion, we shall use the term *code-switching* to include:

All phenomena where elements from at least two linguistic systems (separate languages, or distinguishable varieties of one language) are used in the same speech situation.

For our purposes, the term speech situation includes the participants, their motivations and agenda, the constraints on language use imposed by various factors, as well as the talk (or writing) that is produced by the participants.[1] We also presuppose, through this definition, the existence of different, distinguishable linguistic systems. In other words, for the moment we take it for granted that it is relatively straightforward to distinguish psychological, and social, entities called "languages" or "language varieties." This is not necessarily an unproblematic assumption, especially for example in early child language acquisition. The term *code-switching* itself also contains this assumption, namely that a changeover, a switch is involved from one meaning-making, or symbolic system (a code) to another. For descriptive purposes, we can let this assumption stand for now. However, one may wish to reserve judgment as regards the underlying psychological reality.

Our definition includes what many researchers would classify as code-mixing, namely intrasentential code-switching (see, e.g., Kamwangamalu, 1992; Muysken, 2000), as in example (1a), as well as intersentential code-switching (example (1b), which also shows what we would classify as a borrowing). We deliberately do not draw a distinct line between code-switching (or code-mixing) and nonce or spontaneous borrowing, since we are of the opinion that in many cases, the distinction is blurred at best. We also include switches that involve more than one speaker, but take place within the same speech situation, as in example (1c):[2]

(1) a. Ro'wn i'n   enormous. (Welsh–English)
         was-1s I PRT enormous
         'I was enormous.'
     b. Mae ganddi boyfriend newydd. He's just gorgeous!
         (Welsh–English)
         is   with-3sf boyfriend new
         'She has a new boyfriend.'
     c. A: Ti eisiau mynd am   baned o goffi?
         you want going about cup   of coffee
         'Do you want to go for a cup of coffee?'
         B: Sure. Absolutely. (Welsh–English)

A very basic, but also very important characteristic of CS is that it is not random. Just as monolingual speech or writing is rule governed, so is speech or writing that involves more than one language or language variety. There are systematic patterns we can observe; one might say that CS has its own grammar, and the patterns we observe are constrained by the patterns available in the languages (or varieties) involved. In this short overview chapter, we do not have the room for a detailed discussion of the various constraints on code-switching that have been discussed in the literature. For some key works, the reader is referred to the references, and the section on further reading. In investigating code-switching we must try to avoid an assumption that might be intuitively appealing especially for monolinguals, namely, that CS is an exception, something that needs to be explained in light of monolingual language practices. Rather, we should assume that CS can, and does, occur, whenever more than one linguistic system is available to the participants in a speech situation. In other words, bilingual (or multilingual) people in bilingual situations will code-switch.

CS *as product or process*

The phenomena included under our (deliberately wide) heading of CS can be described under many headings, and analyzed from many angles. A first distinction that comes to mind is that of CS as *product*, or as *process*. In other words, we can distinguish whether our focus of analysis is going to be the language (talk, writing) produced, and preserved in some medium (tape-recording, transcript, written text), or the process of producing language. If our focus of analysis is CS as a product, we look at CS as a feature of a text or texts.[3] We typically think of CS as a feature of spoken rather than written texts, and one typically finds that for example in educational contexts, spoken contexts tend to be more tolerant of CS than written ones. However, CS is not unknown in written contexts, although possibly less widely investigated. Illustrations from medieval Ireland that involve both Latin and Irish are given in examples (2) and (6).

An analysis of CS as a feature of text can involve a variety of questions. For example, we can investigate the possible role of CS in textual organization (see, e.g., Müller, 1999), CS as a marker for different text genres or types; we can look at stylistic features or levels of formality, or at CS as a projection of a writer's or speaker's cultural and linguistic identity in the text. We can also investigate the grammar of CS; aspects of language structure as they manifest themselves from the spoken or written data before us. In short, the basic questions we ask are where does CS occur, and how is CS patterned in the text?

If the target of our investigation is CS as a *process*, we can draw further distinctions. We may view CS primarily as a *behavior*, i.e., an aspect of a speaker's linguistic *performance*, influenced by various factors such as situational requirements, personal preference, and differential linguistic competence, or we may be more interested in any conclusions we can draw as to the nature of the speaker's *linguistic knowledge* or *competence*. Since the investigation of competence typically rests on the investigation of behaviors, and behaviors result in the production of texts, the distinction between a process focus and a product focus sometimes becomes somewhat blurred in language research.

CS at the level of the sentence and the text

As pointed out above, CS in a text may occur between sentences, or within sentences. One approach to the study of intrasentential CS is to distinguish between *base language* or *matrix language*, and *embedded language*, elements of which are *inserted* into the matrix language. In Myers-Scotton's Matrix Language Framework (e.g., Myers-Scotton, 1993a, 1995), the matrix language provides the grammatical frame, such that in mixed constituents, morpheme order will be that of the matrix language. Further, in mixed sentences, grammatical or systems morphemes are drawn from the matrix language. Into this frame, content morphemes (e.g., nouns, verbs, adjectives) from the embedded language are inserted. A constraint in this framework is expressed by the so-called blocking hypothesis: only content morphemes from the embedded language that fulfil three congruence conditions can be embedded into the matrix language. In order to be embeddable, a content morpheme has to have a match in the matrix language that has the same grammatical status, takes or assigns the same thematic roles (or participant roles), and fulfills equivalent discourse and pragmatic functions. In addition, intra-sentential CS may also involve "islands" from the embedded language, that is, constituents (for example, whole noun phrases, or verb phrases) that are formed from grammatical and content morphemes in the embedded language. Example (1a) illustrates the embedding of an English adjective into the predicative slot in a Welsh sentence. Example (2) shows an "island" (a prepositional phrase) of Latin in a medieval Irish sentence (from Müller, 1999: 77):

(2) Co   tainic Deman chuice in nocte i richt aingil
     (med. Irish/Latin)
     so-that came devil   to-her in night in shape angel-gs
     '(Irish) And the Devil came to her (Latin) during the night (Irish) in the shape of an angel'

Myers-Scotton's framework rests crucially on the concept of *insertion*. Other discussions of intra-, and intersentential, CS are based on the notion of *alternation*, i.e., more properly a switching back and forth between two language systems. An example is the title of a classic paper on the topic, Poplack (1980), in example (3):

(3) Sometimes I'll start a sentence in Spanish *y   terminó en español.*
                                                  and finish   in Spanish.

According to Poplack (1980; Sankoff and Poplack, 1981), CS is most likely to occur at switch-points of *equivalent constituent order*, such that the order of the constituents on either side of the switch point must be grammatical according to the rules of both languages that are involved in the switch. In other words, the combination of morphemes and words resulting at the switch point must not violate the grammar of either language. Poplack (1980: 585–6) also formulated the *free morpheme constraint*: "Codes may be switched after any constituent in discourse provided that constituent is not a bound morpheme." According to this principle, the English elements "files" and "download" in the German sentence in example (4) would presumably be treated as (nonce) borrowings, rather than CS, since they violate the free morpheme principle (English nouns are used with German determiners, and an English infinitive with a German infinitive ending, i.e., bound morphemes):[4]

(4) Manfred will sich   noch schnell die Files vom   Internet downloaden.
    M.   wants himself still quickly the files from-the internet download-INFIN.
    'Manfred still/just wants to quickly download the files from the internet.'

Indeed, a case could be made for treating the English elements here as borrowings, since typically such items are adapted in terms of their phonological realizations to German.

Muysken (2000) discusses *congruent lexicalization*, "where the two languages share a grammatical structure which can be filled lexically with elements from either language," as in example (5), where we find a German name and a German verb *mein(en)* ("to believe, to be of an opinion," but also "to mean" in the sense of "intending to express a meaning"[5]) inflected in English (Clyne, 1987: 756, quoted from Muysken, 2000: 12):

(5)   That's what *Papschi mein*-s to say   (English–German)
               P.   'mean'-s

Intersentential CS is probably most easily conceptualized in terms of alternation, such that in a text, a speaker or writer alternates between using syntactically complete structures in two (or more) languages, as in example (6) (medieval Irish/Latin; from Müller, 1999: 75):

(6)   Rofiarfaig Brigit dia   coic . . . in   raibi biad aici   dona
      hepscopaib. Dixit illa non.
      asked   B   to-her cook . . . PRT was   food at-her to-the
      bishops   said   she no
      '(Irish) Brigit asked her cook . . . whether she had any food for the
      bishops. (Latin) She said no.'

It would lead us too far to analyze the implications of *insertion*, *alternation*, and *congruent lexicalization* at greater length here. For a detailed summary and critique, the reader is referred to Muysken (2000: 16ff.).

CS at the level of the speaker within a speech situation

Thus far, our considerations have mainly been of patterns in text, of language structure. We need to keep in mind that it is speakers (or writers) who produce CS, and thus can legitimately ask not only *when or where* in speech or writing CS occurs, but also *how* and indeed *why*. The questions of *when or where*, rest, again, on the observation of patterns in the product of CS, whether intra- or intersentential (thus intra-speaker), or indeed inter-speaker. The questions *how* and *why*, as we understand them, address the psychological reality of a speaker using two or more linguistic systems, within the requirements of a speech situation. It is of course rather less straightforward to observe said psychological reality; rather, we need to rely on our best inferences based on what we can observe directly, namely speakers' behaviors and their results (i.e., products, or texts). We can also ask what the neurological base for CS might be.

In the rest of this section, we shall consider some of the factors that may impact on CS, beginning with the speakers themselves. CS does, of course, presuppose the ability to use two languages or language varieties. Further, CS is only effective, communicatively, when all participants in a speech situation share the languages or varieties involved; otherwise communication breaks down. The knowledge when and how CS is appropriate and acceptable thus is part of the communicative competence of a bilingual or multilingual speaker.

It might be tempting to think that CS is often due to a lack of fluency or competence in a target language, and that the speaker has to draw on his or her first language for concepts that cannot, or cannot yet, be expressed in the target language. We do indeed encounter such situations; see, for example, Dabène and Moore's (1995) discussion of *functional* as compared to *complementary* bilingualism in two generations of a Spanish-speaking immigrant family in France: The younger generation used elements from both Spanish and French strategically to fulfill pragmatic and stylistic functions, whereas the older generation would use both languages to compensate for insufficient resources in either. Especially intrasentential CS of the insertion type can also sometimes be accounted for by momentary difficulties with *access to*, rather than *knowledge of* a target item (lexical or phrasal), especially in a context that is otherwise strongly dominated by one language. Thus the first author of this chapter, living in the USA in an English-speaking household, occasionally will insert an English word or phrase into a German telephone conversation with her sister, with whom she shares German as a first language, and who is also a competent English speaker (see Grosjean, 2001, on differential activation of languages in bilingual and monolingual situations).

However, we regularly encounter CS where there can be no question of a lack of competence, or of a lexical gap in a base language that may have occasioned an insertion. Thus the person who produced example (1) above is fluent in both Welsh and English, and indeed works as a Welsh language teacher. It is thus less than likely that accessing the Welsh equivalent to "enormous" (*enfawr*) would have been a problem for her. Similarly, it is extremely unlikely that the writer of the Irish examples above would have been unfamiliar with the Irish equivalents of the Latin phrases he used.

We can thus move beyond questions of linguistic knowledge, or competence, and think of CS in terms of *speaker choices*. Formulating a message involves many choices on the part of the speaker, including for example the choice of lexical material (e.g., the use of "died" or a euphemism such as "passed away"), syntactic structures (active or passive; simple sentences, or complex embedded structures), phonological systems and their phonetic realizations (the choice of a particular accent), and indeed the choice of language, for bilinguals. The presence of two or more languages of course multiplies the resources that a speaker has at her or his disposal. In order for communication to be maximally effective on all levels, the choices made have to be appropriate interpersonally, situationally, and transactionally. Let us briefly consider CS in light of these three categories.

The term transactional refers to the informational aspects of a message, and concerns the effective transmission of information. A transactional motivation for CS may be founded in lack of knowledge or momentary access difficulties, but CS may also have an organizational or textual function. For example, it has been argued that many of the switches into Latin in data examined in Müller (1999) have a function that is not dissimilar to that of underlining or italics in a modern printed text, namely to highlight certain elements of the message.

Situational and interpersonal appropriateness, of course, overlap to a certain extent. However, situational appropriateness in a narrower sense concerns chiefly the physical and functional context of a speech situation, including the communicative modes involved, rather than primarily the participants. A good example would be an elementary school with a policy of monolingual instruction in English, in which, however, some of the children are from other language backgrounds, say, Spanish. In such an environment, we can expect that CS by children will be considered more appropriate during recess than during lessons. We may also find that CS in a lesson context may be more acceptable for certain activities (maybe "show and tell") than for others (for example literacy-based activities, such as retelling a story previously read) (see, e.g., Cloud, Genesee, and Hamayan, 2000, for a discussion of code-switching in the context of bilingual instruction).

Interpersonal appropriateness essentially concerns the appropriate choice among communicative resources in light of the participants involved and their relationship with each other. In other words, we can expect CS to be influenced by factors of communicative politeness. Seemingly the simplest choice to be made rests on whether an interlocutor shares the same languages. However, this consideration, or knowledge, may not be trivial at all for young children starting their pre-school careers, surrounded by unfamiliar people. CS, or its avoidance, can also express group identity or intra-group solidarity, and at the same time inter-group demarcations. The peppering of Welsh with English expressions by many teenagers in Welsh-medium schools can be seen in such a light. The teenage girl who produced example (7) was in a position to signal intra-generational solidarity to her classmates as well as rile her teacher in one elegant swoop. Again, there can be no reason to assume that the Welsh equivalent of the word "love" would have been unknown to her:

(7) Dw'i'n   love-o 'ny.
am I prt loving that
'I love that.'

Interpersonal and situational considerations of CS are of course closely connected with questions of language choice in general in bilingual persons, groups and situations (see Edwards, Chapter 4, this volume). The consideration of such factors leads us to the topic of the second part of this chapter, diglossia.

Diglossia

Original definition of diglossia

The phenomenon of *diglossia* was first described in detail by Ferguson (1959: 336). He defined it as:

> a relatively stable language situation in which in addition to the primary dialect of the language, which may include a standard or a regional standard, there is a very divergent, highly codified, often grammatically more complex, superposed variety, the vehicle of a large and respected body of literature, heir of an earlier period or another speech community, which is learned largely by formal education and is used for most written and formal purposes, but is not used by any sector of the community for ordinary conversation.

A linguistic situation that is often referred to in discussions of diglossia is that of the Arabic world (see Kaye, 1970). Here, we have a superposed variety (usually termed the "H," or "high" variety) of Standard Arabic (the term "Classical Arabic" is usually restricted to older forms of this standard language), which is very much the same across different Arabic-speaking countries. This variety is used for literature, education, and formal modes of discourse. It is, indeed, the heir to the Koranic tradition of classical Arabic, but would not be used in ordinary, everyday conversations. On the other hand, there also exist a range of local vernacular forms of Arabic (the "L," or "low" varieties). These varieties differ not only from Standard Arabic, but also from each other, in that the vernacular forms of Moroccan Arabic diverge noticeably from those of Iraq, for example. These vernaculars fit well into Ferguson's description of the primary dialect of the language given above. Differences between modern standard Arabic (H) and

Table 5.1 Vocabulary differences in Arabic

Language	"now"	Language	"good, well"
standard Arabic	ʔalʔāna	standard Arabic	xair, ḥasan
Egyptian colloquial	dilwaʔti	Egyptian	kuwayyis
Moroccan	dába	Moroccan	mizyán, wáxxa
Algerian	delwóq, druk	Algerian	mlīeħ
Tunisian	tawwa	Tunisian	ṭayyab
Saudi Arabian	daħħín(a)	Libyan	bāhi
Hassaniya	dark	Lebanese	mnīħ
Syrian	hallaʔ	Syrian	mnīħ
Nigerian	hatta, hassa, dātēn	Nigerian	zēn, ṭayyib

the various vernaculars (L) can be found in all areas of language: lexis, phonology, and grammar. For example, Kaye (1987: 676) lists the vocabulary differences shown in Table 5.1.

We can illustrate major phonological differences through a consideration of the situation in Germany, where standard German (H) is often in a diglossic contrast with regional vernaculars (L) (although we also have to recognize that many speakers today use standard German or a slightly modified version of it, rather than the vernaculars). Example (8) illustrates some of the difference between a local dialect of Palatinate German and standard German (*Hochdeutsch*):

(8) Palatinate German:
   ['hænɐ   'ʃʊn   də 'naɪʲə 'fɪlm 'gsɛːnə] ['welən]
   have-you already the new movie seen   which-one
   Standard German:
   'Habt ihr schon den neuen Film gesehen?' 'Welchen?'
   ['hapt iːɐ 'ʃoːn   den 'nɔɪʲən 'fɪlm gə'zeːn] ['welçən]
   have you already the new   movie seen   which-one
   'Have you already seen the new movie?' 'Which one?'

Finally, we can see major syntactic and morphological differences between the H form of Welsh, and the different L vernaculars found regionally (see Coupland and Ball, 1989, for a discussion of diglossia in Wales). Example (9) shows the use of periphrasis, alternative constructions, different inflectional endings, and different lexis in the L variety (a southern vernacular) as opposed to the H standard:

(9) H: Ni allaf   fyned adref yfory,   oherwydd y   tywydd.
      neg. can+1s go   to–home tomorrow because   the weather
      Dywedodd Lleucu ei bod yn   hoffi'r glaw, ond ni wnaf.
      said+3s   Ll.   her be   PRT like the rain but neg do+1s

   L: Dw'   i ddim yn gallu mynd adre   fory,   achos y tywydd.
      neg+am I not   PRT able go   to–home tomorrow 'cos   the rain
      Fe   wetws Lleucu bod hi 'n   lico'r glaw, ond dwi   ddim yn.
      PRT said+3s Ll.   be she PRT like the rain but neg+am not PRT
      'I am not able to go home tomorrow, because of the weather. Lleucu
      said she likes the rain, but I don't.'

Apart from the case of Arabic, Ferguson (1959) noted three other instances
that fitted well with his description of diglossia. In Haiti the H variety is
standard French, while Haitian Creole is the L form (see Stewart, 1963,
1968); in Switzerland, Standard German (H) is partnered by Swiss German
(*Schwytzertüütsch*) in the L role (see comparisons of Standard and Swiss
German in Trudgill, 2000). Finally, Ferguson listed the linguistic situation
at that time holding in Greece, where an H variety (*Katharevousa*) was in
competition with an L variety (*Dhimotiki*). Interestingly, these two varieties
also had political connotations with, basically, the right supporting the H
form of the language, and the left the L form. Political and constitutional
changes in Greece over the past 25 years or so have resulted in *Dhimotiki*
being promoted to the status of national official language, and a subsequent
decline in the status and use of *Katharevousa* (Frangoudaki, 1992).

   While stylistic differences within a language often seem similar to the
diglossia phenomenon, Ferguson (1972) notes that the inability to use the H
form in ordinary conversation is a major differentiation between diglossia
and more common stylistic differences encountered in all languages.

Extended definition of diglossia

As we saw in Ferguson's definition of diglossia, he saw this as a phenomenon that was restricted to two related linguistic systems: standard and
vernacular Arabic, standard and Swiss German, and so forth. Fishman
(1967) proposed an expanded version of diglossia, where the H and L
varieties did not have to be related languages. One example Fishman noted
of such an instance is found in Paraguay where Spanish occupies the H
position, and Guaraní (an unrelated Andean-Equatorial language) the L

(although we have also to remember that not all speakers in all social classes will speak both languages, or speak them both with equal fluency).

This extended definition of diglossia shows that diglossia and bilingualism can interact (Fishman, 1972c). We can therefore have diglossia with bilingualism, as in German-speaking parts of Switzerland, and the Paraguay example just mentioned. Such a situation requires different groups within an area to speak different languages (where one is H and one L in terms of the society), but where members of one group rarely if ever speak the other group's language. Such situations were common in countries which were colonies of another power; so, for example, Rhodesia (now Zimbabwe), where the L languages were Shona and Ndebele, and the H language was English, and comparatively few members of the population were fluent in both English and either Shona or Ndebele. However, we can also have bilingualism without diglossia when both linguistic codes have equal validity. Verdoodt (1972) describes the situation in German speaking parts of Belgium, where both French and German are in use by most speakers but are not separated into H and L. Of course, a situation where neither diglossia nor bilingualism pertains can be found in monolingual communities, although even here we tend to find stylistic differences that may approach the H–L distinctions of diglossia.

Of course, neat groupings such as these do not account for the wide range of possible interactions between linguistic codes. For example, in Welsh-speaking parts of Wales, we find an interesting form of diglossia. Vernacular forms of Welsh (differing from region to region) constitute the L varieties, but there is competition for the H role between standard Welsh and English. Speakers who have not had access to standard Welsh through either education or attendance at Welsh-language religious services (almost exclusively using standard forms of the language), may well have to switch to English for those contexts where an H linguistic form is required. Others will use standard Welsh in that context. In addition to this, there is the need to use English in interactions with monolingual English speakers.

Further categories of diglossia

This last example leads on to a brief consideration of more complex relations between languages that include some kind of diglossia. Another example where three languages interact is in Tanzania. Abdulaziz Mkilifi (1978) noted that English, Swahili and local languages operated in what he termed a *triglossic* manner. At that time, Swahili was introduced in primary schools as the medium of education and, therefore, took on an H role to the L role of the vernaculars. For those students who went on to secondary school, English was then introduced, and so became the H to Swahili's L. So, at a national level, English and Swahili were in an H–L relation, whereas at a local level Swahili and local languages were also in an H–L relation.

More complex is Platt's (1977) description of *polyglossia* in Malaysia. Here many languages interact with more than one H language (formal Malaysian English and Bahasa Indonesia) and more than one L language (non-dominant Chinese languages). Interestingly, Platt also includes an M level for languages with moderate prestige that fit between the H and L levels (colloquial Malaysian English and the dominant Chinese variety of the particular region). He also notes the existence of what he terms a *dummy high*, that is a language that most speakers look up to as a prestige language but which in fact hardly anyone can actually speak (in this instance the dummy high is Mandarin Chinese).

Diglossia and change

Ferguson (1972) notes that different developments are possible in a diglossic situation. The relatively stable diglossia of his original (1959) definition can certainly be found (for example, in Switzerland), but there are occasions when diglossia can disappear. For example, the Greek situation referred to above saw the adoption of the L variety (in this case that L variety found in the capital city of Athens), and the gradual decline in use of the H variety. In these kinds of circumstances the new "national" language may well take on some characteristics of the former H variety. Ferguson saw the establishment of national languages based on L (but with an admixture of H) as likely scenarios resulting, perhaps, from increased education and literacy. He felt the loss of L together with the adoption of H as a national language to be much less likely, coming about only when a territory was merged with another where the H was the national language with no diglossia.

Why do we need to know about code-switching and diglossia?

Why should students, professionals and researchers in communicative disorders concern themselves with questions of code-switching and diglossia?

The simplest reason is that both concern fundamental realities of our communicative lives. It is unfortunate that most speech–language professionals are monolingual, and that their linguistic and clinical education has operated under the tacit assumption that monolingualism is the norm. Since CS is a normal part of a bilingual's communicative behavior, and since increasing numbers of children and adults referred to speech–language clinics are bi- or multilingual, we cannot ignore what amounts to a substantial part of their communicative repertoires.

Notes

1 See Hymes (1972) for a slightly different definition of speech situation.
2 Examples without citation are from the authors' own linguistic experience.
3 A text can be spoken or written, or signed, or a combination of different modalities.
4 The word "internet" is at this stage a bona-fide English borrowing into German.
5 As in *Ich hab's nicht so gemeint* 'I didn't mean it like that.'

Further reading

Auer, P. (ed.) (1991) *Bilingual Conversation*. Amsterdam: Benjamins.
Auer, P. (ed.) (1999) *Code-switching in Conversation: Language, Interaction and Identity*. London: Routledge.
Fasold, R. (1984) *The Sociolinguistics of Society*. Oxford: Blackwell.
Jacobson, R. (ed.) (1998) *Codeswitching Worldwide*. Berlin: Mouton de Gruyter.
Myers-Scotton, C. (1997) *Social Motivation for Codeswitching: Evidence from Africa*. Oxford: Clarendon Press.
Schiffman, H. (1997) Diglossia as a sociolinguistic situation. In F. Coulmas (ed.), *The Handbook of Sociolinguistics* (pp. 205–16). Oxford: Blackwell.
Wardhaugh, R. (1998) *An Introduction to Sociolinguistics*, 3rd edn. Oxford: Blackwell.

6

Language and Power

Jack S. Damico, Nina Simmons–Mackie and Holly Hawley

Within the social and cultural contexts of modern society the concept of power and its manipulation is pervasive. From the actions of governmental agencies and other institutions to the ways that individuals such as parents, teachers, and managers impose their will on their dependents, we anticipate and accept societal and interactional power and its consequences. As a social construct, power is frequently studied and interest in this phenomenon is justified; power appears to be a primary organizing principle in society (e.g., Weber, 1947; Mills, 1956; Foucault, 1972). Social hierarchies, social classes, and variables such as social status and group identity all appear to be influenced by the concept of power – who has it and how it is manipulated.

However, there is much about this construct that is beyond the scope of applied linguistics and the clinical professions. As emphasized by Fairclough, "power is not *just* a matter of language" (1989: 3). Rather, it has many manifestations in other modalities or dimensions that may be more tangible and influential. Physical force, monetary remuneration, codified oppression, political patronage and even cultural ideology may involve language as a medium of transmission or focus but these manifestations of power can certainly exist outside of the linguistic realm as well. Such manifestations of power will not concern us at present. While we are oriented to the overall foundational construct of power as it correlates with our clinical efforts, we are primarily interested in how power is exercised and enacted through language and within discourse.

This more discourse-oriented focus is appropriate; human beings constantly interact with one another and these interactions involve not only the ways we construct our communicative interactions but also how these constructions correlate with "underlying" social forces such as power and solidarity. Indeed, to understand just how we are able to accomplish social actions and to navigate the complexities of communicative interaction, we must have a functioning understanding of these relations between social forces and their influence on our language and discourse. This chapter will discuss the concept of power in language and discourse with a particular focus on power in clinical contexts.

Interactional power

As an object of discussion, power and power relations are complicated. Much has been written regarding power in language and discourse but often these discussions employ synonymy and referential examples of inter-actional power rather than an actual definition. This is understandable. Power from a social science perspective is a relative term imbued with various qualities that are often more metaphorical than tangible so the process does not lend itself to clear definition (Tannen, 1987). The investi-gation of interactional power follows a fairly standard process: since we are interested in social action, we want to describe not only the objects of this social activity but the relationship between these objects as well. We accomplish this by isolating and defining our social entities in more or less concrete ways (e.g., nations, institutions, codes, interactants) and then we note the complex interplay between two or more of these "social objects." When describing these complex interactions, we see relational differences that are directly and indirectly manifested between the objects and we assign various labels to the targeted relationships we find within these interactions (Gergen, 1991). These relationships are viewed as social dimensions and some of the labels assigned are "power," "control," and "authority."

Since interactional power is more relational than discrete, arriving at an explicit definition is not easily accomplished. This is because interactional power is signaled, constructed, and delineated not only by one's linguistic structure and communicative style but also by subtle and elaborate features of social identity, affect, and implied meanings that reflect both broad social features like role relationships and more narrow social meanings like inter-personal significance (Schiffrin, 1994). Whether describing these various components as "contextualization cues" (Gumperz, 1982), "layered" signals employed to determine various aspects of social or cognitive meaning (Clark, 1996), or relative values based upon collective and dynamic behavioral expectations (Habermas, 1984), these features of language, discourse, and social perception coalesce to create the phenomenon of interactional power.

Consequently, when focusing on interactional power, we tend to view it as a *social construction* of reality that is the outgrowth of interactive processes with others and not a simple mirror of *external* reality.

Operational characteristics

While we cannot easily define interactional power, we can provide several operational characteristics of this social phenomenon that might describe the nature of the construct. Of course, the first characteristic has already been described: Interactional power is a *complex* phenomenon and this complexity must not be ignored if we are to understand this social and interactional phenomenon. It is our attempt to grasp this complexity that leads us to consider the other operational characteristics.

The second operational characteristic is that interactional power is *multimodal* and *multi-dimensional* in nature. This characteristic is closely tied to the first and is one of the reasons for the complexity of interactional power. There are many ways that interactional power may be manifested (hence Clark's "layering of signals" metaphor) and often these various manifestations cross modalities and social dimensions. In any given interaction, therefore, a participant may possess several types of *usable* power across several dimensions (Grimshaw, 1990). For example, the participant may be older than their dyadic partner, may be more informed, and may possess some form of institutional or contextual power (e.g., a therapist in a clinical setting). While the influence of each of these potential vestiges of power is contextually dependent, it is often the amalgam that must be considered since several manifestations – of greater and lesser import – may be employed simultaneously.

The next two operational characteristics also contribute to the complexity of interactional power and how the multiple manifestations are employed. The third characteristic is that the manifestations and vestiges of interactional power are *culturally influenced*; the effectiveness of any variable that might be employed to manifest power is dependent upon the cultural experiences of the participants. For example, Tannen (1985) analyzed the talk of individuals from different geographic regions and found that talking in unison was viewed as a sign of affiliation and solidarity in one group, while another cultural perspective viewed this same behavior as rude interrupting and an indirect play for interactional power. Sociolinguistic research has provided a significant body of knowledge regarding cultural variables that affect and are affected by discourse (e.g., Gumperz, 1982; Brown and Levinson, 1987; Schiffrin, 1987). The research demonstrates that these variables (e.g., timing, prosody, gestures, proxemics, language code, communicative style) transmit a complex web of affective, cultural and linguistic information that creates an interactional power differential and adds to the layer of complexity.

The fact that interactional power is always *contextually relative* is the fourth operational characteristic and it is based on a social science assumption that social action involves contextual relativity (e.g., Hymes, 1967; Bateson, 1972; Halliday, 1973; Goffman, 1974). That is, the contextual variables present in an interactional dyad operate in conjunction with the linguistic features to create a particular range of social action and interpretation. Goodwin and Duranti stressed this critical contextual role when they stated that a focal communicative event cannot be "properly understood, interpreted appropriately, or described in a relevant fashion, unless one looks beyond the event itself to other phenomena" (1992: 3). Consequently, those contextual variables are always important considerations when dealing with interactional power. It is important to remember, however, that the context is much more than a physical "setting." It also involves the interactants who become contexts for each other; what they do and say, where they are located, and their past experiences go into shaping this "context" (Goodwin and Duranti, 1992). As applied to interactional power, contextual relativity means that depending on a host of contextual variables, language usage is differentially employed to accomplish objectives such as the manifestation and manipulation of power.

A result of this contextual relativity is that interactional power is expressed as a matter of degree. It is misleading to think of interactional power as simply absent or present; to consider that one person has power and another does not. Rather, "When people are taking different roles, it may not be the case that one has power and one doesn't, but that they have different kinds of power, and they are exercising it in different ways" (Tannen, 1987: 5). Additionally, research indicates that there are various social dimensions that interact during discourse and depending upon the context one may influence the expression of the other (e.g., Tannen, 1984; Schiffrin, 1987; Hudson, 1996). A classic example of this relativity involves the interaction between power and solidarity. Brown and Gilman (1960) investigated the ways that linguistic marking of social dimensions operated, and power and solidarity were their primary dimensions of interest. For our purposes here, solidarity is concerned with the social distance that exists between two people. For example, if an individual shares many experiences, interests, or various social characteristics with another individual, then the social distance between them may be small and there may be a high degree of solidarity. On the other hand, if two individuals have little in common, they will typically have great social distance between them and far less solidarity. Brown and Gilman found that the same linguistic signals were typically employed to mark both power and solidarity (e.g., alternative pronouns in French, family name versus a given name in English) and that they tended to vary together. When there was a conflict between the two, however, it was generally solidarity that was coded rather than power.

Finally, interactional power is *collaboratively constructed*; it is not static or organized as prepackaged objects waiting to be invoked. Power is a dynamic and generative social dimension that emerges as a complex interaction of variables that mutate from moment to moment (Erickson and Shultz, 1982; McDermott and Tylbor, 1987). Power is not simply delivered by the actions of one participant and passively received and accepted by the other participant in the action dyad. Instead, interaction involves the manipulation of power as an elaborate social exercise that is negotiated in a dynamic fashion by the participating parties. While it is true that an individual may have various vestiges of power when entering an interaction (e.g., higher social standing, greater physical strength, more intellectual ability, valuable new information), these variables and their import must be negotiated during any interaction; power through discourse emerges based upon the manifestations of this dimension and it will be linked to numerous contextual features and then negotiated (Fisher, 1984). While this process may not be lengthy or even at the level of consciousness, there will be manifestations of attempted power and these will be used by all parties to collaboratively establish a potential power differential. Because of this, interactional power is doubly situated: it helps constitute and is constituted by the context (Goodwin and Duranti, 1992). Regardless of the outcome, however, interactional power is always collaboratively negotiated in face-to-face encounters through which we construct the "self" in relation to others and create social roles, power and authority hierarchies and autonomy (Goffman, 1967).

Power manifestations in discourse

Social scientists have identified a variety of culturally conventionalized signals that assist in the interpretation of power during discourse. Each signal acts within the interactional context to assist in the construction of the power relationship that exists. We will discuss some of the more frequently

employed manifestations of interactional power. Three caveats are necessary to properly benefit from this discussion. First, recognize that interactional
power is noticeable when there is a power differential. That is, when one
interactant appears to have more power than the other in discourse. In such
unequal interactional encounters, the power imbalance is collaboratively
constructed by the involved parties and coded by the extent to which the
more powerful interactant employs behaviors or resources to exert control
and constraint on the interaction. When discussing manifestations, remember that these behaviors are typically used to manipulate the interaction to
create and sustain "power asymmetry;" it is through such asymmetry in
communicative behavior that power and authority manifest themselves in
social action (Fairclough, 1989; Grimshaw, 1990; Hudson, 1996).

Second, the interpretation of interactional power is relative to a number of other contextual variables (e.g., solidarity) and the expression of
interactional power will vary with the context – regardless of which of these
manifestations are employed. It would be incorrect to assume that the
linguistic and discourse features must always be employed to manifest power
or to expect that when one of these features is employed it is exclusively for
the manipulation of interactional power. The phenomenon is too complex
for such a simple correlation between a surface manifestation and the social
dimension. Finally, there are a number of other ways that interactional
power may be manifested other than those discussed in this section.

Forms of address

Forms of address are often employed during an interaction to mark
interactional power (Brown and Gilman, 1960). That is, speakers often
locate themselves along the power continuum by the way they name their
addressees. This is possible because there are a number of address forms
available to a speaker in any language and the choice of what to call another
explicitly references their combined social relationship. In English, for example, one may use given names (*Tommy*), family names with or without
title (*Ball, Dr Ball*), role-based names (*son*), or honorifics (*Your Honor*) as
markers of the power differential. In other languages, there may be other
address forms that can also code a potential power/solidarity differential. In
French, for example, choice of the alternative pronouns (*vous, tu*) assists
speakers in locating themselves along a power continuum (Brown and Gilman,
1960). Typically, the individual with more power chooses to use more
intimate forms (e.g., given names) when referring to the subordinate while

the latter uses more formal and distant forms such as a family name with a title (Brown and Ford, 1961). So, for example, we may note power coded when there is an unequal distribution of address forms. For example, *"Tommy, how are you doing today?" "I'm feeling great, Dr Ball."*

Speaking turn negotiation

The negotiation of speaking turns and speaking rights is another manifestation. Halliday (1978) and others (e.g., Sacks, Schegloff and Jefferson, 1974; Brown and Levinson, 1987) have demonstrated that speakers with greater power typically manipulate and control both the range and granting of speaking turns – often through interruptions of the other speaker(s) with little risk of discord. The more powerful interactant can interrupt, choose the next speaker, or extend the turn with long chunks of uninterrupted talk. O'Donnell (1990) provides examples of more powerful participants holding the conversational floor in labor-management talks and Fairclough (1989) illustrated the same when describing how a physician controlled the selection of medical students for turns-at-talk during their interactions. In both cases, speaking rights were directly linked to the exercise of interactional power.

Topic selection and maintenance

The control of topic selection and maintenance of the topic is another manifestation. That is, the more dominant speaker may choose what will be discussed and even the length of the topic. Shuy (1987) and Walker (1987) have suggested that whoever controls the topic is often the person who controls the interaction, not only in face-to-face manipulations of power but in broader applications as well. Fairclough (1989) has demonstrated that even in larger social events such as paneled investigations the balance of topic content and even ideological "spins" are overwhelming in favor of the existing power-holders.

Questioning

The function and form of questions are also used as manifestations of power. Often the dominant individual controls the contributions of the other interactant(s) through questioning. In speech act theory (Searle, 1969) questioning is recognized as a form of control – a directive – intended to get one interactant to do something for another. In many interactions, the more powerful individual often has greater freedom to question. For example, questioning may be used to "put someone on the spot" or to turn a conversation into an interrogation and the individual with less power generally has a greater obligation to respond (but see Goodwin and Goodwin, 1990). The grammatical forms of questions may also transmit potential power asymmetry. For example, negative questions (e.g., *Did we not forget to raise our hand?*), grammatical forms that are reduced to words or minimal phrases (e.g., *Which way?*), and declarative statements with a question tag (e.g., *It was a stupid thing to do, wasn't it?*) are all more likely when there is greater rather than lesser asymmetry along the power differential. While one has to be careful with over-interpretation of questioning as a manifestation of power (Tannen, 1987), it is often a tangible signal of this social dimension.

Use of evaluative statements

In many situations where the power differential is inherent in the context itself, asymmetry is often manifested through evaluative statements. For example, teachers often respond to student interactions with statements such as *that's correct, a fine thought*, or *very good* (Cazden, 1988). When one interactant provides a response to a question or makes a statement and it is evaluated by the other, this is a distinct exercise of interactional power. Of course, in classrooms and some other social settings these evaluative statements are expected. However, evaluative statements are frequently used in other contexts and they also signal power asymmetry.

There are other ways that interactional power is manifested as well. Some of these are as explicitly signaled as these manifestations while some are more subtle, but all may be very effective. The asymmetrical employment of politeness forms (e.g., use of indirect speech acts, expressing gratitude, saying *please*), the lack of mitigation during a difficult interactional situation, and overt statements of power (e.g., announcing the objective of the meeting, statements such as, *Hey, I'll talk and you listen*) are all examples of more explicit signaling. The manner in which one's contribution is interpreted via another individual's dominant interpretive framework (Ulichny and Watson-Gegeo, 1989), the use of various discourse markers (Schiffrin, 1987), unequal physical contact or facial affect, the implied value placed on one dialect versus another are also signals of interactional power – albeit they may be more subtle in nature.

Interactional power in clinical contexts

Whether one is creating social action through general conversation or through targeted teaching/learning encounters, the same social dimensions are operative and one individual typically is more dominant than the other(s). In fact, this asymmetry may be necessary to accomplish the goals of most interactions. It should not be surprising, therefore, that a number of discourse studies reveal that interactional asymmetries exist when professionals such as doctors, lawyers, or teachers provide services for those who require their help (e.g., Erickson and Shultz, 1982; Kedar, 1987; Grimshaw, 1990; Morris and Chenail, 1995); within the therapeutic encounter this is especially true and many clinical studies have provided specific descriptions to support this contention (e.g., Labov and Fanshel, 1977; Panagos, 1996).

Often, the same manifestations discussed in the previous section are employed to establish interactional power and therapeutic authority. For example, Prutting and colleagues (1978) investigated how speech clinicians controlled therapeutic interactions through topic selection, dominance of speaking turns, and evaluative statements, Scheflen (1973), Panagos, Bobkoff and Scott (1986), McTear and King (1990), Cicourel (1992), and Lahey (2004) have provided data on the importance of asymmetrical discourse sequences (i.e., tripartite hierarchical structuring such as request–response– evaluation sequences) in constraining the various clinical and therapeutic contexts, and Kovarsky (1990) and Lahey (2004) investigated employing particular discourse markers (e.g., *okay, oh, so, well, now*) and pronouns as ways to structure therapeutic discourse. Even when reacting to the contributions of others, interactional control can be employed. Simmons-Mackie, Damico, and Damico (1999), for instance, analyzed feedback as a control mechanism in aphasia therapy and found that it was asymmetrically employed for various functions including as a constraint on therapeutic discourse routines. Similarly, Damico and Damico (1997) demonstrated how dominance is negotiated through the clinician's response framework while interpreting the students' attempts at interaction. By employing these dominant interpretive frameworks, clinicians frequently influence not only the interactions but also how children think about issues.

These attempts at control of therapeutic situations are actually manifestations of interactional dominance that are necessary for successful therapeutic encounters (Kovarsky and Duchan, 1997). If clinicians are to assist children in becoming effective language users and learners, they have to employ interactional power to set the agenda and guide the interaction.

A number of researchers have generated similar findings in various teaching encounters (e.g., McDermott and Gospodinoff, 1979; Mehan, 1979; Cazden, 1988; Delpit, 1988; Ulichny and Watson-Gegeo, 1989; Ballenger, 1992; Eriks-Brophy and Crago, 1994; Strum and Nelson, 1997; Westby, 1997).

Conclusion

There are several clinical implications that may be derived from this sociolinguistic review of interactional power. First, we must *recognize the complexity* of interactional power. Just as with any other social dimension, power is a complicated interaction between a number of social, affective, and linguistic factors that are forged into a operating phenomenon via the dynamic pressures that exist within the social context. To understand this complexity, the interested clinician should pursue more detailed information. Of course, the brief descriptions and references provided within this chapter will serve as an excellent starting point. The key, however, is to abandon the naïve conception of power as simplistic, unitary, and pre-packaged. Such a conception will only lead to poor clinical results.

The second implication is that the clinical professional should *contextualize this knowledge into action*. The clinician should determine how this knowledge can be employed to benefit clients. This may mean, for example, that you determine which manifestations of power are most relevant to the cultural background of your client(s) or how you can best use interactional power to propel your client toward independence. Above all, you should be aware of the mechanisms of power that might cause difficulty within your therapeutic context and strive to reduce or eliminate those behaviors and expectations that serve to alienate and marginalize students. Contextualizing your knowledge requires an understanding of power manipulation as an instructional practice through which proficiency and progress emerge.

Finally, implicit in the first two implications is the third – each clinician must *take responsibility for the clinical encounter*. Ultimately, the success or failure of any clinical effort resides with the individual with authority – the clinician or teacher. You must establish the goals and agenda of the therapeutic encounter and continually monitor the interactions to determine whether there is sufficient movement toward those goals. This is the reason that interactional power is employed in the clinical context in the first place.

For nearly three decades there has been an interest in the dimension of power and its role in structuring clinical interaction. It has been shown that this social dimension is both pervasive and powerful; it may be implicated in much of the social action that occurs in the clinical context. To effectively appreciate this social dimension, we must recognize both its complexity and its potential. This chapter has attempted to describe both the character of interactional power and the various ways that it has been manifested in the clinical context. Based on the work reviewed here, a more dynamic view of this social dimension – a view that embraces the complexity of the phenomenon and strives to both understand it and incorporate it into one's therapeutic planning – is suggested. As with any complex social dimension, power can be employed to accomplish a number of objectives. Whether these objectives are valued or not is dependent on the goals and the social context within which one exists. Regardless of the value or quality, however, the effective clinician should strive to understand this phenomenon and realize that it can be employed as a strategically powerful tool in the pursuit of therapeutic effectiveness and efficacy.

Further reading

Anderson, L. and Trudgill, P. (1990) *Bad Language*. Oxford: Blackwell.

Atkinson, J.M. and Drew, P. (1979) *Order in the Court: The Organisation of Verbal Interaction in Judicial Settings*. London: Macmillan.

Collins, R. (1975) *Conflict Sociology*. New York: Academic Press.

Gumperz, J.J. (ed.) (1982) *Language and Social Identity*. Cambridge: Cambridge University Press.

Milroy, J. and Milroy, L. (1995) *Authority in Language: Investigating Language Prescription and Standardisation*. London: Routledge.

Tannen, D. (1986) *That's Not What I Meant! How Conversational Style Makes or Breaks Your Relations with Others*. New York: William Morrow.

7

Language and Culture

Nicole Taylor and
Norma Mendoza-Denton

The aim of this chapter will be to provide a broad overview of language and culture scholarship that focuses on the concept of linguistic co-construction and then to illustrate these concepts through a more detailed analysis of cultural differences that focuses on (1) the ways in which verbal and non-verbal communication interact with the social and physical environment; and (2) the ways in which discourse markers become emblematic of groups.

Currently, the concept of co-construction emerges in studies of how group and individual identities are constructed through language interaction that occurs within a specific social and cultural context. The notion that identities are constructed within and through social contexts is a well-established anthropological area of discussion (Mead, 1934; Sapir, 1949; Whorf, 1956). Jacoby and Ochs define co-construction as "the joint creation of a form, interpretation, stance, action, activity, identity, institution, skill, ideology, emotion, or other culturally meaningful reality" (1995: 171). In other words, social meaning and individual and group identities are not created by individuals; instead, they are created jointly through language interaction. The concept of "co-construction" has theoretical roots in phenomenology, symbolic interactionism, and conversation analysis as well as Bakhtin's (1935) theory of dialogism.

Symbolic interactionists, such as Mead (1934) and Goffman (1959) believed that meaning is socially constituted through communicative interaction rather than mental processes. Mead identified three necessary phases of social interaction from which meaning emerges: (1) an initial gesture (either verbal or non-verbal) by one person; (2) the interpretation of and response to that gesture by another person; and (3) the subsequent phases of social interaction. In addition to requiring all three phases of interaction, for Mead, meaning-making also required a level of intersubjectivity among participants. According to Mead, an individual is able to internalize the "attitudes" of other individuals and groups of which he is a member so that their experiences and behaviors are manifested within him. This shared experience among participants is what enables them to incorporate others into their self and thereby govern and direct their own conduct in relation to those they communicate with.

Although Goffman (1959) did not overtly focus on meaning-making through social interaction as Mead did, the concept is implicit in his discussion on "maintenance of expressive control." In reference to the "sign accepting tendency" of the audience, Goffman discusses the ways in which intentional signs can be misunderstood by the audience and ways in which unintentional signs can be received by the audience. In this process of giving/giving off signs and having them received and interpreted/misinterpreted, meaning emerges (Goffman, 1959: 51). The most important contribution of symbolic interactionists, such as Mead and Goffman, to the concept of "co-construction" has been the idea that meaning-making is an interactional process requiring more than one individual, whether it be a self and an other (Mead) or a performer and an audience (Goffman).

Garfinkel (1967) problematized the assumption that all humans share intersubjectivity and focused instead on the processes by which "trouble" is negotiated during social interaction when interlocutors falsely assume intersubjectivity. While Schutz's notion of social interaction was wholly theoretical, Garfinkel's notion of social interaction is more empirical, based on data of naturally occurring speech that he collected and analyzed. Thus, Garfinkel drew the focus away from theoretical communication models toward the analysis of micro-level communication processes whereby participants co-negotiate meaning during interaction. While his research indexed the importance of analyzing micro-processes of actual social interaction in order to understand how meaning is co-constructed, Garfinkel did not actually propose a model for doing so.

Conversation analysts, such as Sacks, Schegloff and Jefferson (1974) picked up where Garfinkel left off, conceiving of a conversational model that would allow for the systematic analysis of how meaning is co-constructed through social interaction. Conversation analysts examine the specific ways in which conversation is managed moment-to-moment, taking as their unit of analysis the turn of talk. The CA model is broad enough to allow for an infinite set of potential turn-taking sequences, which vary according to elements such as turn order, length, and number of speakers. However, the CA model is "context-sensitive" in the sense that participants are attuned to cues within the conversation that guide their participation, such as turn-taking boundaries, selection of next speaker, and appropriateness of turn length. This context-sensitivity is closely tied to the CA assertion that conversations are "locally managed." Within the constraints of the conversation model, speakers have choices such as whether to select next speaker or to allow the next speaker to self-select and the listeners have choices as to the content of their response. These constrained choices are made moment-to-moment during individual turns at talk. Thus, within the constraints of this conversation model, interlocutors negotiate and co-construct meaning moment-to-moment through turns at talk.

Bakhtin (1935) conceived of human communication (in addition to texts) as heteroglossic in nature. That is, utterances as well as ideas are the products of previous, current, and hypothetical future dialogues with other interlocutors. He writes, "Of all words uttered in everyday life, no less than half belong to someone else" (p. 339). In contrast to the notion of a "self" (versus an other), Bakhtin conceived of a "dialogic self" that is socially constituted through past interactions with other people as well as internal interactions between and among hypothetical subject positions. Irvine (1996) expands Bakhtin's notion of multivocality from the self to the speech interaction. She writes, "Rather than multi-vocal, we might consider a speech situation to be multiply dialogical: it is not just the speaker who is doubled (or multiplied) by other voices, but a set of dialogic relations that are crucially informed by other sets – shadow conversations that surround the conversation at hand" (1996: 151–2). Thus, meaning in the present interaction is co-constructed not just by the interlocutors engaging at that moment, but by past conversations and past interlocutors as well.

At this point in the chapter, we will illustrate more concretely the ways in which these theories of meaning-making through communication are utilized in anthropological studies of human interaction across cultures. We will illustrate this through focused discussions of two major areas of study: (1) language and gesture; and (2) discourse markers.

Language and gesture

Language and gesture scholars have long been concerned with the ways in which meaning is co-constructed by interlocutors through both verbal and non-verbal communication processes, specifically with regard to how verbal and non-verbal modes of communication work together to produce meaning. Most contemporary gesture scholars who work within the communicative framework agree that because speech and gestures are often produced together, they must be viewed as two aspects of a single process, and therefore equally valuable (Kendon, 1980, 1986, 1997). Furthermore, gesture scholars have come to view gestures as referential acts rather than incidental physical movements, a shift in focus that was crucial to moving the field beyond analyses of hand movements as peripheral accompaniments to speech, toward an understanding of the ways in which interlocutors draw upon semiotic resources, including gesture, speech, physical environment, and the communicative event itself, to co-construct meaning (Goodwin, 1986, 2000; Goodwin and Goodwin, 1992; Haviland, 1993; Streeck, 1994; Basso, 1996; Ochs et al., 1996). The Goodwins' research (Goodwin and Goodwin, 1992; Goodwin, 2000, 2003) has been significant in foregrounding context in gesture analysis. They explore the ways in which participants mutually orient toward their physical environment to co-construct meaning through language and gesture.

Goodwin (2000) argues that human action is produced and interpreted through the moment-to-moment configuration and reconfiguration of semiotic resources available to participants. He illustrates, through detailed video analysis of turns-at-talk, the ways in which a girl playing hopscotch combines linguistic resources, such as lexico-semantic content, a specific syntactic frame, and use of a rhythmic pitch contour to demonstrate how her co-participant has violated the rules of the game. Additionally, this linguistic exchange is embedded within a larger rule-bound activity (the game of hopscotch) that is grounded in a physically constructed spatial field (the actual grid), toward which participants mutually orient. Goodwin argues that it is the framework of mutual orientation within a constructed, physical space and a rule-governed activity that allows sign systems other than talk to function. Goodwin shows how co-participants shift their mutual orientation from hand signs that emphasize and reconstruct the hopscotch transgression within the "empty" transactional space between them to one participant's deictic stomping on the grid as a further means of illustrating the transgression. Goodwin illustrates the ways in which participants recombine and re-orient toward objects moment-to-moment within the physical environment through both language and gesture, to co-construct meaning.

McNeill et al. (1993) explore the creative, generative properties of deictic gestures by illustrating the ways in which pointing during narrative telling redefines seemingly "empty space," creating referents that are mutually oriented to during interaction. The authors examine how pointing at "empty space" during a narrative may either index a physical environment known to participants or imaginatively build a physical environment within which the narrative takes place. In doing so, the participants are co-constructing more than meaning. Participants are also co-constructing an imagined or remembered narrative space toward which they may orient.

Basso's (1996) research on the Western Apache builds upon this idea, exploring the ways in which physical spaces, infused with moral messages through narratives, are invoked in everyday conversation, thereby redefining participants' mental spaces and creating referents that are mutually oriented to by participants. The Western Apache narratives are told repeatedly and passed down to younger generations so that everyone in the community knows them. Additionally, they are often told at the physical site where they are imagined to have taken place so that everyone has a similar mental picture of the space where the narrated events happened.

Basso illustrates how the physical space is reconfigured through gesture during narrative telling: "Reaching out his hand to the fields of growing corn, he performs a scooping motion that seems to gather them up, drawing them together as though cradled in his palm and setting the stage for a place-world about farming and the origin of clans" (1996: 19). For example, in telling a story about the ancestors' first encounter with the place that is now Cibeque, Charles picks up a handful of mud, squeezing it so that water spurts from between his fingers. He then says in reference to this gesture, "There. Water and mud together, just as they were when our ancestors came here" (p. 12). In this way, physical spaces are reconfigured through gesture and speech so that a desolate, dried-up spring consisting mostly of large rocks may be co-imagined as a space filled with fresh water where ancestors came often or a tree-covered knoll may be co-imagined as a space filled with brush-covered armadas interspersed with farms inhabited by ancestors.

The Western Apache historical narratives often explain causes and consequences of poor social conduct, moral failings that can be indexed through the simple utterance of a place name, such as "Shades of Shit," a process the Western Apache refer to as "speaking with names." Through this process, Basso explains that place names may be used as a semiotic resource in everyday conversation: "[L]andscapes are always available to their seasoned inhabitants in more than material terms. Landscapes are available in symbolic terms as well, and so, chiefly through the manifold agencies of speech, they can be 'detached' from their fixed spatial moorings and transformed into instruments of thought and vehicles of purposive behavior" (p. 75). Furthermore, the place names, through their syntactic structure, imply specific positions for viewing locations. Names such as "Water Flows Inward under a Cottonwood Tree" and "White Rocks Lie Above in a Compact Cluster" direct participants to mutually orient to the space in the same way even when place names are uttered out of their physical context. Thus, when people "speak with names" they are mutually orienting to a shared, albeit absent, space in much the same way as Goodwin's girls mutually orient to the hopscotch grid. Similarly, they are redefining space, creating mental referents that are mutually oriented to during interaction.

Basso also discusses the communicative functions of "speaking with names" in everyday conversation. By simply uttering a place name in the same utterance or in an adjacent utterance as a person's name, interlocutors are able to co-construct moral identities of other community members. For example, in the following exchange:

LOUISE: "My younger brother . . ."
LOLA: "It happened at Line of White Rocks Extends Up and Out, at this very place!" (1996: 79)

The interlocutors mutually orient to shared past knowledge of a mistake made by Louise's younger brother as well as the imagined physical space and the narrative associated with that space. In doing so, they co-construct Louise's little brother as "stupid and careless" without embarrassing Louise by saying so explicitly (p. 92). Furthermore, meaning in the present interaction is co-constructed not just by the interlocutors engaging at that moment, but by indexing shared knowledge of past narratives as well; past narratives for which meaning was co-constructed through gesture, speech, and a shared sense of place.

Haviland (1993) adds another dimension to the ways in which participants orient to space during interaction. He illustrates the ways in which speakers of Guugu Yimithirr (GY) in Queensland shift between unanchored interactional space that is co-constructed in the same way that McNeill et al. (1993) describe and anchored local space that orients participants toward a specific local geographical location via reference to cardinal direction (north, south, east, and west) that the narrated event occurred in relation to. This deictic orientation anchored in cardinal directions mimics the linguistic practices of GY speakers, for whom accurately portraying the compass direction is important. Haviland points out, for example, that GY speakers use "compass direction words" almost to the exclusion of other linguistic directional devices. Similarly, GY speakers often point to indicate the specific direction or place where a narrated event took place.

However, GY speakers often shift between actual space and interactional space. For example, in one instance, the narrator, who is facing west, shifts his body to the right to reenact a scene he is describing in which the protagonist was looking north. Haviland notes that the narrator usually switches to unanchored, interactional space during scene setting, framing, narrative meta-commentary, and direct engagement with his interlocutors. For example, the narrator shifts from anchored local space to unanchored interactional space during the framing comment, "you see he was in charge of the dormitory," by tracing a small "dormitory" circle in front of him. Haviland asserts that these shifts back and forth between anchored local space and unanchored interactional space index the interlocutors' shared knowledge about local geography, local interaction etiquette, compass direction, and relationships among local people. It is this shared knowledge that allows participants to co-construct meaning for narratives within which the narrator is constantly shifting mutual orientation from interlocutors (if they or someone they are related to is involved in the narrated event), to anchored local space, to unanchored interactional space.

Taylor's (2002) work on adolescent girls in the United States focuses on the ways in which teenage girls construct and communicate body norms and ideals through a combination of verbal and non-verbal communication (presented at the "Gesture: The Living Medium" conference in June 2002). Using video-taped segments of 19-year-old girls talking in one of their apartments, Taylor has analyzed the ways in which these girls draw upon both verbal and non-verbal modes of communication to critique another girls' body parts and body presentation through clothing and non-verbal behavior. During this meta-commentary, the girls' integrated use of gesture and reported speech allow them to simultaneously do the following: (1) ridicule the girl they criticize through exaggerated performance; (2) perform their own thoughts and evaluations regarding the behavior and body presentation of the girl they criticize; (3) form an alliance with each other and against the girl they criticize; (4) construct their identities as mature and controlled in contrast to the inappropriate, wild, sexual behavior the girl they criticize; and (5) co-construct norms for the ways in which a woman should present herself publicly.

Through verbal and non-verbal communication, these young women police the female body, socialize participants regarding body norms, negotiate their own identities in relation to those norms, and construct alignments with each other and the body norms they communicate. Using this data, Taylor has explored the ways in which the multifunctionality of gesture and speech allows speakers to access, appropriate, and entextualize the behavior and appearance of others in creative ways as a means for constructing and communicating female body norms.

Discourse markers: culture and identity in small packages

The question of the relationship between language and culture touches not only on language itself but on extralinguistic forms including gestures and what is in the general population referred to as "filler words," known in the literature as discourse markers. Some examples of discourse markers are words and constructions such as *you know, I mean, like,* and *evidently.* According to Fraser (1990), discourse markers (henceforth DMs) are particles of speech that serve to structure discourse-internal relations (i.e., relations between clauses) and to manage the interaction between speakers without making an impact on the logical and truth-conditional interpretation of sentences. This characteristic has caused DMs to be widely ignored in semantics, the area of linguistics that deals with word and sentence meaning. The richest literature on the topic of discourse markers is in the area of pragmatics and of sociolinguistic discourse studies, where discourse markers have long been recognized as serving crucial functions of language processing, language coherence, and identity-marking. It is the latter issue that will serve as the focus for the remainder of this chapter.

Discourse markers are popularly thought of, and may be presented to clinicians as conveying unstructured thinking or lack of organization. In certain clinical situations they are even presented as symptomatic of learning disability itself (Seldin, 1998). Widely derided in employment-interview handbooks and in proper-language advice columns, discourse markers are age-graded, indexing the speakers' generation. While many people believe that youth make greater use of discourse markers (to wit stereotypes of "California girls" and "Surfer dudes," peppering their speech with *like* and *dude*), in fact older generations are also using DMs, though employing distinctive ones such as *evidently, as it were,* or *if you will* (the latter humorously examined in Pullum, 2003).

The aim of this section is to consider discourse markers in their reality-generating capacity, as makers of identity and stance, and as linguistic traces of the complex structuring of face-to-face interaction. With regard to language and gender as recently as Robin Lakoff's *Language and Woman's Place* (1975), linguists have observed that women use more "empty words" than men, and more evaluative, "meaningless" constructions such as "that's lovely." Recently, Mehl and Pennebaker (2002) used electronically activated recording to sample the daily activities and speech of 52 college students. They found that female students used more discourse markers, more modals, more first-person references and one-quarter of the swear words that male students use. How can one interpret these results? In Lakoff's account, DMs might be thought to signal insecurity and uncertainty, and many scholars today continue to assign them that interpretation. There is a contrasting possibility that the distribution of discourse markers might mean that women were simply more attuned to subtle communicative aspects of the interaction with their interlocutors, and used DMs as a marker of stance.

We will summarize two examples of discourse marker usage from Mendoza-Denton's research among Latina adolescents in Northern California to illustrate what is meant by stance-taking and identity-marking.

Discourse markers and stance-taking

The data that will be analyzed in the next two sections comes from research conducted from 1993 to 1997 by Mendoza-Denton in a Northern California Bay Area high school. To maintain the privacy of the study participants, this public high school has been assigned the pseudonym Sor Juana High School (SJHS). Despite being located in the wealthy Silicon Valley area, SJHS nevertheless has a fair share of working-class students, many of whom are immigrants from Latin America, particularly from Mexico. A full ethnographic account is given in Mendoza-Denton (1997) and Mendoza-Denton (forthcoming). Of the 1,200-person student body, approximately 20 percent are Latina/o. Within this larger group are Spanish-speaking Traditional Rural Girls (TRGs) and Mexican Urban Middle Class (MUMCs) immigrants, California English-speaking Latina Jocks, and strategically bilingual Norteña and Sureña gang members.

Mendoza-Denton (1999) observes in a recording of a group of five Spanish-speaking friends (of mixed TRG and MUMC backgrounds) the use of the Spanish discourse marker *no* when arguing about social class. Part of the transcript is reproduced below. Transcription conventions are shown in the Appendix:

1 GRACIELA: [Yo- e:hh- ahh:]
2 ANDREA: [YO CREO QUE] HACEN MÁS AMBIENTE: UNOS DE
            BARRIO que todos unos pinches fresas, me caen bien mal.=
2t   I THINK THAT THE ATMOSPHERE IS BETTER WITH
            PEOPLE FROM THE BARRIO than with a (expletive) bunch
            of fresas [spoiled rich brats], they get on my nerves.=

3 LAURA:	=Bueno, > de↑pende no ? porque si estás e<n:: (.) >depende como te sientas tu a gusto<, no? porque si te sientes a gusto en la ↑onda de: (.) de con los de barrio, pus - se te [va-]=
3t	=Well, it depends no?, because if you're in (.) it depends where you feel comfortable no?, because if you feel comfortable with the, the barrio thing, then you're-]
4 GRACIELA:	[Pero-]
4t	[But-]
5 LAURA:	=s'te va a hacer lo máximo.
5t	=then you'll think it's the best.
6 MARISOL:	↓~Yo soy del ba:RRio:~=
6t	↓~I'm from the baRRio:~=
7 LAURA:	=Aha:,=
7t	=Aha:,=
8 ANDREA:	=<u>NO, no, no</u>, yo no digo que si están revueltos los dos, yo digo que- [(0.3) que (.) ve-]
8t	=NO, no, no, I'm not talking about when they're both together, I'm saying that- [(0.3) that (.) see-]
9 LAURA:	[NO, pero, no, pus,] o sea, tu sabes, no, cada quien,=
9t	[NO, but, no, pus,] o sea, you know, no, each one,=
10 ANDREA:	= no, claro, propia onda=
10t	= no, of course, own thing=

In this example, *no* is serving to index and modulate the stance that different social class speakers are taking toward each other. *No* can be used in multiple ways; turn-finally to mean something equivalent to English *isn't it?* or *you know?*; turn-initially it is actually ambiguous between a negation marker and an agreement marker! For instance, in line 10, *no* is followed by *claro*, a usage that might appear contradictory and which remains ambiguous in the discourse. Because of the polysemous nature of this marker, and because of its ubiquitousness, a group of five close friends is able to use it to modulate a substantial disagreement about social class, to take epistemic stances with respect to each other and to give themselves more time for processing exactly how the disagreement will be worked out.

Discourse markers and identity marking

The next example comes from the English spoken among the same population of Latina girls in Sor Juana High School. This time, the marker is an indeterminate pronominal form, a Pro-form that has been dubbed TH-Pro by Mendoza-Denton (1997). TH-Pro is a family of related constructions that all involve the thing pronoun in some way: *and everything; or nothing; or something; that's the thing.* In this particular speech community, Norteña and Sureña girls who are deeply involved in gangs are much more likely to be frequent users of TH-Pro. This does not mean, however, that there is a perfect correlation between DM usage and gang membership. Many different groups in the school use DMs, and many different kinds of students use TH-Pro. In order to understand the correlation between a particular linguistic feature and social membership, it helps to know not only that TH-Pro is used in combination with other linguistic features (such as vowel height and fortition of consonants, but also that TH-Pro is used in grammatically innovative ways. For core Norteña and Sureña gang members, their innovative use consists of fronting, dislocating and heightening the frequency in the use of common discourse material. Consider this example, from Mendoza-Denton (1997):

> 1 YADIRA: That's how it started.
>   But the thing is that, my dad was engaged in El Salvador.
>   But he called the wedding off because he wanted to get married
>   to my mom.
> 2 NORMA: h!hh! Oh my God. [2.73 seconds]
> 3 YADIRA: And everything, and like umm so like my mom, she decided to
>   marry him.

In normative prescriptive grammars it is simply not possible to use a TH-Pro element to begin a phrase as in turn (3), uttered after a very substantial silence. By tracking not only the pronunciation of the internal parts of the TH-Pro element but also the grammatical usage of the form, Mendoza-Denton concludes that a new group of discourse markers has emerged, one that is both intelligible within the wider community and yet has a deeply structured community-internal use. It is the latter function that allows this small and seemingly inconsequential bit of language to serve as a marker of identity.

Conclusion

Research on discourse markers and on gesture has contributed to the theoretical ideas surrounding language and culture by illustrating the ways in which participants draw upon a variety of semiotic resources as well as local, interactional, imagined, and remembered space to co-construct meaning in interaction.

Appendix: Transcription conventions

Standard CA (conversation analytic) transcription procedures have been employed.

Bold, <u>underline</u>	Talk in bold, italics or underlined has received special emphasis.
:::	Colons indicate lengthening of segments.
(1.2)	Numbers in parentheses mark gaps – silences in seconds and tenths of seconds.
><	The combination of "less than" and "more than" symbols indicates that the talk between them is compressed or rushed.
↑↓	Upward and downward arrows mark sharp intonation rises and falls, or resettings of pitch register.
~talk~	Talk between tildes is spoken with creaky voice, or laryngealization.

The following punctuation symbols are used to mark intonation:

- . A period indicates a falling contour.
- ? A question mark indicates a rising contour.
- , A comma indicates a fall–rise.
- – A dash indicates a cutoff of the current sound.
- [ ] A left bracket marks the precise point at which an overlap begins. When the end of the overlap is itself overlapped, a right bracket defines the ends of the overlapped segments.
- = An equal sign indicates "latching," i.e., when there is no interval between units of talk by the same or different speakers.

Further reading

Atkinson, J. M. (1984) *Our Masters' Voices: The Language and Body Language of Politics*. London: Methuen.

Farnell, B. (1999) Moving bodies, acting selves. *Annual Review of Anthropology* 28: 341–73.

Hanks, W. (1990) *Referential Practice: Language and Lived Space among the Maya.* Chicago: University of Chicago Press.

Kita, S. (ed.) (2003) *Pointing: Where Language, Culture and Cognition Meet.* Mahwah, NJ: Lawrence Erlbaum Associates.

8

African American English

Walt Wolfram

African American English is by far the most scrutinized – and controversial – dialect of American English. Little about this sociocultural variety has escaped debate, and even its name has become a matter of contention. What we refer to here as African American English has gone through at least a half dozen name changes over the past several decades, including Nonstandard Negro English, Black English, Vernacular Black English, Afro-American English, Ebonics, African American (Vernacular) English, and African American Language. Though popularly referred to as Ebonics, most linguists prefer more neutral terms such as African American English (AAE) or African American Language. Notwithstanding the academic arguments over its genesis and development, the continuing public controversy over AAE demonstrates how language functions as a proxy for wider social issues relating to racial categories and ethnic identities in American society.

In discussing AAE, it is still necessary to start with a disclaimer about language and race. There is absolutely no foundation for maintaining a genetic base for the kind of language differences shown by some black Americans. Nonetheless, myths about the physical basis of AAE persist, so that there is a continuing need to confront and debunk claims about language and race. In our ensuing discussion, it should be understood that a label such as African American English refers to a socially constructed, ethno-cultural language variety rather than a genetically determined racial group.

In this discussion, we consider several issues related to AAE. First we consider its origin and early development, which has now gone through several paradigmatic shifts. Then we consider its present path of development and outline some of its structural traits. Finally, we consider the clinical and educational implications of these differences for the speech-language pathologist (SLP).

The origin and early development of AAE

Though the present-day structure of AAE can be described apart from its past, it is difficult to fully appreciate its dynamic status without understanding its historical evolution. Unfortunately, a half-century of debate over its genesis and early development has not led to a consensus position. Major disputes concern the validity of language data used to document its earlier development, the nature of the early language contact situation between Africans and Europeans, and the sociohistorical circumstances that framed the speech of earlier African Americans. There are a couple of major hypotheses about the origin and early development of AAE, with some variation within these primary positions. One major hypothesis is the *Anglicist hypothesis*, which maintains that the roots of AAE can be traced to the same sources as earlier European American dialects, the dialects of English spoken in the British Isles. This position maintains that the language contact situation of African descendants in the United States was comparable to that of other groups of immigrants, and that African slaves simply learned the regional and social varieties of surrounding white speakers within a couple of generations. Given their early concentration in the rural American South, African Americans ended up speaking varieties of English indistinguishable from those of the regional benchmark white varieties found in these areas. This position was originally associated with American dialectology in the mid-1900s (Kurath, 1949; McDavid and McDavid, 1951), but it has been revived in the past decade, based on the examination of newly uncovered written documents and the study of speech among expatriate, transplant communities of African Americans who left the US in the early 1800s for remote locations such as Nova Scotia and the peninsula of Samaná in the Dominican Republic (Poplack and Tagliamonte, 1991, 2001; Poplack, 1999). The primary difference between the original Anglicist hypothesis and the so-called Neo-Anglicist hypothesis is that the former position maintained that current-day AAE was still comparable to Southern rural European American English whereas the latter position maintains that contemporary AAE has since diverged from Southern rural European American varieties. In the words of prominent sociolinguist William Labov (1998: 119), "many important features of the modern dialect [AAE] are creations of the twentieth century and not an inheritance of the nineteenth."

Language contact hypotheses stand in opposition to the Anglicist position. These positions argue that earlier AAE developed distinctly due to the enduring structural effects from the original contact situation between speakers of African languages and speakers of English. A strong version of the contact hypothesis is the *Creolist hypothesis*, which maintains that AAE developed from a creole language, a special language developed in language contact situations where the vocabulary from a primary language, in this case English, is imposed on a specially adapted, universally based grammatical structure. Those who support the Creolist hypothesis assert that the creole language that gave rise to AAE was fairly widespread in the antebellum South (Stewart, 1967, 1968; Dillard, 1972). This creole shows a number of similarities to well-known English-based creoles of the African diaspora such as Krio, spoken today in Sierra Leone and along the coast of West Africa, and English-based creoles of the Caribbean such as those spoken in Barbados and Jamaica. In the United States, Gullah, more popularly called "Geechee," is an acknowledged creole still spoken by some African Americans in coastal South Carolina and Georgia. Creolists maintain that some of the vestiges of this creole predecessor are still reflected in contemporary AAE. For example, prominent AAE structures such as the absence of the copula in *You ugly* or *She nice* and various types of inflectional -*s* absence (e.g., *Mary go_*; *Mary_ hat*), as well as phonological characteristics such as consonant cluster reduction in items (e.g., *wes' en'* for *west end*) show a strong affinity with creole language structures.

Closer scrutiny of the sociohistorical situation in the antebellum South has raised important questions about the Creolist hypothesis. For example, the distribution of slaves in the Plantation South was not particularly advantageous to the perpetuation of a widespread Plantation Creole (Mufwene, 1996, 2001), as had been postulated by proponents of this position. In fact, the vast majority of slaves lived on smaller farms with just a few slaves per household rather than in the large, sprawling plantations with large numbers of slaves as pictured in popular portrayals of the antebellum South. Whereas expansive plantations with large numbers of slaves might be conducive to the development and spread of a plantation-based Creole, as was the case in coastal South Carolina, over 80 percent of all slaves in the American South were associated with families that had less than four slaves per household.

One situation that provides insight into earlier AAE is the historically isolated community, where language change may be quite conservative. Research on long-term, historically isolated enclave communities of African Americans in coastal North Carolina (Wolfram and Thomas, 2002) and in Appalachia (Mallinson and Wolfram, 2002; Childs and Mallinson, 2004) suggests that earlier African American speech converged with localized varieties of English spoken by their European American cohorts. Though this may seem to support the Anglicist hypothesis, it is essential to note that there is, at the same time, strong evidence for a persistent ethnolinguistic divide that is most reasonably attributed to enduring structural influence from the early contact history between Africans and Europeans. For example, structures vulnerable to alteration during language contact, such as inflectional suffixes and redundant agreement patterns, distinguished earlier African American speech from that of its regional European American counterparts even though many other regional dialect traits were shared. Earlier African American speech may have accommodated local dialect features to some extent, but there also has been lasting language influence from the earlier language contact situation between Europeans and Africans, referred to as a *substrate effect*. The Substrate hypothesis maintains that there has been durable influence from an earlier contact situation between African language and English, but does not insist on the existence of a widespread Plantation Creole, as posited under the earlier Creolist hypothesis. Current research suggests that there was more regional influence than assumed under the Creolist hypothesis but more durable substrate effects from the early language contact history than assumed under the Anglicist positions. In effect, earlier AAE was a product both of the distinct language contact situation that characterized the African diaspora and the regional influences that provided a context for its development in the US.

The contemporary development of AAE

The roots of present-day AAE were established in the rural South, but its development into a distinct sociocultural variety in the twentieth century is strongly associated with its use in urban areas. The emergence of urban AAE was due in part to the Great Migration in which African Americans moved from the rural South to large metropolitan areas of the North in the early and mid-twentieth century. In 1910, almost 90% of all African Americans in the US lived in the South and 75% of that number lived in communities of less than 2,500. Starting with World War I and continuing through World War II and beyond, there was a dramatic relocation of African Americans, and by 1970 almost half of all African Americans lived outside of the South, and over three-quarters of those lived in urban areas. The large concentrated populations of African Americans in cities led to a social and cultural environment that was conducive to the maintenance and augmentation of a distinct ethnolinguistic variety.

Perhaps more important than population demographics was the establishment of contemporary cultural and language norms related to African
American youth culture. The center of African American culture today is
primarily young and urban, and many models for behavior, including language, seem to radiate outward from these urban cultural centers. During
the twentieth century, a couple of noteworthy sociolinguistic trends have
taken place with respect to AAE. First, this variety has taken on an ethnic
significance that transcends regional parameters. That is, there appears to
be a *supra-regional norm* for AAE in that this variety shares a set of distinctive traits wherever it is spoken in the US. Though AAE is still regionally
situated to some extent, many of its linguistic traits supersede the kinds of
regional boundaries associated with European American dialects.

During the twentieth century, AAE also become strongly associated with
cultural identity. This identity is supported through social mechanisms
that range from community-based social networks to stereotypical media
projections of African American speech (Lippi-Green, 1997). Part of the
definition of African American speech is the adoption of distinct dialect
traits in AAE, but part of its characterization is also the avoidance of
features associated with regional, "white speech." *Oppositional identity*, in
which African Americans avoid conduct with strong associations of white
behavior, may thus be an important reason for rejecting regional dialect
features that have strong white connotations (Fordham and Ogbu, 1986).
Studies of contemporary urban AAE show further that some of its structures are intensifying rather than receding and that new structures are
evolving. For example, the use of habitual *be* in sentences such as *Sometimes
they be playing games* is escalating, to the point of becoming a stereotype of
AAE. While older speakers in rural areas rarely use this form, some younger
speakers use it extensively. Similarly, younger speakers use the auxiliary *had*
with a past or perfect form of the verb to indicate a simple past tense action,
as in *They had went outside and then they had messed up the yard . . .* for *They
went outside and then they messed up the yard.* Earlier descriptions of AAE do
not mention this feature at all, but more recent descriptions (Rickford and
Théberge, 1996; Cukor-Avila, 2001) observe that this construction is often
quite frequent in the narratives of some preadolescents.

Our own research on language change in a historically isolated community of African American residents in coastal North Carolina demonstrates
how AAE is moving toward a more supra-regional norm (Wolfram and
Thomas, 2002). Since the early 1700s, a small group of European Americans and African Americans had lived in a remote, marshland coastal community in North Carolina, with regular overland access only starting during

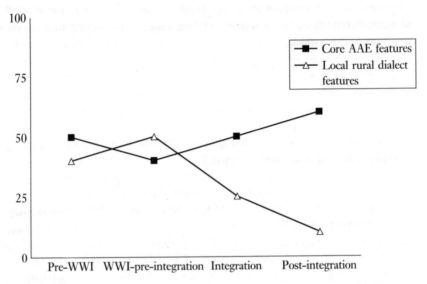

Figure 8.1   Idealized trajectory of changes for African Americans in Hyde County (adapted from Wolfram and Thomas, 2002: 200)

the middle of the twentieth century. Elderly African Americans, who traveled little outside of the region, adopted many of the distinct regional dialect traits of coastal North Carolina while maintaining a core set of AAE features. Over time, regional dialect features have receded and core AAE features have intensified. The idealized paths of change with respect to the local, regional dialect features and core AAE features based on our analysis of different generations of speakers are plotted in Figure 8.1. The graph represents four sociohistorical periods: speakers who were born and raised in the early twentieth century up through World War I; speakers born and raised between World War I and school integration in the late 1960s; speakers who lived through the early period of school integration as adolescents; and speakers who were born and raised after legalized institutional integration.

It is noteworthy that during and following the period of institutionally mandated integration, African Americans abandoned local dialect features while intensifying their use features associated with AAE, in effect, showing a growing consciousness of the role of language in maintaining ethnic identity. Such studies show the establishment of a contemporary supra-regional norm for AAE, in opposition to regional dialect norms that have strong symbolic associations with white speech behavior (Wolfram, Thomas and

Green, 2000). Studies such as this demonstrate that the vernacular speech norm for African Americans today is urban and generic rather than rural and local, and that norms of behavior, including language, follow the lead of speakers in urban areas.

Structural features of AAE

The structural details of AAE, which have now been cataloged in a number of descriptive overviews (Fasold and Wolfram, 1970; Labov, 1972a; Wolfram and Schilling-Estes, 1998; Rickford, 1999; Green, 2002) range from the minute phonetic features of vowel and consonant segments to generalized conversational routines and discourse strategies. In Northern urban contexts, most of the features of AAE are distinct from surrounding European American varieties, but their ethnolinguistic distinctiveness in Southern rural contexts is more debatable. As noted above, some structural traits of AAE (e.g., inflectional -*s* absence, copula absence, consonant cluster reduction, etc.) are quite durable, and apparently have been associated with AAE for centuries now. Other traits, such as habitual *be* and past tense auxiliary *had*, appear to be innovations of the twentieth century. Furthermore, it is important to recognize that AAE, like any other variety, is also currently changing. Recent descriptions of *be* (Alim, 2001), for example, show that its meaning is extending beyond the habitual reference noted previously. Invariant *be* is now being used in sentences such as *I be the truth* or *Dr. Dre be the name* in a way that seizes upon its iconic status as a marker of black speech rather than its aspectual reference to habitual action. Under earlier analyses, such stativity would have been considered ill-formed or ungrammatical AAE, since it is incompatible with a habitual meaning. We thus see a shift in the function of this form, led by its use in hip hop, within the last decade.

There are also structures in AAE that appear on the surface to be very much like those in other dialects of English; however, upon closer inspection they have uses or meanings that are unique. These types of structures are called *camouflaged forms* because they bear surface resemblance to constructions found in other varieties of English even though they are used differently. One of these camouflaged constructions is the form *come* in a construction with an -*ing* verb, as in *She come acting like she was real mad*. This structure looks like a common English use of the motion verb *come* in structures like *She came running*, but it actually has a special use as a kind of verb auxiliary indicating annoyance or indignation on the part of the speaker (Spears, 1982). Similarly, the use of *ain't* for *didn't*, as in *I ain't go there yesterday*, appears to be quite like the use of *ain't* for the perfect *have* (e.g., *I ain't been there* for *I haven't been there*) or *be + not* (e.g., *She ain't here* for *She isn't here*) in other vernacular varieties. Upon closer inspection, however, it turns out to be a distinctive structural use of *ain't* in AAE, since other varieties do not use *ain't* for *didn't*.

It is not possible to catalog the complete inventory of features characteristic of AAE in this overview (see Rickford, 1999; Bailey, 2001; Cukor-Avila, 2001; Green, 2002, for more comprehensive inventories). In the illustrative list of grammatical traits of AAE provided, we limit ourselves to some of the major traits, and some representative features shared with other vernacular varieties. Traits that are unique, or predominantly associated with AAE, are marked with an asterisk:

*habitual *be* for intermittent activity:
  e.g. *Sometimes my ears be itching.*
*absence of copula for contracted forms of *is* and *are*:
  e.g. *She nice. They acting all strange.*
*present tense, third person -*s* absence:
  e.g. *she walk_* 'she walks'
*possessive -*s* absence:
  e.g. *man_ hat* 'man's hat'
*general plural -*s* absence
  e.g. *a lot of time* 'a lot of times'
*remote time stressed *béen* to mark a state or action that began a long time ago and is still relevant:
  e.g. *You béen paid your dues a long time ago.*
*simple past tense *had* + verb:
  e.g. *They had went outside and then they had messed up the yard.*
**ain't* for *didn't*:
  e.g. *He ain't go there yesterday.*
regularized *was* for past *be*:
  e.g. *We was there.*
completive *done*:
  e.g. *She done ate the food.*
irregular verbs: past for participle:
  e.g. *I had went.*
participle for past:
  e.g. *I seen it.*

bare root past form:

    e.g. *Yesterday I run fast.*

regularized past form:

    e.g. *I knowed it.*

finna auxiliary 'plan to':

    e.g. *I finna do it.*

negative concord:

    e.g. *She ain't do nothing.*

preverbal indefinite:

    e.g. *Nobody don't like it.* 'Nobody likes it.'

negative inversion:

    e.g. *Didn't nobody like it.* 'Nobody liked it.'

*stative locative *here go*:

    e.g. *Here go the pencil.*

*regularized *mines*:

    e.g. *It's mines.*

existential *it* or *they*:

    e.g. *It's a J Street in DC. They's a J Street in DC.* 'There's a J Street.'

subject relative pro deletion:

    e.g. *It's a man took it.* 'There's a man who took it.'

Some of the prominent phonological traits of AAE are illustrated in the list below. The structures involve syllable-structure processes, in which the canonical shape of the syllable is altered in some way; substitutions in which one sound simply corresponds to a different sound in other varieties of English; and prosodic details such as stress and intonation. The selective list is based on Wolfram (1994), Bailey and Thomas (1998), Rickford (1999), and Bailey (2001). Again, traits found predominantly in AAE are indicated by an asterisk. Conventional orthography is used rather than phonetic symbols to indicate the phonetic differences:

*prevocalic consonant cluster reduction:

    e.g. *wes' en'* 'west end'

unstressed syllable deletion:

    e.g. *sec'tary* 'secretary'

**skr* for *str* clusters:

    e.g. *skreet* 'street', *skraight* 'straight'

f and *v* for medial and final *th*:

    e.g. *toof* 'tooth', *smoov* 'smooth'

stopping of word-initial voiced *th*:
   e.g. *dese* 'these'
*transposed *sk* and *sp*:
   e.g. *aks* 'ask', *waps* 'wasp'
stopping of voiced fricatives before nasals:
   e.g. *wadn't* 'wasn't'
postvocalic *r* and *l* loss:
   e.g. *fou'* 'four', *he'p* 'help'
*devoicing of final voiced stops:
   e.g. *goot* 'good'
*vowel nasalization for final nasal segments:
   e.g. *ma'* 'man'
diphthong ungliding:
   e.g. *tahm* 'time', *bohl* 'boil'
primary stress movement:
   e.g. *pólice* 'políce', *Júly* for 'Julý'
intonation differences:
   e.g. more varied intonation

Though it is possible to compare the structures of AAE with those of other American dialects on an item-by-item basis, this type of comparison does not represent the true status of AAE; its uniqueness lies more in the particular combination of structures that make up the dialect than it does in a restricted set of distinct structures. It is the co-occurrence of a set of grammatical structures along with a set of phonological characteristics that best defines the variety rather than a subset of uniquely AAE structures.

Studies of listener perceptions of ethnic identity certainly support the contention that AAE is distinct from comparable European American vernaculars, but sorting out the precise points of this differentiation is still under investigation. Recent experimental investigation by Thomas and Reaser (2004) suggests that minute phonetic differences, including vowel differences and voice quality differences, may have as much to do with the perceptual determination of ethnicity as do some of the more prominent grammatical differences.

There are also many lexical items that are associated with AAE, particularly in its association with youth culture (Wolfram and Schilling-Estes, 1998). Many lexical differences fit into the general category of *slang*, that is, euphemistic terms that serve an informal, group reference function. Prominent among these differences are terms for labeling people (e.g., *dawg*, *homes*, *playa*, etc.), terms for evaluating people, activities, and situations (e.g., *saditty* 'conceited', *bougie* 'high class, privileged', *bopper* 'woman seeking material gain', etc.), and terms for leisure activities (e.g., *get my chill on* 'rest', *get my groove on* 'dance', etc). Many lexical differences are also associated with particular conversational routines, such as addressing (e.g., *money, homes, cuz*, etc.), greeting (e.g., *sup, yo, word*, etc.) leave-taking (e.g., *bounce, push-off, and one*, etc.), or empathy (e.g., *feel, we're here*, etc.), so that lexical differences may converge with different pragmatic functions of language use (Green, 2002). One noteworthy lexical process is *semantic inversion*, where an adjective describing a negative attribute in the Standard American English lexicon is used to express a positive quality; for example, adjectives like *bad, ugly, fresh*, and *ill* may be used to indicate positive attributes, as in *That outfit is bad* or *Those lyrics are ill*. There are also many lexical differences of AAE that extend well beyond the slang associated with youth culture, such as *ashy* 'pale, whiteish color', *the hawk* 'cold and windy', *cut eye* 'scornful gesture made with the eyes', and so forth (Smitherman, 1994), so that it is important not to limit the discussion of lexical items in AAE to slang. Though most linguists tend to limit their descriptions of AAE to the structural patterns of phonology and grammar, lexical differences and language use conventions are certainly as indexical as any other level of language in establishing symbolic ethnic boundaries between African Americans and European Americans (Labov, 1992; Green, 2002).

There are generational, regional, and social status differences associated with African American speech, and it is important to note that not all African Americans speak this variety. At the same time, one of the most noteworthy aspects of AAE is the common set of features shared by vernacular speakers from different regions. Features such as habitual *be*, copula absence, inflectional -*s* absence, among a number of other grammatical, phonological, and lexical features, are found in locations as distant as Los Angeles, California; New Haven, Connecticut; and Meadville, Mississippi. The set of common AAE features that surfaces regardless of where it has been studied in the United States attests to its strong ethnic association and supra-regional dimension in its contemporary form.

Clinical and educational applications

Though other chapters in this volume (see chapters by Oetting, Damico, and Isaac) deal with the educational and clinical aspects of language differences in specific detail, it must be recognized that an important motivation for studying AAE over the past half-century has been a concern for the potential educational and clinical significance of the language differences associated with this variety.

One of the obvious venues for sociolinguistic application is speech and language assessment. Historically, the field of speech-language pathology relied on a battery of standardized, quantifiable discrete point tests normed on majority ethnic groups and dominant social classes, so that norms of "correctness" were limited to populations whose language represented Standard American English. Many of these tests did not allow for legitimate regional, social, or ethnic language variation. Furthermore, these tests tended to focus on the more superficial aspects of language organization rather than underlying categories and relationships (Vaughn-Cooke, 1980). Current assessment instruments have undergone several types of revisions. Many standardized tests now allow for alternative dialect forms as "correct" responses in the scoring guidelines, so that it is not uncommon for a standardized, discrete point test to offer dialect alternates that should be scored as correct if the test taker speaks AAE or another vernacular variety of English. Other projects involve designing tests that specifically target the developing structures of vernacular dialects such as AAE, as in the test developed by Seymour and Roeper (www.umass.edu/synergy/fall98/ebonics).

Another trend in assessment departs from discrete point testing of superficial grammatical differences to focus on deeper levels of language organization, for example, units that constitute underlying semantic categories and relationships (Bloom and Lahey, 1978; Vaughn-Cooke, 1983; Stockman and Vaughn-Cooke, 1986; Lahey, 1988). This development is based on the assumption that the more superficial the language capability tapped in a testing instrument, the greater the likelihood that the instrument will be inappropriate for populations beyond the immediate population on which it was normed.

The increasing concern with language functions *vis-à-vis* language form within communication disorders has also moved the field of communication towards a more broadly based ethnographic vantage point. Under the loosely defined rubric of "pragmatics," developing interest in speech acts, speech events, conversational routines, and discourse has expanded evaluation beyond the limits of the clinical setting. It is more common to include in an assessment battery a line of inquiry that can tap representative dimensions of language functions (Gallagher, 1991). A functionally oriented perspective has obvious implications for the type of data collected with respect to communication disorders, the procedures used in collecting data, the contexts in which data are collected, and the analytical tools used in analyzing and interpreting data. For example, in many instances, this focus compels clinicians to gather more qualitative types of data as viewed from the vantage point of an ethnographer and to adopt appropriate ethnographic roles *vis-à-vis* the traditional clinical context.

One of the expanding roles for SLPs today involves a more proactive educational role with respect to sociolinguistic diversity. Though the sociolinguistic model has now become entrenched within the field of communication disorders, it is often not given the necessary focus in the day-to-day clinical setting (Supple, 1993: 24), and there is a continuing need for information about linguistic diversity. Furthermore, the ascribed role of the SLPs as recognized "language experts" places them in a position to be heard on language matters. When speech and language pathologists speak about language, people listen. Adger et al. (1993) observe that the speech and language pathologist is the cultural guardian of language in education, so that even when educators and administrators do not listen, the clinician still bears the moral authority to speak out about issues of diversity.

Finally, in many educational settings there is an expanding role for speech and language pathologists in mainstream classroom education (Simon, 1987). For example, in the United States it is becoming increasingly common for speech and language pathologists to augment language activities in the mainstream classroom, in addition to their traditional "pull out" therapy sessions with students. SLPs are taking a more active and a more collaborative role related to general educational activities involving language, and they may therefore use some of these collaborative educational opportunities to introduce students and professional colleagues to the orderly nature of sociolinguistic diversity as it pertains to AAE and other vernacular varieties of English.

Acknowledgments

Support for research reported here came from NSF Grants 9910024 and 0236838, HHS Grants MCJ-370599 and MCJ-370649, and from the William C. Friday Endowment at North Carolina State University.

Further reading

Green, L. J. (2002) *African American English: A Linguistic Introduction.* New York: Cambridge University Press.

Lanehart, S. J. (ed.) (2001) *Sociocultural and Historical Contexts of African American English*. Philadelphia, PA: John Benjamins, especially pp. 53–92.

Rickford, J. R. and Rickford, R. J. (2000) *Spoken Soul: The Story of Black English*. New York: Wiley.

Wolfram, W., Adger, C. T., and Christian, D. (1999) *Language Variation in Schools and the Community*. Mahwah, NJ: Erlbaum.

9

Language Change

Dominic Watt and Jennifer Smith

A common belief in the western world, where nation states have generally developed highly focused linguistic standards, is that there is one and only one "correct" way of using the language . . . [This] popular model of language . . . often influences judgements of speakers' language abilities even in *professional* contexts where language is the explicit focus of attention and where a realistic concept of its variable and patterned nature is a matter of practical importance.

Milroy (1987: 199–200)

All living languages[1] inevitably change. No known period in the history of any living language is identifiable as an era of stability or uniformity. Indeed, we might best not ask why languages change, but rather why they do *not* change more or faster than they do. Related questions – e.g., why particular varieties of particular languages undergo particular changes at particular times while others apparently equally susceptible to the same changes do not, how changes get started in the first place, and how they then spread and become "embedded" in languages – are also uncertain.

These questions, to which linguists are only starting to provide answers, may seem of little clinical relevance. In this chapter we argue, however, that anyone working with living language varieties should acknowledge them as "moving targets" often with properties we do not expect either because they have not yet been described in sufficient detail, or because they have changed since last described. Languages vary across geographical and social space, but also across surprisingly short spans of time. We must recognize the importance of variability in all three dimensions to fully understand the nature of the language(s) we work with.

Lack of space precludes discussion of the explanations for language change that have been proposed over the centuries; instead, we refer readers to J. Milroy (1992), McMahon (1994), Lass (1997), Croft (2000), Aitchison (2001) and Hickey (2003). We introduce here some key concepts involved in sociolinguistic accounts of language change, illustrating with some phono-logical and morphosyntactic changes in contemporary British English. We conclude by stressing our belief that an appreciation of the ubiquity and social significance of language change is vital among practitioners and stu-dents of the clinical language sciences if addressing patients' communicative needs is to be accomplished.

Popular perceptions: change as decay

Most people know that the languages we speak have changed over time in various ways. English speakers appreciate, for example, that the language of the King James Bible or the Gettysburg Address is "old-fashioned" and now used only in special circumstances. Lincoln's *four score and seven* ("eighty-seven"), for instance, is wholly obsolescent. Changes, moreover, are perceived to be mostly for the worse: as Labov (2001: 6) points out, "no-one has ever been heard to say, 'It's wonderful the way young people talk today. It's so much better than the way we talked when I was a kid.'" (See further entries in Bauer and Trudgill, 1998.) English is, some say, increasingly vulnerable to contamination from non-standard dialects and other languages, and only by resisting the adoption of new forms used indiscriminately by the undereducated and impressionable, and especially the young, can we pre-serve the language for future generations.

Consider, in this light, remarks made by a Scottish "speech therapist" (quoted in Paterson, 2002).

> Clear speech is a problem in all children in Scotland . . . I had a boy who first came to me when he was four and he was unintelligible. His school teacher was determined he was deaf but he wasn't, it was just that nobody had ever corrected him.

Paterson reports the most common "offences" perpetrated by children sent for therapy (here, actually elocution) to be "the glottal stop, where the t's and d's are dropped from the end of words, and the distortion of vowel sounds." But for the intervention of experts, apparently, many Scottish children would grow up speaking unclearly, even unintelligibly, and pep-pering their speech with "offensive" pronunciations.

Children's language more generally is harshly criticized. A recent BBC report on a package entitled "Speaking, Listening, Learning" produced for English primary schools states that "headteachers had claimed that the behavioural and verbal skills of children starting school were at an all-time low, with some five-year-olds unable to speak properly."[2]

A recurring popular perception of innovations in non-standard varieties, and in the speech of young speakers of any variety, is that of "sloppiness" or "laziness." For instance, the pronunciation of final /k/ in *back* as [x] in Liverpool English is often attributed to lazy or careless articulation, as are the aforementioned substitution of [ʔ] for non-initial /t/ (in e.g., *matter*, *set off*) and "[*h*]-dropping" (in e.g., *happy*) in many British accents. Via institutions such as the BBC or newspaper letters pages, constructions like *different than* or *to* (versus *different from*), *none are/were*, *between you and I*, and *everyone . . . their* (as in *Everyone must submit their assignment tomorrow*) are attacked for their perceived ungrammaticality, and taken to signal ignorance of or even contempt for "correct" grammar (see Wardhaugh, 1999).

Such judgments, however, usually depend on flawed assumptions, e.g., that pronunciation should follow spelling, or that grammatical rules are "logical." Ideas of linguistic correctness are usually arbitrary, being based largely on the preferences of individuals (self-)appointed as authorities on language use.

Standard varieties, despite their stable and unchanging image, are like any other varieties in being susceptible to change. British Received Pronunciation (RP) recorded in the 1930s is markedly different from contemporary RP. This holds even for individual speakers, as a recent "real-time" analysis of Queen Elizabeth II's vowels over several decades of Christmas broadcasts demonstrates (Harrington et al., 2000).

Real versus apparent time

Studies across such protracted timespans are, however, rarely feasible. Instead, linguists compare speech samples drawn from different age groups, on the assumption that speech habits essentially fossilize in youth. We can thus observe a community's linguistic behavior in "apparent time" (Labov, 1972c), and thereby deduce what has happened to the language since the sample's oldest speakers were young.

We cannot provide here a comprehensive summary of theory and methods used in the investigation of language change; for this, see Chambers (2003), Chambers et al. (2002), or Milroy and Gordon (2003). We describe, however, some central issues involved in the analysis and interpretation of patterns of linguistic variation and change, and relate these to practice in the remedial domain. We begin by introducing a basic methodological concept which has been used, in one form or another, by historical linguists, dialectologists and sociolinguists since the emergence of these disciplines.

The linguistic variable

Until the mid-twentieth century linguists generally assumed that language change was imperceptibly gradual, and only observable after completion. This was challenged, then invalidated, by Labov's early work on American English and the subsequent proliferation of research using similar approaches. The linguistic variable – a set of at least two distinguishable variants which have equivalent linguistic meanings but which may carry differing social meanings – emerged as the key investigative tool from this work. The occurrence of each variant is not predictable from linguistic structure; rather, variants have greater or lesser *tendency* to occur depending upon linguistic or non-linguistic factors. Distributional patterns are thus quantifiable by expressing a variant's frequency in proportional terms (e.g., in a 45-minute recording, for a variable X with two variants y and z, speaker A used y 27% of the time and z 73% of the time).[3]

Consider, for example, the pronunciation of words like *car* or *form*. In many accents (most of those in England and Wales, in New York City, the southern US, Australia, etc.) no post-vocalic /r/ is pronounced. *Paw* and *pore* are thus homophonous. Such accents are said to be "non-rhotic." To suppose that they lost rhoticity instantaneously is absurd. Rather, we must posit an intermediate stage. At time A, rhoticity was "categorical" (invariant), for all English speakers. By time B it had become variable, because certain speakers had stopped consistently pronouncing post-vocalic /r/. They may, for instance, have produced /r/-less pronunciations when conversing informally with friends and family, using post-vocalic /r/ only in careful speech. At C, non-rhoticity had diffused through the community to the extent that /r/ in *cart* or *bird* was never pronounced – i.e., non-rhoticity had in these words become categorical – with the historical /r/ in words like *four* or *hear* only being pronounced in pre-vocalic contexts (e.g., in *four apples*, *hear about*).[4]

We can schematize the progression of such changes using an S-curve (Figure 9.1). Innumerable studies of historical and contemporary language changes yield results approximating this shape, so the model's theoretical validity is quite certain.

The linguistic variable's value depends on understanding that variation is not random but systematic, and that non-standard varieties – often stigmatized

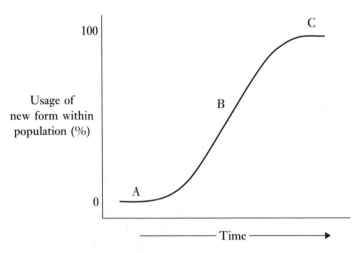

Figure 9.1 The S-curve of diffusion

as illogical, "degraded" forms of the language – are as structured and rule-governed as standard ones. It also allows explicit linkage of synchronic (contemporary) variation to change ("diachronic" variation), without proposing that changes occur "overnight."

Rhoticity in English, moreover, exemplifies the arbitrariness of the stigmatization of certain changes. Post-vocalic /r/ in American and English accents is viewed in opposite, but equally subjective, ways. In England, pronunciations like [haɹt] *heart* or [fiːɹd] *feared*, which are (stereo)typical of accents of the southwest and of southern Lancashire, tend to be evaluated reasonably positively elsewhere, but are nonetheless considered amusing, rustic and perhaps indicative of low intelligence. They are certainly not considered as "correct" as non-rhotic [haːt] and [fɪəd]. In US English, conversely, pronunciations like [paɹt] *part* or [kɔɹn] *corn* are standard, being considered more correct than non-rhotic pronunciations typical of speakers from southern states, urban New Yorkers, and African-Americans. The latter, indeed, are frequently described negatively even by speakers who themselves use them (Labov, 1966). Consider, for instance, this selling point for Wellborn's (1997) *Accent Reduction Made Easy* course: "The purpose of this program is to help you change the muscle habits of your mouth by saying correctly over and over again the 5 or 6 sounds which you personally need . . . There are sounds for Southerners such as the 'r' . . . which Southerners often skip." Prestigious and "correct" features in one variety, then, may be stigmatized in others. The rhoticity example demonstrates the importance of identifying normal linguistic behavior in a given community, and seeing past the subjective evaluations of laypeople. We return to this point later.

Changes from above and below

To sociolinguists, language change is not something that languages do to themselves without their speakers "having a say." There are changes which speakers realize they are making, and on which they overtly comment (like rhoticity). In the morphological domain, we might cite the invariant tag *innit* (Stenström and Andersen, 1996), which has become identified with urban British teenagers from a range of ethnic backgrounds, and which appears often to have been deliberately adopted to signal in-group identity.

An innovative syntactic feature in British English is quotative *be like*; see Tagliamonte and Hudson (1999: 147):

(1)   She's like, "Right, you know we're taking you out." I was like, "Ah, I don't want to go out."

Unlike invariant tags, this feature is seen as originating in North America, and particularly among university students (Ferrara and Bell, 1995: 285). It has subsequently spread dramatically through British English, and may soon supersede the traditional quotative *say*.

Changes consciously adopted like this are called *changes from above* (Labov, 1972c). *Changes from below*, conversely, operate below conscious awareness, and go generally unnoticed. They can also proceed very slowly; some take centuries. One such change involves the complementizer *that*. *That* presence, as in example (2a), was once almost categorical (Warner, 1982). In contrast, modern spoken English shows near-categorical *that*-deletion in these contexts, as in example (2b) (Tagliamonte and Smith, forthcoming).

(2)   a.   I wish *that* forty or fifty years ago I'd as much confidence.
       b.   I wish Ø I'd had it then.[5]

Another apparently largely unnoticed change involves structures expressing obligation/necessity. The traditional form was *must*, as in example (3a). *Have to*, example (3b) then appeared, but is increasingly being replaced by *have got to*, example (3c) (in some varieties *got to*, as per example (3d)). Examples (from Tagliamonte et al., 2004) are:

(3) a. . . . next time I'm in the doctors I *must* ask to see the physio.
     b. And I *have to* wear a hearing aid.
     c. You're told you*'ve got to* speak properly.
     d. You *got to* watch her food cos she'd get like the side of a house.

Such examples demonstrate that change is endemic at many levels and in all varieties, regardless of speakers' awareness of it. They tend to excite neither overt social nor derogatory comment, and often become part of the standard. Changes from below are, moreover, far commoner than changes from above. This appears to contradict popular perceptions of language change, but changes from above are (by definition) more conspicuous than those from below, often becoming foci of attention and sometimes concern among the population.

Change versus innovation

How do changes get started? According to J. Milroy (1992), they begin life as innovations, the innumerable variations in pronunciation or grammar occurring as normal byproducts of language in use. Innovations only rarely become changes; most remain either idiosyncrasies of the innovator's speech, or just disappear again. They qualify as changes if adopted by sufficient numbers of speakers, a process dependent on (1) their perceptibility; (2) positive evaluation (either overt or covert); and (3) reasonably frequent use in the adopters' speech. Even then, some are only temporary, and later disappear (see, e.g., Boberg and Strassel, 2000).

Linguists cannot yet predict which innovations will become changes. Chance undoubtedly figures heavily. Certain pathways, however, seem more likely to be followed than others. For example, lenition – "softening" of stops to fricatives, or voiceless consonants to voiced ones – is far more common cross-linguistically than fortition ("hardening" or "strengthening;" see, e.g., Lass, 1997: 218ff. for an example from the history of English).

Innovation versus pathology

Occasionally a change arises that will be interpreted as the spread of a "defect," because it resembles a hitherto rare and unambiguously pathological form. The use of labial [ʋ] for /r/ is an example. Labial pronunciations have traditionally been viewed as infantilisms occurring in the normal phonological development of young English-speaking children, generally being superseded by lingual pronunciations such as [ɹ] (e.g., Grunwell, 1981: 111). In many regions of England, however, [ʋ] is fast becoming the norm (Foulkes and Docherty, 2000, 2001; Docherty and Foulkes, 2001). Older attitudes nevertheless prevail among many British people, to the extent that use of [ʋ] is still commonly considered a "speech impediment" for which, if a child uses it beyond infancy, remediation should be sought.

The persistence of negative views of linguistic innovation in Anglophone countries, in which the notion that there is only one correct form of the language is subscribed to so widely, is understandable. By definition, deviations from this form are "incorrect" and can be deemed potentially pathological, especially if they carry the taint of immature speech. But negative reactions to non-standard forms (including innovative non-standard forms) manifest themselves worryingly frequently among language professionals as well as among laypeople. Niedzielski's (2002) survey of language assessment methods in the US reveals in their design disturbingly little account being taken of normal non-standard variation. The Rice/Wexler Test of Early Grammatical Impairments (TEGI), for instance,

> contains tests for so-called "inaccurate" constructions such as "he happy," "he walking," "yesterday she walk to my house," and "(do) he like me?", each of which is purported to signal a syntactic disorder. Other tests check for "correct" usage of plural or possessive markers (so that "two cat" and "Gramma house" are "incorrect"). While these syntactic productions may in fact signal a disorder in children whose dialects do not contain such constructs, in many dialects these sentences are well-formed, grammatical utterances, and there are millions of normal, non-disordered children and adults who use them. However, there is no statement regarding these dialects anywhere on articles about the TEGI, websites advertising the test, and SLP websites mentioning the test. (Niedzielski, 2002: 4)

If TEGI is typical of current procedures, many US clinicians must be continuing to deny the validity of non-standard morphosyntax, thus perpetuating the situation Crystal et al. (1976) lambaste in their review of tests then used in the UK. This would be worrying even were varieties of English fixed and unchanging, which they are quite obviously not. The risk of misdiagnosing normal language behavior as pathological becomes markedly higher if the variety is changing, since what might be categorized as disordered speech could be an incipient change which has not yet affected all members of the community, as per [ʋ] in British English.

Much of the problem in distinguishing normal from disordered forms lies in the unavailability of detailed information on normal patterns of variation in the community in question. Sociolinguistic surveys entail long lead-times: years can pass between the initial identification by linguists of variables worth investigating and publication of the final results. Often, these are published in journals not generally read by clinicians, or presented at conferences only attended by other sociolinguists. Sociolinguistics is a fairly new discipline, and sociolinguists are relatively few: many therapists work in communities (sometimes even large cities) in which very little or no systematic sociolinguistic research has previously been conducted. In the next section, we consider an example from the current remediation literature illustrating this point.

GOAT fronting in West Yorkshire

With a population of around 1.2 million, the Leeds/Bradford conurbation of West Yorkshire, northern England, is one of the UK's largest. However, there exists to the best knowledge of the authors no modern widely available descriptive linguistic survey of West Yorkshire English (WYE) to provide information on community norms (see Khattab, 2002).

Further, the phonology of WYE is apparently far from static. Comparison of contemporary WYE with sources such as Petyt (1985) reveals several changes over recent decades. One involves fronting of the GOAT vowel (Wells, 1982) from a back monophthong [ɔː] to a more centralized quality in the region of [θː]. This may be part of a wider pattern affecting other urban vernaculars in Yorkshire, notably Hull English, in which GOAT is characteristically [ɜː] (as in RP *bird*). This feature is stereotyped in Hull, as reflected by the joke spellings *Kirker Curler* ("Coca Cola") and *there's ner snur on the rurd* ("there's no snow on the road") printed in the *Hull Daily Mail* (16 March 1999).[6] GOAT, furthermore, seems to be participating in a chain shift (see Docherty and Watt, 2001) also involving NURSE, whereby words such as *skirt* and *worm* are pronounced [skɛːt] and [wɛːm].

WYE exhibits similar GOAT fronting, which may be linked to the Hull pattern. Comparison of two speakers' GOAT productions plotted in the F1~F2 plane (open circles in Figures 9.2 and 9.3, both from Watt and Tillotson, 2001), suggests that Debbie produces a wider range of pronunciations in the front–back dimension than does Ray. Her GOAT overlaps with NURSE, even encroaching on KIT. These effects are not so rare or subtle that instrumental

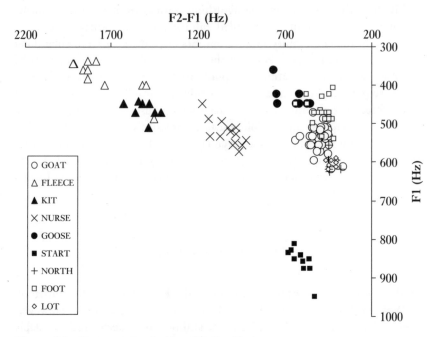

Figure 9.2   Formant plot for Ray, 29, Bradford

analysis of WYE is needed to detect them: it was, indeed, strong auditory impressions of GOAT centralization that prompted acoustic investigation.

We have trouble, therefore, interpreting assertions made by Reynolds (1990), and repeated in substantially the same form in Reynolds (2002), to the effect that such pronunciations – which are typical of WYE – should be grouped within the constellation of abnormal features present in the speech of a group of phonologically disordered Leeds children recorded in the 1980s. Reynolds, a senior Speech-Language Therapist (SLT) based in Leeds, states that "diphthong reduction" of /oʊ/ to [ɵː] (or [oː], in Reynolds, 2002) by some children is one of many vowel disorders they exhibit (2002: 120).

This is doubly problematic. Reynolds nowhere explains why WYE GOAT should be considered underlyingly a diphthong, and the monophthongs he lists as errors are actually *commoner* than diphthongs in non-disordered WYE. Reynolds presumably sees /oʊ/ as the basic, "target" pronunciation of GOAT, leading him to regard the monophthongs as so deviant as to be classifiable as pathological, or least idiosyncratic. His assumption that the underlying non-disordered WYE system corresponds to that obtaining in more standard(-like) accents also underpins his assessment of monophthongal

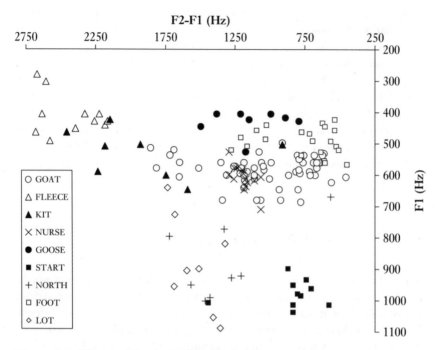

Figure 9.3   Formant plot for Debbie, 27, Bradford

[aː] in items like *kite* or *side*, a variant we believe should *not* be considered disordered, since pronunciations like ['naːʔklʊb] *nightclub* or ['waːʔ 'kʰɒfɛ] *white coffee* are perfectly normal in WYE.[7]

Reynolds, in fairness, indicates that monophthongal pronunciations of GOAT and its "partner" vowel FACE are used in non-disordered WYE (Reynolds (1990: 116, 2002: 117) state that [oʊ] and [oː] coexist). The Leeds children were doubtlessly seriously disordered, their pronunciations in other respects being unambiguously deviant. Nevertheless, if normal, well-established pronunciations like monophthongal GOAT in WYE are occasionally interpreted as errors or abnormalities, it is more likely still that innovative forms like the [əː] variant will be labeled deviant. Clearly, such misdiagnoses are potentially wasteful of time and resources, and may cause unnecessary distress to children and parents. We concur with Howard and Heselwood's (2002: 62) stipulations that "one . . . has to try to distinguish between a speaker using a new variant, and one using a pathological deviant variant. Confronted by these in a pediatric SLT clinic the temptation might be to intervene without taking the time to distinguish the sociolinguistic from the pathologic." It is therefore "imperative that before diagnosing or remediating any vowel disorder, SLTs should be well acquainted with the vowel system of the client's speech community" (p. 62).

As noted above, clinicians may experience difficulty locating sources on the local variety which are detailed and current, even if these exist. Growing availability of relevant online resources[8] may help alleviate this problem – although here the reliability issue is of especial concern – while journals (e.g., *Journal of the International Phonetic Association*) increasingly contain relevant materials (e.g., Hillenbrand, 2003; Watt and Allen, 2003).

We next consider some data exemplifying change in the grammatical domain.

Morphosyntactic variability in Buckie

The data discussed below come from Buckie, a small fishing port in northern Scotland. In this variety, young children can be heard using various non-standard grammatical features alongside their standard equivalents. Examples (4–8) are drawn from recordings of pre-schoolers aged 3;0 to 3;5 in interaction with primary caregivers (Smith and Steele, 2003):

(4) a. I *did* Belle and Cinderella.
     b. Look what you *done* to my mam's bridge! (Isabel, 3;0)
(5) a. I do *na* see *any* bears.
     b. I do *na* want *nothing*, just a sweetie. (Kerry, 3;2)
(6) a. Cos the bunnies *are* out.
     b. The leaves *is* falling off the tree. (Luke, 3;5)
(7) a. I *do na* want a bath.
     b. I Ø *na* like baths. (Ellie, 3;5)
(8) a. *This* are mine.
     b. *These* are sharp bits. (Luke, 3;5)

Significantly, some of these non-standard constructions have been associated with Grammatical Specific Language Impairment (G-SLI; see Leonard, 1998; van der Lely et al., 1998), of which in G-SLI children "the most prominent characteristic . . . is an impairment in inflexional morphology and complex syntax" (Nelson and Stojanovik, 2002: 134). Such behavior may signal potential difficulties for the child in later years, so early diagnosis may be crucial. Alternatively, these non-standard uses may simply reflect

Table 9.1 Classification of Buckie speakers in sample

Age	Male	Female
Young (22–31)	8	8
Middle (50–60)	7	7
Older (80+)	4	5

Source: Smith (2000).

adult norms. How, then, can we differentiate individual usage – perhaps resulting from language impairment – from the use of rule-governed norms by larger populations of speakers? Isolated examples like those above provide few insights. We turn, therefore, to more in-depth analysis of two variables: *do* absence in negative declaratives, and use of irregular verbs.

Recordings of subjects from three generations, as shown in Table 9.1, were analyzed. Inspecting distributional patterns of use across linguistic structure, in addition to analyzing change in apparent time across the three generations, helps establish (1) whether this variability is idiolectal (and/or a sign of some language disorder) or is the product of rule-governed use by large numbers of speakers; and (2) the existence of variation in the dialect with or without change (remembering that variation precedes, but does not entail, change).

Do *absence*

We start by assessing the frequency of (non-standard) *do* absence in Buckie speech. Table 9.2 shows it to be common, at around 40 percent. Of 39 speakers, 35 use both standard and non-standard forms variably. Consequently, Ellie's utterance (7b) is no anomaly.

Table 9.2 Overall distribution of *do* in present tense negative declaratives

	with	without	Total
N	451	305	756
%	59.7	40.3	

Source: Smith (2000).

Examining the use of *do* absence across the three generations we can next establish whether more specific patterns of use exist within the grammar, and whether the feature is undergoing change.

Initial observations of linguistically-conditioned patterning suggest that grammatical person predicts *do* absence. We distinguish, therefore, between 1st singular, as in example (9), 2nd singular, as in example (10), and 1st plural, as in example (11). Third person pronouns, as in examples (12) and (13), were categorized separately from full NPs as in examples (14) and (15):

(9)   *I Ø na* ken far my ain face is here.
(10)   *Ye Ø na* hear o him onywye.
(11)   *We Ø na* hae raffles.
(12)   *It doesna* cost nothing to walk ower the hill.
(13)   *They Ø na* lose trade.
(14)   *Willy doesna* play much golf.
(15)   *My crowd divna* like barley.

Figure 9.4 shows that not all contexts of use are variable: both singular and plural full NPs show categorical use of standard *do* as do the 3rd person singular pronouns *he*, *she* and *it*; Buckie speakers are never heard to utter

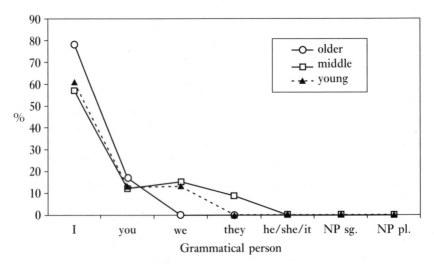

Figure 9.4 Distribution of *do* absence by grammatical person and age (%)

examples such as **It Ø na cost nothing to walk ower the hill*, for instance. Other contexts are variable. This analysis reveals that *do* absence is not random but rule-governed.

These patterns are consistent across age, indicating little or no change in (apparent) time for this feature. However, and more crucially for present purposes, this variability is not idiolectal or symptomatic of pathological disorder, but is the consequence of rule-governed use by a large number of speakers in this community.

Irregular verbs

Another characteristic of G-SLI is "errors with regular and irregular past tense" (Nelson and Stojanovik, 2002: 135; see also Ullman and Gopnik, 1999). Example (4b) might be considered to qualify for this category. However, Buckie adults also demonstrate much non-standard use in this respect.

Table 9.3 shows that non-standard forms account for around 21% of 5,403 contexts of use of irregular verbs. We might ask here whether for 21% of the time the speakers were simply confused as to which form to use. However, closer examination reveals five major areas of variability: use of past participle forms in preterit contexts with the verbs *seen*, *done* and *taen* (*taken*), as in example (16); *-en* retention with past participles, as in example (17); regularization of forms unique to Scottish dialects, as in example (18); use of *come* in preterit contexts, as in example (19); and use of preterits in past participle contexts, as in example (20):

(16) a.   I *seen* his death in the paper.
      b.   I *done* it in Aberdeen, like.
      c.   It *taen* a long time.

Table 9.3 Overall distribution of forms in strong verb paradigm

standard		non-standard	
N	%	N	%
4,285	79.3	1,118	20.7

(17)   a.   We've *haen* your dad across.
     b.   They were *putten* ben the house.
     c.   She's *gotten* a mixer but she winna use it.
(18)   a.   It was your granny that *telt* me.
     b.   The more you *selt*, the bigger the commission.
     c.   His bones *gied* rattling up against the wa.
(19)   a.   He *come* to me ae day and he says, "Was ever ee in Uig, John?"
     b.   It depended how much herring *come* in.
(20)   a.   Since they've *went* to a trawler they've haen problems.
     b.   I had *drove* home fae Elgin heaps of times.

Figure 9.5 shows that in contrast to *do* absence, which exhibited little or no change in apparent time, the irregular verb system demonstrates major change across the generations. Could Buckie speakers, particularly the young, simply be ignorant of the rules of irregular verb formation? If so, it would be unsurprising if pre-schoolers used the "wrong" forms. Closer examination reveals, however, the emergence of a "slimlined" version of past tense

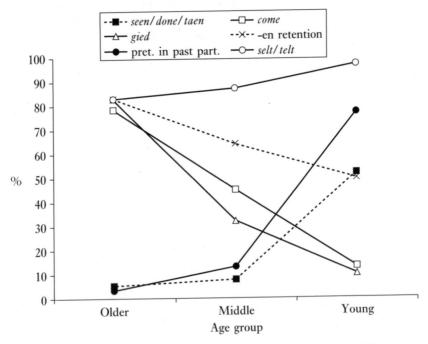

Figure 9.5   Distribution of non-standard irregular verb forms by age (%)

verb marking. Regular verbs have only two forms: e.g., *live/ lived/ lived*, *walk/ walked/ walked*, as indeed do many irregular verbs e.g., *buy/ bought/ bought*. Verbs which in current standard English have three forms, such as *forget/ forgot/ forgotten* or *see/ saw/ seen*, now conform to this pattern of use in Buckie, especially for young speakers (thus *forget/ forgot/ forgot*, *see/ seen/ seen*, etc.). Such use of one verb form instead of two – the outcome of what historical linguists call *change by analogy* (Hock, 1986) – features in many other dialects of English worldwide.

Buckie is not special in this regard: virtually any non-standard variety of English will exhibit comparable levels of conditioned morpho-syntactic variability. It would be easy, however, for a clinician lacking a thorough grounding in the particularities of the local dialect(s) to misidentify grammatical features like those above as "ungrammatical" and potentially symptomatic of G-SLI. "Overregularization errors at age 9–12," as documented by Eyer and Leonard (1995), should also be treated as possible signs of G-SLI "when such errors are not expected" (Nelson and Stojanovik, 2002: 135). Clearly, clinicians must have enough current background knowledge of the variety to be able to anticipate "overregularized" forms like *went* and *seen* in contexts disallowing them in the standard variety, and to see these features as normal elements of the linguistic repertoires of some communities of speakers (such as children) but not others.

Conclusion

We have attempted to avoid approaching these topics with, in Niedzielski's words, "guns blazing, mouths frothing, and demanding more accountability *vis-à-vis* dialect issues from communication disorders professionals" (2002: 1), and we recognize that there is truth in her assertion that "linguists spend very little time with speakers such as Speech-Language Pathologists' (SLPs') clients, and thus hurl their accusations from the tops of their ivory towers, while *they* [SLPs] are the ones who must answer to the education system, the parents of the clients, and the clients themselves" (p. 1). We identify with Niedzielski's position when she states, "As someone who has researched and published a great deal on folk linguistics, language attitudes, and speech perception, I am acutely aware of the myths and misconceptions surrounding language varieties" (p. 9) and agree that "those whose job it is to help children and adults learn to communicate better need to absolutely not operate with any of those myths and misconceptions" (p. 9).

We have highlighted two such "myths and misconceptions" in the fore-going discussion. The first is that the structural rules of standard varieties somehow underlie, and are necessarily pertinent to, description and inter-pretation of non-standard varieties. The second myth (actually more mis-conception) is that SLTs should provide treatment without considering that the local variety might have changed substantially and rapidly, such that their knowledge of it – perhaps owing to the shortcomings of existing descriptive sources – is unrepresentative of the variety in its current form.

Responsibility naturally cuts both ways. Sociolinguists should be pre-pared to attempt to keep track of the findings of language disorder research as far as possible, and to take note of developments in the clinical field. Sociolinguists, after all, do not have a monopoly on the detection of incipient language change. It should be acknowledged that "researchers with the greatest contact with children – namely SLPs – should be able to most accurately gauge what kinds of variables are found in a given community" (Niedzielski, 2002: 8) and that much more is at stake for clinicians who misdiagnose normal behavior as pathology, and their patients, than there is for sociolinguists who fail to identify changes as such. That most SLT degrees taught in the English-speaking world now feature sociolinguistics modules is a trend we take encouragement from, as is the increased toler-ance of linguistic variation and change among educational policy-makers, employers, and the general public (in the UK, at least). Regular dialogue between sociolinguists and clinicians is desirable and beneficial for both camps, and we trust that this book will contribute to making the necessity of such interaction more obvious.

Notes

1   Those with native speakers, unlike dead languages like Latin or Pictish.
2   "TV children taught how to talk", *BBC News Online*, 4 November 2003, http://news.bbc.co.uk/1/hi/education/3239861.stm
3   Deciding whether two variants do indeed have the "same" linguistic meaning is often difficult, and is particular problematic in the study of grammatical and lexical variation, in which variants are arguably not exactly synonymous (see Lavandera, 1978).
4   In some varieties (e.g., Tyneside) /r/ occurs non-categorically even in these contexts, glottal stop [ʔ] being inserted instead between the vowels flanking the word boundary.
5   Ø denotes the "zero variant." It is used to indicate where a variant of a variable could *potentially* occur but doesn't.

6 See also http://www.greengates.karoo.net/hull/speak.html. The time-lag involved in dissemination of sociolinguistic survey results means that informal sources such as newspapers often provide useful clues to the progress of incipient changes.

7 The first author has on several occasions been served white coffee in Leeds when black was requested, a misperception presumably stemming from the similarity of the vowels of *white* [waːt] and *black* [blak] in WYE.

8 For example, http://ling.man.ac.uk/Info/Staff/SMB/accents.html

Further reading

Campbell, L. (2004) *Historical Linguistics: An Introduction*. 2nd edn./Edinburgh: Edinburgh University Press.

Fennell, B. (2001) *A History of English: A Sociolinguistic Approach*. Oxford: Blackwell.

Hock, H.-H. and Joseph, B. (1996) *Language History, Language Change and Language Relationship*. Berlin: Mouton de Gruyter.

Keller, R. (1994) *On Language Change: The Invisible Hand in Language*. London: Routledge.

Trudgill, P. (2002) *Sociolinguistic Variation and Change*. Edinburgh: Edinburgh University Press.

10

Language Planning

Humphrey Tonkin

Plans and planners

All societies, and groups within them, use language to communicate, cooperate, and compete. The explicit and premeditated strategies that societies and communities employ to advance or change their use of language, for example through government policy or educational practice, are known as *language planning*. While professional language planners normally try to make the process objective and rational, language planning is a highly political and ideological activity, and is normally policy-driven.

Language policy "is usually formulated by a government or by an agency appointed . . . by a government" to support official goals (Cluver, 1993). All language policy implies intervention in the existing language ecology (Haugen, 1972; Calvet, 1999). While governments may adopt language policies with good intentions, such efforts almost inevitably favor one group over another (Tollefson, 1991; Myers-Scotton, 1993b), and the outcome, as with intervention in the physical environment, may be positive or negative.

Language planning is often a by-product, intended or unintended, of some other planning enterprise. Thus the spread of universal education in the nineteenth century fostered standard linguistic practices among teachers and in textbooks, and in some cases – France and Britain for instance (Hechter, 1975; Bourdieu, 1991) – led to suppression of local dialects and regional languages. An expanded government bureaucracy promoted standard linguistic forms, as did changes in technology. Even the ancient practice of examinations for state service in China was a form of language planning, at least in its effect – the promotion of a standard written Chinese.

But language policy and planning are not confined to governments. In the 1580s the Accademia della Crusca was founded to advance Italian as a language of arts and letters, and the Académie française followed in 1635. Today, many countries and languages have their quasi-official academies. England never created one, but the Royal Society, founded in 1660, favored development of a standard, lucid form of English for science and philosophy (Howell, 1956: 388). Johnson's monumental dictionary of 1755 was also an attempt to standardize English and sharpen its semantics, as was Webster's *American Dictionary of the English Language* (1828), which helped stabilize and reinforce English in America but made it different in certain details (such as spelling), so that a distinctive American national language could emerge (Lepore, 2002). Academies, by insisting on norms and encouraging what they regard as good language practices, engage in what is sometimes called *language cultivation*; dictionaries and other normative linguistic compilations practice *language standardization* (Weinreich, 1953).

The term *language planning* (first used in print by Haugen, 1959) was unknown in Webster's or Johnson's day but these examples fit the definition: where the normal, unplanned processes of *language change* or *language shift* leave off, and premeditated intervention begins, we have language planning. Language planning (sometimes called *language engineering* or *language management*) seeks to redirect or arrest the processes of language change and redistribute language use. Laws on the use of Spanish in US voter registration, or on bilingual education (Brisk, 1998; Cummins, 2000; Reagan, 2002), or the controversial decision of the Oakland, California, school district in 1996 to recognize the existence of Ebonics (African American Vernacular English: McWhorter, 1998) constitute language policy, but the term can also describe such non-government policies as rules for foreign-language interpreting in hospitals, or for the use of English in a company. Even a bilingual family's decision to have father talk to the children in language A and mother use language B is a form of micro-policy.

Policy becomes planning when intentions are implemented. When a lexicographer compiles an influential dictionary, or a grammarian a grammar; when the government requires educators to use a language in a particular way, or one language rather than another; when judges are required to use one language, or several languages, in court, or to provide translation and interpretation; when a newspaper uses a particular uniform style or a radio station a particular accent; when a school offers one foreign language rather than another – these activities are language planning, derived from language policy.

Planning and policy

Language planning and *language policy* are interactive. Ideally, planning takes place to explore policy options, based on a comprehensive study and inventory of actual language practices. Out of this process emerge policies (in some cases, legislation) which again require a plan to put them into effect; thus, desire for policy begets planning, planning begets coherent policy, and policy is implemented through planned action. Unfortunately, policies are often developed with no plan, or planning occurs without policy.

Rubin and Jernudd (1971) describe language planning as an effort to find solutions to language problems "by formulating alternative goals, means and outcomes." Decolonization after World War II stimulated interest in language planning (Weinstein, 1990; Laitin, 1992; Schiffman, 1996; Mazrui and Mazrui, 1998), which coincided also with the emergence of sociolinguistics (Paulston and Tucker, 1997): language planning is a form of applied sociolinguistics. Language is a crucial practical and symbolic element in nation-building, economic development, and political participation, and language experts were called in by newly independent nations to help rationalize the often chaotic postcolonial language situation (Le Page, 1964). Should such countries continue to use the language of their colonial masters, or adopt indigenous languages? Which ones? Could these indigenous languages be developed for modern communication, with up-to-date terminology and standard forms, backed by mass communications? Using one language rather than another may isolate sections of the population, but using all languages is probably unworkable, particularly when a country lacks basic resources. Can we strike a realistic and economically feasible balance among maximizing participation, promoting efficiency in government, improving productivity, and expanding education – while also addressing such issues as regional development and human rights? Initially, experts were optimistic that equitable solutions could be found. Today we see that special interests, political pressures, and lack of capital often undermine good intentions.

Language planning goals

Why engage in language planning? Nahir (1984) offers an eleven-point classification of language-planning goals:

1 Language purification (to remove foreign elements, or "errors").
2 Language revival (to restore "a language with few or no surviving native speakers" as "a normal means of communication").
3 Language reform (to improve effectiveness).

4 Language standardization (to turn "a language or dialect spoken in a region" into one "accepted as the major language").
5 Language spread (to expand the domains and speakers of a language).
6 Lexical modernization (to create terminology).
7 Terminology unification (to standardize existing terminology).
8 Stylistic simplification (to make technical or legal language comprehensible, and reduce bureaucratese).
9 Interlingual communication (through planned languages, translation and interpretation, etc.).
10 Language maintenance (to preserve the domains in which a language is used).
11 Auxiliary code standardization (to create norms for language-related activities, e.g., transliteration and transcription).

Since Nahir developed his list, the Internet has arrived and the internationalized computer market has mushroomed. The sudden rise of Microsoft as language planner, with its development of character sets, recognition of certain languages and not others, and the development of Unicode, has reshaped interlingual communication and auxiliary code standardization (Jordan, 2002). With expanding globalization and increased capital flows among countries, the role of non-governmental agents expands and is often hard to document, while governments engage in language planning not only within their own territories but also across boundaries, as in the United Nations – whose language regime, established in 1945 by the victors of World War II, has never been substantially modified (Tonkin, 1996) – or the European Union, which in 2004 almost doubled its official languages with its eastward expansion (Phillipson, 2003). Language planning and policy are fraught with many perils, but *failure* to plan and *lack* of policy may be equally destructive: the outdated regime at the UN and the unworkable rules at the EU, developed when that body was much smaller, are good examples. Under cover of the unworkability of present policies, English has gained a stronger hold in both bodies, and other languages, disabled by internecine quarrels, are unable to mount coherent resistance. Linguistic unity through the medium of English may seem admirable, but it advantages some and disadvantages others.

A need for language planning is most likely to arise in situations in which the users of given languages or language forms compete for influence: most language planning takes place in multilingual or diglossic settings, though it is also often concerned with the development of norms and standard forms. Haarmann (1990: 123) calls it "a form of conflict management."

Rubin and Jernudd refer to *solutions* to *language problems*. In practice, it is hard to define what constitutes a "language problem," and fixing one problem may simply create another. If Rubin and Jernudd describe a largely top-down approach, today we recognize that *language choice* – decision-making by the users of a language – is equally important (Pütz, 1997): we can either tell people what to do (top-down) or we can offer them tools to make choices (bottom-up). For the latter we must understand how choices are made (Daoust, 1997: 437–8). It is easier to change language use in controlled, formal settings (primarily written texts) than in informal settings (primarily spoken language), such as the family, where outside controls are absent; but influencing informal use may be strategically important.

Corpus planning

Our questions about newly emerging nations fell into two categories: (1) how to expand and standardize a given language; and (2) what language to use under what circumstances. Language planning comes in two forms: *corpus planning* (language-centered) and *status planning* (society-centered). The first changes the structure and content of a language (its *corpus*), the second changes its *status*. Most instances of language planning contain elements of both.

Some years ago, the Dutch abandoned the capitalization of nouns, a practice that continues in Germany; this was *corpus* planning. The new South African Constitution recognizes eleven languages with official status; this is *status* planning (though to be effective it also requires *corpus* planning).

A much cited instance of corpus planning (aided by status planning) is the emergence of Modern Hebrew a hundred years ago (Fellman, 1973), particularly through *lexical modernization*: the invention of new terms for concepts unknown in the ancient language. The Bible and other ancient writings yielded terms whose semantics could be expanded or adjusted to accommodate new meanings, or words were borrowed from other languages, e.g., Arabic (Nahir, 2002). Recent decisions by the Former Soviet Republics of Azerbaijan, Turkmenistan and Uzbekistan to abandon Cyrillic script in favor of Roman are also corpus planning (specifically, *graphization*, the selection of a writing form, either among competing forms or to transcribe the language for the first time).

Writing a language down is an important step in *standardization*. Writing has to be taught; it also offers models that endure over time and can be transmitted through space (Roberts and Street, 1997). It is thus an important stabilizer, promoting emergence of standard forms. Other factors in standardization include mass media, both print and electronic, and education. Literacy planning is closely related to language planning: literacy requires a standard language and reinforces it. Written language and spoken language are not identical, however: in some languages written and spoken forms are widely divergent.

Corpus planning, then, comprises three major elements: writing a language down (graphization), codifying it (standardization), and expanding it (modernization). Even these apparently innocent activities may have political or ideological implications: Azerbaijan's choice of the Roman alphabet, presented as an effort to open the country to international contacts, also symbolically redefined the country and its language – as non-Russian and Turkic (Turkish uses Roman script – an outcome of an earlier case of language planning, by Kemal Atatürk, who made Turkey into a modern secular state by, among other things, abandoning Arabic script, identified with Islam and the East, in favor of Roman script, identified with modernist Europe and the West). In many countries even neologisms bring political division, between those wishing to exclude foreign borrowings by creating new terms and those open to foreign borrowings. Some languages accommodate borrowings easily; heavily inflected or agglutinative languages often do not.

Status planning

Status planning takes many forms. It may involve, for example, promoting one language or language variety over another, among several competing possibilities (Le Page, 1964; Fishman, 1972a; Coulmas, 1988), or guaranteeing language rights to minorities, indigenous peoples, or immigrants (May, 2001). Skutnabb-Kangas and Phillipson (1995: 80) suggest a continuum from outright prohibition of a language (Kurdish in Turkey) or denial of its existence (Macedonian in Greece) at one end, to active promotion at the other. Recently interest in rights of language minorities has increased sharply, along with the negotiation, writing, promulgation and application of language laws, declarations on language, and international instruments (Peñalosa, 1981: 183–94; Skutnabb-Kangas and Phillipson, 1995; Turi, 1995; Kibbee, 1998; Kontra et al., 1999).

The German Romantic writer Johann Gottfried Herder (1744–1803) saw language and nation as closely related. A one-nation/one-language principle emerged in Europe, culminating in the disintegration of the multilingual Russian and Austro-Hungarian Empires and their replacement by new nations whose impulse for existence lay in part in rapid cultivation of formerly low-status provincial languages like Estonian, Serbian and Finnish. Nationalist movements in these countries discovered a new history for their languages – a history rooted in notions of incipient nationhood supported by long-lost epics and shadowy kings (the Finnish epic *Kalevala*, fashioned in the nineteenth century out of existing folk tales, is a good example).

Modern language planners are sometimes seduced by this European model into imposing linguistic unity on countries and regions at such political and cultural cost that it has led to disunity rather than unity: today planners tend to be more sympathetic to multilingual solutions. Kaplan and Baldauf (1997: 30) suggest that "a state must have a language(s) in which it can communicate with its citizens," but the choice must also allow a right to reply: messages in the language of the state may not be heard by the citizenry, and citizens may lack the power to reply in a language they know – leading to political instability.

Such difficulties are well illustrated by the highly political (and largely unplanned) process undergone by East Timor, recently independent of Indonesia. Its choice of languages lay among official adoption of the local vernacular, Tetum, one of sixteen indigenous languages, widely used as a lingua franca; Bahasa Indonesia, the language of East Timor's oppressor but largest trading partner (hitherto the official government language); or Portuguese, the language of an earlier oppressor but also a world language (used by seven UN members). East Timor adopted Portuguese as its official language of wider communication, Tetum for local use, and all the other indigenous languages as "national languages." Can Portuguese be introduced in education and government when there are very few people able to teach and use it, and are the resources available to expand the corpus of Tetum? Portuguese is little known among young people, who are more attuned to English and the Australian sphere of influence; and Indonesian may continue in use in the mainstream even if ideologically unacceptable.

Even in Europe the one-nation/one-language model applies less and less. Urbanization and migration and the growing importance of written and electronic communication have weakened the connection between language and place. More or less everywhere in the world we are condemned, or privileged, to live in a multilingual environment, and language planners and policy-makers must take this reality into account.

It is clear that language is a powerful social and political institution (Fairclough, 1989; Bourdieu, 1991) whose importance is often underestimated. A community's language is as much an institutional force as its banks, government offices and universities: it is the software that drives these items of sociopolitical hardware. Those who command the institution of language command power to include and exclude.

Acquisition planning and prestige planning

Education straddles both types of planning: status issues include choice of a language of instruction or which foreign languages to teach; corpus issues include the actual teaching of linguistic elements and the choices involved. This ambiguity caused Cooper (1989: 33–4) to propose a third category of language planning, called *acquisition planning* (or *language-in-education planning*), covering language teaching and learning. Israeli services to help immigrants learn Hebrew are acquisition planning; so is the decision of a given US school district to teach Spanish and French as foreign languages but not Italian. Many experts believe that early education, and particularly literacy, are best pursued in a child's mother tongue (a complex issue, however: see, for example, Skutnabb-Kangas, 2000: 597–600; Reagan, 2002: 135–6).

As Cooper added acquisition planning to status and corpus planning, Haarmann (1990) sees prestige planning as a separate category, related to status (making English the official language of the USA, for example) or corpus (efforts to keep a language pure of foreign influences). Seeing prestige planning as a separate category does highlight some of the less obvious motives behind language planning, such as the relationship between language planning and ideology, language planning and identity planning, and language planning intended to exclude certain groups (so-called elite closure: see Myers-Scotton, 1993b). Making English the official language of the USA may seem a commendable confirmation of the obvious – but it may be motivated less by a desire to accentuate national unity than by the wish to exclude recent immigrants or marginalize non-native-English speakers.

Levels of language planning

We can chart language planning on a continuum, between relatively minor adjustments to status and corpus at one end, to the wholesale creation or destruction of languages at the other. Cornish largely disappeared from south-western England in the sixteenth century, a victim of the centralized Tudor state, economic change, and the shift from Latin to English in the (Protestant) Church. The Cornish rebellion (1549) against the English prayer book marked resistance to Protestantism (and poverty), but may also have been a reaction to efforts to redefine the relative standing of Latin, Cornish and English: the Cornish were used to the Latin of their priests, but the English of their oppressors was another matter. While it may look as though the Cornish *chose* to abandon the old language, the linguistic cards were stacked against them. Many other examples of such *language death* could be cited (Dorian, 1989; Grenoble and Whaley, 1998; Crystal, 2000; Hagège, 2000; Nettle and Romaine, 2000; Dalby, 2003). Language death generally results from specific language policies, not simply a failure to institute policies to preserve the language in question (preservation activities are variously known as *language maintenance, language revival,* or *reversing language shift,* depending on their nature: see Fishman, 1991).

Radical in a different way are efforts to plan entire languages (Large, 1985; Eco, 1995). Sprat and others in seventeenth-century England confined themselves to making the English language more precise and consistent (attracted by the notion that a language should mirror thought and, rather more radically, the notion that a logical language might stimulate logical thinking), but other members of the Royal Society, among them its secretary John Wilkins, were attracted by the idea of constructing an entirely new language on fully rational principles. Wilkins's language worked like a Dewey Decimal System, with concepts grouped into broad categories and then divided and subdivided into ever more precise sub-categories. He supplied a writing system to articulate the resulting words. Such universal-language systems were related to interest in mathematical logic: others interested in planned languages included Descartes, Leibnitz and Newton (Knowlson, 1975; Slaughter, 1982; Stillman, 1995; Rossi, 2000).

More recently, there have been many efforts to create international languages as bridges between ethnic languages, on the principle that everyone might speak his or her local language or languages, plus a planned international language. Best known is Esperanto, launched in Warsaw in 1887 by Lazar Ludwik Zamenhof (Janton, 1993; Nuessel, 2000). Esperanto's lexicon comes from Europe, but its grammatical elements are less obviously European and are based on structural principles akin to those explored by Jan Baudouin de Courtenay in Russia and later Ferdinand de Saussure in Switzerland (Ferdinand's brother René was among Zamenhof's earliest recruits). Most such projects do not get beyond corpus planning (a grammar and dictionary), but Zamenhof emphasized status planning, creating a community of users, publishing literary works, and insisting that the language belonged to its speakers and not to him (on developmental stages of planned languages, see Blanke, 2000).

The goal here is nothing less than the establishment of a new international linguistic order. Pool and Fettes (1998; Fettes, 2003) suggest five possible approaches to the creation of a fully functioning global linguistic regime: (1) World English (English as standard language of wider communication); (2) Esperantism (a neutral international language in this role); (3) Language Brokers (translators and interpreters mediating between languages); (4) Plurilingualism (advances in language teaching allowing use of several languages internationally); and (5) Technologism (translation and interpretation, and other modes of cross-language communication, done by machines).

Less radical than creating a whole new language, but highly interventionist, was the adoption of Indonesian, Bahasa Indonesia, by the new state of Indonesia (Kaplan and Baldauf, 1997: 33). As the language of resistance to the Dutch the early nationalists chose the form of Malay widely used in the East Indies as a trading language, rather than Javanese, the more highly developed language spoken by the largest group of Indonesians. Bahasa Indonesia was built from the ground up – but the fact that it was not perceived as the power base of one particular group had a decisive influence on the creation of a sense of national unity following independence. Across the water, in India, the nationalists decided differently, selecting Hindi and English as languages of government – the first the language of many of the independence leaders and the second an interim measure until Hindi could be developed as the language of all Indians. The effort failed: English remained powerful, and resistance to Hindi, particularly in the south, led to bloodshed and linguistic stalemate.

The adoption of Hindi or Indonesian had significant macropolitical outcomes embracing both status planning and corpus planning. Less radical with respect to corpus but equally radical as to status were Belgian efforts to reach a solution to language quarrels that threatened the country's very existence. An uneasy truce between the speakers of French in the south and Dutch in the north has led to a *modus vivendi* along geographical lines, based on separate but equal status.

In Canada, another example of language planning *in extremis*, much of Quebec's wealth was owned by an English-speaking elite and provincial affairs were conducted largely in English, excluding lower-status and less powerful French-speakers, but a political power shift led to radical economic realignment, allowing the French-speaking majority to gain control of the means of communication by widespread use of French and legally-backed limitations on English. The English-speaking minority protested – and the resulting battles showed how politically charged the question of language can be, and how the language rights of the individual (the English speaker wishing to use his or her language in all domains) and those of the collective (French speakers wishing to use their language more widely than heretofore) can clash.

Most language planning issues are less cataclysmic than these. Languages change over time, with or without planning. For the most part, language planning is concerned with hastening, arresting or deflecting such change.

The methodology of language planning

Language planning can be effected in many ways: the methods used will depend on goals, the disciplinary background of the planner, and the degree of political or social pressure fueling the planning process (Phillipson, 1992; Pennycook, 1994, 1998). Cooper (1989: 46) suggests that language-planners face four tasks: "(1) to describe, (2) predict, and (3) explain language-planning processes and outcomes in particular instances, and (4) to derive valid generalizations about these processes and outcomes."

The process begins with establishment of facts – both the sociolinguistic situation and its larger context (Reagan and Osborn, 2002: 113). Kaplan and Baldauf (1997: 103), citing Cooper (1989), suggest that "an understanding of the linguistic situation derives from answering a complex set of questions: who speaks what to whom under what conditions and for what purpose?" Thus sociolinguistic surveys or an ethnographic survey to map characteristics of a particular language and the language behavior of its users (Hymes, 1974; Saville-Troike, 1989) may be required. But research cannot stop there: many language planning efforts have foundered because they were tied too tightly to language and neglected the larger political, economic and social setting.

Many surveys can serve as models (Whiteley, 1984; Kaplan and Baldauf, 1997: 102–3). Some, backed by political will and adequate financing, involve multidisciplinary teams, using questionnaires and other instruments (Kaplan and Baldauf, 1997, describe the process of preparing, administering and analyzing such questionnaires), but most language-planning efforts are more limited in scope and resources, and demand of the researcher an ability to cross disciplinary lines easily (Eastman, 1983). All efforts, large or small, must engage the public. Thus, a study of the advisability of providing language services in a city hospital should, at a minimum, involve data-gathering among patients and staff, a survey of any groups currently excluded from care through language difficulties, a survey of the language attitudes of all populations involved, an inventory of language resources (and resources and people likely to assist in implementation), a thorough review both of the services that might be provided and of the likely competence of the providers, an informed estimate of probable expenditures and cost-savings, and a review of the policy context. It might involve a comprehensive cost-benefit analysis, and, since it will be acted on by non-linguists, it should address expectations: non-linguists often have unrealistic expectations, for example, about the quality of interpreting and translation.

Reagan and Osborn (2002) describe the second stage as "determination and articulation of goals, strategies and outcomes." This stage could be colored by the hypotheses and policy assumptions that prompted the study in the first place, and it may be hard to separate preconceptions from hard data. Even the design of the initial fact-finding effort risks being influenced by the desire for particular outcomes: Reagan and Osborn (2002) cite Cobarrubias (1983), who describes four ideologies lying behind language policy and likely to affect design and outcomes: (1) assimilationism, or belief in linguistic unity; (2) pluralism, emphasizing language diversity and language rights; (3) vernacularization, stressing local languages as means of in-country communication, and (4) internationalization, emphasizing links with the larger world. There are many planning approaches to this second phase: Cooper (1989) finds models in the study of innovation, marketing, the sociology of power, and decision-science; Selten and Pool (1991) apply strategies from game theory; Mac Donnacha (2000) turns to strategic planning models used by business; Grin (1996) and Vaillancourt (1983) assign economic values to language-planning choices. Underlying most of these approaches is what Daoust (1997: 439) calls "a general social planning framework."

Once analysis has taken place, plans have been drawn up, and recommendations and options laid out, decisions can be taken by the body that commissioned the language-planning effort and the stage is set for implementation. This third stage may require several iterations as planners and policy-makers come to an understanding of how the plan will be executed, what resources will be available, and how the process will be monitored.

The fourth, implementation stage (see Rubin and Jernudd, 1971; Eastman, 1983; Kaplan and Baldauf, 1997) may require new educational programs, personnel training, endorsements and advocacy, information campaigns, and the like. It may involve some kind of formative evaluation process. It should be followed by a fifth stage – evaluation of the effectiveness of the project as a whole and of its outcomes. This stage should be prolonged: effective language planning is for the long term, not for the achievement of short-term goals.

Conclusion

"When language planning began to develop as a field of inquiry in the 1950s and 1960s," writes Paulin Djité (1994: 67), "it was first conceived as an efficient, neutral and scientific mechanism for the determination of answers to questions related to the use of language(s) in various societies." Today, in an era of competing rights, conflicting visions, and belief in market forces, the early days of language planning seem unattainably pristine, like the lines of a modernist building. Post-modern language planning, by comparison, is a messy and political affair. But the notion that it is possible to intervene in language processes to make them more responsive, more equitable, and ultimately more effective, lives on. Indeed, such intervention, benign or malign, goes on all the time. It is best directed by coherent and proactive language policy and practice.

Further reading

Cooper (1989) and Kaplan and Baldauf (1997) offer more detailed introductions to language planning. See also Bernard Spolsky, *Language Policy* (Cambridge: Cambridge University Press, 2004) and Sue Wright, *Language Policy and Language Planning* (Basingstoke: Palgrave Macmillan, 2004). On language policy and planning in the United States, see James Crawford, *At War with Diversity* (Clevedon: Multilingual Matters, 2000).

11

Dialect Perception and Attitudes to Variation

Dennis R. Preston and
Gregory C. Robinson

Language and people

It is perhaps the least surprising thing imaginable to find that attitudes towards languages and their varieties seem to be tied to attitudes towards groups of people. Some groups are believed to be decent, hard-working, and intelligent (and so is their language or variety); some groups are believed to be laid-back, romantic, and devil-may-care (and so is their language or variety); some groups are believed to be lazy, insolent, and procrastinating (and so is their language or variety); some groups are believed to be hard-nosed, aloof, and unsympathetic (and so is their language or variety), and so on. For the folk mind, such correlations are obvious, reaching down even into the linguistic details of the language or variety itself. Germans are harsh; just listen to their harsh, guttural consonants. US Southerners are laid-back and lazy; just listen to their lazy, drawled vowels. Lower-status speakers are unintelligent; they don't even understand that two negatives make a positive, and so on. Edwards summarizes this correlation for many social psychologists when he notes that "people's reactions to language varieties reveal much of their perception of the speakers of these varieties" (1982: 20). In the clinical fields of speech-language pathology and audiology, these perceptions can have major implications. Negative attitudes about the individuals who use certain linguistic features can pervade service delivery causing testing bias, overrepresentation of minorities and nonmainstream dialect speakers in special education, and lack of linguistic confidence in children. Although folk correlation of stereotypes to linguistic facts has little scientific basis in reality, an understanding of this correlation is particularly important to the clinical fields of speech-language pathology and audiology. Folk beliefs can pervade clinical practice via school teachers, parents, peers, spouses, physicians and other medical professionals, as well as fellow speech-language pathologists and audiologists.

Research into folk perceptions and attitudes about language variation has been scarce within the fields of speech-language pathology and audiology; however, the domains of sociolinguistics and social psychology have contributions that can benefit the clinical professions greatly. In this chapter, we will discuss some of the studies that shed light on folk perceptions and attitudes regarding linguistic variation that have significant implications for clinical professionals.

The apparent difficulty in establishing language-and-people connections was, at first, a great concern to social psychologists. The person-in-the-street might not be so willing to own up to racist, sexist, classist, regionalist, or other prejudicial attitudes. Questionnaires, interviews, and scaling techniques (which asked about such characteristics directly) were suspect data-gathering methods since they allowed respondents to disguise their true feelings, either to project a different self-image and/or to give responses they thought the interviewer might most approve of.

Several methods have been used to circumvent such suspected manipulation of attitudes by respondents (Osgood et al., 1957; Lambert et al., 1960; Giles and Powesland, 1975). These studies involved "guises" in which the respondents are told to rate something that is apparently distinct from language in scales of opposites (e.g., fast–slow, heavy–light). Although this work was not without criticism (for its artificiality and other drawbacks, e.g., Agheyisi and Fishman, 1970), it set the standard for such studies for quite some time and managed to provide the first important generalization in language attitude studies – that of the "three factor groups." Analyses of large amounts of data seemed to group together paired opposites which pointed to *competence*, *personal integrity*, and *social attractiveness* constructs in the evaluation of speaker voices (summarized in Lambert, 1967). A great deal of subsequent research in this mode confirmed that these constructs were very often at work, and, more interestingly, that standard (or "admired accent") speakers were most often judged highest on the *competence* dimension while nonstandard (or regionally and/or ethnically distinct speakers) were rated higher for the *integrity* and *attractiveness* dimensions. Subsequent work has often conflated the two latter categories into one, usually referred to as *solidarity*, e.g., Edwards (1982).

Even early on, however, it became clear that the path from stimulus to group identification to the triggering of attitudes towards the group so identified was not a trouble-free one. There is evidence to suggest that when respondents assign attitudinal judgments from linguistic stimuli they may not first assign group membership. In fact, the linguistic features themselves may trigger the attitudes. This was evident in one particular study in which attitudinal responses were statistically significant between speakers of different dialectal groups in Great Britain in spite of the fact that respondents were inaccurate in the identification of the area from which the speakers came (Milroy and McClenaghan, 1977). Irvine (2001) suggests that this has to do with the "iconicity" of linguistic features. Thus, individuals semiotically link social attitudes toward various groups to the common linguistic features that have been noted within those groups. Milroy and McClenaghan (1977) suggest that this is below the level of consciousness for most individuals, and that attitudes, therefore, may be assigned without first assigning group membership. Extremes of such iconicity in American English might include "ain't" and multiple negation, both of which apparently trigger negative evaluations with no need for any (specific) group association.

Although this program of social psychological research into language attitudes has been productive, we believe it has left much to be done. If Irvine is correct, there are at last two very large areas left relatively unexplored:

1   What linguistic features play the biggest role in triggering attitudes?
2   What beliefs (theories, folk explanations) do people have about language variety, structure, acquisition, and distribution which underlie and support their attitudinal responses, and how might we go about finding them out and using them to supplement and even guide future language attitude research?

The linguistic detail

Research on perception of linguistic details has been relatively scarce in the clinical literature. The core of this research is reflected in determination of "dialect rate," or the rate at which a speaker uses features associated with a particular dialect. Researchers in speech-language pathology have used several methods for determining "dialect rate" (see Oetting and McDonald, 2001, for a summary of these methods). These methods either rely totally on listener perception for group identification or they rely solely on researcher identification of linguistic "tokens." These tokens are added together and divided by some linguistic unit (e.g., C-unit, sentence, word, etc.) and usually consist of syntactic tokens rather than phonological tokens. These methods are very different from similar research being conducted by sociolinguists.

Sociolinguists have sought to determine if certain linguistic features (tokens) affect the perceptions and attitudes of listeners, and their findings suggest that such tokens are not always equally weighted in the perception of listeners, as is assumed in many of the methods for coding dialect rate in the clinical literature. Several sociolinguistic studies make it clear that language attitudes can be related very specifically to individual linguistic features, but it is equally clear that that relationship is not a simple one.

In some cases, precise acoustic features appear to trigger accurate identification. In a study by Purnell, Idsardi, and Baugh (1999), a single speaker said the word "hello" in three dialects: Standard American English (SAE), Chicano English (ChE), and African American Vernacular English (AAVE). Variation in the frontness or tenseness of the vowel and pitch prominence on the first syllable of "hello" was enough to elicit significantly accurate identification of the dialects by listeners. When the stimulus was expanded to include "Hello, I'm calling about the apartment you have advertised in the paper," in actual calls to landlords, the SAE speaker guise was given an appointment to see housing at roughly the 70 percent level. Both the AAVE and ChE guises were given appointments only about 30 percent of the time.

In other cases, an acoustic feature appears to be so strongly identified with a group that it can overcome all other surrounding evidence. In a study by Graff, Labov, and Harris (1983), the [æ] onset to the /aʊ/ diphthong was enough of a marker of European-American identity in Philadelphia that when the sound was superimposed onto the recording of a speaker of African American English (AAE), respondents identified him as European-American in spite of the presence of other phonological features of AAE.

On the other hand, some sociolinguistic studies seem to confirm the idea that "rate" is important, even for an individual feature. In a study by Labov (1966), inconsistent use of "r" in New York City was shown to affect the judgments of respondents regarding the occupation that the person would be suited for.

In other studies, a great deal of inaccuracy in both self-report of the use of a specific feature has been detected. For example, in a study by Trudgill (1972) in Norwich (England), men over-reported the use of the nonprestigious form of the vowel in the word "ear," while women under-reported its use. Also, in a study by Niedzielski (1999), the identification of the vowel quality of a specific feature was influenced simply by the words "Canadian" and "Michigan" superimposed at the top of the response sheet for Detroit respondents.

. The three areas of perception, evaluation, and production are so intimately connected that it is not surprising that the findings of these studies are not simple and clear-cut. It is also worth noting that the areas of perception, evaluation, and production are so intimately connected in the clinical practice of speech-language pathology and audiology that it is clear that these studies are vitally relevant to the issues of least-biased assessment procedures and treatment of culturally and linguistically diverse clients.

To help explain the complexity of the findings of these studies, Preston (1996a) suggests that some of these differential responses to a variety of linguistic details may operate along a continuum (or several continua) of consciousness or "awareness" (just as language use involves degrees of "monitoring" or "attention to form," e.g., Labov, 1972b: 208). Preston (1996a) reviews a number of these possibilities for "folk linguistics," suggesting that folk-linguistic facts (i.e., linguistic objects as viewed by nonlinguists) may be subdivided for "awareness" along the following clines:

1 *Availability*: Folk respondents range in their attention to linguistic features from complete disregard for to frequent discussion of and even preoccupation with them.
2 *Accuracy*: Folk respondents may accurately, partially accurately, or completely inaccurately represent linguistic facts (and their distribution).
3 *Detail*: Folk respondents' characterizations may range from *global* (reflecting, for example, only a general awareness of a variety) to *detailed* (in which respondents cite specific details).
4 *Control*: Folk respondents may have complete, partial or no "imitative" control over linguistic features.

An important fact about these clines is their relative independence. For example, a respondent who claims only a general awareness of a "foreign accent" may be capable of a completely faithful imitation of some of its characteristics. On the other hand, a respondent who is preoccupied with a variety might have no overt information about its linguistic makeup but be capable of performing a native-like imitation of it.

Perhaps the range of so-called language attitude effects ought to be treated in a similar way. That is, attitudinal responses which are based on the respondents' association of a sample voice with a particular social group may be different from ones based on reactions to linguistic caricatures such as *ain't*. Responses which may be based on some sort of cline (e.g., masculine–feminine, degree of "accent") may be different from those based on the recognition of "categorical" features (e.g., correct–incorrect).

Attitudes and folk perceptions

Since linguists know, however, that linguistic details have no value of their own (in spite of the "life" they seem to achieve by virtue of their social associations), it will be important to return to the second of the questions suggested above: what underlying beliefs, presuppositions, stereotypes, and the like lie behind and support the existence of language attitudes? Ultimately, it seems to us, this will require linguists to give something like an account of a folk theory of language. Such a theory can illuminate the causes of some of the issues that are pervasive in the clinical professions when treating or assessing clients from culturally and linguistically diverse backgrounds.

In doing language attitude research, perhaps it is important to first determine which varieties of a language are thought to be distinct. Preston (1989) has complained that language attitude research did not determine where respondents thought regional voices were from and, worse, did not know if respondents even had a mental construct of a "place" where a voice could be from; that is, their mental maps of regional speech areas might not include one with which a sample voice could be identified. So Preston (1996b) asked Michigan respondents to draw lines on a map of the US to denote where linguistically distinct places were in America (see Figures 11.1 and 11.2).

Hartley and Preston (1999) analyzed each of these individual maps (and others) to study the stereotypic labels assigned to various regions; and Preston and Howe (1987) utilized a digitizing pad which feeds the outlined area of each salient region into a computer so that a more precise numeric determination can be made of the "boundary" of each hand-drawn region. Figure 11.3 shows a computer-determined map for the mental map of US regional speech areas derived from the hand-drawn maps of 147 southeastern Michigan respondents (from a variety of status and age groups, male and female).

Armed with this "cognitively real" map of the dialect areas of the US (as seen by Michiganders), we might now approach the study of attitudes towards these regions in a classically social psychological manner. What characteristics would be relevant to an investigation of attitudes to these speech areas? Again, the best method is to go to the respondents themselves. Characteristics for judging were elicited by showing a large number of Michigan respondents a simplified version of Figure 11.3 and asking them to mention any characteristics of the speech of those regions which

Figure 11.1 A Michigan respondent's hand-drawn map

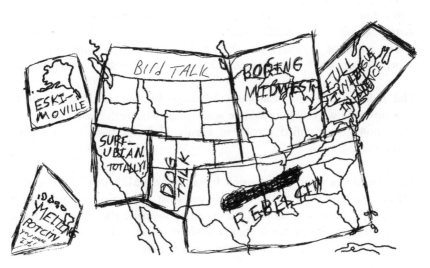

Figure 11.2 Another Michigan hand-drawn map

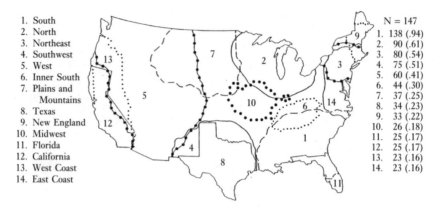

1. South
2. North
3. Northeast
4. Southwest
5. West
6. Inner South
7. Plains and
   Mountains
8. Texas
9. New England
10. Midwest
11. Florida
12. California
13. West Coast
14. East Coast

N = 147
1. 138 (.94)
2. 90 (.61)
3. 80 (.54)
4. 75 (.51)
5. 60 (.41)
6. 44 (.30)
7. 37 (.25)
8. 34 (.23)
9. 33 (.22)
10. 26 (.18)
11. 25 (.17)
12. 25 (.17)
13. 23 (.16)
14. 23 (.16)

Figure 11.3   Computer-assisted generalizations of hand-drawn maps showing where south-eastern Michigan respondents believe speech regions exist in the US

came to mind. The most frequently mentioned items were selected and arranged into the following pairs:

slow – fast	formal – casual	educated – uneducated
smart – dumb	polite – rude	snobbish – down-to-earth
nasal – not nasal	normal – abnormal	friendly – unfriendly
drawl – no drawl	twang – no twang	bad English – good English

The judges (85 young, European-American lifelong southern Michigan residents who were undergraduate students at Michigan State University) were shown a simplified version of Figure 11.3 and given the following instructions:

This map shows where many people from southern Michigan believe speech differences are in the US. We will give you a list of descriptive words which local people have told us could be used to describe the speech of these various regions. Please think about twelve of these regions, and check off how each pair of words applies to the speech there.

For example, imagine that we gave you the pair "ugly" and "beautiful."

ugly ____ ____ ____ ____ ____ ____ beautiful
     a   b   c   d   e   f

Table 11.1 The two factor groups from the ratings of all areas

Factor group #1		Factor group #2	
Smart	.76	Polite	.74
Educated	.75	Friendly	.74
Normal	.65	Down-to-earth	.62
Good English	.63	(Normal)	(.27)
No drawl	.62	(Casual)	(.27)
No twang	.57		
Casual [Formal]	−.49		
Fast	.43		
Down-to-earth [Snobbish]	−.32		

Notes: Parenthesized factors indicate items which are within the .25 to .29 range; "−" prefixes indicate negative loadings and should be interpreted as loadings of the opposite value (given in brackets).

You would use the scale as follows:

If you very strongly agree that the speech of a region is "ugly," select "a."

If you strongly agree that the speech of a region is "ugly," select "b."

If you agree that the speech of a region is "ugly," select "c."

If you agree that the speech of a region is "beautiful," select "d."

If you strongly agree that the speech of a region is "beautiful," select "e."

If you very strongly agree that the speech of a region is "beautiful," select "f."

Through statistical analysis, it was determined that the 12 scales could be conflated into two groups (see Table 11.1).[1] The first (which we will call "Standard") contains those characteristics which we associate with education and the formal attributes of the society. Note, however, that the last three items in this group ("Formal," "Fast," and "Snobbish") are not necessarily positive traits. Group 2 (which we will call "Friendly") contains very different sorts of characteristics (including two which are negative in Group 1 but positive here – "Down-to-earth" and "Casual").

These two groups will not surprise those who have looked at any previous studies of language attitudes. As already noted, many researchers have found that the two main dimensions of evaluation for language varieties are most often those of *social status* ("Standard") and *group solidarity* ("Friendly").

The Michigan respondents rated Michigan highest in all of the "Standard" attributes, while they rated the South highest in almost all of the "Friendly" attributes. Since many of the hand-drawn maps of US dialect areas by Michigan respondents label the local area "standard," "normal" (as in Figure 11.1), "correct," and "good English," there is obviously no dissatisfaction with the local variety as a representative of "correct English." What is the source of the preference for the southern varieties along the "friendly" dimensions? Perhaps a group has a tendency to use up what might be called the "symbolic linguistic capital" of its variety in one way or the other (but not both). Speakers of majority varieties have a tendency to spend the symbolic capital of their variety on a "Standard" dimension. Speakers of minority varieties usually spend their symbolic capital on the "Friendly" dimension.

Perhaps many northerners (here, south–eastern Michiganders) have spent all their symbolic linguistic capital on the standardness of local English. As such, it has come to represent the norms of schools, media, and public interaction and has, therefore, become less suitable for interpersonal value. These young Michiganders, therefore, assign an alternate kind of prestige to a variety which they imagine would have more value than theirs for interpersonal and casual interaction, precisely the sorts of dimensions associated with Group 2.

Already armed with the information that respondents tend to evaluate language variety along these two dimensions, Preston took an even more direct approach to eliciting judgments about such variety, again with no recourse to actual voice samples. He asked south–eastern Michigan respondents to rate the 50 states (and Washington, DC, and New York City) for "correctness." The results are shown in Figure 11.4.

Again, it is clear that the south fares worst. On a 1–10 scale (with one being "least correct"), Alabama is the only state which reaches a mean score in the 3.00–3.99 range, and, with the exception of New York City and New Jersey, the surrounding southern states (Texas, Arkansas, Louisiana, Mississippi, Tennessee, and Georgia) are the only other areas rated in the 4.00–4.99 range. In short, the importance of southern speech would appear to lie in its distinctiveness along one particular dimension – it is incorrect English. It is only Michigan which scores in the heady 8.00–8.99 means score range for language "correctness."

What parallel can we find in such work as this to the scores for the attributes in Factor Group 2 ("Friendly") already reported? Figure 11.5 shows what Michigan raters have done in a direct assessment of the notion "pleasant" (as was shown above in Figure 11.4 for "correctness"). As Figure 11.5

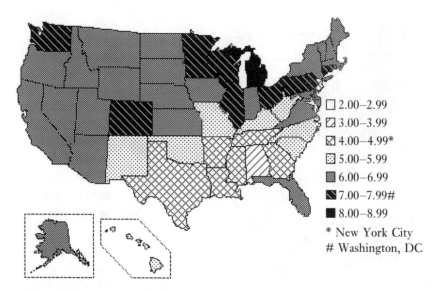

Figure 11.4 Means of ratings for language "correctness" by Michigan respondents for US English
Note: On a scale of 1 to 10, where 1 = least and 10 = most correct.

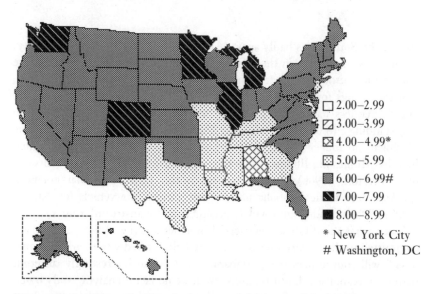

Figure 11.5 Means of ratings for language "pleasantness" by Michigan respondents for US English
Note: On a scale of 1 to 10, where 1 = least and 10 = most pleasant.

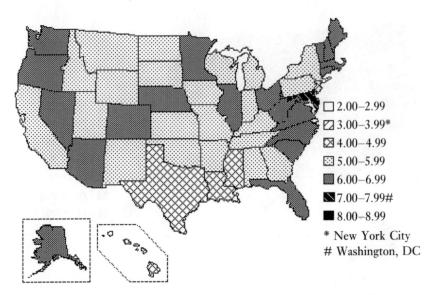

□ 2.00–2.99
▨ 3.00–3.99*
⊠ 4.00–4.99
▨ 5.00–5.99
■ 6.00–6.99
◣ 7.00–7.99#
■ 8.00–8.99

* New York City
\# Washington, DC

Figure 11.6   Means of ratings for language "correctness" by Alabama respondents for US English
Note: On a scale of 1 to 10, where 1 = least and 10 = most pleasant.

shows, the South fares badly again. Alabama (tied here by New York City) is the worst-rated area in the US, and the surrounding southern states are also at the bottom of this ten-point rating scale. One may note, however, that the ratings for the "pleasantness" of the English of southern states are one degree less harsh than those for "correctness." Similarly, there is no "outstanding" (8.00–8.99) rating as there was for "correctness," making Michigan no longer the uniquely best-thought-of area (since it is joined here by Minnesota, Illinois, Colorado, and Washington). In previous work (e.g., Preston, 1996b), Preston has taken this to indicate that northern speakers have made symbolic use of their variety as a vehicle for "stand-ardness," "education," and widely accepted or "mainstream" values.

Then what about US southerners? If northerners (i.e., Michiganders) are committed to their "correctness" but only half-heartedly to their "pleasant-ness," will southerners (e.g., Alabamians) show an interestingly different pattern of responses? Unfortunately, we have no factor analytic study based on the cognitive maps of southerners, but we can show you how they have responded to the "correct" and "pleasant" tasks already discussed for Michiganders (see Figures 11.6 and 11.7).

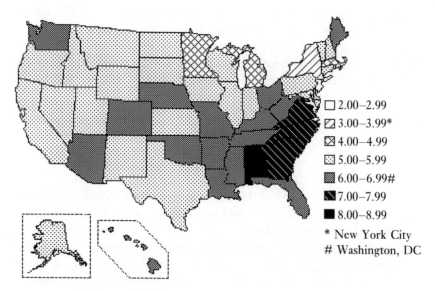

Figure 11.7 Means of ratings for language "pleasantness" by Alabama respondents for US English
Note: On a scale of 1 to 10, where 1 = least and 10 = most correct.

Just as one might have suspected, as Figure 11.6 shows, Alabamians are much less invested in language "correctness" (and well they should not be, since they are constantly reminded in popular culture and even personal encounters that their language is lacking in this dimension). Imagine the horror of a Michigander in seeing Figure 11.6. Their own "correct" English-speaking state scores no better than the fair-to-middling "5" which Alabamians assign to many areas, including their own (showing no break in correctness on a trip from Alabama all the way north to Michigan!).

Upon inspection, Figure 11.7 resembles Figure 11.4, indicating that Alabamians are invested in something, just as Michiganders are, but it is clearly "pleasantness," not "correctness." This simple task shows very straightforwardly the sort of differential investment in local varieties discussed above.

In one sense, of course, such studies are "language attitude" studies; in another sense, however, they form important background understandings for the study of attitudes among different social and regional groups. How can we study more detailed aspects of language attitudes unless we know that a group is investing in "correctness" or "solidarity"? And, of course, as we hope to have shown in this entire section, how can we measure language attitudes unless we know something of the cognitive arrangements our respondents have made of the terrain we want to explore. Although part of the game belongs to linguists (the linguistic detail), the real territory (as perhaps in any linguistic work) lies within the cognitive maps (whether of geographic or social facts) of those we study.

Conclusion

What of the larger promise? How can we go about fashioning a more general folk theory of language, one which surely underlies all attitudinal responses? Also, what implications does this folk theory of language have for speech-language pathologists and audiologists? We believe much of the attitudinal data outlined above, including the mental maps of and attitudinal responses to regional varieties of US English, is dominated by the notions of "correctness" (the more powerful) and "pleasantness." We also believe a great deal of folk belief and language ideology stems from these facts. Speakers of "correct" dialects do not believe they speak dialects, and educational and even legal repercussions arise from personal and institutional devaluing of "incorrect" varieties. On the other hand, speakers of stigmatized varieties (like stigmatized groups in general) derive solidarity from their distinct cultural behaviors, in this case, linguistic ones.

In a more direct attempt to get at this underlying fact, some attitude researchers have collected and analyzed overt folk comment about language (e.g., Labov, 1966; Niedzielski and Preston, 1999). These include complex (and rewarding) conversations about social and regional varieties of US English which may be analyzed to show not only relatively static folk belief and attitudes but also how these beliefs and attitudes are used in argument and persuasion. Such investigations are particularly important in showing what deep-seated presuppositions about language are held (e.g., Preston, 1994). Many of these conversations (and their parallels and contrasts to professional opinion) are given in Niedzielski and Preston (1999), but we will provide only one here. We think, however, it is an especially representative one which supports the claim that correctness dominates in US folk perceptions of language and which also allows a slightly deeper look at what sort of theory might allow that domination. H (the fieldworker) has asked D and G (his respondents) if there is any difference in meaning between the words "gift" and "present."[2]

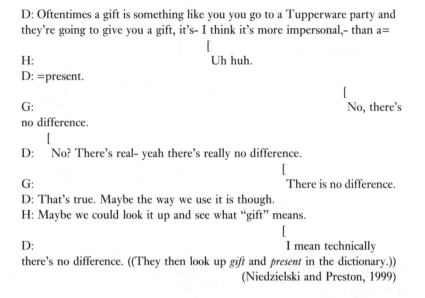

D: Oftentimes a gift is something like you you go to a Tupperware party and
they're going to give you a gift, it's- I think it's more impersonal,- than a=

                  [

H: Uh huh.

D: =present.

                                           [

G: No, there's
no difference.

   [

D: No? There's real- yeah there's really no difference.

                                       [

G: There is no difference.

D: That's true. Maybe the way we use it is though.

H: Maybe we could look it up and see what "gift" means.

                                  [

D: I mean technically
there's no difference. ((They then look up *gift* and *present* in the dictionary.))

                                   (Niedzielski and Preston, 1999)

Although there are several interesting folk linguistic (and of course discoursal)
facts about this short excerpt, the shock for linguists comes in D's remark
that there is no difference in the meaning except in "the way we use it." Of
course, what other difference could there be? We believe this remark (and
many others noted in the course of surveying "folk linguistic conversations") points to a folk theory of language in which language itself is somehow external to human cognitive embedding – somewhere "out there."
Figure 11.8 illustrates the essential difference between folk and professional
theories.

In the linguistic theory, one moves up (and away from) the concrete
reality of language as a cognitively embedded fact in the capacities of individual speakers to the social constructions of language similarity. These
higher-level constructs are socially real but considerably more abstract than
the "real" language, embedded in individual speakers.

In the folk theory, just the opposite is true. A Platonic, extra-cognitive
reality is the "real" language – such a thing as English or German or
Chinese, a level which has only an abstract or social reality in the linguists'
world. Speakers who are directly connected to this ideal speak a fully
correct form (the only rule-governed variety), although one may deviate
from it comfortably not to sound to "prissy." Go too far, however, and
error, dialect, or, quite simply, bad language arises. Since this connection to
the rule-governed, exterior "real" language seems a natural (and even easy)

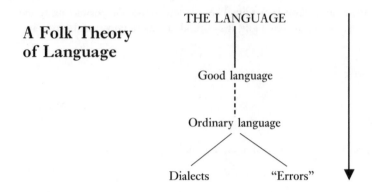

A Folk Theory
of Language

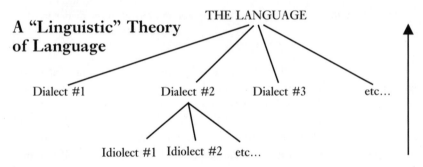

A "Linguistic" Theory
of Language

Figure 11.8   Folk (above) and "linguistic" theories of language

one, many folk find it difficult to understand why nonstandard speakers, for example, persist in their errors (and often find them simply lazy or recalcitrant).

If this is the theory of language for most nonlinguists, the implications for clinical professionals are numerous. If professionals involved in positions of power over speakers of stigmatized dialects operate with such a theory of language, major repercussions can occur (e.g., over-/under-diagnosis of speech-language disorders, inadequate service delivery, etc.). Since "correctness" is deemed the governing factor in attitudinal judgments of regional dialects, the pervasive attitude is that individuals who speak nonmainstream dialects are speaking "incorrectly." What happens when a child moves mid-year from an area that uses a stigmatized dialect to an area with high linguistic security? Although no research that we know of has been conducted that tests this scenario directly, the literature regarding the folk theory of language suggests that the child's speech has a high likelihood of being labeled "incorrect" by anyone who operates under the folk theory (teachers, peers, medical professionals, and even fellow speech-language pathologists and audiologists). The more we understand about folk theories of language, the more we can hope to understand the underlying sources of much behavior previously studied as "language attitude" and to solve these ever-present problems within the clinical professions.

Notes

1   Although the paired opposites were presented to the respondents with "negative" and "positive" sides randomly distributed, the "positive" poles were all moved to the high (i.e., "6") end of the scale for all the quantitative analyses reported below. I (Preston) realized after I did this that there might be cultural misunderstandings of what I consider to be the "positive" end. They are "Fast," "Polite," "Down-to-earth," "Educated," "Normal," "Smart," "Casual," "Good English," "Not nasal," "Friendly," "Speaks without a drawl," and "Speaks without a twang." I apologize to readers who disagree with my assignments. That should not detract from the contents of the chapter.

2   Since H is not a native speaker, such a question seemed "reasonable."

Further reading

Garrett, P., Coupland, N., and Williams, A. (2003) *Investigating Language Attitudes: Social Meanings of Dialect, Ethnicity and Performance.* Cardiff: University of Wales Press.

Long, D. and Preston, D. R. (eds) (2002) *Handbook of Perceptual Dialectology*, Vol. 2. Amsterdam: Benjamins.

Milroy, L. and Preston, D. R. (guest eds) (1999) *Journal of Language and Social Psychology* (special issue: Attitudes, Perception, and Linguistic Features) 18(1).

Preston, D. R. (ed.) (1999) *Handbook of Perceptual Dialectology*, Vol. 1. Amsterdam: Benjamins.

Ryan, E. B. and Giles, H. (1982) *Attitudes towards Language Variation: Social and Applied Contexts* (*The Social Psychology of Language* 1). London: Edward Arnold.

Part II
A Clinical Sociolinguistics

12

Acquisition of
Sociolinguistic Variation

Julie Roberts

What do children learn when they learn language? A speech-language pathologist (SLP) studies the process of language acquisition and knows, for example, that language acquired by children can be broken down into components. Sometimes these are called semantics, syntax, morphology, phonology, and pragmatics. Sometimes other words are used, such as form, content, and use (Bloom and Lahey, 1978). In either case, the emphasis is on a more-or-less orderly progression of language skills, in which a child acquires a form by becoming more and more consistent in its appropriate use and more and more proficient in its production. Variation was considered to be located within the individual child and often related to the rate of acquisition rather than the order. Bates, Dale and Thal (1995), for example, conducted a study with an unprecedented subject sample of more than 1,800 children. They used a parent-report methodology and found high variability in the rate of language acquisition among children, particularly after the age of 12 months in all areas of language studied.

In the past few years, it has been more frequently acknowledged that children do vary greatly in the order of acquisition as well as the rate. For example, Lahey, Liebergott, Chesnick, Menyuk and Adams (1992) demonstrated that the order of morpheme acquisition, assumed stable since established by Brown's landmark study (1973), was, in fact, less orderly than previously thought. Lahey et al.'s study marked a change toward the recognition of variation as a normal occurrence in language acquisition, but the focus remains on individual differences, often assumed to be secondary to skill level or learning style.

The study of sociolinguistic variation, on the other hand, as discussed in Part I of this volume, is the systematic variation that is both inherent and socially meaningful among and within speech communities. Acquisition of this type of variation, then, is not a by-product of the learning process, but an integral part of acquisition itself. In order to be a competent speaker of a language, a child must acquire variable structures in the same manner as she acquires invariable, or categorical, language rules. At the same time, as caretakers provide a model of a language's regular rules and patterns, they also must provide a model of language in all of its systematic variability.

Acquisition of variation is a relatively new field of study, one that involves the interaction of psycholinguistics and sociolinguistics. It also involves recognizing that the language learning of children encompasses a broader and more complex set of features than previously studied by researchers. In other words, children not only must learn categorical rules, so that they may sound like a proficient native speaker of their language, but they must also acquire variable rules and patterns so that they will sound like a proficient speaker of their speech community! How a child acquires these rules and patterns, and when this learning takes place is the focus of the study of the acquisition of variation.

Nurturing language acquisition, naturally

Ochs and Schieffelin (1984: 308) stated the following: "What child says, and how he or she says it, will be influenced by local cultural processes in addition to biological and social processes that have universal scope." They were discussing the influence of various cultural language socialization practices on the acquisition of language in three very different societies. Although their analysis was primarily at the level of pragmatics, or use, of language, the points they made are germane to the acquisition of regionally and socially based dialects as well. Ochs and Schieffelin demonstrated in their comparison of early mother–child interaction in Papua New Guinea, Western Samoa, and Western middle-class society, that the type of early social input that children are exposed to is crucially and intricately influenced by the cultural norms of the society. For example, mothers among the Kaluli in Papua New Guinea do not simplify their language when speaking to babies in the manner that is often characterized as universal child directed speech (CDS). Rather, they provide practice in multiparty interaction, which is typical of communication in this community, by holding the infant facing out from the mother and speaking for her to one or more listeners. As the child grows, this same mother will instruct the child on what to say to a third party in a particular interaction. The result of this language socialization process is, at least, two-fold. First, the Kaluli child, like the Western child and the Samoan child, learns to speak her language competently, even without the Western-style CDS. Second, she learns to speak that language in such a way that she becomes not only competent in the Kaluli language but in the Kaluli interactional style as well.

Ochs and Schiefflin's work demonstrates that culture and its variation are far from incidental to language socialization and acquisition. In fact, it is the context within which meaning is made and taught. Children become members of their individual communities, and their speech reflects and demonstrates this identity. Just as the above ethnographic work shows that language takes meaning within interactions and causes us to ask new questions about socialization, a more local examination of language acquisition within speech communities allows us to ask new questions about the environment in which language is acquired, the mechanisms that foster this acquisition, and the interactions that facilitate changes not only in the language learner but in the language itself.

The Language Acquisition Environment (LAE)

Anyone who has read language acquisition literature knows that when Noam Chomsky changed the world for linguists in the 1950s, he changed psycholinguistic thinking as well. Learnability, or how easily a language model can account for language acquisition by a native speaker, became a critical linguistics construct (Chomsky, 1957, 1959). The search was on for linguistic universals, those language features that, as they were present in all human languages, could be postulated to be innate. The innate, or "hard-wired" neurological construct present in each person from birth that contains these universals was sometimes termed the Language Acquisition Device (LAD). The description of the "device" has changed over the years, but the importance of innateness to language acquisition study has not. As previously noted, much of psycholinguistic study, influenced by universal grammar, has been focused on a search for linguistic similarity among the languages of the world, and most of the exploration of difference has centered on the individual and their learning styles. It is not the purpose of this chapter to dispute the importance of the heritability of language. However, it is critical to look as well at the context in which language is learned, how that context is influenced by society, and how the systematic influence of society is enacted by the child as the child grows up and becomes a contributing member to the language of the society. Therefore, we will discuss the Language Acquisition Environment, or LAE, as a partner to the LAD.

Child directed speech: variation and systematicity

As many researchers have noted, an essential component to the LAE is the child's earliest interactions with caretakers. However, like language learning itself, the LAE was originally thought to be more invariant than was borne out by later research. Charles Ferguson (1977) first noted that mothers tend to modify their speech when talking to very young children and that this modification could be systematically described. This work spawned a very large body of work on the nature, the universality, and the linguistic benefit of what Ferguson termed "baby talk" but what has come to be called CDS. The similarity among caretakers' speech in the cultures initially studied led researchers to hypothesize that CDS might be universal, and that it might be beneficial, maybe even necessary, to language learning. Schieffelin's work with the Kaluli in Papua New Guinea was the first to demonstrate that child directed speech was not universal, although subsequent work showed that it differed in either kind or quantity in other cultures as well (Ward, 1971; Heath, 1983). If an input process is not universal, it cannot be considered necessary to language acquisition because children do learn to talk in cultures where CDS is absent or rarely used. This realization did not end researchers' interest in the phenomenon, however, it did broaden the nature of the inquiry considerably. If caretakers were not using a universal language register to teach language, what was going on in these early acquisition environments, and what, if anything, was being taught? We have already discussed the body of work demonstrating the importance of CDS as a critical component of language socialization and the passing along of cultural information from one generation to the next. On the other hand, there was little or no information on whether or not child directed speech was instrumental in transmitting more specific linguistic information to the young child. Psycholinguists have very logically assumed that language-specific forms are learned, and there is a large body of work on this process. We are considerably less well informed about dialect-related CDS and dialect acquisition.

Some preliminary findings on this topic were presented in the following study. Roberts (2002) presented data from four white middle-class mothers

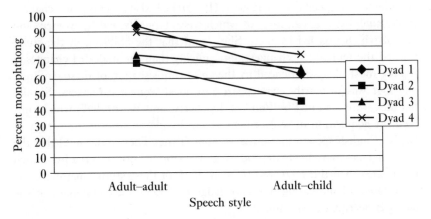

Figure 12.1 Memphis mothers' speech to an interviewer as compared with their children. Monophthongization of long /aɪ/

from Tennessee talking with their toddlers, aged 18 to 19 months, and with an interviewer. These mothers were all speakers of the Southern shift American English dialect, which has as one of its features the pronunciation of long /aɪ/ as in "might" as a fronted monophthong, or closer to "mat." All four mothers used both types of /aɪ/ but produced more of the Southern /aɪ/ in their speech to the adult interviewer than with their children. This was true even though the interviewer was, in most cases, not a speaker of the Southern shift as shown in Figure 12.1. However, the main finding of this work was not that the mothers used significantly more of the more "standard" pronunciation of /aɪ/ to their children. In fact, the sample size is too small to show significance. Rather, the important point is that the speech directed to the children by their mothers was highly variable. The children heard both the standard sounding and the southern sounding variable in the speech of their mothers. They were presented with examples of what sounds within their dialect could vary and in what ways. Just as the caretakers studied by Schieffelin, Ochs, Heath, Ward, and others found that the language environment of the children comprised culturally specific and culturally significant information, the above results suggest that child directed speech also contains the elements necessary for producing the variable dialect forms spoken by the community of which the child will be a part.

Although work exploring CDS from a variationist perspective is extremely scarce, two studies looked at the potential result of this process and found that young children do appear to be influenced by the early language environment in specific ways. Roberts (1997b) looked at several sound changes in Philadelphia English, most of which were, typically, led by women, and one of which was led by men. She found that the children in the study learned the female-led changes more quickly than the male-led changes, a finding most likely influenced by the child care situation of these children, one that was primarily characterized by local women caretakers. Similar findings were obtained by Foulkes, Docherty, and Watt (1999) who examined the acquisition of replacement of /t/ by glottal stop in the variety of British English spoken in Newcastle upon Tyne. They, too, found that the children were more likely to produce glottal stop features favored by women in the area than those favored by men. Both of these studies highlight the importance of increasing our knowledge of CDS as a component of the language learning environment.

Dialect production by children

Fortunately, there is somewhat more research on children's acquisition and use of their native dialect than on dialect-related CDS. As we look at this research, our focus will be on two questions:

1   What does children's acquisition of their native dialects tell us about child language acquisition in general?
2   What can children's acquisition of their native dialects tell us about the future of the dialects themselves?

In other words, we are interested not only in what impact the dialect environment has on the child but also in what impact the child will have, in return, on the dialect. As regards the first question, study of children's dialect acquisition shows us that children are even more impressive in their ability to learn language than we may have previously thought. Speech-language pathologists have long been aware that children learn an immense number of language features, whatever their native language. For example, children must learn how to produce a variety of phonemes and which of these phonemes are utilized in their native languages. Further, children learn words, grammatical morphemes to add on to the words to give them number, tense, agreement, etc. They learn to put these words and morphemes in grammatical order to make sentences. The study of acquisition of variation allows us to add to all of this that very young children can and do produce phonemes specific to their regional and social dialects, and they vary these phonemes in such a way as to sound like speakers of their communities.

Before we look at a specific example, however, it is first important to consider the developmental process of dialects as a whole. Wolfram (1989) notes that if the dialect of the child and the more standard dialect of a language share a feature, then the assumption is made that the acquisitional process will be the same for a child speaking a more non-standard and a more standard dialect. However, he cautions that this is an assumption, not an empirically explored assertion, and it remains so today. A different but related question is, what is the developmental process if a feature is present in the non-standard dialect and not present or differently present in the corresponding more standard dialect?

Dialect acquisition differences can be especially puzzling when a dialect has a rule or process that allows for a phoneme or morpheme to be variably deleted. Since features are variable when they first enter a child's linguistic repertoire, how does one decide when such variation becomes dialectal rather than developmental? Some of the first studies of the acquisition of variation looked at just this question with limited but instructive results.

Here are two examples. In the first, Wolfram (1989) studied the speech of 12 African American children, ages 18 to 54 months, over a period of 18 months. He was particularly interested in final nasal deletion with nasalization of the preceding vowel as this phenomenon is common in adult speakers of African American English (AAE). Although nasal segments rarely appeared at all in the youngest children, they were produced often by the 36- and 54-month-olds. These children demonstrated a pattern of deletion that bore strong similarity to the adult AAE pattern. For example, final /n/ was far more likely to be deleted than final /m/ or /ŋ/, and nasals at the end of an utterance were more likely to be deleted than those followed by another word, particularly if that word began with a vowel. In addition, there was little change in the nasal patterning of the 36- and 54-month-olds. In other words, the nasalization pattern appeared to have stabilized in the 3-year-old speakers and was maintained afterward.

The second example also involves a pattern of deletion, found in many, and quite possibly, all dialects of English. Sociolinguists have known for a long time that English speakers often delete /t/ or /d/ in consonant clusters at the ends of words such as "list" or "told" (Guy, 1980). Further, dialects vary in how much /t, d/ deletion is allowable in particular environments (e.g., what sound precedes and follows the cluster, what part of speech the word with the cluster is, etc.) Roberts (1997a) found that 3- and

4-year-old children in Philadelphia also reduced these consonant clusters. This finding may not seem the least bit surprising to speech-language pathologists, who know that consonant cluster reduction is a one of the most common natural phonological process in children developing language (Vihman, 1996: 21–2). However, the difference is that these children reduced these clusters in the environments predicted by analyses of adult Philadelphia speakers. For example, they were more likely to reduce clusters when they were at the end of an utterance and followed by a pause than in other environments, just like adult Philadelphians, but unlike adult New Yorkers (Guy, 1980). Second, the children were more likely to reduce the cluster by omitting a /t/ or /d/ that had no specific meaning (as in *mist*) than one that did (as in *missed*). The only time they did not follow the adults' lead was when the /t/ or /d/ was in a particular type of irregular past tense verb in which it accounted for only part of the past tense meaning (such as *slept* or *told* in which past is signaled by a vowel change and a /t/ or /d/.) In this case the children omitted /t/ or /d/ at the same rate as when they had no meaning at all.

How much of our question about the process of acquiring social and regional variation do these studies answer? Both of these examples emphasize the need for studies of younger speakers and with more intensive longitudinal analysis. In both cases, children were well on the way, if not complete, in their acquisition of the variable patterns examined. It will be important for future research to examine this early acquisitional stage to enable us to answer questions involving the earliest emergence of dialect forms. Second, the children demonstrated variable patterns first in those environments that are most transparent: phonetic environments (e.g., (-t, d) followed by consonant, vowel, pause, /n/ followed by a pause vs a vowel) and grammatical environments that contrast words with no morphological segmentation (e.g., *list*, *melt*) with those containing overt tense morphemes (regular -ed past tense marking). In more ambiguous contexts, such as the verbs that contain redundant irregular marking, the children rely on their own "analysis" and show no evidence of interpretation of the final /t/ or /d/ as a tense marker. In other words, these two studies capture an early piece of the process, in which acquisition is partial or final, but not the earliest stage.

Although the above examples demonstrate that children can and do learn complicated patterns of language, (-t, d) and /n/ deletion are the features usually associated with dialect difference. Far more diagnostic of regional and social variation is how different words are pronounced in different communities. Usually this pronunciation is associated with a difference in

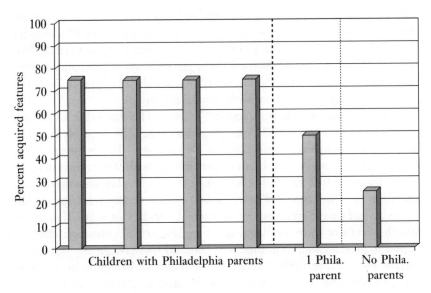

Figure 12.2 Proportion of Philadelphia vowel changes learned by children with local and non-local parents

vowel production. Philadelphia English, for example, has a very complicated dialect pattern called the short *a* pattern (Trager, 1940; Labov, 1989). Short *a* (/æ/ as in *cat*) is a vowel that often varies by dialect. Sometimes it is raised and tensed so that it sounds like *ey-uh* or [ɪə] or even [iə]. This occurs in Philadelphia, but only in some environments. It is such a complicated system that Payne (1980) found that older children who had moved to Philadelphia could not learn the system unless they learned it early and had parents who came from Philadelphia. In another study of six of the same 3- and 4-year-old children discussed above, Roberts (1997b) found that they had made great strides in the mastery of this system but that their progress was greatly dependent on the background of their parents. The children who were furthest ahead in their dialect acquisition were those who had only Philadelphia influences at home as shown in Figure 12.2. The child who had only one parent from Philadelphia made more "errors" in vowel raising than the others, and the one whose parents both came from Italy had not learned the system at all, even though he sounded very much like a native speaker of English.

The children in this study continued to learn the patterns of vowel placement long after they learn the vowel itself. That is, none of the children had adopted a vowel that sounded like anything other than short *a*. However, they were still in the process of acquiring the intricacies of Philadelphia short *a*. We can suggest that a variable vowel pattern may, as Payne (1980) noted with second dialect learners, be quite difficult to learn and require more time to acquire than its corresponding "standard" phoneme, and may not be fully acquired by those with insufficient input.

These findings beg a larger question: When do children become speakers of their speech communities? Psycholinguists engaged in the study of infant babbling have explored similar issues. Anyone who listens to an infant babble can observe that children's earliest sounds are not restricted to those in the language that surrounds her. At least three explanations have been given for this "international" early sound play generally relating to vocal tract size and shape, emerging motor control, and lack of acquisition of the speech sounds of their own language (Ferguson, 1978). Although children appear to produce sounds of their own language more frequently than other sounds even at the earliest stages (Cruttenden, 1970), they increasingly come to resemble adult speakers of their native language. A child can be said to be a native speaker of his language when he produces words in that language, a point that can be admittedly difficult to determine. However, the transition to speaker of a particular speech community is even more difficult to define for researchers of variation, but the studies discussed here and similar ones show that the answers lie in in-depth studies of the speech of very young children themselves.

Future leaders of dialect variation?

There is at least one more topic of great interest to dialect acquisition researchers. Clearly, the input of caretakers and others in the child's early life is of prime influence in the acquisition of dialect features. Just as obviously, children are the mature dialect speakers of the future, who will influence the direction of language change. Is it possible, then, to detect any influence of the effect of these young speakers on the dialect itself?

The previous discussion suggests that caretakers present models of variation to their young children. The presence of systematic variation in CDS offers to the child sites of modification. These features must be learned by the children as they learn the local linguistic norms of their communities. However, they also provide the learners with the locations of segments that offer the potential of future modification. For example, Roberts and Labov

(1995) found that in a new short *a* raising environment, /æ/ between /l/ and /n/ as in *planet*, the 3- and 4-year-old children were significantly more likely to raise short *a* than adults. Although they did not extend the domain of raising to similar environments (such as *Janet*), their pattern of raising does suggest that they have found sites of variation and modified them slightly.

This small bit of evidence, in conjunction with the information provided by studies of CDS, presents us with another fascinating and critical area for future research: how variation is transmitted through interaction and subsequently modified by the learner to result in patterns of language change.

Conclusion

Speech-language pathologists know that the practice of assessment and treatment of children with speech and language disorders depends crucially on knowledge of normal language acquisition. We also know that the diversity of the SLP's caseload has become of prime importance in day-to-day practice, both because the children on the caseloads themselves are increasingly diverse in their social characteristics and because we are increasingly recognizing the social diversity that has always been present. If knowledge of diversity is to become a part of clinical practice in the twenty-first century, then the emphasis on universality in the study of language acquisition must be supplemented by knowledge of acquisition as it occurs in local speech communities around the world. It is impossible to separate language difference from language disorder without understanding the range of normal variation as it occurs in the speech and language of typically developing children. This is not an easy task, and the information needed is far from complete; however, the interaction of speech-language pathologists and sociolinguists is of vital importance to the progress of both fields.

Further reading

Heath, S. B. (1983) *Ways with Words*. New York: Cambridge University Press.

Ochs, E. and Schieffelin, B. B. (1984) Language acquisition and socialization: Three developmental stories and their implications. In R. Shweder and R. Levine, *Culture Theory: Essays in Mind, Self and Emotion* (pp. 276–320). New York: Cambridge University Press.

Payne, A. (1980) Factors controlling the acquisition of the Philadelphia dialect by out-of-state children. In W. Labov (ed.), *Locating Language in Time and Space* (pp. 143–78). New York: Academic Press.

Roberts, J. (2002) Child language variation. In J. K. Chambers, P. Trudgill and N. Schilling-Estes, *The Handbook of Language Variation and Change* (pp. 333–48). Oxford: Blackwell.

Wolfram, W. (1989) Structural variability in phonological development: Final nasals in Vernacular Black English. In R. W. Fasold and D. Schiffrin (eds), *Language Change and Variation* (pp. 301–32). Amsterdam: Benjamins.

13

Bi- and Multilingual Language Acquisition

Zhu Hua and Li Wei

This chapter outlines some of the central issues in the study of bi- and multilingual acquisition. For convenience, we shall use the term "bilingualism" or "bilingual" to cover both bilingualism or bilingual and multilingualism or multilingual.

Routes to bilingualism

People become bilingual for a variety of reasons and in a variety of ways. With regard to *motivation* and *style of learning*, we can distinguish between *planned* bilingualism and *unplanned* bilingualism. Planned bilingualism is a result of deliberate decisions regarding language learning and use with a specified goal of producing a bilingual individual. For example, some parents decide that one of them speaks one language to the children and the other speaks a different language, even if one of the languages spoken may not be native to either parent. A more commonplace case of planned bilingualism is when individuals attend bilingual education programs or language classes, with the aim of becoming bilingual in the target languages. Unplanned bilingualism, on the other hand, occurs where some environmental factor determines that the individual has to operate with two or more languages in order to function in their immediate community. For instance, children of bilingual parents become bilingual themselves not through any formal teaching and learning but through everyday interaction. Likewise, people who have married speakers of languages other than their native ones may pick up their spouses' languages and use them regularly in social interaction, and immigrants become bilingual as a result of living in a community whose language is different from their first language(s).

Although most cases involve some degree of internal motivation, unplanned bilingualism is primarily motivated by external factors. In other words, planned bilingualism is primarily by choice while unplanned bilingualism is not.

In terms of developmental course, we can distinguish between *simultaneous* bilingualism and *successive* bilingualism. The latter is also sometimes known as *consecutive* or *sequential* bilingualism. Simultaneous bilingualism refers to a child acquiring two languages at the same time very early in life. For instance, in a family where the two parents have different first languages and one parent speaks one language to the child while the other speaks a different language, the child may learn both languages simultaneously. This kind of situation has been described as "bilingual first language acquisition" (e.g., Meisel, 1990) or "bilingualism as a first language" (e.g., Swain, 1972). Successive bilingualism refers to a child acquiring one language first and adding another language later in childhood. An example of successive bilingualism is when, say, a child of Mexican–American parentage learns Spanish at home, then goes to an English-speaking nursery or elementary school and learns English as a second language. There are good theoretical reasons for maintaining the distinction between simultaneous and successive bilingualism. Speakers who have never been monolingual, as in the case of simultaneous bilinguals, may well process the languages very differently from those who learned one language after another. Likewise, anything a child learns in one language might have a subsequent effect on the language learned later. However, the distinction is not always easy to maintain in practice. For example, it has been suggested that acquisition of more than one language up to age 3 should be considered simultaneous, and that after the age of 3 should be successive (e.g., McLaughlin, 1978). The reason for this age boundary is that younger learners tend to achieve a relatively higher level of language proficiency, in its global sense, than older learners. Nevertheless, research evidence indicates huge individual variations. Setting a rigid age boundary for the two types of bilingualism can only be arbitrary and has little scientific value.

Researchers who prefer to maintain the distinction between simultaneous and successive bilingualism often point to the *context* and style of acquisition. Generally speaking, simultaneous bilingualism takes place very early in a child's life and in a naturally-occurring context without formal instruction. In other words, simultaneous bilingualism tends to happen in an unplanned fashion. Successive bilingualism, on the other hand, happens later in childhood and tends to involve formal teaching and learning, often in an educational setting and in a systematic and planned way. However, early simultaneous bilingualism can also involve some elements of formal instruction. Parents can plan which language to use with the children as well as the specific ways in which they speak to the children. In the meantime, there is a movement towards making language learning more naturalistic in an educational setting, emphasizing meaning-making over grammatical accuracy and developing communicative competence in a less formal way. This is particularly true when the learners are very young.

Instead of such dichotomies, it may be useful to consider the following questions when describing various types of childhood bilingualism (Baker, 2001: 87–8):

1 What is the linguistic repertoire of the parents? In some family situations, the parents or guardians may both be bilingual. That is, both parents may be able to speak both the languages of the particular community. Alternatively, both parents may be monolingual. The child acquires the second language from neighbors, friends and other people in the local community. In other families, one parent may be practically bilingual, the other virtually monolingual. Many studies of bilingual families have reported a difference in language proficiency and use between fathers and mothers.

2 What is the parents' strategy in speaking to the child? While parents have the ability to speak both languages to their children, there is often a conscious decision or a latent understanding about which language to use with the child from birth upwards. A bilingual parent may choose to use both the languages with the child. A different situation is when one parent speaks one language to the child, the other parent speaks a different language. A third circumstance is when bilingual parents both speak the "home" language, while the child learns a different language outside the home.

3 What is the sociolinguistic situation of the community at large? Language contact is a dynamic process. Bilingual communities have different degrees of stability. The linguistic experiences of individuals from more or less stable language contact environments are likely to impact on their attitudes towards bilingualism and may well result in different patterns of language behavior. Differences in the social status of the languages concerned will also impact on the linguistic experience of the bilingual child. Some languages have no institutional support whereas others may play a crucial role in a child's education and everyday social life.

Considering such questions, Romaine (1995) classified the main types of early childhood bilingualism into six categories. Five of them were described also by Harding and Riley (1986: 47–8):

Type 1: "One-person-one-language"
Parents: The parents have different native languages with each having some degree of competence in the other's language.
Community: The language of one of the parents is the dominant language of the community.
Strategy: The parents each speak their own language to the child from birth.

Type 2: "Non-dominant home language" or "One-language-one-environment"
Parents: The parents have different native languages.
Community: The language of one of the parents is the dominant language of the community.
Strategy: Both parents speak the non-dominant language to the child, who is fully exposed to the dominant language only when outside the home, and in particular in nursery school.

Type 3: "Non-dominant home language without community support"
Parents: The parents share the same native language.
Community: The dominant language is not that of the parents.
Strategy: The parents speak their own language to the child.

Type 4: "Double non-dominant home language without community support"
Parents: The parents have different native languages.
Community: The dominant language is different from either of the parents' languages.
Strategy: The parents each speak their own language to the child from birth.

Type 5: "Non-native parents"
Parents: The parents share the same native language.
Community: The dominant language is the same as that of the parents.
Strategy: One of the parents always addresses the child in a language which is not his/her native language.

Type 6: "Mixed languages"
Parents: The parents are bilingual.
Community: Sectors of community may also be bilingual.
Strategy: Parents code-switch and mix languages.

Examples and discussions of the various types of childhood bilingualism can be found in Romaine (1995).

Input and context in bilingual acquisition

One of the key questions about bilingual acquisition concerns the role of input and social context. The three headings Romaine used to classify the six types of childhood bilingualism – the language(s) of the parents, the sociolinguistic situation of the community, and the discourse strategies of the parents and other immediate carers – are critical factors not only in the process of bilingual acquisition but also in the type of bilingual speaker the process produces. Arguably, the six types of bilingual children would grow up as different types of bilinguals with different mental representations of the languages and different patterns of language behavior. So how do input and context affect bilingual acquisition?

To answer this question, we need to know, first of all, the quantity and quality of the input. Unfortunately, very few studies have examined the quantity of input in simultaneous bilingual acquisition systematically or in sufficient detail to warrant any specific claims. It is generally assumed that more input in a particular language, either at the macro-community level (e.g., living in a community with a clearly dominant language) or at the micro-interactional level (e.g., conversational exchanges with parents and other care-givers) leads to faster development, more frequent use and higher proficiency in that language. In her study of two children, Tomas and Siri, acquiring Norwegian and English simultaneously, Lanza (1997) finds that the amount of input of each language does play a role in the children's language development. Tomas's preference for Norwegian, for example, can be partly attributed to the fact that he had more active contact with Norwegian playmates and adults in an organized outdoor play school, while Siri, who did not have such contact, used more English than Tomas did. But once Siri's contacts with her Norwegian environment expanded, she began to mix the two languages much more. There is also evidence that changes in the quantity of input can have significant effect on bilingual children's language development. Kessler (1984) suggested that young bilingual children will experience some kind of language loss or attrition if input in one of their languages suddenly cease for prolonged periods of time. Yukawa's (1997) analyses of lexical and grammatical development of two early Japanese–Swedish bilingual children show that their ability to use specific linguistic items and structures are very closely related to the changing exposure to the two languages as the children move between Japan and Sweden.

Input, however, is much more than simply the amount of exposure to each language. The quality of input plays a very crucial role in bilingual acquisition. Some in fact argue that "the quality of input takes precedence over the quantity" (Dopke, 1988: 103). Nevertheless, there are no generally accepted criteria for determining the quality of input; rather, most researchers seem to equate quality to parental discourse strategies or interactional styles. Dopke (1992) studied the role of interactional strategies employed by parents in bilingual acquisition and showed how the considerable differences in the quality of interaction could account for the different linguistic outcomes in six German-English bilingual children in Australia. One boy (Keith) and one girl progressed significantly between the time of Dopke's first recording and the second (a period of six months) as measured in terms of increase in MLU and auditory comprehension. Three other children, however, had not progressed and did not want to speak German, while another child had progressed but no longer wanted to speak German. The apparent success of Keith is particularly noteworthy, as neither of his parents were native speakers of German. His main German input came from his father, who not only talked more to Keith than did the mother, but his interactions were more child-centered and intensive than the mother's. Dopke concluded that there were two key factors that facilitated the child's bilingual development: one was the parents' consistency of choice of language and the other was their insistence that the child respects the "one-parent-one-language" principle. There are some noticeable gaps in the existing studies of the input factor in bilingual acquisition. For example, most studies focus on parents as the only or main source of input. There is no systematic study of the role of siblings and peers in bilingual acquisition. Romaine's (1995) typology of childhood bilingualism does not include peers as a key factor. However, observations in bilingual communities often suggest that siblings and peers are a major contributing factor in bilingual children's language development and use, and their input may well be contradictory to that from the parents. For instance, bilingual children from the so-called ethnic minority families in the USA and in Europe tend to use the "majority" language (e.g., English in the USA and the UK, German in Germany and French in France) as their primary language of communication in peer-group interaction, while their parents have a preference for the ethnic languages. Young children born into families with siblings often form a separate social network with other children of similar age and speak the "majority" language among themselves (Li, 1994). This input from siblings and peers is bound to have some impact on the acquisition and development of the two languages in the bilingual child's linguistic repertoire.

The significant role of input in bilingual acquisition seems undeniable. Nevertheless, language acquisition, bilingual or not, takes place in social context. The impact of that context on the acquisition process can also be highly significant, especially in bilingual situations. The languages a bilingual child has to learn may represent very different values and have different social status in the community in question. Some may receive institutional support, for example, in mainstream schools, while others may be stigmatized. Consequently, attitudes towards children's learning of the different languages may be very different for the extended family, the school, and society at large. There are frequent reports that children who have acquired "minority" or "immigrant" languages at home refuse to speak and to be spoken to in those languages in public. In any case, "minority" and "immigrant" languages are usually confined to specific social contexts and have only limited value in daily social interaction. Even if the language is generally considered a high-status language, different individuals may react differently to becoming bilingual.

Another aspect of the social context in which bilingual acquisition takes place is the social economic status (SES) of the family and of the language group in the wider community. In a recent large-scale study of Spanish–English bilingual children in Miami (Oller and Eilers, 2002), SES was found to interact with home language and school language in interesting ways. One might have expected high SES to afford a child certain advantages for any language acquisition, in that belonging to a higher SES group might give great access to stimuli and opportunities for enrichment, or perhaps from the possibility that the "norms" being tested might come from prescriptive norms related higher SES groups. However, results showed that while children from the higher SES group had the advantage for English, children from the lower SES group had the advantage for Spanish. The best explanation appears related to the amount of exposure to the two languages that SES entailed. High SES bilingual children may have had more opportunities to interact with native speakers of English; low SES bilingual children often came from homes in which the parents were fluent native speakers of Spanish and felt weak in their command of English.

Interaction between languages I: the one–system–or–two debate

A central issue in bilingual acquisition is the relationship between a bilingual child's two languages. A number of scenarios have been mentioned in earlier studies, ranging from complete fusion to complete separation of the two languages. Volterra and Taeschner's (1978) study of the simultaneous acquisition of Italian and German by the second author's two daughters was the first to propose a developmental model, which suggested that bilingual acquisition went through three key stages:

Stage I: The child has one lexical system comprised of words from both languages

Stage II: The child distinguishes two different lexicons, but applies the same syntactic rules to both languages

Stage III: The child speaks two language differentiated both in lexicon and syntax, but each language is associated with the person who uses that language

Although some studies both before and after Volterra and Taeschner's had evidence supporting the model, there has been much criticism particularly of the claims made regarding the first two stages. This is generally known as the "one-system-or-two" debate, i.e., do bilingual children begin with a fused linguistic system and gradually differentiate the two languages, or do they start with a differentiated system? Part of that debate centers around the question: what counts as evidence for differentiation or fusion? Volterra and Taeschner (1978) and Taeschner (1983), for instance, based their decision on whether the child made appropriate sociolinguistic choices, i.e., whether the child spoke the "right" language to the "right" person. It was argued that awareness of the two languages as distinct plays a crucial role in deciding the issue of differentiation, and a child's ability to make appropriate language choices reflects that awareness. However, as McLaughlin (1984) points out, the argument that bilingual children separate the languages when they are aware there are two systems is circular unless some criterion is provided for assessing what is meant by awareness other than that children separate the languages. In any case, we need to bear in mind that a child's apparent (in)ability to choose the right language for the right addressee is a rather different issue from whether the child has one or two linguistic systems. Part of the problem is the familiar one of what we can infer about competence from performance.

One piece of evidence that has often been used in support of the fused system view is language-mixing. Some researchers consider the child to be "truly bilingual" only at the stage where there is complete separation of the two systems (Arnberg and Arnberg, 1985: 21). Language mixing therefore is regarded as indicative of inability to separate the different languages. Leopold (1939–49), for example, said that his daughter, Hildegard, who was acquiring German and English simultaneously from birth, was not really bilingual during the first two years because she mixed the two languages together in her utterances. However, as more and more research shows, bilingual children's language mixing is highly structured and rule-governed. It follows the same structural patterns of code-switching as bilingual adults. It is interesting that no one has questioned whether bilingual adults have one or two systems. So why should language mixing be used an evidence for a fused system of children? Genesee (1989: 189) argues that in order to maintain the one language system hypothesis one would need to show that bilingual children could use items from both languages indiscriminately in all contexts. He further points out that even if a young child at the two- or three-word stage of development produces mixed utterances, it may only mean that the child is drawing on his or her total communicative repertoire in order to be understood.

In a detailed longitudinal study of a girl named Kate who was acquiring Dutch and English simultaneously, De Houwer's (1990) provided strong evidence for the separate development argument. De Houwer reported that Kate used only Dutch with monolingual Dutch speakers, but would occasionally switch to English when interacting with Dutch–English bilinguals. Thus, the child seemed aware of the linguistic abilities of the interlocutors. De Houwer further suggested that Kate used English and Dutch in the same manner as do monolingual children of her respective languages. She was, according to De Houwer, already fully bilingual by the age of 2;7. Although lexical mixing was not a focus of De Houwer's analysis, the phenomenon was discussed. In the majority of Kate's mixed utterances, a single-word item, most often a noun from one language, was inserted into an utterance that was otherwise completely in the other language. These mixed utterances were well formed, that is, structurally grammatical. De Houwer used this as evidence for the child's separate rule systems of the two languages. Citing Poplack (1980: 605), she noted that in order to produce well-formed mixed utterances, "the speaker must . . . know enough about the grammar of each language, and the way they interact, to avoid ungrammatical forms."

Meisel (1989) also took issue with Volterra and Taeschner (1978), criticizing their stage of syntactic mixing for being too vaguely defined; he pointed out that the evidence given by Volterra and Taeschner was not sufficient to support the hypothesis that bilingual children must undergo an initial stage of syntactic mixing, a situation which would need to be explained by the child's processing both languages as a single system. Meisel argued that one could only consider those aspects of grammar where the two adult systems differed as valid empirical evidence for instances of syntactic mixing or of differentiation between systems. In addition, one should try to find evidence for or against a non-differentiated syntax in structural areas where the language production of monolingual children in each language differed. Meisel further suggested that if it could be shown that young bilingual children used linguistic structures in which the two adult target systems (including the respective child languages) differed, this would constitute evidence against the one-system hypothesis.

In his 1989 study, Meisel focused on two children whose parents employed the one-person-one-language strategy in the home; the approximate ages covered range from 2;1 to 3;11. The children were video-recorded interacting separately with an adult interlocutor in each of their languages. Meisel investigated two phenomena that in his view could be rightly regarded as "syntactic" in nature and which could serve as test cases for the problem of language differentiation, since they were distinct in the two languages: word order and subject–verb agreement. The results indicated that both subjects preferred the SV(O) structure in both of their languages; however, language-specific word orders also emerged at the appearance of two- or more-word utterances: VOS or AdvSV(O) for French and AdvVS or OVS sequences for German, that is, the fronting of an adverbial or object which triggered subject–verb inversion in German, a so-called verb-second language; such triggering did not occur in French. Moreover, at the same time, the children started using subjects and verb inflections to encode grammatical person, number, and tense. Meisel (1989: 13), therefore, claimed "strong evidence in support of the hypothesis that bilingual children are, in fact, able to differentiate between two languages as soon as they use what may be interpreted as syntactic means of expression."

Further evidence for the differentiated system argument is provided by Deuchar and Quay (2000) who established that their young bilingual subject, M, who was acquiring Spanish and English from birth, had translation equivalents already from the beginning of speech, thus refuting Volterra and Taeschner's stage model involving lexical development. Similar evidence is reported by David (2004). Deuchar and Quay (2000) further investigated the extent to which the child made appropriate language choices when equivalents were available. The picture that emerged was of a young bilingual child already at the age of 1;10 developing language in contextually sensitive ways.

Interaction between languages II:
the same–or–different debate

While the one–versus–two–systems debate continues to attract new empirical studies, a more interesting question has emerged regarding the nature of bilingual development. More specifically, is bilingual acquisition the same as monolingual acquisition? Theoretically, separate development is possible without there being any similarity with monolingual acquisition. Most researchers argue that bilingual children's language development is by and large the same as that of monolingual children. In very general terms, both bilingual and monolingual children go through an initial babbling stage, followed by the one–word stage, the two–word stage, the multi–word stage and the multi–clause stage. At the morphosyntactic level, a number of studies have reported similarities rather than differences between bilingual and monolingual acquisition. Garcia (1983), for example, compared the use of English morpheme categories by English monolingual children and bilingual children acquiring English and Spanish simultaneously and found no systematic difference at all. Pfaff and Savas (1988) found that their 4–yearold Turkish–German subject made the same errors in Turkish case marking as reported in the literature on monolingual Turkish children. Muller's (1990) study of two French–German children suggests that their use of subject–verb agreement and finite verb placement in both languages is virtually identical to that of comparable monolingual children. De Houwer (1990) found that her Dutch–English bilingual subject, Kate, used exactly the same word orders in Dutch as monolingual Dutch-speaking children, both in terms of types and in proportional use. Furthermore, De Houwer found in Kate parallels to monolingual children for both Dutch and English in a range of structures, such as non–finite verb placement, preposed elements in affirmative sentences, clause types, sentence types, conjunctions, and question inversion.

Nevertheless, one needs to be careful in the kinds of conclusions one draws from such evidence. Similarities between bilingual and monolingual acquisition do not mean that (1) the two languages a bilingual child is acquiring develops in the same way or at the same speed; (2) the two languages a bilingual child is acquiring do not influence and interact with each other. Paradis and Genesee (1996), for example, found that while the 2–3–year-old French–English bilingual children they studied displayed patterns that characterize the performance of monolingual children acquiring these languages separately and they acquired these patterns within the same age range as monolingual children: (1) they used finite verb forms earlier in French than in English; (2) they used subject pronouns in French exclusively with finite verbs but subject pronouns in English with both finite and non-finite verbs, in accordance with the status of subject pronouns in French as clitics (or agreement markers) but full NPs in English; and (3) they placed verbal negatives after lexical verbs in French (e.g., "*n'aime pas*") but before lexical verbs in English ("*do not like*"). Further evidence of cross-linguistic influence has been reported by Dopke, for example, in her study of German-English bilingual children in Australian. They tended to over-generalize the -VO word order of English to German which instantiates both -VO and -OV word orders depending on the clausal structure of the utterance. Dopke suggests that children learning English and German simultaneously are prone to over-generalize S–V–O word order in their German because the -VO order is reinforced on the surface of both the German and the English input they hear.

Most of the studies that have examined cross-linguistic influences in bilingual acquisition focus on morphosyntactic features. One area that has hitherto been under-explored is the interface between phonetics and phonology in bilingual acquisition. Although most people seem to believe that the onset of speech by bilingual children is more or less the same as monolingual children, there are indications that bilingual children seem to develop differently from monolingual children in the following three aspects: the overall rate of occurrence of developmental speech errors, the types of speech errors and the quality of sounds (Zhu and Dodd, 2005). For example, studies on Cantonese-English, Putonghua-Cantonese, Welsh-English, Spanish-English and Punjabi-English bilingual children seem to suggest that bilingual children tend to make not only more speech errors, but also different types of speech errors compared with monolingual children of the same age. These speech errors would be considered atypical if they had occurred in the speech of monolingual children. Chapter 15 of this volume deals further with the issues of difference versus disorder in bilingual children's speech and language development.

There is one area in which bilingual children clearly differ from monolingual children, namely, code-mixing. Studies show that bilingual children mix elements from both languages in the same utterance as soon as they can produce two-word utterances (e.g., De Houwer, 1990; Lanza, 1997; Deuchar and Quay, 2000; David, 2004). Researchers generally agree that bilingual children's mixing is highly structured and grammatically constrained, although there is no consensus on the nature of the specific constraints that organize their mixing. Vihman (1985), who studied her own son Raivo who acquired English and Estonian simultaneously, argued, for example, that the language mixing by bilingual children is qualitatively different from that of more mature bilinguals. She invoked as evidence for this claim the fact that young bilingual children indicate a propensity to mix function words over contentives (e.g., nouns, verbs, adjectives) – a type of mixing that is rare in older bilingual mixing. However, Lanza's (1997) study, while finding similar patterns in the mixing produced by her two Norwegian-English bilingual subjects, argued that children's mixing is qualitatively the same as that of adults; their relatively more mixing of function words is evidence of what Lanza called "dominance" of one language over another, rather than substantial difference from bilingual adults' mixing. Both Vihman and Lanza, as well as other studies of children's mixing, show that bilingual children mix their languages in accordance with constraints that operate on adult mixing. The operation of constraints based on surface features of grammar, such as word order is evident from the two-word/-morpheme stage onward, and the operation of constraints based on abstract notions of grammatical knowledge is most evident in bilingual children once they demonstrate such knowledge overtly (e.g., verb tense and agreement markings), usually around 2.6 years of age and older (see further Meisel, 1994; Koppe and Meisel, 1995). As Genesee (2002) points out, these findings suggest that in addition to the linguistic competence to formulate correct monolingual strings, bilingual children have the added capacity to co-ordinate their two languages on-line in accordance with the grammatical constraints of both languages during mixing. While these studies provide further evidence for the separate development, or two systems, argument, they also suggest that there are both quantitative and qualitative differences between bilingual acquisition and monolingual acquisition.

Multilingual acquisition

So far we have used the term "bilingual" to cover both bilingual and multilingual acquisition. However, acquiring more than two languages involves some processes that are specific to multilingual acquisition. There is a growing body of literature on multilingual acquisition, suggesting that it is much more widespread than was previously assumed. Research has hitherto focused on two key issues: the dynamic process of multilingual acquisition, and the role of bilingualism on third and further language acquisition.

Hoffmann's (1985) case study of her own children's simultaneous acquisition of Spanish, German and English demonstrates the dynamic nature of
the process of multilingual acquisition. The Spanish input was mostly from
the father and au pairs and German from the mother, while English is the
dominant language of the community and peers. The parents followed the
one-parent-one-language rule. However, the children's vocabulary fluctuated
across the three languages. English became dominant as the children's peer
relationships expanded and strengthened. A similar case was reported by
Dewaele (2000), whose daughter learned Dutch from the mother, French
from the father, and English from peers and adults in the community. She
also learned some Urdu from a child-minder. By one year and two months,
she had a passive vocabulary of around 150 words consisting of French,
Dutch, Urdu and English elements. But Dutch seemed to be her dominant
language as the parents spoke Dutch to each other at home. Dutch-French
mixed utterances began to appear when the girl was two years and two
months, but gradually English took over when she began to socialize with
English-speaking peers. Her Urdu eventually disappeared. Both Hoffmann
and Dewaele suggested that the children in the studies could separate the
different languages. In fact, Dewaele reported that his daughter had clear
metalinguistic awareness of which language to speak to whom and when
before her second birthday.

In both of the cases reported by Hoffmann and Dewaele, the children
had two different languages from the parents and another from the community. This turns out to be a very common pattern of multilingual acquisition. There is a difference in the quantity and quality between the input the
child receives from the parents and that from the community; the input
from the parents tends to be more active and dominant in the first couple of
years of the child's life before his or her social network expands to include
significant numbers of peers and non-family adults. Consequently, the
timing of the child's becoming bilingual as opposed to tri- or multilingual is
also different. Recently, a number of researchers have looked into the effect
of early bilingualism on third and further language acquisition in childhood.

It is clear that the experience of bilingualism and the knowledge of two
languages has an effect on the acquisition of further languages. But opinions
differ as to whether the effect is largely a positive one or a negative one.
Some suggested that learning more than two languages at the same time
added to the burden of language acquisition and young multilingual children needed much longer time for their different languages to stabilize and
mature. Others, however, argued that the more language the child learned
the easier the process of language learning became. Children who were

already bilingual under the age of 3 could acquire further languages and achieve native proficiency very easily and quickly (see Cenoz, 2003, for a review). More recent and carefully designed studies show that the picture is much more complex than has previously been painted. While early bilingualism does seem to have a facilitating effect on the general proficiency of the third and further languages, e.g., learning grammatical rules, distinguishing translation equivalents and differences, specific aspects of the third and further languages may well prove to be difficult for the young bilingual child to process, e.g., distinguishing specific sounds, reading and writing particular scripts. A range of factors may influence third and further language acquisition, for example, typological differences between the languages, social status of the languages and the associated support available to learning these languages, context and motivation of learning, and personality features (see the studies reported in Cenoz and Hoffmann, 2003, and reviewed by Cenoz, 2003).

Bilingualism and multilingualism are widespread but not static and unitary phenomena; they are shaped in different ways and they change depending on a variety of historical, cultural, political, economic, environmental, linguistic, psychological and other factors. Bilingual and multilingual acquisition takes place in social contexts. Our understanding of how bilingual and multilingual children acquire, develop and use their languages will grow as research methodology is defined and refined and our attitudes towards bilingualism and multilingualism change to the positive.

Further reading

Cenoz, J. and Genesee, F. (eds) (2001) *Trends in Bilingual Acquisition*. Amsterdam: Benjamins.

De Houwer, A. (1995) Bilingual language acquisition. In Paul Fletcher and Brian MacWhinney (eds) *The Handbook of Child Language* (pp. 219–50). Oxford: Blackwell.

De Houwer, A. (ed.) (1998) Bilingual acquisition. Special issue of *International Journal of Bilingualism* 2(3).

Dopke, S. (ed.) (2000) *Cross-linguistic Structures in Simultaneous Bilingualism*. Amsterdam: Benjamins.

14

Assessing Language in Children Who Speak a Nonmainstream Dialect of English

Janna B. Oetting

"Linda is a girl. Mary is a girl. They are both . . . *pretty?*" This sentence cloze prompt and response should be familiar to anyone who has administered Newcomer and Hammill's (1988, 1991) *Test of Language Development Primary* (TOLD). Taken out of the test's context, a child's response of "pretty" is a good one. Unfortunately when administering the test, "pretty" doesn't receive credit because it doesn't include the expected regular plural inflection (i.e., girls). For an exceptionally strong language learner, the "pretty" response can be easily interpreted as the product of a poorly designed test question, but for children who have undiagnosed language skills, interpreting the "pretty" response is more difficult. Although "pretty" may be the result of an ill-conceived item, it also may be related to a weak language system, because language weaknesses can contribute both to a child's inability to notice parallel grammatical structures offered in prompts and to a child's inability to generate intended grammatical responses.

When multiple interpretations of a response are possible, speech language clinicians are frequently able to collect additional data to support or refute each interpretation. This same type of hypothesis testing is needed when the child being assessed is a speaker of a nonmainstream dialect of English. Since most language tools were not designed to assess children from nonmainstream backgrounds, however, two additional hypotheses must be tested. In the case of the "pretty" response on the TOLD, the first relates to the child being unfamiliar with the sentence cloze nature of the test item, and the second relates to the mismatch between the way the child's dialect and the dialect targeted on the test expresses plurality. With both of these hypotheses, the child's response of "pretty" reflects a language difference rather than a language weakness.

If hypothesis testing is central to the assessment of both mainstream and nonmainstream English speakers, why then is the assessment of the latter so difficult? An obvious answer relates to the limited number of tools and measures that have been designed for, and validated with, children who produce nonmainstream varieties of English. In short, a clinician cannot support or refute hypotheses without data. The aim of this chapter is to review information about a collection of newly developed and/or recently validated tools that should be considered when assessing a child whose native dialect is not mainstream. The tools can be categorized into three types. The first reflects advances in standardized test development, the second reflects advances in language sample analysis, and the third reflects advances in the development of experimental probes.

Standardized tests

Perhaps the most exciting advancement in standardized test development is the recently released *Diagnostic Evaluation of Language Variation* (DELV; Seymour, Roeper, and de Villiers, 2003). The goals of the DELV are to help a clinician formally document a child's status as a mainstream or nonmainstream English speaker, and regardless of the child's dialect, help a clinician formally rule in or rule out the presence of an articulation and/or language impairment. The screener consists of 17 items and is designed for children between the ages of 4 and 12;11 years. The criterion-referenced tool consists of 117 items (25 in syntax, 17 in pragmatics, 50 in semantics and 25 in phonology) and is designed for children between the ages of 4 and 9;11 years. The standardization sample included 1014 children, and 63% of them were nonmainstream English speakers. Moreover, 28% of the children who spoke a nonmainstream dialect and 34% of the children who spoke a mainstream one were independently classified as language impaired.

One of the appealing features of the DELV is that the procedures and test items used to assess a child's language ability were designed for a wide range of English dialects (e.g., African American English, Appalachian English, Cajun English, Standard American English, Southern English). The DELV achieves this by focusing the test items on language patterns that cut across different dialects of English rather than limiting the patterns to only one language variety. The DELV is also appropriate for speakers whose dialects include low, medium, and high densities of nonmainstream patterns. This is an ideal feature of the test because frequency differences in nonmainstream pattern use vary across speakers, even when these speakers are perceived to use the same dialect, and even when they live in the same community and attend the same schools (Washington and Craig, 1994; Oetting and McDonald, 2002). That the authors developed the DELV with an understanding of the overlapping nature of various English dialects, while also considering the variability that exists across speakers of the same dialect, sets this tool apart from all others that have been developed.

Another appealing feature of the DELV is its focus on language content that has been shown, across different dialects of English, to differentiate children with and without speech and language impairments. For example, rather than test children's knowledge of their existing vocabulary, the DELV includes fast mapping tasks to examine how well a child can extract the meaning of a novel word from a sentence (e.g., a child sees a picture and hears "The girl was sugging the man to send the ball," then the child is asked "Which one was sugging?"). Independent support for the use of novel word learning tasks to differentiate children with language impairments from those who are typically developing can be found in a number of studies that have included both mainstream and nonmainstream English speakers (e.g., Ellis Weismer and Hesketh, 1996; Oetting, 1999; Rice, Cleave, and Oetting, 2000; Johnson, 2001).

Other advances in standardized testing involve recent and on-going re-norming attempts by publishers of existing tests. The re-norming of the *MacArthur Communication Development Inventories* (CDI Gestures and Words and CDI Words and Sentences; Fenson et al., 1993) is an excellent example of this effort. Designed for children between the ages of 8 and 30 months, the format of the CDI is ideal for families from diverse language backgrounds because it makes use of caregiver report and encourages caregivers to consider family-particular gestures, words and utterances. The universality of the CDI's testing format is well attested as similar instruments have now been developed in more than a dozen languages (see http://www.sci.sdsu.edu/cdi). The clinical utility of the CDI and its adapted version for Spanish has also been supported with empirical data for bilingual children who are learning English and Spanish in the United States (Marchman and Martinez-Sussmann, 2002).

Unfortunately, the standardization samples of the original CDIs were heavily represented by white children of college-educated mothers who lived on the East and West coasts of the United States. Thus, even though the format and content of the original CDIs were appropriate for children from a wide range of family backgrounds, the normative data were not. The

CDI is currently being re-normed and is expected to be available in late 2004 (Fenson, personal communication). Although the re-norming effort of the CDI does not identify the dialect status of the standardization sample, it now includes children from a range of minority groups (including Asian, African American, Hispanic and mixed). The standardization sample also includes children who live in diverse areas of the country (including the Midwest and South) and children whose families vary in their socio-economic level as measured by maternal level of education.

Language sample analysis

Although language sample data vary as a function of a number of situational and interpersonal factors, conversing with a child in an informal and non-threatening manner remains one of the best ways to get to know how a child uses his/her language to communicate with others. Because of this, most clinicians elicit language samples from children as part of their diagnostic protocol. What is not routine or consistent across clinicians is the ways in which language sample data are used for assessment purposes. For children who speak mainstream varieties of English, at least three different language sample indices are available. These include: mean length of utterance (MLU; Brown, 1973), Developmental Sentence Score (DSS; Lee, 1974), and Index of Productive Syntax (IPSyn; Scarborough, 1991).

Unfortunately, these three language sample measures are rarely recommended for children who speak a variety of English that is not mainstream. One of the reasons for this is a lack of empirical data to support their use with different English dialects. The absence of normative data is not the only reason clinicians avoid these measures, however. Transcending the problem is a long history of criticism garnered against these measures for children who speak a particular type of nonmainstream dialect, that of African American English (AAE; see Vaughn-Cooke, 1983, 1986; Craig, 1996; Gutierrez-Clellen, 1996, Stockman, 1996).

Much of the criticism has been theoretical in nature and rests on the fact that these measures focus on the morphosyntactic surface forms of English, and it is with this aspect of language that AAE is argued to be significantly different from those that are mainstream. The following statements by Craig illustrate this point. "Methods used for collecting language data and the ways in which we approach their scoring and analysis should not be rooted in the majority culture" (1996: 13) and "Language scoring procedures could be improved by creating taxonomies that are largely unaffected by the morphosyntactic nature of AAE" (p. 14).

Contributing to the criticism is the finding that all three language sample measures do not provide an equivalent means by which to score mainstream and nonmainstream expressions of similar language content. To illustrate this point, consider the utterances, "They're gonna catch beads" and "They gonna catch beads." Both of these utterances are acceptable in most nonmainstream dialects of English, but when calculating a child's MLU, DSS, and IPSyn score, the first utterance would be considered more advanced than the other. According to Vaughn-Cooke (1983), without equivalent scoring, nonmainstream surface patterns may be interpreted as "not good enough." To others, scoring systems that do not provide equal treatment to alternative language expressions lack validity (for additional discussion, see Nelson, 1991).

In the 1990s, we began collecting data to examine the validity of the above criticisms against MLU, DSS, and IPSyn for three reasons. First, while deductive methods play an important role in research, the above concerns had never been tested with empirical data. Second, measures of utterance length and utterance complexity are routinely used by researchers who study a wide variety of languages and cultures, so it seemed untenable that similar methods of analysis would be inappropriate for particular varieties of English. Third, although calculations of MLU, DSS, and IPSyn focus on morphosyntax, there are important differences between them in the ways in which morphological structure is viewed and scored. With MLU, only utterances that involve nonmainstream additions and zero-markings are scored differently from utterances involving mainstream forms. With DSS, each utterance within a child's sample that contains a nonmainstream pattern is reduced by no less than two points, and in some cases the point deduction is even greater. Unlike MLU and DSS, IPSyn does not involve the scoring of individual utterances. Instead, a child's entire sample is searched for two instances of 56 different morphosyntactic structures (for a total maximum score of 112), and most (if not all) of these structures can be found in a number of English dialects.

In Oetting, Cantrell, and Horohov (1999), the effects of nonmainstream surface forms on MLU, DSS, and IPSyn were examined using samples from 31 children who spoke a rural version of Southern White English. In that study, IPSyn scores were not affected by the children's use of nonmainstream patterns, but their MLU and DSS scores were. Nevertheless, we interpreted these effects as clinically insignificant because classification of the children as either typically developing or language impaired did not change as a function of whether an utterance with a nonmainstream pattern was, or was not, included in the analysis. Finally, MLU, DSS, and IPSyn scores for the normally developing children were not statistically different from those reported in previously published mainstream English data sets.

In our 1999 study, nonmainstream surface forms occurred in less than 20% of the children's utterances, and the average percentage of utterances within a sample that included a nonmainstream pattern was only 5.3. Thus, the children's low rates of nonmainstream pattern use may have influenced the results. To further test our findings, we have redone the analyses here with 40 additional samples from children who spoke a southern rural variety of AAE. Sixteen of the samples were from 6-year-olds classified as specifically language impaired (SLI), and the rest were from equal numbers of normally developing age-matched (6N) and language-matched (4N) controls (for participant details, see Oetting and McDonald, 2001).

Like the earlier study, the language samples were elicited by a trained graduate student at each child's school, and the stimuli included toys and pictures. The samples contained 7,957 complete and intelligible utterances, 2,293 (29%) of which contained at least one nonmainstream pattern of English. The average percent of utterances with one or more nonmainstream pattern per sample ranged from 7 to 46; group averages for the SLI, 6N and 4N groups were 32% (SD = 9), 26% (SD = 53), and 29% (SD = 10), respectively. As demonstrated by these statistics, the rate of nonmainstream pattern use was higher for this group of children than for those studied in our earlier work. Nevertheless, like our previous study, the children's rates of nonmainstream pattern use were not significantly correlated to their MLU, DSS, or IPSyn scores (Pearson r for MLU = .18, DSS = −.006, IPSyn = −.22).

Table 14.1 presents descriptive information about the children and the samples. Also included are group scores for the children's MLU, DSS, IPSyn Total Score and IPSyn Sentence Score using each child's entire sample and then using only those utterances within each sample that did not include a nonmainstream pattern of English.

Consider first the data from the full samples. These scores were calculated using procedures recommended for children who speak a mainstream dialect of English. One-way anovas indicated that for MLU, DSS, and the IPSyn Sentence Subtest Score, reliable differences existed between the three groups; MLU $F(2,39)$ 4.19, $p = .023$; DSS $F(2,39) = 4.96$, $p = .012$;

IPSyn Sentence Score $F(2,39) = 3.67$, $p = .035$. In each of these cases, scores of the children with SLI were lower than those of their same-age peers; MLU $t(26) = -2.27$, $p = .037$; DSS $= t(26) = -2.19$, $p = .049$; IPSyn $t(26) = -2.57$, $p = .016$.

Table 14.1 Calculations of MLU, DSS, and IPSyn

	SLI	6N	4N
N	16	12	12
Age in months	77.1 (6)	74.5 (4)	56.83 (3)
PPVT – R[a]	71.4 (10)	102.2 (13)	97.8 (8)
Mean C&I Utterances[b]	188.0 (52)	221.0 (79)	192.0 (63)
Total C&I Utterances	3003.0	2652.0	2302.0
Full Samples			
MLU	4.75 (0.90)	5.90 (1.60)	4.98 (0.60)
DSS	6.22 (1.06)	7.67 (2.14)	6.03 (0.75)
IPSyn Total Score	83.25 (11.74)	91.75 (11.69)	85.92 (9.49)
IPSyn Sentence Score	25.00 (4.89)	29.50 (4.33)	27.50 (3.65)
Samples excluding utterances with nonmainstream patterns			
MLU	4.27 (0.93)	5.28 (1.24)	4.58 (0.58)
DSS	6.48 (1.01)	7.88 (1.53)	6.64 (1.35)
IPSyn Total Score	same as above	same as above	same as above
IPSyn Sentence Score	same as above	same as above	same as above
Normative data			
MLU[c]	–	5.49 (0.97)	4.22 (1.20)
DSS[d]	–	9.84 (1.70)	7.40 (1.51)
IPSyn Total Score[e]	–	–	85.80 (4.21)
IPSyn Sentence Score	–	–	24.47 (2.36)

Notes: [a] Standard scores for the Peabody Picture Vocabulary Test – R (PPVT-R; Dunn and Dunn, 1981) are reported; normative mean = 100 and SD = 15.
[b] MLU and IPSyn analyses were completed on complete and intelligible utterances (C&I) of each child's sample, but DSS was completed on a random set of 50 utterances per the guidelines of Lee (1974).
[c] Normative data were from Leadholm and Miler (1992).
[d] Normative data were calculated from Lee (1974).
[e] Normative data, which are limited to 4-year-olds, were taken from Scarborough (1991).

Next compare the results of the full samples to those calculated from samples that excluded utterances with a nonmainstream pattern of English. Like our previous findings, IPSyn scores remained unaffected by the removal of nonmainstream utterances, but within-group differences as a function of the utterance manipulation were found for MLU and DSS. MLU scores were higher when utterances with nonmainstream patterns were included than when they were not. The children's DSS scores showed the opposite pattern, with the full samples leading to lower scores than the samples with utterances excluded. Interestingly, though, visual inspection of the data indicated that it was only the samples with nonmainstream patterns occurring in more than 30% of the utterances that MLU and DSS scores changed at levels we would consider clinically significant (i.e., change resulted in scores that were .50 different from the original scores).

Finally, it is useful to examine how many of the children's MLU, DSS, and IPSyn scores were consistent with their original language diagnosis when normative data from mainstream speakers are considered. For this analysis, scores from the children's full samples were examined. The bottom row of Table 14.1 lists means and standard deviations for mainstream English-speaking 4- and 6-year-olds; however, to improve the diagnostic sensitivity of the measures, we calculated normative cut-offs that took into account each child's age in months. For MLU and IPSyn, −1 standard deviation was used to classify a child as language impaired and for DSS, impaired status was determined when a child's score was below the 10th percentile (approximately −1.25 SD).

The accuracy of MLU and DSS to classify the language status of the children was 72% and 63%, respectively. For MLU, sensitivity (i.e., percentage of SLI children scoring below the cut-off) was low (37%), but specificity (percentage of 6N and 4N children scoring above the cut-off) was high (96%). Results for DSS showed the opposite pattern as this tool yielded high sensitivity (94%) and low specificity (42%). Findings for IPSyn were similar to those found for MLU, with 11 of the 12 (92%) children in the 4N group presenting scores that were in the normal range. Although the ideal pattern of results would have been 100% diagnostic accuracy for all three measures, the above levels of specificity for MLU and IPSyn are particularly impressive given that high specificity is needed to limit the rates at which typically developing children are misdiagnosed as impaired. Note also that very few tools generate high levels of diagnostic accuracy when used in isolation. Indeed, the *Clinical Evaluation of Language Fundamentals-3* (CELF-3; Semel, Wiig and Secord, 1995), a frequently used test for children who are mainstream English speakers, reports a diagnostic accuracy rate of only 57%.

Independent support for measures of utterance length and complexity can be found in AAE studies by Craig and Washington (2000, 2003), Craig, Washington and Thompson-Porter (1998a), Jackson and Roberts (2001), and Smith, Lee and McDade (2001). Some of the relevant findings from these studies have included small but steady increases in utterance length and complexity scores as a function of a child's age, significant within-child correlations between utterance length and utterance complexity scores, and nonsignificant within-child correlations between these scores and their rates of nonmainstream pattern use. In addition, when length and complexity scores of AAE speakers have been compared to those of their non-AAE English-speaking counterparts (and SES and/or maternal education has been controlled), nonsignificant differences have been reported.

Experimental probes

Researchers often begin conceptualizing new assessment tools through the development of experimental probes. While these probes are not always readily available to clinicians, they are important to consider because they represent future possibilities within assessment. One example of an experimental probe that has received widespread attention involves nonword repetition. Nonword repetition (NWR) tasks require children to listen to, and repeat, a series of nonwords that vary from one to four syllables in length. Because the items on NWR tasks are nonwords, the task is thought to measure a child's ability to process language without being dependent upon the child's knowledge of a pre-existing set of words.

The use of NWR to identify children with specific types of language impairments was first documented by Gathercole and Baddeley (1990) and Bishop, North and Donlan (1996). Soon after these studies, the nonbiased nature of NWR was documented by Campbell, Dollaghan, Needleman and Janosky (1997). Their data were from 156 school-age boys, 69% of which were from a minority (African American or Hispanic) background. Whereas a traditional measure of vocabulary knowledge led to group differences between the minority and majority participants, NWR did not.

Since the publication of these early findings, a number of studies have been completed to further test the nonbiased nature and clinical utility of NWR. NWR studies that have included both majority and minority

Table 14.2 Phonemes correctly repeated (%)

Study	AAE	SWE
Cleveland and Oetting (2004)		
6-year-olds		
typically developing	77.5 (9.9)	84.1 (7.1)
language impaired	65.8 (8.8)	65.9 (12.8)
Rodekohr and Haynes (2001)		
7-year-olds		
typically developing	84.7 (3.95)	85.0 (6.0)
language impaired	77.6 (12.36)	74.0 (10.94)

participants have consistently reported nonsignificant findings for the variable of race and/or dialect (Ellis Weismer et al., 2000; Rodekohr and Haynes, 2001; Cleveland and Oetting, 2004). These same studies and a number of others have also documented statistically reliable differences between the scores of typically developing children and those with language impairments (Dollaghan and Campbell, 1998; Conti-Ramsden, Botting and Faragher, 2001; Conti-Ramsden, 2003).

Table 14.2 presents data from 52 6-year-olds studied by Cleveland and Oetting (2004) and data from 40 7-year-olds studied by Rodekohr and Haynes (2001) to demonstrate the consistency that has been found across studies. Both of these investigations included southern AAE and Southern White English speakers, used Dollaghan and Campbell's (1998) NWR stimuli, and reported the children's scores as the percentage of phonemes correctly repeated. Both of these studies also documented significant effects for language ability and nonsignificant effects for dialect.

Finally, in two of the above studies, the accuracy of NWR to identify 5- and 6-year-olds as typically developing or impaired approximated 80% (81% for 5-year-olds in Conti-Ramsden, 2003; 82% for 6-year-olds in Cleveland and Oetting, 2004). In each of these cases, NWR demonstrated low sensitivity (59%, 56%) with high specificity (100%, 92%). When NWR was combined with at least one other tool, however, measures of accuracy and sensitivity increased to levels greater than 85%. In the former study, the research participants were nonmainstream AAE and SWE speakers living in the United States, and NWR was combined with the Comprehension Subtest of the *Stanford-Binet* (Thorndike, Hagen, and Sattler, 1986). In the latter, participants were mainstream English speakers living in the

United Kingdom, and NWR was combined with an experimental past tense probe.

Other promising assessment tools for nonmainstream English-speaking children include Campbell et al.'s (1997) Competing Language Processing Task, Craig, Washington, and Thompson-Porter's (1998b) informal passive probe and Wh-question probe, and Peña, Iglesias and Lidz's (2001) dynamic assessment procedure (see also Ukranitz, Harpell, Walsh and Coyle, 2000). Although each of these tools has been supported by some empirical data, additional studies are needed to evaluate their clinical usefulness for a wide range of dialect speakers.

Existing challenges

Over 20 years ago, the American Speech Language Hearing Association published a position statement on social dialects. Through this document, professionals were charged with the task of developing tools that could be used to assess linguistically-diverse language learners. The tools reviewed in this chapter are, in part, a product of this charge. Although none of the tools identifies childhood language impairment with 100% accuracy, the reviewed empirical data support their use in clinical practice. Data from these tools, when combined with other data (i.e., data from family and teacher interviews, classroom observations, other testing, and trial therapy) should leave the clinician better equipped than in the past to rule in or rule out a diagnosis of impairment, regardless of a child's dialect status.

The charge set forth by ASHA is far from being fulfilled, however. Clinical adoption of the tools reviewed above still presents a number of challenges. For example, one possible challenge of the DELV is its criterion-referenced format. As noted by McCauley (1996), clinicians are sometimes unaware of their reliance on criterion-referenced decision-making processes because service eligibility is often discussed in terms of normative data. One challenge of the DELV, then, may involve a clinician's reluctance to use it within an assessment. Hopefully, this challenge can be overcome by helping clinicians understand the criterion-referenced nature of assessment and the diagnostic value of testing clinical hypotheses with multiple types of data.

The adoption of utterance length and complexity measures within clinical practice is also not without challenges. Although findings from a number of the studies reviewed in this chapter support the use of these measures for nonmainstream dialect speakers, there exists wide variation in the particular types of indices that have been utilized. Some researchers calculate MLU in morphemes while others calculate MLU in words, some report their results in terms of child utterances while others report C-units and T-units, and finally, some search for expanded lists of complex syntax while the searches of others are more limited.

For research purposes, consistency across studies that vary in their methods adds validity to each set of findings, but for clinical practice, multiple versions of a metric make it virtually impossible to directly compare and join individual data sets. This is an unfortunate situation, especially since some of the measurement differences within these studies lead to within-child scores that are highly correlated to each other (e.g., correlations between MLU-words and MLU-morphemes are consistently higher than .90; Craig et al., 1998a; Oetting and McDonald, 2001). One solution to this problem would be the creation of a large normative and/or criterion-referenced database. A normative dataset that also includes a battery of experimental probes would also facilitate the clinical adoption of tasks like NWR.

Normative datasets that include a number of measures would also facilitate a researcher's ability to identify and test (with sensitivity and specificity measures) the clinical utility of different combinations of assessment tools. In addition, this type of effort would also make it easier for researchers to include child speakers of different nonmainstream dialects within theoretically-based studies of child language and child language impairment. The need for under-represented language groups within theoretically-motivated studies cannot be overstated. Theories of child language impairment are now quickly moving toward the identification of specific phenotypic markers and genetic analysis. For the outcome of this work to be relevant to all children, it is critical that this work includes child speakers of a wide range of languages and dialects.

If and when this work is completed, it is critical that researchers describe the participants with as much detail as possible so that interpretations of dialect are not confounded with effects from other variables. Key variables include a child's race, ethnicity, socio-economic status, place of residence (e.g., urban vs. rural), and social network (e.g., open vs. closed). Each of these factors, while at times has been shown to correlate with nonmainstream pattern use, is a separate variable that can affect (in isolation or in combination with other variables) a child's acquisition of language and his/her achievement in school (for example, see research by Hart and Risley, 1995; Dollaghan et al., 1999). Understanding how nonmainstream pattern use relates to these different sociolinguistic variables within the context of different types of families, schools, and communities is an important goal for future studies.

Further reading

de Villiers, J., de Villiers, P., Pearson, B., Roeper, T. and Seymour, H. (2004) *Raising the Standard: New Approaches for Language Assessment*, www.speech pathology.com.

Laing, S. and Kamhi, A. (2002) Alternative assessment of language and literacy in culturally and linguistically diverse populations. *Language, Speech, and Hearing Services in the Schools* 34: 44–55.

Peña, E. (2000) Measurement of modifiability in children from culturally and linguistically diverse backgrounds. *Communication Disorders Quarterly* 21: 87–97.

Roy, P. and Chiat, S. (2004) A prosodically controlled word and nonword repetition task for 2- to 4-year-olds: Evidence from typically developing children. *Journal of Speech, Language, and Hearing Research* 47: 223–34.

Seymour, H., Bland-Steward, L. and Green, L. (1998) Difference versus deficit in child African American English. *Language, Speech, and Hearing Services in the Schools* 29: 96–108.

15

Childhood Bilingualism: Distinguishing Difference from Disorder

Li Wei, Nick Miller, Barbara Dodd and Zhu Hua

Speech and language disorders in children have been attributed to a wide variety of causes including, for example, hearing impairment, mental retardation, brain injury, or certain genetic syndromes. In addition, there is a population of children who suffer none of these conditions but whose language is impaired. These children have been referred to as "specifically language impaired" (SLI). In general, SLI children show a later onset of language skills, speak less frequently and less accurately, process information at a slower rate, produce more errors than their language normal peers, and may never achieve the language skills of their peers even as adults. Speech and language disorders do not respect ethnic, geographical, religious or any other boundaries imposed by society. Research shows that in any population, bilingual or not, one can expect around 5 percent of all children experiencing difficulties in language learning. Nevertheless, bilingual children often show specific speech and language features (see also Chapter 13 of this volume) that are characteristic of their normal development yet different from the developmental norms of their monolingual counterparts – norms that speech and language therapists, whose work is to help people of all ages with speech and language disorders to overcome their communicative difficulties, often rely on in their diagnosis and treatment. Non- or mis-understanding of such features can lead to under- or over-identification of speech and language disorders in bilingual children. In this chapter, we discuss the importance of distinguishing communicative difference from disorder in bilingual children by focusing on notions of "norm" and "standard" in both monolingual and bilingual language development.

The "standard" language and language standard

A person's speech and language are considered to be disordered when they deviate sufficiently from a norm to interfere with communication. The norm is usually defined as the phonological, lexical, syntactic and discourse features of the standard language. The concept of a "standard" in any language is a result of a number of social, political, economic and educational factors. Usually, the language varieties spoken by the socially, politically, economically and educationally privileged and powerful groups come to gain sufficient prestige to become the standard variety of the language. In Britain and the USA, for example, the so-called standard English is the variety of language usually associated with white, middle to upper class, well-educated, English-as-first-language speakers. Such standard forms become tantamount to official versions of the language that hold currency in education, even when no official language has been designated as such by the national government.

A moment's reflection, however, tells us that most people grow up speaking the non-standard varieties of language first, and only acquire the "standard" at a later age, if ever. Language acquisition takes place in social context, and this social context is first and foremost the family and community where the interaction is mostly informal and spontaneous. Nevertheless, young children are capable of style-shifting before they reach adolescence. The following two extracts are taken from an interview by Romaine (1975: 204–5) with a 6-year-old girl in Edinburgh:

(a) I fall out (au-1) the bed. She falls out (au-1) the bed and we pull off the covers. I fell out (au-1) the bed so D. says, "Where are you J?" I says, "I'm down (au-1) here." She says, "Come up. Babies *dinnae* do that. They should be in their cot" (gs-1). So she gets out (au-1) the bed. She falls out (au-1) cause she bumps her head on the wall and she says, "Oh, this is a hard bed too." So she says, "Oh, I'm on the *floor*" (e).

(b) It's a house (au-0), my house (au-0) that I live in now (au-0), cause I flitted (I-2) (gs-1). The house (au-0) is still in a mess anyway. It's still got plaster and I've no fireplace now (au-0), all blocked up. Working (ing-1) men plastered where they used to be, there and there, and they did (I-1) the same to (gs-0) the fireplace. They just knocked it all out (au-0) (gs-1).

We can see that (a) is much closer to the Scots end of this girl's repertoire than (b). All of the variables Romaine studied have non-standard realizations in (a), e.g., (au-1) indicates a pronunciation with /u/ instead of (au) in words like *down*; (gs-1) indicates the use of a glottal stop; (ing-1) indicates the use of [n]. There are also other marked Scots forms in the first extract such as the pronunciation /fler/ for "floor" and the use of the Scots negative form *dinnae* instead of English *don't*. Extract (b) is by comparison much closer to standard Scottish English.

Style-shifting is an important sociolinguistic concept. The ability to move from one speech style to another, according to context, is an integral part of a speaker's communicative competence. In the meantime, sociolinguists suggest that stylistic variations in the speech of individual speakers often echo the variations which exist between speakers of different social background and characteristics. Sociolinguists argue that linguistic features that are commonly found in less formal contexts also tend to be more common in the speech of lower social class speakers generally. Reid (1978) studied the speech of 11-year-old boys in three different schools in Edinburgh, representing three social classes (middle middle class, upper working class, and middle working class). The children's speech was recorded in four situations: reading a text, interview with an adult, peer-group discussion, and playground interaction. Table 15.1 shows the results of two phonological variables (ing) and (gs).

As we can see, apart from the deviation in the playground situation for the variable (gs) i.e., the use of glottal stops, there is a progressive increase in the frequency of use of non-standard variants of both variables from reading style to playground interaction. The slope is somewhat steeper for (gs) than (ing), which perhaps indicates the greater social significance of this variable. The greatest shift occurs between the reading style and the other three spontaneous speaking styles.

Table 15.2 shows the effect of social grouping, in this case three different schools (1–3) representing three social classes (1 = middle working class;

Table 15.1 Percentage of non-standard variations in the speech of Edinburgh schoolboys in four styles

	Reading	Interview	Peer group	Playground
(ing)	14	45	54	59
(gs)	25	71	84	79

Table 15.2 Percentage of non-standard variants (ing) and (gs) in relation to school attended and style

	School	Reading	Interview	Group
	3	0	5	0
(ing)	2	7	21	45
	1	30	96	100
	3	20	37	58
(gs)	2	22	68	85
	1	31	98	100

2 = upper working class; 3 = middle middle class), in relation to three styles (the playground style has been excluded, because the percentages are the same as those for peer-group interaction).

These figures suggest that children of 11 years old are not only capable of adapting their speech style to different contexts (e.g., they use the non-standard variants considerably more in peer-group interaction than in one-to-one interviews than in reading a text.), but are also aware of the "norm" of the social group to which they belong (e.g., children from School 3, representing middle middle class, use the non-standard variants much less, especially in reading style, than those from the other two schools.) Social class differences in speech style already exist among young children. In fact, the patterns of social and stylistic variation in the speech of these Edinburgh boys are strikingly adultlike. Reid (1978: 169) observes that "It is as true of the eleven year old Edinburgh boys as of older informants investigated previously in a similar way in the United States and in Britain that there are features of their speech which relate in a systematic way to their social status and to the social context in which their speech is produced."

Studies such as Romaine's and Reid's give rise to two important sociolinguistic principles worthy of speech–language pathologists' attention:

1   The principle of style-shifting. There are no "single-style" speakers of a language. Each individual controls and uses a variety of linguistic styles appropriate to the situation.
2   The principle of non-conformity. Although speakers of similar social background and characteristics (e.g., age, sex, social class, social network, ethnicity) tend to share certain linguistic features, no two speakers speak in exactly the same way in all circumstances.

Speakers, young and old, are generally aware of the language standard of the situation in which they find themselves as well as that of the social group to which they belong, and this "standard" has nothing to be with the so-called "standard" language, but is defined by the context of use and the user of the language.

Language standard in bilingual and multilingual populations

The issue of language standard is by no means confined to monolingual speakers of major world languages such as English. Over half of the world's population is born and brought up in bilingual, or even multilingual, families and communities. Many people learn a second or third language at school and some use it regularly at work. There is a growing body of literature on language development and behavior of bilingual and multilingual speakers (see Chapter 13 of this volume). Table 15.3 is taken from a study of language choice patterns of British-born Chinese children in Britain (Li Wei, 1994: 94–5). As we can see, there is a wide range of variation in both in terms of the addressee types and speakers of different ages and sexes.

As in style-shifting of monolingual speakers, bilingual and multilingual speakers can switch from one language to another according to whom they are talking to, the social context of the talk, the function and topic of the discussion. Bilingual and multilingual children learn the rules of code-switching from the community of adults and other children, and are capable of assessing the appropriate language choice of the situation, the topic and the language preference of the listener.

It is important to remember that bilingual and multilingual speakers develop domains of competence in each language, and equal knowledge of all the languages in a bilingual or multilingual speaker's repertoire is rare. For example, a child may learn to speak Spanish as a home language with his or her parents and siblings, and later on enters an English-as-the-language-of-instruction school and interacts with English-speaking children on a daily basis. He or she may have acquired a fairly large "domestic" vocabulary, while the "academic" vocabulary is mostly English. The rate of language development, in terms of vocabulary and grammar, of both languages of such a child may not be equal to that seen in a monolingual child speaking only Spanish or English. Research has shown that bilingual children at different stages of development often show signs of dominance in one of

Table 15.3 Language choice by British-born Chinese children

Age	Addressee types											
	Family members						Non-family members					
	1	2	3	4	5	6	7	8	9	10	11	12
16	CE	C	CE	CE	–	CE	CE	C	CE	CE	E	E
15+	–	C	CE	CE	CE	–	CE	C	CE	CE	E	E
14	–	C	CE	CE	–	CE	CE	CE	CE	CE	E	E
12+	CE	C	CE	CE	CE	CE	CE	C	CE	CE	CE	CE
12	–	–	CE	CE	CE	–	CE	C	CE	CE	CE	CE
11+	–	C	CE	CE	CE	CE	CE	CE	CE	CE	E	E
10+	–	C	CE	CE	CE	–	CE	CE	CE	CE	E	E
10	C	C	CE	CE	–	CE	CE	C	CE	CE	E	E
9+	–	C	CE	CE	CE	CE	CE	C	CE	CE	E	E

Notes: + = girls; C = Chinese; E = English
Addressee types:
1 = grandparent, male; 2 = grandparent, female; 3 = parent, male; 4 = parent, female; 5 = brother; 6 = sister; 7 = grandparent generation, male; 8 = grandparent generation, female; 9 = parent generation, male; 10 = parent generation, female; 11 = child generation, male; 12 = child generation, male

their languages, and even for the so-called "simultaneous bilinguals," i.e., children who are exposed to two languages from birth, one language often develops faster than the other, crossing all the thresholds (e.g., words and phrases, simple sentences, complex sentences) first.

Moreover, normally developing bilingual speakers sometimes show speech patterns which may be considered atypical or even disordered in monolingual speakers. In a study of phonological development of 16 British-born Cantonese–English bilingual children between the age of 25 and 51 months, Dodd, So and Li Wei (1996) report that the children's phonological error patterns were very different for their two emerging languages, and that these error patterns reflected delay or were atypical of monolingual children's developmental errors (see Table 15.4).

While delayed phonological acquisition may not be surprising – given the need to master two phonological systems in the preschool years and perhaps proportionately less exposure to each language compared with monolingual children – the observation of so many atypical error patterns was unexpected.

Table 15.4   Expected, delayed, and atypical error patterns in Cantonese and English

Cantonese	English
Expected	
Final consonant deletion (2)	Final consonant deletion (1)
Stopping (3)	Stopping (1)
Fronting (4)	Fronting (1)
Affrication/Frication (1)	Cluster reduction (2)
Deaspiration (1)	Weak syllable deletion (2)
Deaffrication (1)	Gliding (3)
	Voicing (1)
	Consonant harmony (2)
Delayed	
Final consonant deletion (9)	Final consonant deletion (7)
Fronting (4)	Fronting (3)
Affrication/Frication (4)	Cluster reduction (10)
Deaffrication (5)	Consonant harmony (1)
Consonant harmony (3)	Weak syllable deletion (1)
	Voicing (2)
Atypical	
Initial consonant deletion (3)	Initial consonant deletion (1)
Voicing (8)	Voicing (2)
Backing (7)	Deaffrication (2)
Aspiration (4)	Affrication (2)
Addition (7)	Addition (2)
Gliding (4)	Nasalization (1)
	Transposition (1)

Note: Number of children evidencing the error pattern.

Many of these errors are usually associated with phonological disorder in English and Cantonese respectively. However, it seems unlikely that all of the children in the sample were phonologically disordered, given an incidence rate for phonological disorder of about 3–5 percent for English-speaking children. Rather, it seems plausible that bilingual children have their special language learning strategies and the bilingual environment results in the development of rather unique speech patterns (see also studies of Cantonese-English (Holm and Dodd), Putonghua-Cantonese (So and Leung), Welsh-English (Ball, Müller, and Munro), Spanish-English (Yavas and

Goldstein) and Punjabi-English (Stow and Pert) bilingual children's phono-logical development, in Zhu Hua and Dodd, 2005). The language standard for bilingual and multilingual speakers, therefore, cannot be defined with-out careful consideration of all the social, psychological, developmental and linguistic factors affecting language learning.

Cultural norms and standard

The notions of "norm" and "standard" are not confined to language form but relate to norms of interaction and interpretation. Wide cultural vari-ation exists in the regulation of speech, of entries, exits, interruptions and topic changes (Philips, 1976, and Kochman, 1981). Variation also exists in the uses to which language is put and its role in society. One particular aspect of this which could easily lead to misdiagnoses of language disorder is the use of silence. In Britain and North America, generally, to be verbally fluent, though not verbose, is socially prestigious, while to be silent, espe-cially when introduced to someone for the first time, when a relationship/ situation is ambiguous, or at parties, would be impolite and interpreted as rudeness, disinterest or distress. In the bilingual assessment context it may be misinterpreted as non-comprehension or as inability to respond. Testers would need to be assured that the subcultural acceptable silence was not masking a true language disorder.

Within the British-American cultural sphere, too, there are times when silence is appropriate, as for instance during solemn (religious) ceremonies, in libraries, and, as taught to many children, in the presence of adults, especially a stranger in what is seen as a socially higher ranking position. This might include clinicians and educationalists. A main source of dissatis-faction in medical consultations stems from the clinicians' reluctance to impart detailed explanations, but also from the consultees' reticence regard-ing social-interactive reasons to interrupt, request information, discuss mat-ters they have not been asked about and question decisions made. Dumont (1972) examined the silence of Sioux and Cherokee children and the misin-terpretation of this by white teachers, while Basso (1970) described the respect of silence among Western Apaches in family reunions, courtship and encounters between strangers. A contrast to this was reported by Reisman (1974) in Antigua, where conversational rules seemed anarchic compared even with the pressure to talk exerted by British-American conventions. There were apparently no constraints on how many people would be talking simultaneously; pauses and eye contact were not signaled to permit another to join in or leave. One simply started speaking when one felt ready, and if there was no success at joining the exchange, one repeated the opening remark until heard by someone, or gave up. Further examples of cultural variations in paralinguistic and prosodic features leading to misunderstanding in cross-cultural encounters are provided by Gumperz (1977) and Adler (1981).

Implications for language pathology

The above discussion of norms and standards has wide-ranging implications for language pathology. The most important one has to do with attitudes towards language variation. Speech and language pathologists must see language variation as a normal phenomenon and not as an indicator of communication disorder. Awareness of the range of "language standard" in different communities is a necessary, and indeed critical, first step for developing speech and language programs compatible with the types of language likely to be heard in various communities.

Another important implication of sociolinguistic research concerns the definition of pathological speech. Traditional definitions of speech disorder have typically categorized speech as being pathologic if it deviates sufficiently from a rather rigid, unicultural, middle-class set of linguistic norms. Recent sociolinguistic studies provide a theoretical orientation and database for defining pathology from the perspective of language norms generated by various speech communities. Where existing data are inadequate to permit a cultural orientation to defining and diagnosing communication disorder, clinicians and researchers can utilize the procedures developed by sociolinguists in collecting and analyzing language samples.

This brings us to the issue of assessment in speech and language clinics. English-speaking speech and language pathologists are fortunate to have both standardized tests and "normative" data on monolingual children's language development, on which they rely heavily. However, most standardized tests are based on linguistic presuppositions consistent with "standard" English and do not take into account regional and social variations. For this reason many of these tests, when administered and scored according to prescribed norms, yield data that unfairly penalize speakers of non-standard dialects and give the inaccurate impression of a communication disorder when in fact no disorder exists. Consider only phonological disorder for a moment: it is fairly easy to envisage a situation where aspects of social class or regional variation in speech can complicate a clinical assessment. Assuming a client presents with a fricative simplification process, whereby target labio–dentals and interdentals are realized as labio–dentals and target alveolars and palato–alveolars as alveolars, we might feel we have a relatively common and uncomplicated simplification of contrasts to deal with. However, if this client originates from a region, such as London, where the merger of interdentals with labio–dentals is common and is from a social group likely to use this feature, then this analysis must be challenged. It may well be that what we have there is simply a process affecting the alveolar versus palato–alveolar contrast, with the loss of interdentals simply reflecting community norms.[1] Other speaker variables such as age and sex should also be considered in clinical assessment. Certain variants of specific linguistic variables may reflect older community speech norms, or may be markers of sex differences.

Stylistic variations in speech must also be considered in clinical assessment, if only because so much of the data speech-language pathologists rely on is obtained in ways which are unusual to say the least in comparison with normal, casual conversations. It must be remembered that a client's normal context of interaction is with family, friends and colleagues, not with speech-language clinicians. If all we can gain on occasions is a speech style radically different from that used by the speaker with their friends and family, then we are in great danger of making a false analysis of the linguistic repertoire and abilities normally open to the patient. It would be necessary, therefore, to consider a speech therapy session as a particular communicative event and take into account all the factors involved therein in analyzing and interpreting the language data.

Apart from issues of assessment, the planning of remediation programs must be reconsidered. In the case noted above, serious consideration must be given as to whether training in the production of the contrast between interdental and labio–dental fricatives should be given, when such a contrast may not exist, or exist only peripherally in the client's speech community.

The difficulty of defining what is normal language behavior becomes more acute when bilingual and multilingual communities are concerned. Recent sociolinguistic studies have highlighted the significance of language choice, code-switching and code-mixing among bilingual and multilingual speakers. Nevertheless some people, including professionals in the social, educational and health services who routinely work with the bilingual and multilingual population, still regard a normal speaker as having perfect knowledge of both or all the languages and rarely if ever mixing them in conversation. The notion of *semilingualism*, developed by educational psychologists, is sometimes used to describe a condition where bilingual children are said to know neither of their two languages well enough, according to monolingual criteria, to sustain the advanced cognitive processes which enable them to benefit from mainstream education. As Martin-Jones and Romaine (1985) point out, this line of reasoning is suspiciously like a new version of language deficit theory and cannot easily be sustained in the face of sociolinguistic evidence.

An additional difficulty in assessing bilingual and multilingual speakers, especially children, is that at present it is hard to specify what is developmentally normal. As the study of Cantonese-English-speaking children cited above suggests, bilingual speakers may acquire language patterns in a different way from their monolingual counterparts. Speech-language pathologists therefore cannot simply follow their usual practice of assessing the language abilities of bilingual and multilingual speakers using standardized tests and normative data. Taylor, Payne and Anderson (1987) recommend speech-language pathologists working with bilingual and multilingual speakers should engage in a number of assessment activities that involve cultural considerations. At the pre-assessment level, these activities include:

1 Familiarization with cultural, social and cognitive norms of the individual's community.
2 Familiarization with linguistic and communicative norms of the individual's speech community.
3 The selection of appropriate, unbiased, standardized and criterion-referenced tests.
4 Preparation of culturally appropriate natural elicitation procedure.

At the assessment level, culturally valid procedures must be employed to obtain a sample of the client's communicative behavior. Three essential elements of this process involve:

1 The administration of unbiased evaluation procedure.
2 The collection of idiosyncratic sociocultural and communicative behaviors.
3 The elicitation and observation of spontaneous communicative behavior in a variety of settings.

Following the collection of data from formal tests and natural language samples, the speech-language pathologist must then engage in several post-assessment, culturally based activities. They are:

1 Scoring and error analysis of data from structured and spontaneous elicitations.
2 Consideration of peer and/or community definition of communication pathology.
3 Peer and/or community corroboration of test and natural data.

Because speech and language disorder affects common processes underlying the surface difficulties, some argue that a bilingual child is unlikely to have a disorder in one language and not in the other. This does not mean, however, that the disorder will have exactly the same manifestation in the two languages. In the training of speech and language therapists, it is important to stress the following points:

- The bilingual child's language performance should be compared to that of other bilingual children who have had similar linguistic and cultural experiences, not to that of monolingual children in either language.
- For a bilingual child who has acquired one language later than the other, "errors" in the second-learnt language are to be expected and must not be viewed as evidence of a disorder.
- Mixing two languages or changing rapidly from one to another in the same utterance is normal practice of bilingual speakers and is not an indicator of a language problem.
- Bilingual speakers, especially young children, may use their languages creatively and playfully; for instance, knowingly adding a sound which exists in one of his or her languages to the beginning or end of words of the other language or putting words from one language in an order only acceptable (grammatical) in the other language. Such creative use of the languages often indicates the child's linguistic awareness and competence rather than disorder.
- Language loss is a normal phenomenon in bilingual and multilingual speakers when opportunities to hear and use one of the languages are withdrawn or minimized.

Nevertheless, if we do regard bilingual children as "normal," then it is expected that around 5 percent of them would experience problems at some stage during language learning like their monolingual peers, where the underlying difficulty is a disorder, as opposed to merely issues in acquiring a second or subsequent language. The following is a list of possible symptoms of potential speech and language disorders in bilingual children:

- Inability to produce certain sounds which are common in the speech of children of similar age no matter which language he or she is encouraged to speak.
- Inability to understand words which are familiar to children of similar age no matter which language you use to speak to him or her.
- Inability to say words which are common in the vocabulary of children of similar age no matter which language he or she is encouraged to speak.
- Inability to remember the pronunciation of new words no matter which language is being taught to him or her.
- Inability to express himself or herself in grammatical sentences no matter which language he or she is trying to speak.

The following situations would be more likely to indicate less than perfect acquisition of one of the languages, but not disorder:

- Knowing many more words in one language than the other, and seldom or never using one of the languages for some words.
- Making pronunciation errors in one language but can produce the same or similar sounds in another language.
- Keen to learn new words in one language but not the other.
- Able to express himself or herself grammatically in one language but not the other.
- Fluent in one language but not the other.
- Occasionally choosing the "wrong" language to the "wrong" person.

It is important to stress that bilingual children are no more or less at risk of developing speech and language disorder than monolingual children. While we need to know a lot more about normal developmental patterns of bilingual children's language behavior, the fact that a child has two or more languages in his or her repertoire does not in itself lead to speech and language disorder.

Acknowledgments

This chapter is based on Li Wei and Zhu Hua (1999), Sociolinguistics and language pathology, in F. Fabbro (ed.), *Concise Encyclopaedia of Language Pathology* (pp. 149–55), Amsterdam: Elsevier Science; Li Wei, N. Miller, and B. Dodd (1997), Distinguishing communicative difference from language disorder, *Bilingual Family Newsletter* 14: 3–4; and N. Miller (1984), Language problems and bilingual children, in N. Miller (ed.), *Bilingualism and Language Disability* (pp. 81–103), London: Croom Helm.

Note

1   We have taken the examples from Ball (1992).

Further reading

Duncan, D. (ed.) (1989) *Working with Bilingual Language Disability*. London: Chapman and Hall.

Isaac, K. (2002) *Speech Pathology in Cultural and Linguistic Diversity*. London: Whurr.

Kayser, H. and Kayser, H. G. R. (eds) (1995) *Bilingual Speech-language Pathology: A Hispanic Focus*. San Diego, CA: Singular.

Mattes, L. and Omark, D. (eds) (1991) *Speech and Language Assessment for the Bilingual Handicapped*, 2nd edn. Oceanside, CA: Academic Communication Associates.

16

Speech Perception, Hearing Impairment and Linguistic Variation

Cynthia G. Clopper and David B. Pisoni

Speech perception may be thought of as a process of decomposition of the complex acoustic signal into a number of psychologically-real perceptual dimensions. Klatt (1989) outlined three basic sources of information in the acoustic speech signal: the linguistic message, the attributes of the talker, and the communication channel. Variability is inherent to each of these three sources: the linguistic content of the message is affected by segmental, word-level, and prosodic interactions; talkers differ in terms of their dialect, age, and gender and a single talker can produce a variety of different voice qualities and speaking rates; and the communication channel can be affected by filtering (such as over the telephone), background noise, and degradation. From this complex and highly variable signal, the listener must determine not only the content of the linguistic message (i.e., the meaning intended by the talker), but also use attributes of the signal to obtain information about the talker and the communication setting.

During World War II, research on speech intelligibility focused on extracting the linguistic content of the message from a noisy signal over telephone and radio communication equipment (Miller, 1946). More recently, however, Pisoni (1997) and his colleagues have explored the role of talker-specific information in a range of spoken language processing tasks. Talker-specific, or "indexical," information includes properties of the talker such as gender, age, regional or social dialect, and emotional state. Abercrombie (1967) defined indexical properties as those aspects of the speech signal which index some characteristic of the talker, such as his or her identity, group membership (e.g., race, ethnicity, or region of origin), or current emotional state. In cases where the talker is familiar to the listener, this information may also include the explicit recognition and identification of the talker. Recent studies have shown that speech perception is a "talker-contingent" process and that the indexical properties of the talker can both facilitate and interfere with speech perception under different experimental conditions. For example, in spoken word recognition tasks in noise with normal-hearing adults, talker familiarity has been shown to facilitate performance (Nygaard, Sommers and Pisoni, 1994), whereas talker variability interferes with performance (Mullennix, Pisoni and Martin, 1989). Talker variability interference effects have also been reported for hearing-impaired adults (Kirk, Pisoni and Miyamoto, 1997), adult cochlear implant users (Sommers, Kirk and Pisoni, 1997), and normal-hearing children (Ryalls and Pisoni, 1997). Infants, however, demonstrate facilitation effects for talker variability in word recognition, suggesting that early exposure to indexical variability in development helps in the formation of robust lexical categories (Houston, 1999). The facilitation effects due to talker familiarity suggest that speech perception involves the encoding of both linguistic and indexical information in memory and that these memory traces can be used later in explicit word recognition tasks with familiar talkers. The interference effects of talker variability, on the other hand, reveal the integral nature of speech processing across a number of different populations. The indexical and linguistic properties of speech are processed together in speech perception.

In addition to its well-documented role in speech perception, talker-specific information, such as the identity of the talker, his or her gender, and regional, social, or ethnic dialect, is also important in communicative settings. Participants in a conversation can learn a lot about each other from the indexical properties of a talker's speech and can use this information to better communicate. In fact, participants often respond to the talker-specific properties of their interlocutors through explicit (although potentially unconscious) accommodation towards, or away from, the speaking style of their audience for any number of social reasons (Bell, 1997; Giles and Powesland, 1997). Given the importance of indexical information in speech processing and social interaction, it is important to understand how this information is processed and encoded by normal and clinical populations. Traditional clinical assessments of hearing impairment have focused almost exclusively on the perception of linguistic elements such as words or phonemes. However, the importance of talker-specific information in spoken language processing cannot be denied. In this chapter, we will focus specifically on the perception and processing of talker-specific features such as identity, gender, and dialect. After an introduction to these topics in normal-hearing populations, we will discuss recent findings on hearing-impaired populations, particularly deaf children and adults who use cochlear implants.

Perception of talker variation by normal populations

Talker identification

The ability to identify familiar voices was first examined 50 years ago by Pollack, Pickett and Sumby (1954) who explored effects of utterance length, filtering, and voice quality on voice identification. Not surprisingly, they found that listeners were quite good at identifying familiar talkers, even under degraded listening conditions such as filtering or whispered speech. More recently, these results have been extended to other transformed signals such as sinewave replicas of speech[1] (Remez, Fellowes and Rubin, 1997).

The robustness of talker identification to degradation has also been found in perceptual learning studies of unfamiliar talkers. In one early study, listeners were able to learn to identify ten unfamiliar talkers by name in just nine sessions in a forced-choice training paradigm with feedback using monosyllabic words (Nygaard et al., 1994). In a generalization task administered on the tenth day, the participants identified the same set of talkers producing novel utterances with the same level of accuracy as on the final day of training. This finding demonstrated that listeners were able to learn indexical attributes of a talker's voice that were independent of the specific stimulus materials used in training. More recently, Sheffert, Fellowes, Pisoni and Remez (2002) trained listeners to identify ten unfamiliar talkers using normal, reversed, and sinewave speech with sentence-length utterances. While initial perceptual learning was slower in the degraded conditions, listeners were able to generalize to the other conditions and identified talkers above chance regardless of the training or test materials (normal, reversed, or sinewave). Sheffert et al.'s results suggest that talker identity can be extracted from both segmental information (such as that found in sinewave speech) and prosodic information (such as that found in reversed speech).

Familiar and unfamiliar talker identification has also been examined in normal-hearing children. Several studies have found that 4- and 5-year-old children are able to identify the voices of their classmates and teachers with above chance performance in both normal and reversed speech conditions (Bartholomeus, 1973). In addition, 3-, 4-, and 5-year-olds were able to identify the voices of familiar cartoon characters (Spence, Rollins and Jerger, 2002). Performance on the voice identification task improved with age, but even the 3-year-olds were able to identify the voices with above-chance performance and all age groups performed more accurately on the more familiar voices. In experiments on voice discrimination, 6- and 8-year-olds performed more poorly than older children and adults in a same–different task, but the 10-year-olds' performance was statistically equivalent to that of the adults (Mann, Diamond and Carey, 1979).

In general, familiar voice identification and unfamiliar talker discrimination are relatively easy tasks. Normal-hearing adults and normal-hearing children show reliably above-chance performance even under degraded listening conditions. Moreover, preschool children can identify familiar voices and the ability to discriminate unfamiliar talkers appears to be fully developed by around the age of 10. Learning to accurately identify unfamiliar talkers is more difficult for adult participants, but that learning is also robust to signal degradation.

Gender identification

Research on the identification and discrimination of talker gender has also revealed that normal-hearing adults and children exhibit few problems with these tasks. Not surprisingly, adult listeners are quite accurate in gender identification in normal conditions, but they also perform well in low-pass filtered and whispered conditions (Lass, Hughes, Bowyer, Waters and Bourne, 1976). Performance in the low-pass filtered condition was almost equivalent to the scores obtained in the normal condition, while the whispered speech caused significantly poorer performance. These results suggest that although fundamental frequency is an important cue used for gender identification, it is not absolutely necessary for accurate identification. Bennett and Montero-Diaz (1982) reported that 6- to 8-year-old children could also accurately identify talker gender in normal and whispered conditions. In fact, the performance of the children in the normal condition was identical to that of adults, suggesting that children learn to distinguish and identify male and female voices at an early age.

High levels of gender discrimination ability have also been found in speeded classification tasks with irrelevant stimulus variation. Adult participants in a study by Mullennix and Pisoni (1990) had no difficulty identifying the gender of the talker as quickly as possible while ignoring the linguistic content of the utterance. When listeners were asked to identify target phonemes and ignore talker gender, however, Mullennix and Pisoni found significant interference of talker variability on phoneme perception, suggesting that indexical properties of the talker such as gender are processed automatically along with the linguistic content of the message, regardless of the task demands. This talker variability interference effect is even stronger in children, who seem to show greater gender discrimination than adults in this type of classification task (Jerger et al., 1993). Moreover, 7-month-old infants are sensitive to gender differences and show less generalization in word learning across gender than within gender (Houston and Jusczyk, 2000).

Normal-hearing adults and children show extremely accurate performance in explicit tests of gender identification and discrimination. Performance is robust to various kinds of degradation, including whispered speech. In addition, like the effects of talker variability in general, irrelevant variation in talker gender appears to interfere with linguistic processing in speeded classification tasks for both children and adults.

Dialect identification

The study of dialect identification and categorization is fairly recent in both the sociolinguistic and speech perception literatures. While there is a long history of research on dialect attitudes dating back to the 1960s that examined participants' judgments of voices on subjective dimensions such as politeness, intelligence, and laziness, perceptual studies of explicit dialect identification have only been carried out in the last decade. Preston (1993) found that naïve adults were able to make broad north–south distinctions among nine talkers representing nine cities between Dothan, Alabama, and Saginaw, Michigan. Purnell, Idsardi and Baugh (1999) reported that adults could also make ethnic and racial distinctions based on short samples of speech. More recent research in the Netherlands, United Kingdom, and the United States has revealed that naïve listeners can categorize unfamiliar talkers in forced-choice tasks with above chance performance (Van Bezooijen and Gooskens, 1999; Van Bezooijen and Ytsma, 1999; Williams, Garrett and Coupland, 1999; Clopper and Pisoni, 2004). Van Bezooijen and Gooskens (1999) also reported that adults can accurately categorize unfamiliar talkers by dialect in low-pass filtered and monotonized conditions, suggesting that both prosodic and segmental information contribute to accurate dialect identification.

The only study of explicit dialect categorization in children was conducted in Wales by Williams et al. (1999). The results of their study revealed that the children performed more poorly than adults, but the children's performance was still above chance. Nathan, Wells and Donlan (1998) have also shown that children between the ages of 4 and 7 years old show interference effects in a word repetition task when a non-native dialect is used for the stimulus materials. We again find evidence of interference of talker-specific information in linguistic processing tasks in children, suggesting that the automaticity of processing indexical information is achieved early in perceptual development.

Overall, adults and children with normal hearing are not nearly as proficient at dialect identification of unfamiliar talkers as they are at familiar talker or gender identification, where performance is near ceiling. In addition, the results of the research with children suggest that the development of dialect identification skills may be somewhat delayed relative to that of gender identification. Additional research on dialect perception in normal-hearing children is needed to understand the development of dialect categorization abilities and the effects of early linguistic experience.

Research on the perception and processing of indexical characteristics of the talker such as his or her identity, gender, and dialect has made great strides in the last few decades. Researchers have employed a number of different experimental methodologies that have revealed both facilitative and interference effects on linguistic processing, and various kinds of degradation, which demonstrate the importance of both segmental and prosodic information in the identification of indexical properties of speech. In general, normal-hearing adults and children are able to reliably perform explicit tasks of talker, gender, and dialect identification even in cases of signal degradation such as filtering and reversed, whispered, and sinewave speech. We now turn our attention to the speech perception abilities of adult and pediatric cochlear implant users.

Perception of talker variation by post-lingually deafened adult cochlear implant patients

Almost all of the clinical research on the speech perception abilities of post-lingually deafened adult cochlear implant (CI) users has focused on the processing of linguistic information, such as word recognition and phoneme discrimination. However, Kirk and her colleagues (Kirk, Houston, Pisoni, Sprunger and Kim-Lee, 2002; McDonald, Kirk, Krueger and Houston, 2003) have recently begun to examine talker discrimination abilities in deaf adults with cochlear implants. Adult CI users showed poorer overall performance than normal-hearing adults on talker discrimination tasks using word-length and sentence-length stimuli. In addition, the CI users responded more slowly overall than the normal-hearing control group (Kirk et al., 2002).

Unlike the research discussed above for normal-hearing populations that explored both familiar and unfamiliar talker identification, the research on adult CI users has been limited to studies of unfamiliar talker discrimination abilities. Case studies of brain-damaged patients, however, have revealed a double dissociation between familiar voice recognition and unfamiliar voice discrimination in phonagnosic patients (Van Lancker, Kreiman and Cummings, 1989). In particular, lesions in the right parietal lobe led to impaired voice recognition whereas temporal lobe damage in either hemisphere led to impaired voice discrimination. These results suggest that talker recognition and discrimination are fundamentally different processes that draw on different neural circuits, even in the absence of peripheral sensory deficits such as hearing impairment. Clearly, more research on hearing-impaired listeners' abilities to recognize familiar talkers is needed to explore this aspect of talker identification. To our knowledge, no research on the problem of familiar talker recognition has been carried out with hearing-impaired adults or cochlear implant patients.

Gender identification has not explicitly been examined in adult CI users, but the results of the talker discrimination studies have shed some light on this issue. In particular, McDonald et al. (2003) used both same-gender trials and different-gender trials in the different-talker condition in their talker discrimination task. They found that the CI users performed better on the different-gender trials than the same-gender trials. In fact, CI users performed at the same level of accuracy as the normal-hearing listeners in the different-gender trials when the linguistic content was also varied across the two talkers. These results suggest that CI users are able to discriminate male from female talkers and use that source of information to correctly identify two talkers as being different. In cases where the linguistic content varied and was potentially distracting, adult CI users performed at the same level as normal-hearing listeners in gender discrimination.

In a recent case study of dialect categorization performance by a single adult CI user, Mr "S.," we also found evidence that he was able to extract enough indexical information from the speech signal to perform certain tasks at levels similar to normal-hearing adults. The patient was a postlingually deafened 40-year-old CI user with eight years of implant experience who participated in a six-alternative forced-choice categorization task of American English regional dialects without feedback (see Goh, Pisoni, Kirk and Remez, 2001; Herman and Pisoni, 2002, for more details about Mr "S."). Mr "S." became deaf at age 30 and was implanted at age 32. The categorization task was modeled after our earlier studies with normal-hearing adult listeners (Clopper and Pisoni, 2004).

Mr "S."'s performance on a six-alternative forced-choice categorization task was statistically above chance and was within one standard deviation of the mean performance of a group of normal-hearing controls. In an interview following the task, our patient expressed his frustration with the difficulty of the task, noting that he felt he was losing his auditory memory for dialect variation. Despite his frustration, however, Mr "S." was still able to reliably identify where a set of unfamiliar talkers were from using sentence length utterances. In addition, the pattern of his errors was similar to those made by normal-hearing adults in our earlier studies. Mr "S." made more errors on the less-marked dialect regions such as the West and the Midland areas than on the more marked areas such as New England and the South.

One of the most interesting aspects of Mr "S."'s performance on the dialect categorization task was that he had participated in an earlier perceptual learning study using a similar methodology and similar materials three years prior to his participation in the categorization study. In the perceptual learning study, Mr "S." also performed statistically above chance on the learning trials, but his performance during generalization was at chance. In addition, his performance was more than one standard deviation below the mean of a normal-hearing control group during both learning and generalization.

One explanation for the difference in performance between the earlier perceptual learning experiment and the categorization task without feedback is the difference in task demands. In the perceptual learning task, Mr "S." needed to learn to associate one voice with one region over a number of trials during learning and he may have been trying to pick out specific attributes of the speech signal to use, adapting his strategy based on the feedback he received about the accuracy of his responses. In the categorization task without feedback, however, Mr "S." was not required to learn anything new and was not given any feedback or information about his performance on the categorization task. Therefore, he may have used a more general strategy that permitted him to better access his long-term representations of dialect variation that he acquired prior to the onset of his deafness, which may have led to better overall performance.

Taken together, these two sets of results suggest that, like normal-hearing adults, adult CI users are able to extract both linguistic and indexical information from the speech signal they receive through their cochlear implant. In some cases, performance by adult CI users is indistinguishable from the performance of normal-hearing adults. The results of the talker discrimination and dialect categorization studies with adult CI users are promising, but further research with a variety of methods is necessary to explore the full range of CI patients' perceptual abilities and deficits in processing non-linguistic aspects of the speech signal.

Perception of talker variation by pre-lingually deafened pediatric cochlear implant patients

The literature on the perception of talker-specific information by pediatric CI users is more extensive than the findings obtained for adults. In a series of studies on talker discrimination, Cleary and Pisoni (2002) found that pediatric CI users generally performed worse than normal-hearing children. When asked to discriminate two talkers based on sentence-length utterances, the normal-hearing children performed very well, but the pediatric CI users performed statistically at chance. Cleary, Pisoni and Kirk (in press) then conducted a study using digitally-processed natural speech to examine the degree of pitch difference required for normal-hearing and hearing-impaired children to discriminate two voices as being different. They found that the pediatric CI users required a much greater pitch difference to discriminate the talkers than the normal-hearing children and that some of the CI children were unable to perform the task reliably at all. Cleary et al. (in press) also reported that the CI children's performance on the talker discrimination task was significantly correlated with other speech and language measures such as spoken word identification. These correlations provide additional evidence for the link between indexical and linguistic information in spoken language processing, even in hearing-impaired children.

The perception of talker gender has also been explored in more depth for hearing-impaired children than adults. In an explicit test of gender identification, children with cochlear implants were able to reliably discriminate male from female voices (Osberger et al., 1991). In addition, children's performance on gender identification tasks showed steady improvement over time after implantation (Staller, Dowell, Beiter and Brimacombe, 1991). Finally, in a speeded classification task with interference, mildly to severely hearing-impaired children showed normal gender discrimination abilities relative to normal-hearing children (Jerger, Martin, Pearson and Dinh, 1995). These findings support the proposal that the perception of talker-specific information is an automatic, integral part of speech perception even in hearing-impaired children and pre-lingually deafened pediatric CI users.

While no studies of dialect categorization have been conducted with pediatric cochlear implant users, one recent paper examined the performance of children with speech delays using a lexical decision task with familiar and unfamiliar dialects (Nathan and Wells, 2001). The results revealed normal performance by the speech-delayed children for the familiar dialect, but more impaired performance relative to a typically developing control group for the unfamiliar dialect. Again, the results suggest that indexical information is perceived and processed in both normal and delayed populations and that these sources of information in the speech signal can interfere with processing of the linguistic content of the message. Given that children with hearing impairment typically exhibit speech and language delays and that they can clearly process some indexical properties, such as gender, more research is needed to examine their abilities to identify and discriminate different regional, social, and ethnic dialects of unfamiliar talkers.

Conclusion

The research reviewed above clearly demonstrates that indexical information is processed automatically and simultaneously with linguistic information in a range of spoken language processing tasks. Indexical information in speech is encoded and stored in memory and can be explicitly retrieved for the identification of talkers by name, gender, or dialect. In addition, the simultaneous processing of linguistic and indexical information can lead to interference of indexical information in linguistic-oriented categorization, classification, and discrimination tasks. These generalizations are true for normal-hearing and hearing-impaired children and adults.

The use of several different experimental methods to collect data on these perception effects provides broad converging support for the results presented above. In particular, the results of the case study on Mr "S." suggest that similar tasks with different goals might encourage the use of different strategies in clinical populations which can lead to different outcomes. In addition, much of the research discussed above involved explicit identification of specific properties of the talker while explicit studies of discrimination (such as same–different tasks) were fairly rare. Given the results of the lesion study by Van Lancker et al. (1989) discussed above, more research is needed that assesses performance in both identification and discrimination tasks to provide converging evidence about the abilities of normal and hearing-impaired populations to access and process indexical information in the speech signal.

Another recurring theme in the research discussed above was the relative importance of segmental and prosodic information in identifying indexical properties of the talker. Research on talker, gender, and dialect identification all reveal that both kinds of information in speech are important, but that neither is entirely necessary. Talker gender can be identified in the absence of pitch information and dialect can be identified in the absence of segmental information. Future research on the perception of talker-specific properties of speech should consider not only the perception of variation, but also the production of variation in speech in order to determine which features of the signal are important for identification of talker attributes at both segmental and prosodic levels.

While variation due to gender and regional, social, and ethnic dialects has been studied fairly thoroughly by sociolinguists, the implications of this variation for speech perception processes in clinical populations have been left largely unexplored until recently. Sociolinguistic research has shown that normal adults use variation in the speech signal to make a number of judgments about the talker, from attitudes about personality to social status to gender and ethnicity. Adults make these judgments quickly and easily, but little is known about how that information is processed or stored, much less how hearing-impaired individuals cope with the variability they encounter in their daily lives. The limited evidence accumulated so far suggests that hearing-impaired adults and children are able to extract both indexical and linguistic information from the highly degraded signal they receive and they can use these sources of information in typical ways in some cases. More research is clearly warranted for both normal and clinical populations to understand the role of indexical information in spoken language processing.

The integral nature of linguistic and indexical information in speech perception has been shown in infants, children, and adults and in clinical populations, including hearing-impaired adults and children, brain damaged adults, and children with speech delays. Clearly, the sources of variation in the speech signal that Klatt (1989) described are relevant for everyone, not just normal-hearing adults with typical speech and language skills. The mental representations of speech must include information about the abstract linguistic symbols that are linked to semantic memory, as well as utterance-specific information about who the talker is, where she or he is from, and the contextual setting of the conversation. While the phonological and lexical representations of clinical populations might be expected to differ from those of normal populations in some ways due to impaired peripheral sensory systems, these representations still reflect the variable sources of information that contribute to the complex speech signal.

Acknowledgments

This work was supported by the NIH NIDCD T32 training grant DC00012 and R01 research grant DC00111 to Indiana University. The authors would like to thank Luis Hernandez for his technical advice and support, Brianna Conrey and Caitlin Dillon for their help with the case study, and Mr "S." for his patience and willingness to participate in our perceptual experiments.

Note

1   Sinewave speech is synthesized from natural tokens of speech using three or four sinewaves that follow the trajectory of the first three formants and, optionally, the frequency locus of fricatives. If listeners are told that the sinewave pattern is synthetic speech, they are typically able to understand the utterances after a short period of exposure.

Further reading

Johnson, K. and Mullennix, J. W. (eds) (1997) *Talker Variability in Speech Processing*. San Diego, CA: Academic Press.
Murphy, G. L. (2002) *The Big Book of Concepts*. Cambridge, MA: MIT Press.
Pisoni, D. B. and Remez, R. E. (eds) (2005) *Handbook of Speech Perception*. Oxford: Blackwell.
Preston, D. R. (ed.) (1999) *Handbook of Perceptual Dialectology*. Amsterdam: John Benjamins.

17

Aphasia in Multilingual Populations

Martin R. Gitterman

Research on aphasia (language loss following damage to the brain, frequently the result of a stroke) has been the focus of study for many years. This multifaceted research has focused on classifying types of aphasia (based on the specific language deficits manifested), advancing hypotheses about the organization of language in the brain, speculating on differences in the monolingual and bilingual brain, attempting to design appropriate methods of assessment, and recommending appropriate therapy, to name a few areas. In our current society, which is increasingly sensitive to the needs of the multitude of people who are bilingual, work on bilingual aphasia has fortunately intensified. As Paradis notes, "Until rather recently, because of a long-standing habit, most hospital staff involved in the assessment and treatment of aphasia did not take into consideration the fact that patients spoke more than one language" (1998: 35–6). As our knowledge of aphasia increases, our understanding of the complexities of the human brain grows as well. Grosjean asserted, "the bilingual brain is still very much terra incognita" (1982: 267). Although work in neurolinguistics and aphasiology is ongoing, most would agree that this assertion is in large measure still applicable (see, for example, Fabbro, 2001b). While research on bilingual aphasia is of great interest from a purely theoretical perspective, there exists a very clear, and at least equally important, applied dimension to its study. This dimension includes the assessment of patients with aphasia (aimed at specifying the nature of their language loss) in addition to understanding the dynamics of the therapy used in treatment. Clearly, the stronger the theoretical grounding, the more confident one can feel about decisions made regarding the assessment and treatment of bilinguals with aphasia.

In this chapter the issue of the organization of language in the bilingual brain will be addressed. Reference to the numerous recovery patterns observed in bilinguals with aphasia will be incorporated. The suggestion by some that the bilingual brain might be organized differently from the mono-lingual brain will be discussed as part of a broader framework, one in which language-specific factors hypothesized to influence language representation in the brain are noted. These language-specific factors include the visuospatial dynamic inherent in sign language as well as the unique linguistic role assigned to pitch in a tone language. Next, advances made in recent years in assessing bilingual patients with aphasia will be outlined. Finally, reference will be made to treatment, with particular focus on the extent to which improvement resulting from treatment in only one of the languages of a bilingual is thought to carry over to the other language. While the term *bilingual* refers to those who speak two languages, its use in this chapter is extended to include those who speak three or more languages (multilinguals).

Language organization in the brain

It is agreed that the left hemisphere is dominant for language in most people, with such dominance estimated to exist in over 95 percent of right-handers (Fabbro, 1999). While reported figures on left-hemisphere domin-ance in left-handers vary somewhat, it is, nevertheless, established that left hemisphere dominance in left-handers is much lower (e.g., reported to exist in about 70 percent of this population by Restak, 1988; see also, Bryden, 1982, and Porac and Coren, 1981, for additional discussion, including refer-ence to bilateral representation found in a number of left-handers). The nature of possible differences in the participation of the right hemisphere in monolinguals and bilinguals has received much research attention. Albert and Obler, subsequent to a thorough review of the relevant literature, suggest a possible increased right hemisphere role in bilinguals. They state, "The evidence suggests a need for revision of the traditional concept of cerebral dominance for language" (1978: 243). The suggestion of a greater right hemisphere role in organizing language in bilinguals has been contro-versial, with numerous skeptics. Mendelsohn (1988), for example, asserts that the frequent revisions in models depicting an increased right hemi-sphere involvement in bilinguals are the result of no single model being able to account for all the data. She concludes, "Taken together, clinical and experimental data provide at present no unequivocal evidence that lateralization in bilinguals is 'exceptional' in any way" (p. 284). Reports of a greater incidence of aphasia following a right hemisphere lesion in right-handers (known as crossed aphasia) among bilinguals have served as evidence of a greater involvement of the right hemisphere in bilinguals (e.g., Albert and Obler, 1978; Galloway, 1980). Mendelsohn rejects such reports, however, arguing that these cases of crossed aphasia are not typical (see also Paradis, 1998). In fact, Paradis argues that "neuroanatomically" and "neurofunctionally" there is one system applicable to both monolinguals and bilinguals. Any reported differences in right hemisphere participation in bilinguals can be explained by the need to rely more on modalities of communication associated with the right hemisphere (e.g. pragmatics). He notes that greater use of the right hemisphere in the second language of a bilingual, assuming it is the weaker language (and thus at a somewhat earlier stage of grammatical development), is understandable as the individual might be more dependent on pragmatic aspects of language to facilitate communication. Research comparing monolinguals and bilinguals has not been limited to hypothesized inter-hemispheric differences. Within-hemisphere differences have been suggested in many studies as well. In a frequently cited study involving electrical stimulation, Ojemann and Whitaker (1978) found that in the two bilinguals they tested (one left hemisphere dominant and the other right hemisphere dominant), there was differential within-hemisphere impairment in a naming task. Interestingly, they also found the second language to be organized in a somewhat larger area of the hemisphere dominant for language than the first language.

A within-hemisphere focus on the role of subcortical as opposed to corti-cal structures has also drawn the attention of researchers. Fabbro and Paradis, for example, noting that advances in neuro-imaging have enabled researchers to learn much more about the role played by the thalamus and basal ganglia, present findings on four bilingual patients with aphasia resulting from lesions "confined mainly to left-hemisphere subcortical structures" (1995: 140). Focusing on these subcortical lesions, their three research questions were aimed at understanding the role of the basal ganglia in language processing, learning whether the languages of bilinguals may be differen-tially impaired, and, finally, ascertaining whether the ability to translate may be negatively affected. They conclude, "Indeed, the basal ganglia of the left hemisphere apparently serve specific linguistic functions, since all our patients presented symptoms of agrammatism, verbal and semantic paraphasias, poor comprehension and echolalia" (p. 144). Also evident are differences in degree of impairment across the languages of a bilingual patient and an apparent link between subcortical lesions and a reduction in translation ability. Regarding differential impairment, the authors note that their findings are essentially consistent with a model suggesting languages acquired with "implicit strategies" are organized more in subcortical regions, while those learned with "explicit strategies" are linked more with cortical representation.

The literature is replete with illustrations of bilingual patients with aphasia where the languages do not recover in a parallel fashion. The fact that such cases exist is consistent with, but not irrefutable evidence in support of, a neurolinguistic model of the bilingual brain in which the languages are subserved by different cerebral areas. Based on a review of 138 published cases, Paradis (1977) delineates various recovery patterns. Parallel recovery refers to those cases in which the languages of a bilingual manifest similar deficits and recover at the same pace. This pattern of recovery was evident in 56 of the 138 cases analyzed. Paradis suspects that the actual percentage of cases in which parallel recovery occurs is higher than suggested by these figures, but notes, nevertheless, that the existence of other recovery patterns, those which are "atypical" in nature, is undeniable. (See Paradis, 1977, 1998, for details of the patterns of recovery along with supporting case studies and additional discussion.)

Albert and Obler (1978) provide detailed information on 108 studies of bilinguals with aphasia (three of which they conducted), including a number of the cases reported by Paradis. The level of detail provided by Albert and Obler on the participants in the each of the studies (see pp. 109–39) makes evident the degree of heterogeneity in this population. Among the factors included in their outline summaries are sex, handedness, native language and other languages, education, details about lesion, aphasia classification, information on manner of acquiring the nonnative language(s), and whether the patient was receiving therapy (see complete list on pp. 110–11). Providing information, when available, on a multitude of factors in addition to the type of recovery pattern, is very useful in comparing patients across studies (see pp. 139–53). The study of the organization of language in the bilingual brain, including the suggestion that the languages of a bilingual might be organized differently in the brain, is better understood when assessed in a broader framework, one in which research on aphasia in allied areas is addressed. Just as some researchers have hypothesized that bilingualism might be a factor influencing where a particular language will be organized, others have questioned whether language-specific factors might determine where a particular language will be localized. Two such factors are the visuospatial characteristic present in sign language and the phonemic status of pitch in tone languages. These areas of investigation are related in that they all attempt to determine whether nonbiological factors are predictors of cerebral organization of language (see Sies, Gitterman and Foo, 1989; Gitterman and Sies, 1990).

The visuospatial nature of sign language has motivated researchers to examine whether sign language will be organized more in the right hemisphere (as the right hemisphere is associated with visuospatial activities not related to language, e.g., drawing). Poizner, Klima and Bellugi (1987), for example, in a study of six right-handed deaf ASL signers, three with left hemisphere lesions and three with lesions in the right hemisphere, find no basis for claiming a difference in cerebral dominance in sign and spoken language. All three signers with left hemisphere lesions manifested symptoms of sign aphasia, while such symptoms were not evident in the signers with right hemisphere lesions. A description of Gail D., who had symptoms of sign aphasia similar to Broca's aphasia is of interest (pp. 76–7):

> Indeed, Gail D.'s particular pattern of language impairment strongly resembles the pattern that is called Broca's aphasia in hearing patients. The characteristics of this syndrome include production that is awkward and dysfluent, lacks grammatical formatives, and is syntactically impoverished; comprehension, however, is relatively spared. . . . Although the modality is different, Gail D.'s signing fits the description of a Broca's aphasic remarkably well, and tests of her comprehension (the BDAE and her responses to the examiner in conversation) show that it is good; her scores on the BDAE comprehension test fall in the range typical of hearing Broca's aphasics.

Of note, right hemisphere damage was shown to disrupt performance in visuospatial tasks not related to language. Sarah M., for example, with right hemisphere damage, an excellent artist prior to her stroke, clearly lost much of her visuospatial skill (see p. 175 for sample artwork before and after her stroke). Poizner et al. point out, "This severe loss of her ability to draw after her right-hemisphere stroke brings out in a pronounced way the spatial loss seen in right-lesioned signers across a variety of visuospatial nonlanguage tasks" (p. 174). In short, their research suggests similar hemispheric organization for sign and spoken language (left hemisphere) as well as for nonlanguage visuospatial activities (right hemisphere). Similarly, Emmorey (2002) concludes her review of research on sign language users (both brain damaged and non-lesioned) by emphasizing that the left hemisphere subserves both sign and spoken language.

Speculating that sign language (visuospatial in nature) might be organized in the right hemisphere, based on the fact that nonlinguistic visuospatial tasks are right hemisphere activities, is analogous to speculating that tone languages might involve greater right hemisphere participation, as nonlinguistic tone (e.g., expressing sadness, happiness, or fear in one's tone of voice) is associated with the right hemisphere (see, for example, Ross, 1981).

In tone languages, pitch changes contrast meanings, with the number of pitch contrasts varying depending on the particular tone language. Understandably, some reported cases of crossed aphasia in speakers of Chinese, a tone language, have served to heighten speculation that its tonal component may have contributed to a greater right hemisphere organization.

In one such study, April and Han (1980) report on a 74-year-old Chinese-English bilingual, who acquired English as a second language after coming to the United States from his native China. April and Han speculate that the crossed aphasia which developed in this man might be attributable, at least in part, to the fact that Chinese is a tone language. They allude to research on nonlinguistic tone (specifically, the ability to distinguish pitch in music) in hypothesizing that the right hemisphere might have an increased role in processing a tone language. Of note, they focus on the nonalphabetic nature of Chinese as a possible determinant of this patient's right hemisphere dominance for language. They ask, "Could it be that reading ideographic characters is processed by visuospatial systems of the right hemisphere to a greater extent than reading phonetic letters of alphabetic Western languages?" (p. 345). This reference to visuospatial characteristics is of particular interest when considered in conjunction with the discussion of sign language above. Regarding language loss in Chinese and English, April and Han report their participant demonstrated a similar degree of impairment in both languages, a finding which is inconsistent with the findings of some other studies (e.g., April and Tse, 1977, where impairment was greater in Chinese in a 54-year-old Chinese-English bilingual with crossed aphasia). April and Han note, "students of dissociative trends in Chinese-English bilingual aphasic patients will have to wait for a substantial number of case reports before conclusions can be reached" (p. 345).

Critically, however, April and Han report that a review of records at two hospitals in New York (one with a large number of Chinese patients) covering a two-year time span, as well as information gathered on patients at the National Taiwan University Hospital, provides no evidence of a greater incidence of crossed aphasia in this group of patients. Numerous additional studies have been conducted on Chinese speakers, without providing any basis, however, for concluding that it involves greater right hemisphere involvement. Hoosain, after an extensive review of the literature on Chinese aphasia, concludes, "In aphasia studies, there is again little evidence to suggest any overwhelming neurolinguistic effects of Chinese language uniqueness" (1991: 162).

The study of bilingual aphasia, of interest from many perspectives, has clearly played a central role in attempts to gain a greater understanding of language organization in the brain. As research evolves, our knowledge about possible differences in localization (inter- or intrahemispheric) will become more definitive, and, of primary importance, so will our understanding of the factors that contribute to particular patterns of cerebral representation. Such research will, undoubtedly, increase our knowledge not only about bilingualism, but about neurolinguistic processing in areas whose study is integrally related (e.g., tone, sign, and nonalphabetic languages) as well. What seems obvious, and what is of particular relevance to students of clinical sociolinguistics, is that an understanding of bilingual aphasia will continue to play a central role in this research. This research endeavor will certainly be facilitated by the use of modern techniques in neuroimaging (see, Goral, Levy and Obler, 2002, for a related discussion, including an interesting overview of types of imaging, along with representative studies with each).

Assessment: the bilingual aphasia test

Before the development of the *Bilingual Aphasia Test* (BAT), there existed no truly satisfactory method of assessing the languages of bilinguals with aphasia. The BAT, developed by Paradis and his colleagues, aims to provide clinicians with a valid measure of impairment in bilinguals with aphasia. As Paradis notes, "for a true evaluation of the patients' linguistic communicative capacities, all of their languages should be tested, and should be tested with an equivalent instrument" (1987: x). It certainly would be incorrect to assert that any clinical setting that does not assess bilinguals in both languages is providing less than adequate care. What does seem reasonable to assert, however, is that even those settings reported to be successful (see Wiener, Obler and Taylor Sarno, 1995, for details of one such setting) can only be strengthened by administering the BAT to its bilingual patients. The BAT contains three parts (all outlined in Paradis, 1987). Part A ("History of Bilingualism") consists of a questionnaire in which information about the patient's language background is elicited. In Part B, after some additional background questions, a series of language tasks (both expressive and receptive, at varying levels of complexity) are administered in each language of the bilingual patient. Finally, Part C consists of three translation tasks and one task requiring judgments of grammaticality. A brief overview of each of the parts follows.

Part A

The questionnaire is designed with a broad spectrum of patients in mind, including those with a number of languages in their background. The "branching format" of questions in Part A means that the number of questions to be answered will vary (from 17 to 50, to be specific) across patients depending on a particular patient's language history. Individuals close to the patient may respond in cases where the patient is unable to supply information (see Paradis, 1987, pp. 48–9, for a complete list of the questions).

Part B

The numerous language tasks in this part of the BAT, Paradis notes, will provide the clinician with data permitting comparisons across the languages for each skill tested. The tasks are designed to achieve the goal of "cross-language equivalence" (see Paradis, 1987, pp. 50–141, for a description and accompanying comments for all tasks in Part B). A small sampling of the tasks are as follows:

1   Complex Commands – The patient is instructed to do something with three objects for each item in this part (e.g., "Here are three books. Open the first one, turn over the second, and pick up the third one," p. 56). Language equivalence is achieved by using the same commands for all languages. (Simpler commands are included elsewhere in Part B.)
2   Synonyms – The patient hears a word followed by four other words (all representing common objects) for each item in this part and is asked to select the word most closely related to the initial word (e.g., canoe: match, boat, newspaper, tree, p. 90). Language equivalence is achieved by using the same words translated across languages, to the extent possible. (The BAT also contains two tasks involving antonyms.)
3   Verbal Fluency – The patient hears three sounds (all consonants) and has to say as many words as possible beginning with each of the sounds. For English, the sounds are /t/, /f/, and /k/ (see p. 107), with language equivalence achieved by choosing the sounds in other languages based on their frequency of occurrence in word initial position. Part B contains more than 25 additional tasks (e.g., syntactic comprehension, sentence repetition, sentence reading comprehension, text reading comprehension).

Part C

For all four tasks, each of which is administered in each of the two languages (see Paradis, 1987, pp. 141–51, for details on each task), the patient is assessed in both directions. The four tasks in this part are as follows:

1 Word Recognition – The patient sees and hears a list of five words in one language and is asked to identify translation equivalents from a list in the other language. The second part of this task follows the same design, but the direction of translation is reversed.
2 Translation of Words – The patient hears a number of words (equally divided between concrete and abstract nouns) and is instructed to translate each word into the other language. The opposite direction of translation is similarly assessed.
3 Translation of Sentences – The patient hears a number of sentences (representing different levels of complexity) in one language and is asked to translate them. Performance on an equal number of sentences (and similarly contrasting difficulty levels), but with the direction of translation changed, is also assessed.
4 Grammaticality Judgments – The patient is asked to judge whether each sentence heard is correct or incorrect. There are an equal number of correct and incorrect sentences in both languages, with the error in each incorrect sentence traceable to interference from the other language (a design feature aimed at achieving "cross-language equivalence").

The BAT, available in an extensive number of languages and pairs of languages, will, undoubtedly, be instrumental in continuing to raise awareness about the value of assessment across languages. In providing a valid instrument for assessing bilinguals with aphasia, it clearly represents a milestone in the evolution of clinical intervention (see Fabbro, 1999, 2001a, for related discussion).

Treatment

Research to date suggests that bilingual patients with aphasia being treated in only one language, a common and frequently advisable clinical practice, tend to show improvement in the language not being treated as well (see

Fabbro, 1999, 2001a). Fredman (1975), for example, in a study conducted in Israel involving 40 bilingual adults with aphasia, found that therapy provided only in Hebrew resulted in similar improvement in both Hebrew and the "home language" spoken by the individuals studied. All the participants emigrated to Israel, except two, for whom Arabic was the other language. The range of "home languages" was broad (e.g., Hungarian, Polish, German), thus incorporating languages with a degree of structural heterogeneity (an issue serving as the focus of other studies, see below). Fredman notes, "It is believed that the results obtained in this study will encourage speech pathologists in other parts of the world to treat adult aphasics even when their home language is not that of the country in which they live" (p. 68). Similar findings are reported by Junque, Vendrell, Vendrell-Brucet and Tobena (1989) in a study of 30 Catalan-Spanish bilinguals with aphasia. Therapy was given only in Catalan, the native language of all participants in the study. Significant improvement was evident in both languages following therapy, though more improvement was demonstrated in Catalan (the treated language) than in Spanish.

Improvement based on therapy in only one of a bilingual patient's languages is believed to carry over even to languages that are not structurally similar (Fabbro, 1999, 2001a). Some findings, while not inconsistent with this assertion, do, however, suggest that structural similarly between languages is a factor in degree of carryover to the untreated language. One such example, reported by Sasanuma and Park (1995), is of a Korean-Japanese bilingual evaluated in both languages prior to and following three months of therapy in Korean only. The participant's post-treatment performance revealed improvement in both languages in all areas assessed (auditory comprehension, reading comprehension, oral production, writing), but with gains in writing in Korean much greater than in Japanese. Sasanuma and Park speculate that the differences in the writing systems (Hangul, in Korean; Kana, in Japanese) contributed to the marked dissociation in performance in writing following therapy. Sasanuma and Park also suggest that the similarity in Korean and Japanese syntax helps explain the high degree of transfer from Korean (the treated language) to Japanese (the untreated language) evident in the comprehension tasks, in particular (see, in addition, related discussion in Ijalba, Obler and Chengappa, 2004).

In sum, research to date on bilinguals with aphasia seems to indicate that gains resulting from therapy in one language tend to be accompanied by gains in the other language, albeit not necessarily to the same extent. Overall, however, these findings should provide a measure of reassurance to clinicians with bilingual clients receiving therapy in one language only.

Conclusion

The extensive ongoing research devoted to the study of bilingual aphasia is certain to increase our understanding of language organization in the brain. There exists a multitude of unanswered questions awaiting additional findings, with very few questions definitively answered at present. It is indeed fortunate that clinicians are increasingly aware of the needs of the bilingual population.

The publication of the BAT has undoubtedly already played a major role in improving assessment of bilinguals with aphasia. It is only hoped that effective assessment (with the BAT or other appropriate measures) will continue to be a high priority in clinical settings. Valid assessment, all would agree, is needed to design appropriate therapy. While research suggesting that there is some carryover from the treated to the untreated language of a bilingual with aphasia is reassuring, additional research will, it is hoped, continue to advance our understanding of this process.

Acknowledgment

I wish to acknowledge the helpful suggestions made by Loraine K. Obler. I am most appreciative.

Further reading

Caplan, D. (1992) *Language: Structure, Processing, and Disorders*. Cambridge, MA: MIT Press.

Kayser, H. (ed.) (1995) *Bilingual Speech-language Pathology: An Hispanic Focus*. San Diego, CA: Singular Publishing.

Menn, L., O'Connor, M., Obler, L. K., and Holland, A. (1995) *Non-fluent Aphasia in a Multilingual World*. Amsterdam: Benjamins.

18

Designing Assessments for Multilingual Children

Janet L. Patterson and
Barbara L. Rodríguez

Children who acquire more than one language encounter different experiences with each language, interact in different types of social situations with each language, and experience different opportunities for learning each language. The circumstances in which each language is acquired reflect the languages used in multilingual children's social environments – in their homes, schools, and communities. Because the contexts in which they experience each language differ, multilingual children typically develop different skills and types of knowledge in each of the languages they acquire.

The social contexts of acquisition and use for each language have important implications for language assessment in multilingual children. First, in order to obtain a comprehensive picture of the child's language skills, assessment must include all languages with which the child has had significant experience. Testing in one language does not tell us what the child can do in the other language(s). Second, the assessment of each language must be done in contexts that are congruent with the child's experience with that language. Even adults who are proficient in two languages have limitations when asked to talk about a topic in one language that they usually discuss in the other language (Romaine, 1995).

Because social contexts are so important in the multilingual child's experiences with language, assessments should be designed with social contexts of language use as the organizing element. Domains of use, such as education, home, and religious activities are comprised of clusters of settings, participants, and topics (Fishman, 1972b). Although domains are useful starting points in identifying the contexts in which children hear and use each language, more than one language may be used within a domain, depending on the participants, topics, and purposes of specific interactions

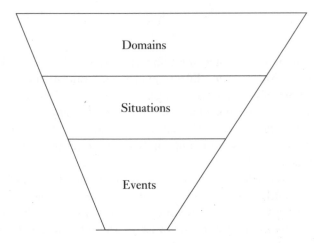

Figure 18.1 Hierarchy of social-communicative contexts

within a domain. For example, in one Head Start preschool classroom in Albuquerque, number and calendar routines were done in English and then in Spanish, reading stories aloud was done in English, and directives to the children regarding behavior were done in English and in Spanish, depending on the proficiency of the child in each language.

Because language use varies within domains, it is important to consider the languages children experience within particular communicative situations (e.g., recess, math, Show and Tell), and the language(s) used in the specific communication events that occur within those situations (Saville-Troike, 2003) (see Figure 18.1). Examples of consistently occurring communication events in "English as a Second Language" sessions that Saville-Troike observed were free play, claiming seats at the table, opening routines using the calendar, a teacher-directed lesson, a follow-up art activity or game, and ending routines.

In bilingual and multilingual environments some communication events will be more likely to occur in one language than another, some events will be conducted in both languages, and the language(s) used also will vary depending on the participants. Therefore, the participants, setting, and topic/purpose elements of communication events, situations, and domains are the organizing elements in a sociolinguistic framework for designing language assessments. These elements are used in gathering case history information, identifying the assessment languages and contexts, selecting specific assessment procedures, and interpreting language assessment findings.

Case history

The cornerstone of assessing multilingual children's linguistic skills is a thorough case history. A case history guides the formulation of assessment questions, provides a basis for selecting assessment procedures and contexts, and frames the interpretation of assessment results. The information gathered should provide the clinician with an understanding of the children's language experiences, a description of family language-related history, and an account of family and teacher concerns.

A detailed case history can be gathered through parent and teacher interviews using open-ended questions that are designed to explore the child's unique language learning experiences. The first issue the clinician needs to inquire about is the timing or order of the introduction of multiple languages. The order in which children learn languages is reflected in the broad distinction between simultaneous and sequential bilingual language acquisition (McLaughlin, 1978). Some children begin acquiring two or more languages simultaneously during infancy. Others learn languages sequentially, with additional languages introduced after the child's first language is established. For example, a child learns Spanish in the home and community, and is introduced to English upon entering school. These differences in the timing of the introduction to the languages are crucial assessment considerations because different patterns of development are often associated with simultaneous and sequential acquisition. For example, a child who acquires multiple languages sequentially may experience a silent period. The silent period has been described as a time during which there is much listening and little output in the most recently introduced language (Roseberry-McKibben, 1995). Conversely, a silent period would not be expected among simultaneous learners who have had continuous experience with each language.

Children's language experiences also vary with regard to the proportion of input for each language. Input refers to the language that is addressed to the child. The amount of input in each language varies and as a result the amount of language acquired in each may be dissimilar. For example, multilingual children may have a larger vocabulary in one of their languages because the amount of input in that particular language is greater. The amount of input for each language also varies across contexts. For example, a child may be addressed most of the time in Spanish at home and in English at school. The child may then be familiar with the Spanish vocabulary for household items and the English vocabulary for colors and numbers.

Patterns of vocabulary acquisition develop systematically in response to the language exposure in the environment (Pearson, Fernández, Lewedeg and Oller, 1997; Bialystok, 2001). During the interview, clinicians need to ask about the amount of input the child receives and obtain an account of the contexts associated with the input of the various languages.

The social contexts of language acquisition are of paramount importance when designing a language assessment for a child who acquires more than one language. From this perspective, the clinician needs to investigate the range and type of contexts to which the child has access. Descriptive interview questions that are broad and general, allow parents and teachers to describe the various contexts of language learning (Westby, 1990). For example, "Tell me about a typical day for Mario" or "Tell me about a typical day in your classroom." These broad or "grand tour" interview questions will reveal the general domains of language use. Specific information about clusters of settings, participants and topics can be obtained through a series of follow-up questions. For example, "Tell me about dinner time" or "Tell me about circle time." These focused or "mini-tour" interview questions will elicit a description of a specific activity or event within a particular situation. Grand tour and mini-tour interview questions can be used to gather a thorough description of the social contexts of language acquisition including the languages used in the communication domains, situations, and events in which the child participates.

The case history interview should also probe the nature of the family's language-related history. An extensive family history of academic, speech, and language problems is crucial in identifying multilingual children suspected of having language difficulties (Restrepo, 1998). Therefore the case history includes asking whether the parents, siblings, aunts, uncles, and grandparents have had a history of problems. In addition to the family language-related history, the clinician gathers information about the family's perception about the child's speech and language development. Clinicians also need to inquire about a variety of skills that are expected for the child's age and how these skills compare with those of the child's peers.

Another important function of the initial interviews is to identify the parents' and teachers' concerns. Clinicians can ask parents and teachers about the specific concerns they have about the child's language skills and what questions they'd like answered as a result of the assessment. This is important because different types of information are needed in order to address different assessment questions. In this chapter, we consider two questions that clinicians commonly encounter: (1) does the child have a language impairment?; and (2) does the child meet a particular agency's

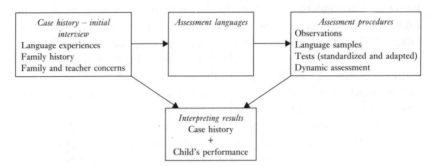

Figure 18.2   Multilingual assessment process

criteria for receiving speech-language pathology services? We do not address other types of assessments in this chapter, such as determining intervention priorities, or measuring progress for children receiving intervention services.

In summary, the case history information provides the clinician with guidance in formulating the assessment questions and an understanding of the role each language plays in the child's daily life. Clear assessment questions and knowledge of the child's experiences with each language, in turn, provide a basis for determining the languages of assessment, selecting appropriate assessment procedures, and interpreting the results of the language assessment, as shown in Figure 18.2.

The languages of assessment

The assessment should include all languages with which the child has significant experience. The basis for identifying the assessment languages is the case history information on the child's language learning experiences. The languages of assessment are *not* determined by results of language dominance or language proficiency testing (Gutierrez-Clellen, 1996). In the past, assessment was conducted in the multilingual child's "dominant" language; that is, the language in which the child had the greatest degree of proficiency. This was typically determined by administering a language dominance test or using language proficiency scales to compare the child's proficiency in each language. However, testing only in the dominant language assumes that the multilingual child should perform like a monolingual

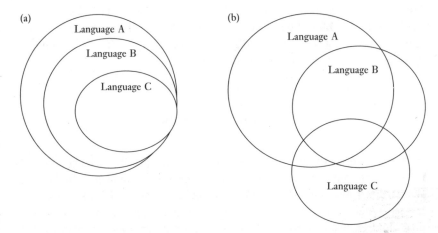

Figure 18.3   (a) Language dominance model, (b) Sociolinguistic model

in their stronger language, and that a multilingual child will have all the skills in their dominant language that they also have in their "weaker" or non-dominant language, as illustrated in the "Language Dominance Model" (see Figure 18.3a). Both of these assumptions are invalid for the multilingual child.

The language knowledge of multilingual children is distributed across languages, as each language is acquired and used within different communicative domains, situations, and events. Although there are overlapping areas of knowledge and many equivalent skills across languages, there are also differences in the knowledge and skills a multilingual child has in each language, as illustrated in the "Sociolinguistic Model" (see Figure 18.3b). For example, among Spanish-English and German-English bilingual toddlers, an average of about 30% to 45% of the children's expressive vocabulary items are expressed in both languages (Junker and Stockman, 2002; Pearson, Fernández and Oller, 1995); the rest of the child's vocabulary items are expressed by a child in one, but not both languages. Quay (1995) found similar results in a detailed longitudinal study of a Spanish-English bilingual toddler. This child had no equivalent Spanish words for about 75% of her English vocabulary and no equivalent English words for about 50–60% of her Spanish vocabulary. A vocabulary inventory or test that counted vocabulary in only one language would seriously underestimate the vocabulary size of this child and other multilingual children. Partial overlap, but also differences in semantic knowledge and skills in two languages also has been documented among Spanish-English bilingual preschool and school age children (Ordoñez, Snow and McLaughlin, 2002; Peña, Bedore and Zlatic-Giunta, 2002). Therefore, assessment in each language in contexts that are congruent with the child's experiences is necessary for a comprehensive assessment for multilingual children.

Assessment procedures

In this section we discuss four types of assessment procedures: (1) observations of communication in daily life; (2) recorded language samples; (3) standardized instruments; and (4) dynamic assessment. Because there is a limited range of assessment procedures designed specifically for multilingual children, we discuss considerations in adapting some procedures that are used with monolinguals. In many cases, the clinician will need to collaborate with an interpreter (Langdon, 2002).

Observations of children communicating in naturalistic or daily life contexts is essential in the evaluation of a multilingual child. Observations provide information on how the child communicates in particular communicative situations and they also inform the clinician about features of the contexts in which a child is learning and using language. If the clinician is not proficient in one or more of the child's languages, observations should be done in collaboration with a proficient speaker.

Contexts for observations are chosen based on the initial interview information on the child's communication in different domains, situations, and events, and the languages used within those contexts. For example, Head Start teachers in a Native American pueblo in which both Keres and English are spoken were concerned about a 4-year-old child from a Keres-speaking home who never spoke during the first few months in their classroom. The mother reported the child spoke fluently in Keres at home, but she was willing to have the child's speech and language evaluated due to the teachers' concerns. The evaluation began with the teachers and the Speech-Language Pathologist observing the child speaking fluently in Keres with her mother in a play area, and the teachers' concerns were immediately allayed. Although the teachers also spoke Keres, the major language used in their school program was English. Apparently the child was in a "silent period" common for early L2 acquisition among preschool children, and she was reluctant to speak Keres in a largely English-speaking environment.

In another case, a 6½-year-old boy from a primarily English-speaking home had had some early experience with Spanish when his family lived in

Mexico, and then later began attending a school in the United States in which most of the school day was conducted in Spanish in kindergarten and first grade. He communicated fluently in English with his brother and mother as they sat in our university clinic waiting area. During an observation at his school, he demonstrated comprehension of all teacher and peer comments, directions, and questions that were addressed to him in Spanish, but he spoke primarily in English or occasionally in short utterances in Spanish, a pattern that was typical of children in the classroom from English-speaking homes.

Observation findings can be recorded by describing significant interactions and events in field notes; this is the approach that was taken in the two examples described above. Another method for recording observations is to use checklists of behaviors that are appropriate for the child's age, observational context, and parent and teacher concerns. There are some checklists that were designed specifically for multilingual children (e.g., Rice, Sell and Hadley, 1990; Mattes and Omark, 1991); however, other communication observational checklists can be adapted for use with multilingual children by making a column for each language so that the observer can indicate the language(s) in which each behavior was observed.

Language samples provide clinicians with opportunities to conduct more in-depth analyses of communication behaviors than is possible with on-line observations in daily life contexts. We restrict our discussion to analyses of oral language samples (including conversations and narratives), but similar principles apply to analyses of written language samples.

A key consideration is collecting language samples in appropriate contexts. Samples should be collected in situations in which the setting, participants, and topic or activity are all consistent with situations in which the target language is used in that child's experience. For example, a sequential learner from a Spanish-speaking home might be recorded talking with his mother in one conversational sample, and with an English-speaking classmate at school in another conversational sample. Language samples recorded with clinicians or others who are proficient in two (or more) languages the child speaks can yield information on the child's ability to use both languages with other multilinguals, including effective use of code-switching.

Language sample analysis should include consideration of the child's effectiveness as a communicator, comparison with developmental data, and consideration of language transfer and the possibility of language attrition (language loss). The child's effectiveness as a communicator can be assessed by the clinician and by native speakers. The clinician can use procedures that focus on specific aspects of language use for samples in each language, keeping in mind the discourse conventions appropriate for the setting, participants, and topics. Native speakers can provide broad judgments of the appropriateness of the child's language use in conversational or narrative contexts. For example, McCabe and Bliss (2003) provide a narrative analysis system that includes clinician analyses of topic maintenance, event sequencing, informativeness, referencing, conjunctive cohesion, and fluency, in addition to native speaker judgments of the adequacy of the narrative.

The child's use of each language in language samples can be compared to developmental expectations. Given the multitude of language combinations and language learning contexts possible, normative data appropriate for multilingual children are rarely available (e.g., mean length of utterance, grammatical stage assignments, age of acquisition of particular phonemes). In general, the child's development should be broadly similar to monolinguals in at least one language on features shared across languages (Bialystok, 2001). Patterns of language use and development that differ from that of monolingual peers in each language will require an explanatory analysis (Damico, 1991). In explanatory analysis, the clinician considers possible interlanguage influences and other cultural and linguistic variables to account for language and communication patterns. For example, specific aspects of form and content that are not shared across languages may differ from monolinguals (Bialystok, 2001; Goldstein, 2004). In addition, the possibility of language attrition should be considered in interpreting the child's performance if the case history information indicates limited opportunities for continued use of a language (Anderson, 2004).

The problems with using standardized tests developed for monolinguals when testing multilinguals are well known (Gutierrez-Clellen, 1996). A major problem is that monolingual tests do not take the distributed knowledge of multilingual child into account. For example, typically developing Spanish-English bilingual children given vocabulary tests in English and in Spanish score low as a group compared to the monolingual English and monolingual Spanish norms. However, their vocabulary combined across the two languages is similar to that of monolinguals (Pearson, Fernández and Oller, 1993). There are few tests developed specifically for multilinguals to date. Developing valid tests for multilingual children is challenging because items that are appropriate for each language must be developed, and the test must be standardized and normed on multilingual children from the appropriate dialectal and language backgrounds.

Many multilingual children acquire combinations of languages for which there are no appropriate standardized tests available. However, in many instances, agencies such as school systems require test scores as part of the assessment process. In addition to educating agency personnel on the pitfalls of using standardized tests inappropriately, the clinician can adapt and administer some standardized tests in each language and explore the child's response to dynamic assessment (described in the next section) for skills the child did not demonstrate. Administering a test in both languages is often done for bilingual children (see Chamberlain and Medeiros-Landurand, 1991). The child receives credit for any item performed correctly in either language. The conditions of administering the test in this way must be described in the report, and scores from this type of non-standard administration must be reported or interpreted broadly, rather than as specific percentiles or standard scores. For example, the clinician might report that when a child's correct answers in either language were credited, the raw score was similar to that of monolingual children who performed within the normal range on the standard version of the test. In contrast, when a child's score appears low, even after the test is translated and adapted for multilingual administration, further assessment should be done, due to the multitude of linguistic and cultural factors that influence children's performance on standardized tests. This can be done through use of dynamic assessment.

Dynamic assessment is an approach to assessment that is based on a Vygotskian, social interactionist view of development. Children's development of language occurs in the context of interacting with more skilled language users (e.g., parents, teachers, older siblings) who provide scaffolding. Scaffolding is the use of strategies that provide a more supportive context, increasing opportunities for the child to participate in the communicative context and develop new skills. In dynamic assessment, the focus is on how the child responds to scaffolding in acquiring new skills, rather than on what the child does independently. Dynamic assessment holds great promise for use with children from diverse cultural and linguistic backgrounds because it does not assume homogeneity of prior experience across children. Instead the assessor is expected to tailor scaffolding techniques in order to provide optimal support for developing new competencies.

Dynamic assessment is used as a follow-up to observations, language samples, and standardized testing. The examiner identifies skills absent during these initial/pre-testing assessment procedures and provides scaffolding to teach a skill the child is lacking. While scaffolding, the examiner notes the child's responses to different types of support. Next, subsequent/ post-testing is done to determine if the child is able to use the skill without support in the initial observational/sampling/testing situation. The examiner considers the child's overall responsiveness to scaffolding, degree of change between pre-testing and post-testing (Peña, Iglesias and Lidz, 2001) and level of post-testing performance (Gutierrez-Clellen and Peña, 2001). High responsiveness to scaffolding and a large improvement on post-testing indicate the child's initial performance may have been due to differences between their cultural and linguistic experiences and those of the examiner, test, or classroom context. In contrast, a more limited responsiveness to a variety of scaffolding strategies and limited gains on post-testing would be expected in a child with a language impairment.

Interpretation of results

Language assessment results are interpreted using the language history information and the child's performance in each language (Figure 18.2). Issues to consider are timing, amount and contexts of exposure for each language, cultural considerations, and family history and perceptions.

The possibility of language attrition should be taken into account for sequential learners. When a child learns new language content, form and use in a second language, but not in the first language, the child's skills in both languages may appear to be more limited than those of monolingual peers in either language (Anderson, 2004).

For sequential and simultaneous learners, language performance is influenced by the amount and contexts of input in each language. Although a child with minimal exposure to a language would be expected to have limited skills in that language, a child with substantial exposure to a language should be making progress in acquiring that language. For example, a sequential preschooler would be expected to have a "silent period" in the initial stages of exposure to the second language; however this is followed by beginning use of routine phrases and/or telegraphic phrases in the second language, and subsequently productive use of the second language (Tabors, 1997).

Considering contexts of the child's experience with each language will help the clinician understand the variability in the child's performance. For example, if language samples are taken in an English-speaking environment, such as a school, a child may not use his or her home language in spite of encouragement to do so. This reflects sociolinguistic awareness, rather than a deficiency in the home language. In addition, cultural influences have a significant impact on children's communicative patterns in daily life contexts, patterns of language use during language samples, and standardized tests (Chamberlain and Medeiros-Landurand, 1991; Langdon, 1992; Kayser, 1995; Cheng, 1996).

Family history of speech, language or academic problems is a key consideration because approximately 77 percent of children with language impairments have a positive family history of speech, language, or academic problems (Tallal, Ross and Curtiss, 1989). Family perceptions of the child's communication skills are also an essential consideration. Restrepo (1998) found that parent perceptions of their children's speech and language skills and family history of speech and language problems accurately discriminated children with normal language skills from children with language impairment.

In summary, language assessments for multilingual children must be designed using social contexts as an organizing framework. If the clinician gathers good initial information, determines the languages of assessment, selects appropriate assessment procedures, and interprets the results from this perspective, the risk of over- or under-identification of language impairment will be reduced.

Further reading

Lidz, C. (1991) *Practitioner's Guide to Dynamic Assessment.* New York: Guilford.

Tabors, P. (1997) *One Child, Two Languages: A Guide for Preschool Educators of Children Learning English as a Second Language.* Baltimore, MD: Brookes.

Westby, C. (1994) Multicultural issues. In B. Tomblin, H. Morris and D. Spriestersbach (eds), *Diagnosis in Speech-language Pathology* (pp. 29–50). San Diego, CA: Singular.

Westby, C., Burda, A. and Mehta, Z. (2003) Asking the right questions in the right ways: Strategies for ethnographic interviewing. *ASHA Leader* 8(8): 4–5, 16–17.

19

Literacy as a Sociolinguistic Process for Clinical Purposes

Jack S. Damico, Ryan L. Nelson and
Linda Bryan

As an applied linguistic specialty, clinical sociolinguistics holds great promise for practicing speech–language pathologists and other pedagogical personnel. With the information obtained from this discipline, practitioners can utilize the methodologies and the data from the long-standing field of sociolinguistics to improve their clinical practices. Specifically, they can address potentially complicated issues with a fresh appreciation for contextual variables and a wealth of accumulated data that can inform them and increase the effectiveness and efficacy of their service delivery.

This chapter may serve as an exemplar of the power and benefits of clinical sociolinguistics. By reporting on some of the sociolinguistic data collected in the area of literacy, this chapter provides the practicing clinician with a richer conception of literacy than most clinicians possess and then demonstrates how this sociolinguistically enriched perspective on literacy can be employed within the clinical context.

A typical literacy perspective

In a recent study, the authors conducted extensive focus group research to determine what conceptions of literacy were being employed by practicing clinicians. These focus groups documented that many practicing speech–language pathologists had a fairly simplistic conception of literacy. That is, literacy was viewed as a straightforward process of decoding and encoding visual text and although it was considered a psychological skill, most clinicians deemed literacy fairly isolated from significant social considerations.

Further, they tended to view literacy as a secondary language system that employed systematically and explicitly taught component skills (e.g., phonemic awareness, phonics, fluency) to create readers and writers. This conception of literacy – though simplistic – was expected. A simplistic approach to literacy instruction has been advocated both within the profession and across a number of other educational disciplines and publications (e.g., Chall, 1967; Moats, 1990; Lyon, 1999). Indeed, this perspective has given rise to a number of political mandates (e.g., National Reading Panel, 2000; Bush, 2001) and has sparked what has been termed the "reading wars" (Lemann, 1997; Goodman, 1998) since there is a debate over whether this isolated conception of literacy is valid and efficacious.

From the perspective of clinical sociolinguistics, however, a different story of literacy can be told. A story involving a more complex and socially relevant phenomenon incorporating the dynamic and the functional qualities of literacy that are so important to its effective use in the real world. To describe this more dynamic perspective, several areas of research involving literacy as a social construct will be discussed and the lessons learned from these data will then be applied to understanding how such sociolinguistic research can inform the literacy practices of clinicians and teachers.

A sociolinguistic consensus of literacy

Over the past two decades, there has been an emerging consensus of literacy as a sociolinguistic phenomenon that takes into account the language and cultural knowledge of the individual and how this knowledge is implemented within society. Scribner and Cole (1981), for example, described literacy as a set of socially organized practices that employed a primary visual symbol system in its own right and that created an adaptable set of technologies for production and dissemination of meaningful content. Inherent in this description is the *socially contextualized* nature of literacy and how societal influence operates to create literacy acquisition (e.g., Bruner, 1984) and to shape literacy practices (e.g., Street, 1993). This focus on literacy as a social phenomenon is crucial to understanding the complexity and the dynamic nature of this meaning-making skill. If we focus on some of the ways that social influence occurs within literacy contexts, we can recognize the paucity of the previously mentioned construct of literacy and we can employ actual data and their implications to guide our pedagogy. Several points about literacy – derived from this focus on social influence

– are detailed below and may serve as examples of the vast data sources available to the practitioner when employing clinical sociolinguistics.

Data source one: the acquisition of literacy is a socially constructed process

As the first demonstration, understanding how literacy is acquired naturally would greatly assist the teacher or clinician since this knowledge could be modified and employed for teaching purposes. With regard to literacy acquisition, nearly thirty years of research has demonstrated that the development of literacy prior to schooling is a socially constructed process (e.g., Holdaway, 1979; Ferreiro and Teberosky, 1982; Heath, 1983; Cochran-Smith, 1984; Wells, 1986).

Literacy acquisition runs parallel to oral language development in that it involves a similar social interaction; the same kinds of mediating events and access to the same kinds of meaningful components described by Bruner (1983) in the acquisition of oral language are employed. This means that the child acquiring literacy is recurrently exposed to authentic literacy skills successfully modeled by proficient readers/writers via reading and writing aloud and through shared reading and writing activities. For his/her part, the child, when ready, has an opportunity to attempt the authentic literacy skills him/herself with the mediation and corrective feedback of the more capable reader/writer. So, for example, during the period of emerging literacy a child and his/her caregiver may pick up a book together and engage in the social act of reading. When this occurs, there is an underlying (and meaningful) social interaction that is employed so that the caregiver collaborates with the child to construct meaning from print. In engaging in this social framework, the caregiver can assist the child's internalization of what the author was trying to say by reading, discussing, questioning, inviting the child to participate, and by responding to the child's questions and other contributions. Clearly, it is through such socialized literacy activities that the child eventually acquires authentic reading and writing skills (Clay, 1979; Holdaway, 1979; Teale and Sulzby, 1986; Cambourne, 1988). That is, the social acts of reading and writing provide many of the conditions necessary for literacy acquisition and learning discussed by Cambourne (1988): the child may be exposed to excellent models of reading and writing, the child is exposed to the specific behaviors that are employed in reading and/or writing, the child can observe and internalize the functionality and meaningfulness of this social act, the child will have the chance to practice and perform, and the child will be able to observe and recognize the joys of literacy – all through social modeling by individuals important to the child.

As with all other forms of meaning-making, literacy acquisition is social, natural and continual. It takes place within a recurrent and meaningful context through social interactions with people the child identifies with and, within any such literacy encounter, the individuals and their personal relationships are at the heart of the process (Smith, 1998, 2003).

Data source two: the concept of literacy is a socially constructed process

Since pedagogical practice is often determined by one's desired end point, it is important to understand the concept of literacy and the stability of this term and its counterparts. That is, if literacy is the objective, exactly what does the term mean and is it a "fixed" or a "moving" target? The sociolinguistic research indicates that while there is frequent discussion regarding literacy, illiteracy, and disorders of literacy (e.g., dyslexia, learning disabilities) in our society, the terms are not set categories. Rather, since literacy is a social construct, the definitions change over time and across various social contexts. Newman and Beverstock (1990), for example, investigated various definitions of literacy over historical periods and found that the conception of literacy changed from very basic skills (i.e., the ability to sign one's name), through the ability to read and write, to attainment of fourth grade reading level. With the current focus on high stakes testing, it is possible that future literacy attainment may not focus on actual reading and writing at all but, rather, on performance scores from de-contextualized standardized tests (Kohn, 2000; Allington, 2002). As a social construct, therefore, the labels or concepts are often just mirrors of the prevailing ideologies that are in vogue at any given time (Baynham, 1995).

This constructed character is also evident in the term *dyslexia*. Monaghan (1980) found that a number of definitions for dyslexia have been employed and that they are always reflective of the current social conditions and "received knowledge" of the time. Boder's (1973) definition, for example, employed a heavy reliance on standardized tests and strategies for reading isolated words and for word decoding rather than authentic reading and writing. This tendency for the social construction of disability and handicapping labels has also been documented in the area of learning disabilities (Coles, 1987). Consequently, we should not simply reify labels such as literacy and dyslexia. Rather, as suggested by Street (1993), the conception of literacy should not be dichotomous (have/have not) but it should be viewed along a continuum that attempts to account for the complexity of this symbolic and social process.

Data source three: literacy is guided by functionality within the social context

One of the most important contributions of sociolinguistics to literacy pedagogy has been the work supporting the contention that literacy is not an isolated skill devoid of context or functionality (e.g., Heath, 1983; Bloome, 1989; Baynham, 1995; Gee, 1996; Hagood, 2002); literacy must have a contextualized purpose for effective acquisition, advancement, or implementation (e.g., Halliday, 1978; Bruner, 1990; Wells, 1990, 1994; Olson, 1994; Hinchey, 1998). When literacy operates within a situated context and when there are practical objectives or goals to pursue, then the literacy activities are more robust, more effective, and motivating for all involved (e.g., Edelsky, 1994; Oldfather and Dahl, 1994; Morgan, 1997; Roberts and Street, 1997; Gee, 2000).

This recognition that literacy is a socially constituted act requiring functional interaction with one's context has manifested itself in many ways. Based upon this functionality, various pedagogical philosophies and orientations have been developed. For example, *critical literacy* has been progressively suggested as a viable and effective component of literacy instruction over the past two decades (e.g., Freire and Macedo, 1987; Shor and Freire, 1987; Graman, 1988; Luke, 1988; Shor, 1992; Edelsky, 1994; Morgan, 1997; Egan-Robertson, 1998). Based upon the ideological work of Freire (1970, 1973), critical literacy is intended to get students to engage in literacy activities by making them more knowledgeable about how texts are used to reflect and advance certain struggles for knowledge, power, representation, and material resources (Cazden et al., 1996). So, for example, students may get more interested in reading and writing when they are doing so with an eye toward understanding how local merchants and the community government make decisions about playground development, or they learn more about how their own cultural backgrounds are reflected in basal readers, or they study the impact of the media on apartheid in South Africa and how it relates to racism in America (Sweeney, 1997).

Other manifestations of this functional interaction between literacy and context involve using literacy to help establish a student's self-concept as a person through reading and writing (e.g., Beach and Anson, 1992;

Egan-Robertson, 1998; Ladson-Billings, 1995) and to investigate how literacy helps individuals shape their own identities (e.g., Halliday, 1978; Kamberelis and Scott, 1993; Hagood, 2002). In each of these examples, literacy is employed as a contextually based tool that is created out of a commitment to understand social conditions, to affect change, and to form a more socially just and equitable society through literacy users' scrutiny of relations between and among language and language users. Additionally, these socially-based efforts typically result in achieving better literacy skills (Graman, 1988; Edelsky, 1994; Morgan, 1997).

Data source four: social adaptations to meet literacy requirements

The final demonstration of how sociolinguistic data can inform the clinician regarding literacy and its complexity involves the various ways that individuals with limited literacy skills create social adaptations to meet their literacy needs. Merrifield and her colleagues (1997) while studying rural and immigrant populations in various areas of the United States found that literacy was often so important that even when individuals were functionally illiterate, they employed social strategies to accomplish their literacy needs. Specifically, four main types of literacy strategies were used when needed. First, there were *other-oriented strategies* that involved using regular designated "readers," asking others for assistant with reading on an ad hoc basis, using other oral information sources, and gaining information through observations of others rather than reading instructions. This set of strategies has been well documented in minority-language populations. For example, Rockhill (1993) and Farr (1994) found that in many recent Hispanic immigrant families the women in the families tended to take on the responsibility of functional literacy for the family while they (or, more likely, their children) worked to gain functional English literacy. In these situations, these women often engaged others to assist them with literacy tasks, they quickly acquired specific sets of English literacy skills for a few frequently occurring literacy contexts, and they operated on a literacy economy wherein those more proficient in literacy helped those less proficient in exchange for other services or favors. Similarly, Metoyer-Duran (1993) found that in some ethnolinguistic communities there were information providers who served as literacy mediators to assist in required literacy activities. Interestingly, she found that literacy was often so important that these individuals – regardless of whether they were "official" literacy mediators or whether they operated on a voluntary basis – became "gatekeepers" between the mainstream society and the minority culture.

The other strategies identified by Merrifield and colleagues (1997) were *self-reliant strategies* including guessing, extensive use of memory, and select- ive use of text, *avoidance of potentially difficult literacy situations*, and *use of substitute technologies* like tape recorders, radios, and televisions to obtain the necessary information. When using these strategies, the illiterate individuals indicated their recognition for the power and necessity of literacy in certain contexts and they employed various social strategies to compensate for their lack of reading and writing proficiency. Their lack of proficiency, however, did not mean they could not participate in literacy activities; they just had to employ different socially-based adaptations.

Clinical applications from the sociolinguistics of literacy

While these four data sources reveal only a portion of the valuable informa- tion that can be derived from the sociolinguistics of literacy, they can be employed to modify literacy service delivery in clinical contexts. First, these data support the conception of literacy as a *complex social phenomenon*. The simplistic conception of literacy as a self-contained psychological ability cannot be justified. Consequently, it is important that the practicing clini- cian adopt a more robust conception of literacy, one that is more socially mediated, more contextualized, more authentic, and more functional. Further, more data from the sociolinguistics of literacy should be obtained to further expand this social construct of literacy.

Second, a more meaning-based and socially-oriented *re-conceptualization of dyslexia* should be employed. Given the fact that labels like dyslexia are socially constructed based upon the available "received knowledge" of the time, given the sociolinguistic data that supports the functional and meaning-based character of literacy, and given the fact that these labels are often transitory rather than permanent, practicing clinicians should employ Weaver's conceptualizations of "reading as constructing meaning" and "dys- lexia as the ineffective use and/or coordination of strategies for constructing meaning" (1998: 320). This re-conceptualization will enable a more proactive pedagogy, enable a greater focus on meaning-based intervention, and not allow unsupported deficit models (such as the traditional definition of dys- lexia) to reduce expectations for overcoming the literacy difficulties (Coles, 1987; Fink, 1995–6; McDermott and Gospodinoff, 1979; Weaver, 1998).

Third, the practicing clinician should employ a *more authentic and socially mediated approach to literacy intervention*. Based upon the data previously discussed from emergent literacy research and from effective literacy practices, approaches should focus on authentic reading and writing for real purposes and the therapeutic effect should be accomplished through the active mediation of a more competent reader and writer (e.g., the clinician). There are several excellent pedagogical frameworks that might be effectively employed to meet this recommendation. For example, Routman's mediational framework (1988) of reading and writing aloud, shared reading and writing, guided reading and writing, and independent reading and writing will supply a general intervention format while many of the meaning-based techniques discussed by Clay (1991), Goodman (1996), and Routman (1988) will provide the functional and social models and feedback needed for the child to overcome any literacy deficits.

Conclusion

As hybrid disciplines such as clinical sociolinguistics are developed and expanded, the practicing clinician should carefully consider the advantages that such a field of study can provide. Often such interdisciplinary endeavors can supply different perspectives and an entirely new database upon which the serious clinician can build new and more effective approaches to service delivery. This short chapter has attempted to demonstrate the power and advantage of clinical sociolinguistics as it might be employed for the remediation of literacy difficulties. The potential of clinical sociolinguistics, however, far exceeds the demonstrations discussed in this chapter. The untapped data and applications await those clinicians willing to pursue these issues further. The advantages for both the clinicians and their clients will be significant.

Further reading

Coles, G. (2003) *Reading the Naked Truth: Literacy, Legislation, and Lies.* Portsmouth, NH: Heinemann.

Edelsky, C. (ed.) (1999) *Making Justice Our Project: Teachers Working toward Critical Whole Language Practice.* Urbana, IL: National Council of Teachers of English.

Ladson-Billings, G. (1994) *The Dreamkeepers: Successful Teachers of African-American Children.* San Francisco: Jossey-Bass.

Smith, F. (1997) *Reading without Nonsense*, 3rd edn. New York: Teachers College Press.

20

The Sociolinguistics of Sign Languages

Ceil Lucas, Robert Bayley and Arlene Blumenthal Kelly

In this chapter, we provide a brief overview of the sociolinguistics of sign languages and then focus on one area, sociolinguistic variation in American Sign Language (ASL). Since Stokoe's (1960) pioneering work, linguists have recognized that natural sign languages are autonomous linguistic systems, structurally independent of the spoken languages with which they may coexist in any given community. This recognition has been followed by extensive research into different aspects of sign language structure and accompanied by the recognition that, as natural sign languages are full-fledged autonomous linguistic systems shared by communities of users, the sociolinguistics of sign languages can be described in ways that parallel the description of spoken languages.

Sociolinguistic studies in the American Deaf community began in the late 1960s, with Stokoe's (1969) characterization of language use as diglossic, following Ferguson's (1959) model.[1] Subsequent studies included examinations of the linguistic outcome of contact between ASL and English, with claims that the outcome was a pidgin (e.g., Woodward, 1973; Reilly and McIntire, 1980), studies of variation in ASL (e.g., Battison et al., 1975; Woodward and DeSantis, 1977a, 1977b), language maintenance and choice (Lee, 1982), language attitudes (Kannapell, 1991) and language policy and planning (e.g., Johnson, Liddell and Erting, 1989; Ramsey, 1989; Nover, 1995). In fact, all the major areas of sociolinguistics have been examined to some extent as they pertain to the Deaf community, including regional and social variation, bilingualism and language contact phenomena, language maintenance and choice, language attitudes, language policy and planning, and language and social interaction (see the chapters in Lucas, 2001, for discussions of research in these areas).

Research has not been limited to the American Deaf community, but has been carried out in many countries. However, even though each of the major areas has at least been touched on, the earliest sociolinguistic research in the Deaf community was shaped and perhaps limited by at least four interrelated considerations:

1 The relationship between the spoken language of the majority community and the sign language, particularly in educational settings.
2 Limited knowledge of the linguistic structure of the sign language.
3 Doubts as to the actual status of the sign language as a "real language."
4 Application of spoken language sociolinguistic models to sign language situations.

As concerns the first, the bulk of early sociolinguistic research in the American Deaf community, for example, had to do with the interrelationship between English and ASL. Considerable attention was given to one outcome of language contact, traditionally known as Pidgin Sign English (PSE), and to characterizations of the sociolinguistic situation as diglossic or as a continuum. We suggest that where linguistic research energy has been directed is a reflection of where societal energy has gone. For example, the focus in American Deaf education since its inception in 1817 has been largely on how to teach English to deaf children, with a variety of philosophies and methodologies. Not until recently has there been any focus on the use of ASL in educational or other social settings. The same is true for Deaf communities around the world. Research on language contact, for example, has focused on contact between spoken and sign languages.

The second and the third considerations contribute to this state of affairs. Normally, sociolinguistic studies of a language accompany or follow linguistic descriptions. That is, it is difficult to describe what sociolinguistic variation looks like in a language until we have at least some basic understanding of the structure of the language. In fact, some early studies of variation in ASL describe as variable features that in fact are not variable at all (Lucas, 1995). Of course, in the case of sign languages, sociolinguistic research was long hindered by the widespread belief that sign languages are not really languages.

The fourth consideration has to do with the application of models developed for spoken languages that may not be entirely suitable for sign languages. For example, Lucas and Valli (1992) investigated a kind of signing that results from the contact between English and ASL and has features of both languages. The description of what the researchers call contact signing naturally led to a review of language contact phenomena in spoken language situations, but it also made clear the necessity for a very basic distinction between contact between two sign languages and contact between a sign language and a spoken language. Clearly this distinction is motivated by the presence of two modalities, so that what happens when two sign languages are in contact will probably differ from what happens when a sign language is in contact with a spoken language. It was in trying to illustrate the distinction with examples that Lucas and Valli realized where the focus in language contact studies has been. That is, although one is able to think of and casually observe examples to illustrate the outcome of contact between two sign languages, empirical research on lexical borrowing, code-switching, foreigner talk, interference, pidgins, creoles, and mixed systems – all as they result from the contact between two sign languages – is just beginning.

Sign languages borrow from each other; bilingual signers code-switch between two sign languages; a native signer of one sign language uses a reduced form of that language with a non-native signer or demonstrates interference when using another sign language; and pidgins, creoles and mixed systems could conceivably come about given the right sociolinguistic conditions. It is not that these things do not happen, but rather that researchers have only just begun to look for them and describe them. Early research attention turned elsewhere, to focus on the relationship between the spoken language and the sign language. The Deaf community has been looked at all too often within the framework of spoken language sociolinguistics, and labels from spoken language situations have been applied too hastily to sign language situations. One problem with this is that it leaves the impression that the situation has been adequately described, when in fact it turns out to be a lot more complex than we thought. For example, the term "pidgin" as applied to the Deaf community needs to be re-examined. Not that pidgins cannot occur, they probably can. Many other terms used in sociolinguistics to describe oral language use such as "lexical borrowing," "code-mixing," "code-switching" and even "bilingualism" also merit re-examination. Indeed, some researchers have already re-examined some terms (see, e.g., Lee, 1982, on "diglossia," and Cokely, 1983, on the term "pidgin").

It is fair to say that each of the four considerations that seem to have governed the study of sociolinguistics in Deaf communities is changing. Our knowledge of the basic linguistic structure of sign languages is increasing every day, and the notion that sign languages are not "real languages" is happily endangered. Research is being undertaken in all areas of sociolinguistics, including multilingualism, bilingualism and language contact, variation, discourse analysis, language policy and planning, and language attitudes. Much of this current work is discussed in this volume. Studies on all aspects of the sociolinguistics of Deaf communities are currently in a period of rapid development. The focus is being extended beyond the relationship between sign languages and spoken languages to the relationship between sign languages (see, e.g., Woodward, 1996; Ann, 2001; Quinto-Pozos, 2002). In addition, research on sign languages is beginning to provide crucial insights into the nature of spoken languages (see, e.g., McNeill, 1992, on the differences between signing and gesturing).

Deaf culture

Sociolinguistic studies of sign languages must also take into consideration the role of Deaf culture, as the sociolinguistic patterns observed have been forged within the socio-cultural networks of Deaf people (Kelly, 2001). As history and experience show us, at the heart of every community is its language (Baker-Shenk and Cokely, 1980: 58). The phenomenon known as Deaf culture consists of a community of people who use sign language to communicate. Equally pivotal are its values, behavioral norms, history, and literature (Kelly, 1998).

For example, residential schools for the Deaf have not only been institutions for academic learning. They have also been the sites of enculturation through socialization with deaf peers. Traditionally, that socialization began upon entry to these schools and bonds were formed that lasted into adulthood because the students lived at the school, away from home. This often led to endogamous relationships, satisfying a natural desire for a domestic partner who shared the same language. Opportunities for leadership and athletics were provided at these schools. Between the 1880s and the early 1970s in the United States, for example, ASL was rarely used as the medium of instruction or taught formally in the classroom. Instead, it was learned through socialization with peers. The Deaf children who came from Deaf, ASL-using homes often served as language teachers or as language models, by virtue of having acquired the language natively from their parents.

In addition to the residential schools, Deaf clubs have been central to the life of the Deaf community. In the late eighteenth century, a Parisian named Pierre Desloges ([1779] 1984) wrote what is believed to be one of the earliest documents by a Deaf person. It described a vibrant Parisian Deaf community, a society whose members regularly interacted and shared a common language. The first formal organization was formed by and for Deaf Americans in 1853 (Van Cleve and Crouch, 1989; Lane et al., 2000). Called the New England Gallaudet Association of Deaf-Mutes, this grew from the desire of Deaf alumni to keep in touch after graduating from Deaf institutions. With the establishment of more residential schools after the mid-nineteenth century, more alumni organizations were formed. In 1880, the National Association of the Deaf, the oldest association of its kind, was founded, to safeguard the rights of Deaf people in education, employment, health care, and social services (Van Cleve and Crouch, 1989; also www.nad.org).

At the beginning of the automobile age, Deaf drivers were discriminated against by insurance companies that imposed higher premiums than were paid by hearing drivers (Baker-Shenk and Cokely, 1980). This discrimination was based on the assumption that Deaf drivers would be at a disadvantage since they could not hear auditory warning devices, i.e., horns, sirens, whistles. In 1901, the National Fraternal Society of the Deaf was formed to provide low-cost automobile and life insurance (www.nfsd.com).

During World War II, Akron, Ohio and Los Angeles, California were the sites of clubs for Deaf war plant laborers who wanted to socialize with other Deaf people (Gannon, 1981; Van Cleve and Crouch, 1989). The clubs allowed face-to-face interactions, and thus became second homes to many Deaf people who spent their working hours among hearing people. Popular activities included weekly open-captioned films and sporting events. The American Athletic Association for the Deaf was formed in 1945 to foster and regulate competition among Deaf clubs, and to host numerous sporting tournaments across the country. It also selects and sponsors American participants in the World Games for the Deaf, which were initiated in Paris in 1924.

As with any minority group, in-group support is crucial for survival in the dominant culture. The experience of communication barriers with members of the dominant culture unites Deaf people, regardless of their birth origin. Most often, Deaf people have closer ties to other Deaf people than to their own kin. For example, family holidays such as Thanksgiving, Christmas, and Passover may be times of celebration, but for most Deaf people, they are often sites of frustration and oppression. Most hearing relatives do not know ASL and Deaf people often resort to watching television, reading, and leaving early. By contrast, residential schools, clubs, and other organizations are the sites of unfettered communication and are key to understanding the sociolinguistics of Deaf communities.

Sociolinguistic variation in sign languages

Systematic research on variation in sign languages began in the 1960s, with Carl Croneberg's two appendices to the 1965 *Dictionary of American Sign Language* (*DASL*) (Stokoe, Casterline and Croneberg, 1965) and continued into the 1970s. A full review of this early work is provided in Lucas, Bayley and Valli (2001). We will focus here on two recent studies of variation in ASL that highlight the main issues and reflect the changing perspective on the nature of sign languages: Lucas et al.'s (2001) study of variation in the form of the sign DEAF[2] and Collins and Petronio's (1998) study of variation in Tactile ASL, the language of the US Deaf-Blind community. Both studies adopted theoretical frameworks that incorporate recent insights into the nature of ASL. Collins and Petronio's (1998) study is exploratory. The authors aimed to understand the parameters of variation in the language variety of a group that had not previously been studied systematically. Lucas et al. (2001) is based on a representative sample of the US Deaf population.

A large-scale quantitative study: Lucas et al. (2001) on DEAF

Lucas et al. (2001) adapted standard sociolinguistic methodology (Labov, 1972b; Milroy and Gordon, 2003) to examine phonological, syntactic and lexical variation in ASL as used throughout the United States. Conversational ASL was videotaped in seven sites (Massachusetts, Virginia, Maryland, Louisiana, Kansas/Missouri, California and Washington State). Participants represented three age groups (15–25, 26–54, 55+) and included male and female, Caucasian and African American, and working–class and middle–class signers. Figure 20.1 provides an overview of the project.

The analysis of the sign DEAF, one of the phonological variables studied, is based on all 1,618 examples present in the data. Although DEAF has many possible forms, only three of these forms were extracted from the videotapes. In the citation form that appears in sign language dictionaries and is taught in sign language classes, the sign begins just below the ear, and ends near the corner of the mouth. A second variant, the "chin to ear" variant, begins at the corner of the mouth and moves upward to the ear. In the third variant, the "contact-cheek" variant, the index finger contacts the lower cheek but does not move up (see Figures 20.2a, 20.2b, 20.2c).

These variants were compared using logistic regression, a statistical procedure that requires many examples as input, but that allows the researcher

Data Collection

Visited seven sites:

1	Staunton, Virginia	5	Fremont, California
2	Frederick, Maryland	6	Kansas City, Missouri/Olathe,
3	Boston, Massachusetts		Kansas
4	New Orleans, Louisiana	7	Bellingham, Washington

Twelve groups at each site, except for Virginia, Maryland, and Bellingham (only white groups)

African American groups:		White groups:	
Middle class	*Working class*	*Middle class*	*Working class*
15–25	15–25	15–25	15–25
26–54	26–54	26–54	26–54
–*	55+	55+	55+

- A total of 207 American Sign Language signers. (Each group consisted of 2–7 signers.)

Overall goal of the project:

- A description of phonological, morphosyntactic, and lexical variation in ASL, and the correlation of variation with external factors such as age, region, gender, ethnicity, and socioeconomic status.

Variables examined:

- Phonological: the sign DEAF, the location of signs represented by the verb KNOW, signs made with a 1 handshape.
- Morphosyntactic: Overt and null subject pronouns.
- Lexical: 34 signs selected to illustrate phonological change as well as lexical innovation stemming from new technology, increased contact with Deaf people in other countries, and contemporary social attitudes.

Figure 20.1 Project on sociolinguistic variation in ASL: overview
* It was not possible in 1994 to locate African American participants 55 and older. Owing to the burdens of double discrimination, very few Deaf African Americans in this age group managed to reach middle-class status.

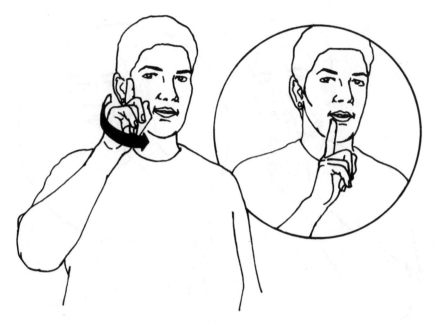

Figure 20.2a DEAF, variant 1: ear to chin

to investigate the effects of many potential constraints simultaneously (Bayley, 2002). Results of the analysis of the 1618 examples indicated that variation in the form of DEAF is systematic and conditioned by multiple linguistic and social factors, including grammatical function, the location of the following segment, discourse genre (narrative or conversation), age and region. The results confirmed the earlier finding of Lucas (1995), which showed that the grammatical function of DEAF, rather than the features of the preceding or following sign, has the strongest effect on a signer's choice of one of the three variants.

The analysis was divided into two stages. First, the citation form was compared with the two non-citation forms. Second, the two non-citation forms were compared with one another. For the choice between citation and non-citation forms, among the linguistic factors, only grammatical function and discourse genre proved to be statistically significant. For the choice between the two non-citation forms, both the grammatical function of DEAF and the location of the following segment proved significant. Among the social factors, only age and region contributed significantly to the observed variation. The other non-linguistic factors for which the researchers coded

Figure 20.2b   DEAF, variant 2: chin to ear

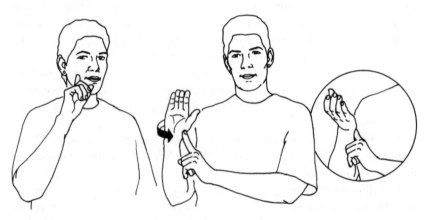

Figure 20.2c   DEAF, variant 3: contact cheek, in the compound

– ethnicity, gender, language background and social class – failed to reach statistical significance.

Specifically, while the youngest and oldest signers in four sites (California, Louisiana, Virginia, and Washington) preferred non-citation forms, in these sites signers aged 26 to 54 were more likely to use citation forms. In Kansas/Missouri, the non-citation form was favored by signers in all age groups, while in Massachusetts non-citation forms were disfavored by signers in all age groups. Finally, in Maryland, older signers preferred the non-citation forms, while the middle age and younger ones preferred the citation form. The results clearly show that DEAF is a classic sociolinguistic variable, and the challenge for researchers is to explain the correlation between the linguistic factors and the social ones. One explanation directly concerns the history of Deaf education in the US.

The history of Deaf education had a direct impact on the recognition of ASL as a language, independent in structure from English. Before 1880, while opponents questioned its status, ASL was accepted widely as a medium of instruction. Between 1880 and 1960, however, the status of ASL was very fragile, even among its users. Recall that in 1960 William Stokoe published the first linguistic description of ASL (Stokoe, 1960), and the recognition of ASL as a viable natural language slowly began to grow. The history of Deaf education and the recognition of ASL appear to be reflected in the patterns of variation in this study. Specifically, in the majority of sites studied, older signers use more non-citation forms. Many of them were attending residential schools at a time when ASL was actively suppressed and forbidden. While they were certainly fluent users of the language, there was very little metalinguistic awareness or prescriptivism accompanying that use. Indeed, many of the older signers in the study could not provide a name for their language – ASL – as the could two younger groups. Rather, many of the older signers still referred to their fluent language production simply as "sign." In contrast, the 26- to 54-year-old signers were in school at the time when ASL was beginning to be recognized and valued as a language separate from English. ASL was still not accepted in classrooms, but there was a rapidly growing awareness in the Deaf community of the need for recognition.

In the late 1960s and early 1970s, formal instruction in sign language began, along with the preparation of teaching materials. This new awareness of the status of ASL helps explain the preference among the 26- to 54-year-old signers in the majority of sites examined for the citation forms of DEAF. The prescriptivism seen here in the use of citation forms may be regarded as a tool in maintaining the hard-won recognition of ASL. Finally, the youngest signers all attended school at a time when, for the most part, the status of ASL was no longer in question. The change in the status of ASL may explain the more frequent use of non-citation forms by younger signers. The status of the language is not threatened by the use of non-citation forms. This would seem to account for the general patterns that we see. Deviations from this pattern, such as the preference in the older Massachusetts signers and the youngest Maryland signers for citation forms, may be explained by the specific history of those communities.

Exploring the dimensions of variation in Tactile ASL

While the ASL of sighted deaf people has been studied for 40 years, the signing of Deaf-Blind people is a new subject of linguistic research. Collins and Petronio (1998) set out to describe changes in signing that occur when ASL is used in a tactile, rather than a visual, mode. The goal was to describe the particular variety of ASL used in the Deaf-Blind community, when Deaf-Blind people converse with other Deaf-Blind people. The authors considered that variation between sighted ASL and Tactile ASL could occur at any level of linguistic structure.

Collins and Petronio collected two sets of Deaf-Blind conversation, one relatively informal and one relatively formal. Informal data were collected at a party attended by 11 Deaf-Blind people. The more formal data came from a set of conversations between three pairs of Deaf-Blind people, all using Tactile ASL to tell stories to each other. The 17 signers had all been born deaf, knew and used ASL prior to becoming legally blind as a result of Ushers Syndrome I,[3] and regularly socialized with Deaf-Blind adult users of Tactile ASL. In Tactile ASL, which can be received with one or both hands, signers' hands are in contact, as shown in Figure 20.3. To limit the possible variation that could occur even within Tactile ASL, only one-handed conversations were included in the data. The researchers focused on the differences and similarities of the phonological form of signs used in visual and Tactile ASL. The features of the signs examined included handshape, location, movement, and orientation.

Early studies of visual ASL sought minimal pairs to determine the distinctive parts of signs. Minimal pairs were interpreted as providing evidence for three parameters: handshape, location and movement, for instance:

- handshape: the signs DONKEY and HORSE use the same location and movement but differ in handshape;

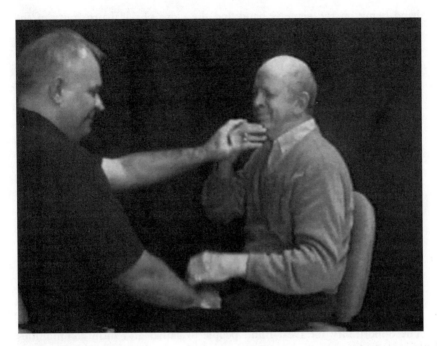

Figure 20.3 Tactile ASL
Source: Steven Collins and Randall Hogue

- location: MOTHER and FATHER use the same handshape and movement but differ in location;
- movement: SICK and TO-BECOME-SICK use the same handshape and location but differ in movement.

Battison (1978) later identified a fourth parameter, orientation, based on pairs such as CHILDREN and THINGS. These two signs have an identical handshape, location, and movement. However, they differ in the palm orientation: the palm of the hand faces upward for THINGS, but toward the floor for CHILDREN. Using these four parameters, Collins and Petronio examined signs in the Tactile ASL data to see if there were any phonological differences between the same sign when it was used in visual or tactile mode.

Collins and Petronio found no variation or changes in the handshape parameter. The other three parameters (movement, orientation and location) displayed the same type of variation due to phonological assimilation that occurs in visual ASL. However, although the same forms of variation occurred in Tactile ASL, this variation was sometimes due to the receiver's hand being on the signer's hand and the close physical proximity of the signer and the receiver. For example, because of the physical closeness, Tactile ASL generally uses a smaller signing space than visual ASL, which usually results in smaller movement paths in signs. In addition, because the signer's and receiver's hands were in contact, the signing space shifted to the area where the hands were in contact; correspondingly, the location of signs articulated in neutral space also shifted to this area. The orientation parameter showed some variation resulting from modifications the signer made to better accommodate the receiver. One change, unique to Tactile ASL, occurred with signs that included body contact. In addition to the signer's hand moving toward the body part, the body part often moved toward the hand in Tactile ASL. This adaptation allowed the receiver to maintain more comfortable tactile contact with the signer.

The variation, adaptations, and changes that Collins and Petronio described are examples of linguistic change that has occurred and is continuing in the US Deaf-Blind community. In the past several years, in addition to an expansion of the American Association of the Deaf-Blind, there has been growth in chapters of this organization based in various US states. Deaf-Blind people are increasing their contact with other Deaf-Blind people. The opportunity for Deaf-Blind people to gather and form communities has resulted in sociolinguistic changes in ASL as Deaf-Blind people modify it to meet their needs. From a linguistic viewpoint, Tactile ASL provides us with a unique opportunity to witness the linguistic changes ASL is undergoing as the Deaf-Blind community adapts the language to a tactile mode.

Conclusion

Most of the variation that we observe in all human languages, whether spoken or signed, is systematic. The linguistic factors that condition the variation have to do with features of the variable in question, the immediate linguistic environment in which it occurs, its function, or with features of the discourse in which it occurs. While many of the social factors that condition variation are the same for spoken and sign languages, some factors, such as language use in the home, are unique to sign language variation. Furthermore, age and region need to be understood specifically within the context of Deaf education. While we see many similarities between the variable units and processes in spoken and sign languages, fundamental differences between the respective structures of spoken and sign languages are reflected in variation. We see this in the strong role that grammatical constraints play in phonological variation in sign languages. Continuing research on variation in a wide variety of sign languages can only enhance our understanding of variation in all languages, while at the same time providing further evidence of the diversity of linguistic resources in Deaf communities.

Notes

1 We have adopted the use of "deaf" (with lower case d) as an adjective referring primarily to hearing loss and the use of "Deaf" (with upper case D) as an adjective referring to social collectivities and attitudes arising from the interaction among people with hearing losses. This distinction is employed throughout this chapter.
2 In accord with convention, ASL signs are written in capital letters. Thus, DEAF refers to the ASL sign, not to the English word.
3 Ushers Syndrome I is a genetic condition in which individuals are born deaf and later, usually in their teen years, start losing vision in varying degrees due to retinitis pigmentosa.

Further reading

For additional information about Deaf culture, see:
Lane, H., Hoffmeister, R. and Bahan, B. (1996) *Journey into the DEAF-WORLD*. San Diego, CA: DawnSign Press.
Padden, C. and Humphries, T. (1988) *Deaf in America: Voices from a Culture*. Cambridge, MA: Harvard University Press.
For additional information about the sociolinguistics of sign languages, see:
Lucas, C., Bayley, R. and Valli, C. (2003) *What's Your Sign for PIZZA? An Introduction to Variation in American Sign Language*. Washington, DC: Gallaudet University Press.
Metzger, M. (ed.) (2000) *Bilingualism and Identity in Deaf Communities* (*Sociolinguistics in Deaf Communities*, vol. 6). Washington, DC: Gallaudet University Press.

For information on methods for conducting sociolinguistic research in Deaf communities, see:
Hoopes, R., Rose, M., Bayley, R., Lucas, C., Wulf, A., Collins, S. and Petronio, K. (2001) Analyzing variation in sign languages: Theoretical and methodological issues. In V. Dively, M. Metzger, S. Taub and A. M. Baer (eds), *Signed Languages: Discoveries from International Research* (pp. 135–62). Washington, DC: Gallaudet University Press.

Lucas, C., Bayley, R., Valli, C., Rose, M., and Wulf, A. (2001) Sociolinguistic variation. In C. Lucas (ed.), *The Sociolinguistics of Sign Languages* (pp. 61–111). Cambridge: Cambridge University Press.

For information about language and Deaf education, see:
Ramsey, C. L. (1997) *Deaf Children in Public Schools: Placement, Context, and Consequences* (*Sociolinguistics in Deaf Communities*, vol. 3). Washington, DC: Gallaudet University Press.

21

Managing Linguistic Diversity in the Clinic: Interpreters in Speech-Language Pathology

Kim M. Isaac

Linguistic diversity within the clinic is gradually attracting more and more interest and acknowledgement as an area of research need. The management of cultural and linguistic diversity has received increasing attention across health care domains, especially within the medical and nursing professions. Yet, despite our profession's interest in communication and interaction, there is a relative lack of literature specific to the management of linguistic diversity, and associated work with interpreters, in speech-language pathology. However, it is likely that the populations we serve will become increasingly diverse in culture and language, given growing rates of international migration and growing acceptance of multiculturalism and multilingualism in many societies world-wide. Interpreters are the ideal option for maximizing effective communication across language boundaries, and many authors in the health care field argue for the need to improve access to and use of interpreting services (e.g., Baker, Parker, Williams, Coates and Pitkin, 1996; Gentile, Ozolins and Vasilakakos, 1996; Hornberger, Itakura and Wilson, 1997; Ozolins, 1998; Roger, Code and Sheard, 2000; Elderkin-Thompson, Silver and Waitzkin, 2001; Isaac, 2002a, 2002b).

A majority of countries offer interpreting services. However, the nature of the services can be vastly different. Ozolins (1998) suggests that interpreting services fall into three broad categories – ad-hoc, generic, and comprehensive – existing along a continuum. Services considered to be comprehensive offer a co-ordinated network across government and private sector domains for establishing and monitoring professional standards, evaluation, and training. Ad-hoc and generic interpreting services operate through individual organizations (e.g., hospitals) with no or little co-ordination within the broader organizational field (e.g., health care system). Due to these differences, the type of interpreting service offered to professionals requiring language mediation can range from professionally trained interpreters with skills specific to the organizational setting (e.g., professional medical interpreters) to untrained bilingual aides, such as bilingual members of staff, family members, or friends.

The theoretical concepts and clinical issues discussed in this chapter relate to working with both trained and untrained interpreters, although the potential barriers to effective interaction are increased when an untrained interpreter is employed in a clinical encounter. This chapter aims to offer a practical and thought-provoking tutorial, drawing on relevant theoretical approaches and clinical processes, in order to explore the barriers and bridges to effective interpreter-mediated speech-language pathology.

Interpreter-mediated interaction

It is generally agreed in the literature that culture has a powerful influence over communication (e.g., Gudykunst, 1993, 1995; O'Sullivan, 1994; Sperber and Wilson, 1995). The way we speak and express ourselves, both verbally and non-verbally, is ultimately influenced by our cultural make-up. Similarly, the way we understand the communication (verbal and non-verbal) of another is also guided by our cultural background. We are able to judge the effectiveness and success of communicative exchanges by comparing them with our knowledge of rules and conventions for interaction, and with our perceptions of what is socially acceptable in different situations. However, when shared cultural background is removed from a communicative dyad, we can no longer rely on our knowledge of rules and conventions or our perceptions of what is socially acceptable interaction, since culture will determine the nature of those rules and standards. If shared language is also removed from the interaction, and communication is mediated by an interpreter, then it is important for message transference to include language and *cultural* interpretation. In order to preserve the *intent* (as opposed to content) of a communicative turn, the interpreter needs to consider the underlying cultural influences, passing the message through a *cultural buffer* before presenting it to the receiving party (see Isaac, 2001). Several authors argue the need for interpreters to take on this cultural-mediation role in addition to the traditional language-mediation role (e.g., Blinstrubaitė, 2000; Elderkin-Thompson, et al., 2001; Isaac, 2002b). Paying attention to the words of a message alone, without considering cultural nuances, can have significant impact on the success and effectiveness of the interpreted message. Pauwels discusses the way in which descriptions of illness and associated symptoms can vary across cultures. For example, she describes the phrase "ants are crawling over my body" (1995: 171) as a general indication of feeling unwell, but argues that it may be misunderstood as a specific symptom, such as numbness and tingling, if the cultural nuance is not conveyed. In describing models for real and ideal interpreter–mediated communication, Buchwald, Caralis, Gany, Hardt, Muecke and Putsch (1993) suggest that for interpretation to be successful, the interpreter must hold similar cultural and linguistic knowledge and perceptions with each conversational partner. Thus, it is not enough for an interpreter to be simply bilingual – they must also be bicultural, and competently so. In a health care context, the cultures of the patient and professional extend beyond a social dynamic. For the patient, this includes sick role behaviors, beliefs and perceptions of illness (including causes, symptoms, and expected treatments), and communicative patterns reflecting those culture-bound feelings and beliefs. For the professional, this includes the culture of the health care system, beliefs and perceptions of illness (including causes, symptoms, and treatments), and communicative patterns reflecting those culture-bound beliefs (very often characterized by jargonistic terminology reflecting a bio-medical approach to health care). Returning to Buchwald and colleagues' (1993) model of interpreter–mediated communication, it seems that even when the interpreter shares language and culture with the patient and professional, additional factors, such as professional culture and sick role culture, have the potential to impact on the success of an interpreted interaction. Using trained medical interpreters is a step towards improving the success of interpreted health care consultations, but a collaborative, information-sharing partnership between the health care provider and interpreter, is considered to be a vital strategy in facilitating effective interaction.

Evaluating interpreter–mediated interaction

Traditionally, interpreter–mediated interactions have been evaluated against a standard of competency, based on accuracy of message transference. The majority of literature describing interpreter–mediated communication in health care contexts have focussed on breakdowns occurring at the level of text, or surface-level difficulties. Such reports have described a rich variety of difficulties in both communication and interaction. Although these studies offer important information about the types of difficulties that may overtly exist in interpreter-mediated interaction, they do not elaborate on the factors underlying those surface manifestations. Wadensjö (1998) pioneered discussion about the deep evaluation of interpreter-mediated communication. She recognized the importance of surface-level analysis, such as descriptions of errors and breakdowns, but she also argued for a deeper analysis to explore the social interaction processes impacting on communicative behaviors and outcomes. In an investigation of the working relationships between speech-language pathologists and interpreters, Isaac (2002a) explored the possible social interaction processes underlying identified and reported surface breakdowns. Some 30 speech-language pathologists and 16 professionally trained interpreters participated in the study, resulting in a rich and unique exploration of professional roles and role dynamics. It was found that a variety of underlying social processes were capable of either impeding or promoting effective interaction between the speech-language pathologist and interpreter during a clinical session. While it is important to identify and describe communication breakdowns occurring at the surface level of interaction, the studies by Wadensjö (1998) and Isaac (2002a) suggest that deep analysis and investigation of social interaction processes should accompany evaluation of surface-level difficulties.

Barriers to effective interpreter-mediated interaction

Numerous barriers have been described in the literature, including inappropriate paraphrasing, use of unexplained professional jargon, lack of linguistic equivalents, language/dialect mismatch, and independent intervention by the interpreter (see Isaac, 2002b, for a detailed discussion of these barriers). Additional barriers have been described by Isaac (2002a), based on her research study of clinician–interpreter interaction in clinical practice:

- ineffective time management, such as either professional arriving late for a session or scheduling insufficient time to complete the goals of the session;
- inexperience and lack of knowledge/skill about managing patients from culturally and linguistically diverse populations and/or through an interpreter, resulting in perceptions of interpreting error, feelings of anxiety, dissatisfaction with session outcomes, and lack of collaborative information exchange between the clinician and interpreter;

- inadequate session planning, such as lack of consideration of how cultural and language differences may impact on session processes and procedures, or inappropriate planning of how the interpreter will be involved in the session;
- limited information sharing between the speech pathologist and interpreter, especially in pre-session meetings (see Isaac, 2002b, for a discussion of pre-session briefing);
- attempts made by the clinician to control information and/or knowledge, resulting in perceptions of the interpreter as language-mediator only and/or suspicion of interpreting error when the interpreted message did not match the original in terms of message length;
- inappropriate assumptions made by the clinician about the interpreter's skills, roles, background knowledge, or commitment to the session.

Linking the barriers

The deep analysis of communication and interaction performed by Isaac (2002a) in her study of speech pathologists and interpreters revealed four broad factors impeding the interaction. These were Inadequate Preparation, Inadequate Communication, Independence, and Assumptions. Some of the more specific barriers described above may be categorized as part of these four broad factors. For example, ineffective time management, lack of knowledge, language/dialect mismatch, and inadequate session planning can be considered components of Inadequate Preparation; use of unexplained professional jargon, unclear communication, lack of linguistic equivalents, and limited information sharing can be considered components of Inadequate Communication; finally, control over information and knowledge, and independent intervention can be considered components of Independence. These and other specific barriers (such as inappropriate paraphrasing and perceived interpreting error) may also occur as a direct result of events or behaviors reflecting one or more of the broader barrier categories. For example, inappropriate paraphrasing may occur due to Inadequate Preparation (such as lack of knowledge and/or inadequate session planning), Inadequate Communication (such as limited information sharing and/or use of unexplained professional jargon) or Independence (such as independent intervention). Thus, each category has the potential to influence any of the other three categories, by either triggering its initiation, or sustaining its development, as illustrated in Figure 21.1.

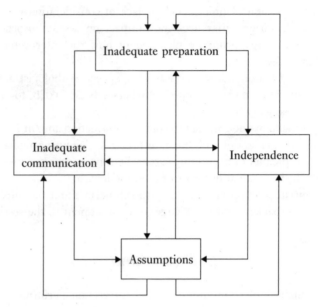

Figure 21.1   Model of barriers to effective clinician–interpreter interaction
(from Isaac, 2002b: 293)

The following text, from Isaac's study, is an actual narrative written by a
speech pathologist describing an interpreter-mediated session she felt dis-
satisfied with. Throughout the text, barrier processes and outcomes are
identified in italics to illustrate their potential circular and sustaining effect.
The barrier processes and outcomes have been modified slightly from the
original example (2002b: 167–8), which describes a session involving the
speech pathologist, the interpreter, and a 54-year-old patient with a moderate
expressive dysphasia:

Example 1
I had pre-arranged to video the session . . . for student use. Everything was
set up in the room. The interpreter came in and had a conversation with the
patient and didn't translate anything (*Independence: speech pathologist feels
excluded*). (I was sitting next to them, waiting to start) (*Assumptions: speech
pathologist suspicious of interpreter's professional intent*). I asked the interpreter
what had been said and explained that I would like to know *all* that is said
(*Independence: control over information*). She was a little annoyed (*lack of
rapport*) and explained that social greetings are important in the culture. I

explained that it was fine to greet but could she just let me know that's all it was (*Independence: control over information*).

I videotaped the patient describing the cookie jar theft picture. The patient did surprisingly well. After the session (video now off) I asked the interpreter how the patient had appeared in Vietnamese. She indicated that the patient hadn't responded well, but because it was being videoed she didn't want to embarrass the patient so she added to the responses to make them more understandable (*Inappropriate paraphrasing: embellishment*) . . . Once I explained **again** (*Assumption that earlier explanation was understood; Inadequate Communication: earlier explanation may have been inadequate or may not have given the interpreter opportunity to clarify her understanding*) what I wanted the interpreter to do (*Repair strategy – clarifying information*), she apologized. The awareness of speech pathology intervention was reduced for this interpreter (even though she had been interpreting for a while) (*Assumptions about background knowledge and experience of speech pathology*). The whole session was wasted (*negative session impact*) – but I learnt heaps.

Learning to build bridges

Although the speech pathologist in Example 1 felt that the entire session had been wasted, she recognized what some of the problems were and used them to her advantage, as a learning tool for future sessions. Building on our knowledge and awareness has the potential to raise our levels of motivation to attempt interpreter-mediated sessions, which will allow us to practice and improve our skills and further build on our knowledge through experience and practical research and discussion. Learning from the barriers is the first step to breaking them down and building the bridges to effective clinician–interpreter interaction. In response to the barriers identified above and described in the literature, many authors have offered suggestions for improving interpreter-mediated communication. Many of these are discussed in the following sections.

Improved time management

Several authors have discussed the importance of improved time management skills, such as allowing for extended session time with the patient and allowing for briefing and, if necessary, debriefing time with the interpreter directly before and after the session (e.g., Lynch, 1992; Poss and Rangel, 1995; Ruiz, 1996; Isaac, 2002a, 2002b).

Comprehensive session planning

Special consideration is required when planning interpreter-mediated clinical sessions. Since culture and language background may influence assessment and treatment techniques, it is important to ensure session goals match the client's needs and expectations, and that procedures and materials are appropriate to the experiences of the client. Where possible, information should be sought before a session regarding the general language and cultural background of the client. In addition, consideration should be given to the expected roles of the clinician and interpreter and interaction dynamics of the session.

It is vital that the clinician has a clear understanding of the session goals, rationales and clinical procedures for achieving those goals, so that she or he is able to confidently and competently discuss the plan with the interpreter. In addition to this, it is important for the clinician to have considered how the interpreter will be involved in the session and how they may be able to help refine the proposed session plan.

Professional development

Breaking down the barriers relies heavily on being able to evaluate what went wrong and then identify effective and practical solutions. Often this involves reading and researching to broaden awareness and knowledge in those areas most likely to contribute to breakdowns (such as cultural and linguistic influences on session plans, clinical skills for working with patients from culturally and linguistically diverse populations, methods of interpreting in speech pathology assessment and treatment sessions, roles and skills of professionally trained interpreters, problems associated with using untrained interpreters such as family members and friends, and so on).

Information sharing

Sharing information with the interpreter about the session, especially as part of a pre-session meeting has been recommended by several authors (e.g., Poss and Rangel, 1995; Ruiz, 1996; Isaac, 2002a, 2002b). Isaac (2002a) found that information exchange was considered to be a crucial element in facilitating effective clinician–interpreter interaction. One speech pathologist commented (p. 188):

Example 2
The interpreter and I met before the session. I asked her about the Arabic language and culture and told her my aims of the assessment and gave her information regarding the client's stroke, medical condition and his communication skills – which I had gained via his family and observations. The interpreter asked very insightful questions regarding his speech/language impairments and was honest in telling me she was new at interpreting in a medical setting. This discussion was very satisfying because I felt confident we both knew the format of the session and had been able to talk about our expectations of each other.

Collaborative discussion, as described in this example, was often thought to result in clearer and more comprehensive communication between the clinician and interpreter with subsequent positive outcomes for the session. Many speech pathologists recognized the value in asking open questions during pre-session briefings to facilitate the interpreter's participation in a collaborative communication style.

Clear communication

Communicating clearly with the interpreter by reducing ambiguity (i.e., from the use of jargon, complex linguistic structures, long sentences, or multiple revisions and restarts due to inadequate linguistic planning) has been supported by several authors (e.g., Launer, 1978; Putsch, 1985; Lynch, 1992; Poss and Rangel, 1995; Ruiz, 1996; Elderkin-Thompson et al., 2001; Isaac, 2002a, 2002b).

Collaborative partnership

Establishing and sustaining a collaborative partnership with the interpreter is considered to be the most crucial ingredient for effective interaction and successful session outcomes. Collaboration was well supported by the speech pathologists and interpreters in Isaac's study and was described in terms of three main functions: (1) the interpreter's involvement in session planning and/or activities, for example (2002b: 194) (see Example 3); (2) the inter-preter's active participation in information exchange before or during the session, and (3) initiation of repair strategies by either professional when actual or potential miscommunication is recognized.

Example 3
In order to attempt treatment using RCS [*Response Contingent Stimulation*], I presented mother, through the interpreter, with the theory and asked for parallel expressions to phrases such as "no bumpy words," "that was a bit bumpy," "nice smooth talking." Together mother and the interpreter were able to work out suitable phrases, which mother wrote down for further sessions and home sessions.

Awareness

Awareness of the interpreter's roles and skills reflects the understanding that an interpreter has much more to offer than just language mediation. Recognizing the interpreter's skill as cultural and linguistic informant (see Isaac, 2002b) in addition to language mediator (especially in the context of speech pathology) can facilitate collaborative interaction at the levels of pre-session planning, implementation, and post-session evaluation. In addition, awareness of the interpreter's skill and the complexities involved in inter-pretation seems more likely to promote confidence in any independent actions (such as establishing rapport with the patient or clarifying a mis-understanding with the patient) which may otherwise have the potential to result in feelings of exclusion and suspicion about the interpreter's skill and professional allegiance.

Linking the bridges

The deep analysis of communication and interaction performed by Isaac (2002a) identified four broad processes with the potential to enhance effective clinician–interpreter interaction – Adequate Preparation, Adequate Com-munication, Partnership, and Awareness. These were found to be in direct contrast with the barrier categories identified in the same study. As with the barrier functions, each individual factor enhancing effective interaction may be classified under the domain of one of the broader categories (e.g., infor-mation sharing and clear communication can be considered components of

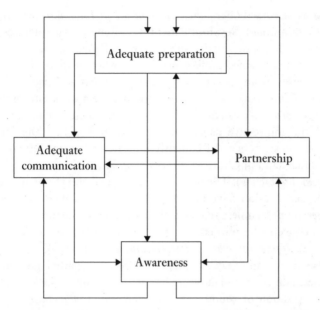

Figure 21.2 Model of bridges to effective clinician–interpreter interaction (from Isaac, 2002b: 296)

Adequate Communication). In addition, each broad category (including the specific functions within them) has the potential to influence and be influenced by the other three bridges to effective interaction (e.g., improving knowledge about cultural and linguistic influences on session procedures can directly impact on pre-session communication with the interpreter, which has the potential to facilitate positive rapport and a collaborative relationship). This bridge-building network can be shown as in Figure 21.2.

The following text helps to illustrate the circular network between the bridge categories (bridge processes and positive outcome are identified in italics and have been modified slightly from the original source). The narrative text, written by the same speech pathologist from Example (1), describes an interpreter-mediated session involving the speech pathologist, interpreter and 60-year-old patient with expressive dysphasia (Isaac, 2002b: 208, 210):

Example 4
Interpreter: presented early to the session (*Adequate Preparation: Effective time management*) to request what the session would be about (*Awareness of roles and information needs*). Briefed well and some cultural information re:

Chinese was discussed (*Adequate Communication: Information sharing; Partnership: Collaboration*). **Session**: Patient describing activity pictures, requiring regular feedback to identify speech errors. Patient was aware of speech rate. Interpreter remained professional for the whole session – i.e., translayed (*sic*) information from speech pathologist to patient and patient to speech pathologist. Comments made by the patient were always interpreted (*Perception of competent interpreting*). Patient demonstrated a "neurological stutter" and the impressive aspect of the session was that the interpreter interpreted the stutters and frequently indicated when the patient was difficult to understand in Chinese (*Awareness of roles and knowledge; Perception of competent interpreting*). The interpreter explained everything to the patient and I felt that I didn't have to repeat myself or clarify (*Perception of competent interpreting*) – unless requested occasionally by the interpreter because of certain concepts he wanted to make sure he explained correctly (*Repair strategy – clarifying information, Partnership: Collaboration*).

We also spent time (patient, interpreter, speech pathologist) discussing the Chinese alphabet and how to use it in therapy – looking at tones/phonemes/position of sounds, etc. (*Partnership: Collaboration*). This was useful for all involved – especially the patient because it was educating him on a metalinguistic level. A Chinese word list was developed on the day and the interpreter actually brought a further list to the next session plus a Chinese alphabet sheet for me (for future reference) (*Partnership: active session involvement*). A debrief session was conducted after the session to review the patient's speech during the session (*Adequate Communication: Information sharing*). I learnt heaps (*improved knowledge and awareness for professional roles and cultural and linguistic influences on session processes and procedures*), the patient's speech improved (*Positive session outcome*) and the interpreter (I hope) felt well utilized in making the session a success.

Crossing the bridges in clinical practice

The models of barriers and bridges to effective clinician–interpreter interaction (Figures 21.1 and 21.2) show how the four broad categories of each model are intricately linked and have the potential to influence and be influenced by the other three categories. It is possible to enter the models at any point and from any base function (e.g., effective time management or awareness of roles and knowledge) and then be shunted through a variety of other barrier or bridge processes subsequently sparked into action. It is proposed though, that education about and improved awareness of the social interactional processes involved in the formation of barriers and bridges can help break down the blockades and begin construction on the bridges to effective interaction. Construction begins in clinical practice and is strengthened through experience across six key areas:

Planning and preparation

- Expect interpreter-mediated sessions to take at least twice as long as same-language clinical sessions.
- Have a comprehensive plan, which considers the patient's cultural and linguistic background and the potential ways that may impact on session goals and procedures.
- Schedule around 10 minutes of briefing time with the interpreter before the patient's appointment – this should allow good opportunity to discuss many issues relevant to the session, including experiences, expectations, roles, and needs. This briefing time is particularly important when the interpreter is untrained in formal interpreting, health care interpreting, or is inexperienced with speech pathology sessions. Pre-session briefing is discussed in greater detail in Isaac (2002b).
- Allow 5–10 minutes with the interpreter after the appointment to discuss the session, the interpreter's perceptions of the patient's performance in the light of cultural and linguistic influences, and plan for the next session (if appropriate).

Improving knowledge

- Investigate the cultural and linguistic diversity of the area in which you work – develop resource manuals for at least the most prominent groups, including information about the language (e.g., morphosyntactic structure and phonology), culture (e.g., important beliefs, religions, child-rearing practices, family structure and dynamics, perceptions of health and illness), meaning and use of common non-verbal behaviors (e.g., hand gestures, body language, eye contact, use of silence), sources of further information (e.g., useful texts and articles, community group libraries, and resource people such as ethnic health workers, interpreters, or cultural liaison officers), and include some common phrases and questions so you can at least greet the patient in their home language.

- Read and research about working with interpreters – the more you understand the complexities of interpreting, the better equipped you will be to facilitate collaborative partnership.

Communicating effectively

- Avoid using professional jargon – plan your words carefully and consider the potential ambiguity of the terms you use. Words we use regularly in a professional context (e.g., hearing assessment, grammar, vocabulary, language, comprehension, dysarthria, swallowing, stuttering, articulation, phonology) may seem common to us, but may be variably understood by the wider community. If you do use jargon terms, try to pair them with a description in lay terms, and check understanding with the interpreter and patient.
- Establish methods for repairing actual and potential misunderstandings or linguistic difficulties with the interpreter prior to beginning the session.
- Plan your sentences to avoid unnecessary and confusing repetition of thoughts, and revision or restart of ideas.
- Facilitate collaborative information exchange by offering the interpreter opportunity to participate in discussion about the session in the pre-session meeting – ask open-ended questions and invite the interpreter's comments or suggestions.

Facilitating partnership

- Remember that speech pathologists and interpreters are communication specialists with unique, but complementary, knowledge and skills. Foster a collaborative partnership based on trust and mutual respect – improved knowledge and awareness, comprehensive planning and preparation, and effective communication will be your stepping stones to a collegial professional relationship.

Avoiding assumptions

- Remember that culture can have a significant impact on beliefs, perceptions, communication styles and expectations – be careful not to judge the interpreter's or patient's behavior based on your own culturally biased perceptions and standards.

- Avoid judging the interpreter's performance and quality of the interpretation based on the length of the interpreted message. If you are uncertain about how the message was received by either party, clarify their understanding by asking checking questions (e.g., "I'd like to be sure that I explained that clearly to you. I'd like you to tell (or show) me how you will practice that at home").

Evaluating the session

- Once a session is complete, reflect on your feelings (and, ideally, the interpreter's feelings) about it. Try to identify problem areas and what may have been underlying those. Similarly, identify successful aspects of the session and the contributing factors. Use your analysis to minimize barriers and maximize bridges in your next sessions.

Conclusion

Linguistic diversity will never go away. In fact, it is likely to become a more prominent part of our everyday and professional lives. Interpreter services are receiving growing recognition around the world and moves are been made in many countries to make access to professionally trained interpreters more equitable. It is probably unrealistic to assume, though, that untrained interpreters will never be needed, or should never be used. Professional interpreting services are often stretched to the limit, and it may be impossible to arrange for a professional interpreter when needed (especially when the need is urgent). Thus, family, friends and bilingual staff will at some time be called upon to assist health professionals assess the immediate needs and health condition of patients. However, it is vitally important for health professionals to be highly aware of the potential risks and problems involved in using untrained interpreters and to be even more aware of the need for comprehensive planning and preparation, clear communication, and cautious collaboration. The barriers and bridges described in this chapter offer an insight into the ways social interaction behaviors and beliefs can influence communication and session success. In the words of one interpreter from Isaac's study (2002a: 213):

When there is a clear view of what is expected of each other's role and agreement of how to work together, there follows the ability to communicate with each other effectively and as a result the session should flow much easier and successfully.

Further reading

Cambridge, J. (1999) Information loss in bilingual medical interviews through an untrained interpreter. *The Translator* 5(2): 201–19.

Kaufert, J. M. and Putsch, R. W. (1997) Communication through interpreters in health care: Ethical dilemmas arising from differences in class, culture, language, and power. *Journal of Clinical Ethics* 8(1): 71–87.

Pöchhacker, F. and Kadric, M. (1999) The hospital cleaner as healthcare interpreter. *The Translator* 5(2): 161–78.

Tebble, H. (1998) *Medical Interpreting: Improving Communication with Your Patients.* Geelong, Australia: Deakin University.

References

Abdulaziz Mkilifi, M. (1978) Triglossia and Swahili–English bilingualism in Tanzania. In J. Fishman (ed.), *Advances in the Study of Societal Multilingualism* (pp. 129–52). The Hague: Mouton.

Abercrombie, D. (1967) *Elements of General Phonetics*. Chicago: Aldine.

Adger, C. T., Wolfram, W. and Detwyler, J. (1993) Confronting dialect minority issues in special education: Reactive and proactive perspectives. In *Third National Research Symposium on Limited English Students' Issues* (pp. 737–62). Washington, DC: Government Printing Office.

Adler, S. (1981) *Poverty, Children and Their Languages*. New York: Grune-Stratton.

Agheyisi, R. and Fishman, J. A. (1970) Language attitude studies: A review and proposal. *Anthropological Linguistics* 12: 131–57.

Aitchison, J. (2001) *Language Change: Progress or Decay?* Cambridge: Cambridge University Press.

Albert, M. L. and Obler, L. K. (1978) *The Bilingual Brain: Neuropsychological and Neurolinguistic Aspects of Bilingualism*. New York: Academic Press.

Alim, H. S. (2001) I be the truth: Divergence, recreolization, and the equative copula in Black Nation Language. Paper presented at NWAV 30, Raleigh, NC, October.

Allington, R. L. (2002) Troubling times: A short historical perspective. In R. L. Allington (ed.), *Big Brother and the National Reading Curriculum: How Ideology Trumped Evidence* (pp. 3–47). Portsmouth, NH: Heinemann.

Altani, C. (1995) Primary school teachers' explanations of boys' disruptiveness in the classroom: A gender-specific aspect of the hidden curriculum. In J. Swann and D. Graddol (eds), *Language and Gender* (pp. 160–79). London: Longman.

American Psychological Association (2000) *DSM-IV TR*. Washington, DC: American Psychological Association Publishing Inc.

Anderson, R. (2004) First language loss in Spanish-speaking children: Patterns of loss and implications for clinical practice. In B. Goldstein (ed.), *Bilingual Language Development and Disorders in Spanish–English Speakers* (pp. 187–211). Baltimore, MD: Brookes.

Ann, J. (2001) Bilingualism and language contact. In C. Lucas (ed.), *The Sociolinguistics of Sign Languages* (pp. 33–60). Cambridge: Cambridge University Press.

April, R. S. and Han, M. (1980) Crossed aphasia in a right-handed bilingual Chinese man. *Archives of Neurology* 37: 342–6.

April, R. S. and Tse, P. C. (1977) Crossed aphasia in a Chinese bilingual dextral. *Archives of Neurology* 34: 766–70.

Aries, E. (1976) Interaction patterns and themes of male, female and mixed groups. *Small Group Behavior* 7: 7–18.

Arnberg, L. N. and Arnberg, P. W. (1985) The relation between code differentiation and language mixing in bilingual three to four year old children. *Bilingual Review* 12: 20–32.

Askew, S. and Ross, C. (1988) *Boys Don't Cry*. Milton Keynes: Open University Press.

Atkinson, K. (1993) Cooperativity in all-female intergenerational talk. Unpublished thesis, University of Wales.

Baetens Beardsmore, H. (1986) *Bilingualism: Basic Principles*, 2nd edn. Clevedon: Multilingual Matters.

Bailey, G. (2001) The relationship between African American Vernacular English and White Vernaculars in the American South: A sociocultural history and some phonological evidence. In S. L. Lanehart (ed.), *Sociocultural and Historical Contexts of African American English* (pp. 53–92). Philadelphia, PA: Benjamins.

Bailey, G. and Thomas, E. R. (1998) Some aspects of African-American English phonology. In S. S. Mufwene, J. R. Rickford, G. Bailey and J. Baugh (eds), *African American English: Structure, History, and Use* (pp. 85–109). London: Routledge.

Baker, C. (2001) *Foundations in Bilingual Education and Bilingualism*, 3rd edn. Clevedon: Multilingual Matters.

Baker, D. W., Parker, R. M., Williams, M. V., Coates, W. C. and Pitkin, K. (1996) Use and effectiveness of interpreters in an emergency department. *JAMA* 275(10): 783–8.

Baker-Shenk, C. and Cokely, D. (1980) *American Sign Language: A Teacher's Resource Text on Grammar and Culture*. Washington, DC: Gallaudet University Press.

Bakhtin, M. M. ([1935] 1981) *The Dialogic Imagination: Four Essays*, ed. M. Holquist, trans. C. Emerson and M. Holquist. Austin, TX: University of Texas Press.

Ball, M. J. (1992) *The Clinician's Guide to Linguistic Profiling of Language Impairment*. Kibworth: Far Communications.

Ballenger, C. (1992) Because you like us: The language of control. *Harvard Educational Review* 62: 199–208.

Bartholomeus, B. (1973) Voice identification by nursery school children. *Canadian Journal of Psychology* 27: 464–72.

Basso, K. (1970) To give up on words: Silence in Western Apache culture. *South West Journal of Anthropology* 26: 213–30.

Basso, K. (1996) *Wisdom Sits in Places: Landscape and Language among the Western Apache*. Albuquerque. NM: University of New Mexico Press.

Bates, E., Dale, P. S. and Thal, D. (1995) Individual differences and their implications for theories of language development. In P. Fletcher and B. MacWhinney (eds), *The Handbook of Child Language* (pp. 96–151). Oxford: Blackwell.

Bateson, G. (1972) *Steps to an Ecology of Mind*. San Francisco: Chandler Press.

Battison, R. M. (1978) *Lexical Borrowing in American Sign Language*. Silver Spring, MD: Linstok Press.

Battison, R. M., Markowicz, H. and Woodward, J. C. (1975) A good rule of thumb: Variable phonology in American Sign Language. In R. W. Fasold and R. Shuy (eds), *Analyzing Variation in Language* (pp. 291–302). Washington, DC: Georgetown University Press.

Bauer, L. and Trudgill, P. (eds) (1998) *Language Myths*. London: Penguin.

Bayley, R. (2002) The quantitative paradigm. In J. K. Chambers, P. Trudgill and N. Schilling-Estes (eds), *The Handbook of Language Variation and Change* (pp. 117–41). Oxford: Blackwell.

Baynham, M. (1995) *Literacy Practices: Investigating Literacy in Social Context*. London: Longman.

Beach, R. and Anson, C. M. (1992) Stance and intertextuality in written discourse. *Linguistics and Education* 4: 335–57.

Bell, A. (1997) Language style as audience design. In N. Coupland and A. Jaworski (eds), *Sociolinguistics: A Reader and Coursebook* (pp. 240–50). New York: Palgrave.

Bennett, S. and Montero-Diaz, L. (1982) Children's perception of speaker sex. *Journal of Phonetics* 10: 113–21.

Bergman, J. R. (1993) *Discrete Indiscretions: The Social Organization of Gossip*. New York: Aldine de Gruyter.

Bergvall, V., Bing, J., and Freed, A. (eds) (1992) *Rethinking Language and Gender Research: Theory and Practice*. London: Longman.

Berko-Gleason, J. (2001) *The Development of Language*. Boston: Allyn and Bacon.

Bialystok, E. (2001) *Bilingualism in Development: Language, Literacy, and Cognition*. Cambridge: Cambridge University Press.

Bishop, D. V. M., North, T., and Donlan, C. (1996) Nonword repetition as a behavioural marker for inherited language impairment: Evidence from a twin study. *Journal of Child Psychology and Psychiatry* 37: 391–403.

Blanke, D. (2000) Vom Entwurf zur Sprache. *Interface: Journal of Applied Linguistics* 15: 37–89.

Blinstrubaité, A. (2000) Interaction in liaison interpreting. *Perspectives: Studies in Translatology* 8(2): 125–33.

Bloom, L. and Lahey, M. (1978) *Language Development and Language Disorders*. New York: Wiley.

Bloome, D. (1989) *Literacy and Classrooms*. Norwood, NJ: Ablex.

Bloomfield, L. (1927) Literate and illiterate speech. *American Speech* 2: 432–9.

Bloomfield, L. (1933) *Language*. New York: Holt.

Boberg, C. and Strassel, S. (2000) Short-a in Cincinnati: A change in progress. *Journal of English Linguistics* 28(2): 108–26.

Boder, E. (1973) Developmental dyslexia: A diagnostic approach based on three atypical reading-spelling patterns. *Developmental Medicine and Child Neurology* 15: 663–87.

Bok, S. (1983) *Secrets*. New York: Vantage Books.

Bourdieu, P. (1991) *Language and Symbolic Power*. Cambridge, MA: Harvard University Press.

Brisk, M. (1998) *Bilingual Education: From Compensatory to Quality Schooling*. Mahwah, NJ: Erlbaum.

Britain, D. (2002) Diffusion, levelling, simplification and reallocation in past tense *be* in the English fens. *Journal of Sociolinguistics* 6: 16–43.

Brown, P. and Levinson, S. (1987) *Politeness: Some Universals in Language Usage*, 2nd edn. Cambridge: Cambridge University Press.

Brown, R. (1973) *A First Language*. Cambridge, MA: Harvard University Press.

Brown, R. and Ford, M. (1961) Address in American English. *Journal of Abnormal and Social Psychology* 62: 375–85.

Brown, R. and Gilman, A. (1960) The pronouns of power and solidarity. In T. Sebeok (ed.), *Style in Language* (pp. 253–76). Cambridge, MA: MIT Press.

Bruner, J. S. (1983) *Child's Talk: Learning to Use Language*. New York: W. W. Norton and Company.

Bruner, J. S. (1984) Language, mind, and reading. In H. Goelman, A. Oberg and F. Smith (eds), *Awakening to Literacy* (pp. 193–200). Portsmouth, NH: Heinemann.

Bruner, J. S. (1990) *Acts of Meaning*. Cambridge, MA: Harvard University Press.

Bryden, M. P. (1982) *Laterality: Functional Asymmetry in the Intact Brain*. New York: Academic Press.

Buchwald, D., Caralis, P. V., Gany, F., Hardt, E. J., Muecke, M. A. and Putsch, R. W. (1993) The medical interview across cultures. *Patient Care* April: 141–66.

Bush, G. W. (2001) *No Child Left Behind: Legislative Proposal*. Washington, DC, January 20. (www.whitehouse.gov/news/reports/no-child-left-behind.html)

Calvet, L.-J. (1999) *Pour une écologie des langues du monde*. Paris: Plon.

Cambourne, B. (1988) *The Whole Story: Natural Learning and the Acquisition of Literacy in the Classroom*. New York: Ashton Scholastic.

Cameron, D. (1992) *Feminism and Linguistic Theory*. Basingstoke: Macmillan.

Campbell, T., Dollaghan, C., Needleman, H., and Janosky, J. (1997) Reducing bias in language assessment: Processing-dependent measures. *Journal of Speech, Language, and Hearing Research* 40: 519–25.

Cazden, C. (1988) *Classroom Discourse: The Language of Teaching and Learning*. Portsmouth, NH: Heinemann.

Cazden, C., Cope, B., Fairclough, N., Gee, J. P., Kalantzis, M., Kress, G., Luke, A., Luke, C., Michaels, S. and Nakata, M. (1996) A pedagogy of multiliteracies: Designing social futures. *Harvard Educational Review* 66: 60–92.

Cenoz, J. (2003) The additive effect of bilingualism on third language acquisition: A review. *International Journal of Bilingualism* 7: 71–88.

Cenoz, J. and Hoffmann, C. (eds) (2003) The effect of bilingual on third language acquisition. Special issue of *International Journal of Bilingualism* 7(1).

Chall, J. (1967) *Learning to Read: The Great Debate*. New York: McGraw-Hill.

Chamberlain, P. and Medeiros-Landurand, P. (1991) Practical considerations for the assessment of LEP students with special needs. In J. Damico and E. Hamayan (eds), *Limiting Bias in the Assessment of Bilingual Students* (pp. 111–56). Austin, TX: ProEd.

Chambers, J. K. (1992) Dialect acquisition. *Language* 68: 673–705.

Chambers, J. K. (2003) *Sociolinguistic Theory*, 2nd edn. Oxford: Blackwell.

Chambers, J. K. and Trudgill, P. (1998) *Dialectology*, 2nd edn. Cambridge: Cambridge University Press.

Chambers, J. K., Trudgill, P. and Schilling-Estes, N. (eds) (2002) *The Handbook of Language Variation and Change*. Oxford: Blackwell.

Cheng, L.-R. L. (1996) Enhancing communication: Toward optimal language learning for limited English proficient students. *Language, Speech, and Hearing Services in Schools* 27: 347–54.

Cheshire, J. (1982) *Variation in an English Dialect*. Cambridge: Cambridge University Press.

Childs, B. and Mallinson, C. (2004) African American English in Appalachia: Dialect accommodation and substrate influence. *English World-Wide* 25: 27–50.

Chomsky, N. (1957) *Syntactic Structures*. The Hague: Mouton.

Chomsky, N. (1959) A review of B. F. Skinner's *Verbal Behavior*, 1957. *Language* 35: 26–58.

Chomsky, N. (1965) *Aspects of the Theory of Syntax*. Cambridge, MA: MIT Press.

Cicourel, A. V. (1992) The interpenetration of communicative contexts: Examples from medical encounters. In A. Duranti and C. Goodwin (eds), *Rethinking Context: Language as an Interactive Phenomenon* (pp. 291–310). Cambridge: Cambridge University Press.

Clark, H. H. (1996) *Using Language*. Cambridge: Cambridge University Press.

Clarricoates, K. (1983) Classroom interaction. In J. Whyld (ed.), *Sexism in the Secondary Curriculum* (pp. 46–61). London: Harper and Row.

Clay, M. M. (1979) *Reading: A Patterning of Complex Behavior*. Auckland: Heinemann.

Clay, M. M. (1991) *Becoming Literate: The Construction of Inner Control*. Portsmouth, NH: Heinemann.

Cleary, M. and Pisoni, D. B. (2002) Talker discrimination by prelingually deaf children with cochlear implants: Preliminary results. *Annals of Otology, Rhinology, and Laryngology* 111(Supplement): 113–18.

Cleary, M., Pisoni, D. B. and Kirk, K. I. (in press) Influence of voice similarity on talker discrimination in normal-hearing children and hearing-impaired children with cochlear implants. *Journal of Speech, Language, and Hearing Research*.

Cleveland, L. and Oetting, J. (2004) The clinical utility of nonword repetition tasks for identification of children with language impairments. Paper presented at the biannual conference of the International Clinical Phonetics and Linguistics Association, Lafayette, LA.

Clopper, C. G. and Pisoni, D. B. (2004) Some acoustic cues for the perceptual categorization of American English regional dialects. *Journal of Phonetics* 32: 111–40.

Cloud, N., Genesee, F. and Hamayan, E. (2000) *Dual Language Instruction: A Handbook for Enriched Education.* Boston: Heinle.

Cluver, A. D. de V. (1993) *A Dictionary of Language Planning Terms.* Pretoria: University of South Africa.

Clyne, M. (1987) Constraints on code-switching: How universal are they? *Linguistics* 25: 739–64.

Coates, J. (1986) *Women, Men and Language.* London: Longman.

Coates, J. (1989) Gossip revisited: Language in all-female groups. In J. Coates and D. Cameron (eds) *Women in their Speech Communities* (pp. 94–122). London: Longman.

Coates, J. (1991) Women's cooperative talk: A new kind of conversational duet. In C. Uhlig and R. Zimmerman (eds), *Proceedings of the Anglistenstag 1990 Marburg* (pp. 296–311). Tübingen: Max Niemeyer Verlag.

Coates, J. (1996) *Women Talk.* Oxford: Blackwell.

Coates, J. (1998) *Language and Gender: A Reader.* Oxford: Blackwell.

Cobarrubias, J. (1983) Ethical issues in status planning. In J. Cobarrubias and J. A. Fishman (eds), *Progress in Language Planning* (pp. 41–85). Berlin: Mouton.

Cochran-Smith, M. (1984) *The Making of a Reader.* Norwood, NJ: Ablex.

Cokely, D. (1983) When is a pidgin not a pidgin? An alternative analysis of the ASL English contact situation. *Sign Language Studies* 38: 1–24.

Coles, G. (1987) *The Learning Mystique: A Critical Look at "Learning Disabilities".* New York: Pantheon Books.

Coles, G. (2000) *Misreading Reading: The Bad Science that Hurts Children.* Portsmouth, NH: Heinemann.

Collins, S. and Petronio, K. (1998) What happens in Tactile ASL? In C. Lucas (ed.), *Sociolinguistics in Deaf Communities*, vol. 4: *Pinky Extension and Eye Gaze: Language Use in Deaf Communities* (pp. 18–37). Washington, DC: Gallaudet University Press.

Conti-Ramsden, G. (2003) Processing and linguistic markers in young children with specific language impairment. *Journal of Speech, Language, and Hearing Research* 46: 1029–37.

Conti-Ramsden, G., Botting, N. and Faragher, B. (2001) Psycholinguistic markers for specific language impairment. *Journal of Child Psychology and Psychiatry* 42: 741–8.

Cooper, R. L. (1989) *Language Planning and Social Change.* Cambridge: Cambridge University Press.

Coulmas, F. (ed.) (1988) *With Forked Tongues: What Are National Languages Good For?* Singapore: Karoma.

Coulmas, F. (ed.) (1997) *The Handbook of Sociolinguistics.* Oxford: Blackwell.

Coupland, N. and Ball, M. J. (1989) Welsh and English in contemporary Wales: Sociolinguistic issues. *Contemporary Wales* 3: 7–40.

Craig, H. (1996) The challenges of conducting language research with African American children. In A. Kamhi, K. Pollock and J. Harris (eds), *Communication Development and Disorders in African American Children* (pp. 1–18). Baltimore, MD: Paul Brookes.

Craig, H. and Washington, J. (2000) An assessment battery for identifying language impairments in African American children. *Journal of Speech, Language, and Hearing Research* 43: 366–79.

Craig, H. and Washington, J. (2003) Oral language expectations for African American preschoolers and kindergarten. *American Journal of Speech-language Pathology* 11: 59–70.

Craig, H., Washington, J. and Thompson-Porter, C. (1998a) Average C-unit lengths in the discourse of African American children from low-income, urban homes. *Journal of Speech, Language, and Hearing Research* 41: 433–44.

Craig, H., Washington, J. and Thompson-Porter, C. (1998b) Performances of young African American children on two comprehension tasks. *Journal of Speech, Language, and Hearing Research* 41: 445–57.

Croft, W. (2000) *Explaining Language Change: An Evolutionary Approach*. London: Longman.

Cruttenden, A. (1970) A phonetic study of babbling. *British Journal of Psychology* 61: 397–408.

Crystal, D. (2000) *Language Death*. Cambridge: Cambridge University Press.

Crystal, D., Fletcher, P. and Garman, M. (1976) *The Grammatical Analysis of Language Disability*. London: Arnold.

Cukor-Avila, P. (2001) Co-existing grammars: The relationship between the evolution of African American and Southern White Vernacular English in the South. In S. L. Lanehart (ed.), *Sociocultural and Historical Contexts of African American English* (pp. 93–128). Philadelphia, PA: Benjamins.

Cummins, J. (2000) *Language, Power and Pedagogy*. Clevedon: Multilingual Matters.

Dabène, L. and Moore, D. (1995) Bilingual speech of migrant people. In L. Milroy and P. Muysken (eds), *One Speaker, Two Languages: Cross-disciplinary Perspectives on Code-switching* (pp. 17–44). Cambridge: Cambridge University Press.

Dalby, D. (2003) *Language in Danger*. New York: Columbia University Press.

Damico, J. S. and Damico, S. K. (1997) The establishment of a dominant interpretive framework in language intervention. *Language, Speech, and Hearing Services in Schools* 28: 288–96.

Damico, J. S. and Hamayan, E. (eds) (1991) *Limiting Bias in the Assessment of Bilingual Students*. Austin, TX: ProEd.

Daoust, D. (1997) Language planning and language reform. In F. Coulmas (ed.), *The Handbook of Sociolinguistics* (pp. 436–52). Oxford: Blackwell.

David, A. (2004) The nature of the developing bilingual lexicon. Unpublished PhD thesis, University of Newcastle upon Tyne.

De Houwer, A. (1990) *The Acquisition of Two Languages from Birth*. Cambridge: Cambridge University Press.

Delamont, S. (1990) *Sex Roles and the School*. London: Methuen.

Delpit, L. (1988) The silenced dialogue: Power and pedagogy in educating other people's children. *Harvard Educational Review* 58: 280–98.

Desloges, P. ([1779] 1984) *Observations d'un sourd et muet sur "un Cours élémentaire d'éducation des sourds et muets," publié en 1779 par M. L'abbé Deschamps*. Amsterdam and Paris: B. Morin. In H. Lane (ed.), *The Deaf Experience: Classics in Language and Education*, trans. F. Philip (1984) (pp. 29–48). Cambridge, MA: Harvard University Press.

Deuchar, M. and Quay, S. (2000) *Bilingual Acquisition*. Oxford: Oxford University Press.

Dewaele, J.-M. (2000) Three years old and three first languages. *Bilingual Family Newsletter* 17(2): 4–5.

Dillard, J. L. (1972) *Black English: Its History and Usage in the United States*. New York: Random House.

Djité, P. (1994) *From Language Policy to Language Planning*. Deakin, Australia: National Languages and Literacy Institute.

Docherty, G. and Foulkes, P. (2001) Variability in (r) production: Instrumental perspectives. In H. van de Velde and R. van Hout (eds), 'r-atics: Sociolinguistic, phonetic and phonological characteristics of /r/. *Etudes and Travaux* 4: 173–84.

Docherty, G. and Watt, D. (2001) Chain shifts. In R. Mesthrie (ed.), *The Pergamon Concise Encyclopaedia of Sociolinguistics* (pp. 303–7). Amsterdam: Elsevier Science.

Dodd, B. J., So, L. K. H. and Li Wei (1996) Symptoms of disorder without impairment: The written and spoken errors of bilinguals. In B. J. Dodd, R. Campbell and L. Worrall (eds), *Evaluating Theories of Language: Implications from Communication Disorders* (pp. 137–61). London: Whurr.

Dollaghan, C. and Campbell, T. (1998) Nonword repetition and child language impairment. *Journal of Speech, Language, Hearing Research* 41: 1136–46.

Dollaghan, C., Campbell, T., Pradise, J., Feldman, H., Janosky, J., Pitcairn, D. and Kurs-Lasky, M. (1999) Maternal education and measures of early speech and language. *Journal of Speech, Language, and Hearing Research* 42: 1432–43.

Dopke, S. (1988) The role of parental teaching techniques in bilingual German–English families. *International Journal of the Sociology of Language* 72: 101–12.

Dopke, S. (1992) *One Parent, One Language*. Amsterdam: Benjamins.

Dorian, N. C. (ed.) (1989) *Investigating Obsolescence: Studies in Language Contraction and Death*. Cambridge: Cambridge University Press.

Dubois, B. L. and Crouch, I. (1977) The question of tag questions in women's speech: They don't really use more of them, do they? *Language and Society* 4: 289–94.

Dumont, R. (1972) Learning English and how to be silent. Studies in Sioux and Cherokee classrooms. In C. Cazden, V. John and D. Hymes (eds), *Functions of Language in the Classroom* (pp. 344–69). New York: Teachers College Press.

Dunn, L. and Dunn, J. (1981) *Peabody Picture Vocabulary Test – Revised*. Circle Pines, MN: American Guidance Service.

Eastman, C. M. (1983) *Language Planning: An Introduction*. San Francisco: Chandler and Sharp.

Eckert, P. (1989) *Jocks and Burnouts: Social Categories and Identity in the High Schools*. New York: Teachers College Press.

Eckert, P. (1993) Cooperative competition in adolescent "girl-talk." In D. Tannen (ed.), *Gender and Conversational Interaction* (pp. 32–62). Oxford: Oxford University Press.

Eckert, P. (2000) *Linguistic Variation as Social Practice*. Oxford: Blackwell.

Eckert, P. and McConnell-Ginet, S. (1992a) Think practically and look locally: Language and gender as community-based practice. *Annual Review of Anthropology* 21: 461–90.

Eckert, P. and McConnell-Ginet, S. (1992b) Communities of practice: Where language, gender, and power all live. In K. Hall, M. Bucholtz and B. Moonwomon (eds), *Locating Power: Proceedings of the Second Berkeley Women and Language Conference* (pp. 89–99). Berkeley, CA: Berkeley Women and Language Group.

Eckert, P. and McConnell-Ginet, S. (1999) New generalizations and explanations in language and gender research. *Language in Society* 28: 185–201.

Eco, U. (1995) *The Search for a Universal Language*. Oxford: Blackwell.

Edelsky, C. (1981) Who's got the floor? *Language and Society* 10: 383–421.

Edelsky, C. (1994) Education for democracy. *Language Arts* 71: 252–7.

Eder, D. (1993) "Go get ya a French!:" Romantic and sexual teasing among adolescent girls. In D. Tannen (ed.), *Gender and Conversational Interaction* (pp. 17–31). Oxford: Oxford University Press.

Edwards, J. R. (1982) Language attitudes and their implications among English speakers. In E. B. Ryan and H. Giles (eds), *Attitudes towards Language Variation* (pp. 20–33). London: Arnold.

Edwards, J. (1994) *Multilingualism*. London: Routledge.

Edwards, J. (2003) Multilingualism. In W. Frawley (ed.), *International Encyclopedia of Linguistics*, 2nd edn (4 vols), vol. 1 (pp. 228–32). Oxford: Oxford University Press.

Egan-Robertson, A. (1998) Learning about culture, language, and power: Understanding relationships among personhood, literacy practices, and intertextuality. *Journal of Literacy Research* 30: 449–87.

Eisikovits, E. (1981) Inner Sydney English: An investigation in variation in adolescent speech. Unpublished thesis, University of Sydney.

Elderkin-Thompson, V., Silver, R. C., and Waitzkin, H. (2001) When nurses double as interpreters: A study of Spanish-speaking patients in a US primary care setting. *Social Science and Medicine* 52: 1343–58.

Ellis Weismer, S. and Hesketh, L. (1996) The impact of emphatic stress on novel word learning by children with specific language impairment. *Journal of Speech, Language, Hearing Research* 39: 177–90.

Ellis Weismer, S., Tomblin, J. B., Zhang, X., Buckwalter, P., Chynoweth, J., and Jones, M. (2000) Nonword repetition performance in school-age children with and without language impairment. *Journal of Speech, Language, and Hearing Research* 46: 1029–37.

Emmorey, K. (2002) *Language, Cognition, and the Brain: Insights from Sign Language Research*. Mahwah, NJ: Lawrence Erlbaum.

Erickson, F. and Shultz, J. (1982) *The Counselor as Gatekeeper*. New York: Academic Press.

Eriks-Brophy, A. and Crago, M. B. (1994) Transforming classroom discourse: An Inuit example. *Language and Education* 8(3): 105–22.

Eyer, J. and Leonard, L. (1995) Functional categories and specific language impairment: A case study. *Language Acquisition* 4: 177–203.

Fabbro, F. (1999) *The Neurolinguistics of Bilingualism: An Introduction*. Hove: Psychology Press.

Fabbro, F. (2001a) The bilingual brain: Bilingual aphasia. *Brain and Language* 79: 201–10.

Fabbro, F. (2001b) The bilingual brain: Cerebral representation of languages. *Brain and Language* 79: 211–22.

Fabbro, F. and Paradis, M. (1995) Differential impairments in four multilingual patients with subcortical lesions. In M. Paradis (ed.), *Aspects of Bilingual Aphasia* (pp. 139–76). Oxford: Pergamon.

Fairclough, N. (1989) *Language and Power*. London: Longman.

Farr, M. (1994) Biliteracy in the home: Practices among *Mexicano* families in Chicago. In D. Spener (ed.), *Adult Biliteracy in the United States* (pp. 89–110). McHenry, IL: Center for Applied Linguistics.

Fasold, R. W. and Wolfram, W. (1970) Some linguistic features of Negro Dialect. In R. W. Fasold and R. W. Shuy (eds), *Teaching Standard English in the Inner City* (pp. 41–68). Washington, DC: Center for Applied Linguistics.

Fellman, J. (1973) *The Revival of a Classical Tongue*. The Hague: Mouton.

Fenson, L., Dale, P., Reznick, S., Thal, D., Bates, E. and Hartung, J. (1993) *The MacArthur Communicative Development Inventories: Users Guide and Technical Manual*. San Diego, CA: Singular.

Ferguson, C. A. (1959) Diglossia. *Word* 15: 325–40.

Ferguson, C. A. (1972) *Language Structure and Language Use*. Stanford, CA: Stanford University Press.

Ferguson, C. A. (1977) Babytalk as a simplified register. In C. Snow and C. A. Ferguson (eds), *Talking to Children* (pp. 209–35). Cambridge: Cambridge University Press.

Ferguson, C. A. (1978) Learning to pronounce: The earliest stage of phonological development in the child. In F. Minifie and L. Lloyd (eds), *Communicative and Cognitive Abilities: Early Behavioral Assessment* (pp. 273–97). Baltimore, MD: University Park Press.

Ferrara, K. and Bell, B. (1995) Sociolinguistic variation and discourse function of constructed dialogue introducers: The case of Be + Like. *American Speech* 70: 265–90.

Ferreiro, E. and Teberosky, A. (1982) *Literacy before Schooling*. Portsmouth, NH: Heinemann Educational Books.

Fettes, M. (2003) Interlingualism: A world-centric approach to language policy and planning. In H. Tonkin and T. Reagan (eds), *Language in the Twenty-first Century* (pp. 47–58). Amsterdam: Benjamins.

Fink, R. P. (1995–6) Successful dyslexics: A constructivist study of passionate interest reading. *Journal of Adolescent and Adult Literacy* 39(4): 268–80.

Firth, J. (1970) *The Tongues of Men and Speech*. Oxford: Oxford University Press.

Fisher, S. (1984) Institutional authority and the structure of discourse. *Discourse Processes* 7: 201–24.

Fishman, J. A. (1967) Bilingualism with and without diglossia; diglossia with and without bilingualism. *Journal of Social Issues* 32: 29–38.

Fishman, J. A. (1972a) *Language and Nationalism*. Rowley, MA: Newbury House.

Fishman, J. A. (1972b) The relationship between micro- and macro-sociolinguistics in the study of who speaks what language to whom and when. In J. Pride and J. Holmes (eds), *Sociolinguistics: Selected Readings* (pp. 15–32). Harmondsworth: Penguin.

Fishman, J. A. (1972c) *The Sociology of Language: An Interdisciplinary Social Science Approach to Language in Society*. Rowley, MA: Newbury House.

Fishman, J. A. (1991) *Reversing Language Shift*. Clevedon: Multilingual Matters.

Fishman, P. (1978) What do couples talk about when they're alone? In D. Butturf and E. L. Epstein (eds), *Women's Language and Style* (pp. 11–22). Akron, OH: Department of English, University of Akron.

Fordham, S. and Ogbu, J. (1986) Black students' school success: Coping with the burden of "acting white." *Urban Review* 18: 176–206.

Foucault, M. (1972) *The Archaeology of Knowledge*. New York: Pantheon Books.

Foulkes, P. and Docherty, G. (2000) Another chapter in the story of /r/: "'Labiodental" variants in British English. *Journal of Sociolinguistics* 4: 30–59.

Foulkes, P. and Docherty, G. (2001) Variation and change in British English /r/. In H. van de Velde and R. van Hout (eds), 'r-atics: Sociolinguistic, phonetic and phonological characteristics of /r/. *Etudes and Travaux* 4: 27–43.

Foulkes, P., Docherty, G. and Watt, D. (1999) Tracking the emergence of structured variation: Realisations of (t) by Newcastle children. *Leeds Working Papers in Linguistics and Phonetics* 7: 1–25.

Fox, S. (2005) New dialect formation in the English of the East End of London. PhD dissertation, University of Essex, Colchester.

Frangoudaki, A. (1992) Diglossia and the present language situation in Greece: A sociological approach to the interpretation of diglossia and some hypotheses on today's linguistic reality. *Language in Society* 21: 365–81.

Fraser, B. (1990) Types of English discourse markers. *Acta Linguistica Hungarica* 38(1–4): 19–33.

Fredman, M. (1975) The effect of therapy given in Hebrew on the home language of the bilingual or polyglot adult aphasic in Israel. *British Journal of Disorders of Communication* 10: 61–9.

Freire, P. (1970) *Pedagogy of the Oppressed.* New York: Seabury Press.

Freire, P. (1973) *Education for Critical Consciousness.* New York: Seabury Press.

Freire, P. and Macedo, D. (1987) *Reading the Word and the World.* Westport, CT: Bergin and Garvey.

French, J. and French, P. (1984) Gender imbalance in the primary classroom: An interactional account. *Educational Research* 29: 127–36.

Gal, S. (1987) Codeswitching and consciousness in the European periphery. *American Ethnologist* 14: 637–53.

Gallagher, T. M. (ed.) (1991) *Pragmatics of Language: Clinical Practice Issues.* San Diego, CA: Singular.

Galloway, L. (1980) Contributions of the right cerebral hemisphere to language and communication issues in cerebral dominance with special emphasis on bilingualism, second, language acquisition, sex differences and certain ethnic groups. Unpublished PhD dissertation, UCLA.

Gannon, J. R. (1981) *Deaf Heritage: A Narrative History of Deaf America.* Silver Spring, MD: National Association of the Deaf.

Garcia, E. (1983) *Early Childhood Bilingualism.* Albuquerque: University of New Mexico Press.

Garfinkel, H. (1967) *Studies in Ethnomethodology.* Englewood Cliffs, NJ: Prentice-Hall.

Gathercole, S. and Baddeley, A. (1990) Phonological memory deficits in language disordered children: Is there a causal connection? *Journal of Memory and Language* 29: 336–60.

Gee, J. P. (1996) *Social Linguistics and Literacies: Ideology in Discourse,* 2nd edn. London: Taylor and Francis.

Gee, J. P. (2000) The new literacy studies: From "socially situated" to the work of the social. In D. Barton, M. Hamilton and R. Ivanic (eds), *Situated Literacies: Reading and Writing in Context* (pp. 180–96). London: Routledge.

Genesee, F. (1989) Early bilingual development, one language or two? *Journal of Child Language* 16: 161–79.

Genesee, F. (2002) Rethinking bilingual acquisition. In J.-M. Dewaele, A. Housen, and Li Wei (eds), *Bilingualism: Beyond Basic Principles* (pp. 204–28). Clevedon: Multilingual Matters.

Gentile, A., Ozolins, U. and Vasilakakos, M. (1996) *Liaison Interpreting: A Handbook.* Melbourne: Melbourne University Press.

Gergen, K. (1991) *The Saturated Self.* New York: Basic Books, Inc.

Giles, H. and Powesland, P. F. (1975) *Speech Style and Social Evaluation.* London: Academic.

Giles, H. and Powesland, P. F. (1997) Accommodation theory. In N. Coupland and A. Jaworski (eds), *Sociolinguistics: A Reader and Coursebook* (pp. 232–9). New York: Palgrave.

Gitterman, M. R. and Sies, L. F. (1990) Aphasia in bilinguals and ASL signers: Implications for a theoretical model of neurolinguistic processing based on a review and synthesis of the literature. *Aphasiology* 4: 233–9.

Goffman, E. (1959) *The Presentation of Self in Everyday Life.* New York: Doubleday.

Goffman, E. (1967) *Interaction Ritual: Essays in Face to Face Behavior.* Garden City, NY: Doubleday.

Goffman, E. (1974) *Frame Analysis: An Essay on the Organization of Experience.* New York: Harper and Row.

Goh, W. D., Pisoni, D. B., Kirk, K. I. and Remez, R. E. (2001) Audio-visual perception of sinewave speech in an adult cochlear implant user: A case study. *Ear and Hearing* 22: 412–19.

Goldstein, B. (ed.) (2004) *Bilingual Language Development and Disorders in Spanish–English Speakers.* Baltimore, MD: Brookes.

Goodman, K. S. (1996) *On Reading: A Common-sense Look at the Nature of Language and the Science of Reading.* Portsmouth, NH: Heinemann.

Goodman, K. S. (ed.) (1998) *In Defense of Good Teaching: What Teachers Need to Know about the "Reading Wars."* York, ME: Stenhouse Publishers.

Goodwin, C. (1986) Gestures as a resource for the organization of mutual orientation. *Semiotica* 62(1/2): 29–49.

Goodwin, C. (2000) Action and embodiment within situated human interaction. *Journal of Pragmatics* 32: 1489–522.

Goodwin, C. (2003) Pointing as situated practice. To appear in S. Kita (ed.) *Pointing: Where Language, Culture and Cognition Meet.* Mahwah, NJ: Earlbaum.

Goodwin, C. and Duranti, A. (1992) Rethinking context: An introduction. In A. Duranti and C. Goodwin (eds), *Rethinking Context: Language as an Interactive Phenomenon* (pp. 1–43). Cambridge: Cambridge University Press.

Goodwin, C. and Goodwin, M. (1990) Interstitial argument. In A. D. Grimshaw (ed.), *Conflict Talk: Sociolinguistic Investigations of Arguments in Conversations* (pp. 85–117). Cambridge: Cambridge University Press.

Goodwin, M. H. and Goodwin, C. (1992) Emotion within situated activity. In A. Duranti and C. Goodwin (eds), *Rethinking Context: Language as an Interactive Phenomenon* (pp. 147–90). Cambridge: Cambridge University Press.

Goodwin-Harness, M. (1980) Directive/response speech sequences in girls' and boys' task activities. In S. McConnell-Ginet, R. Borker and N. Furman (eds), *Women and Language in Literature and Society* (pp. 157–73). New York: Praeger.

Goral, M., Levy, E. S. and Obler, L. K. (2002) Neurolinguistic aspects of bilingualism. *International Journal of Bilingualism* 6: 411–40.

Gordon, E. and Sudbury, A. (2002) Southern hemisphere Englishes. In R. Watts and P. Trudgill (eds), *Alternative Histories of English* (pp. 67–86). London: Routledge.

Graff, D., Labov, W. and Harris, W. (1983) Testing listeners' reactions to phonological markers of ethnic identity: A new method for sociolinguistic research. In D. Sankoff (ed.), *Diversity and Diachrony* (pp. 45–58). Amsterdam: Benjamins.

Graman, T. (1988) Education for humanization: Applying Paulo Freire's pedagogy to learning a second language. *Harvard Education Review* 58: 433–48.

Granovetter, M. (1973) The strength of weak ties. *American Journal of Sociology* 78: 1360–80.

Gray, J. (1992) *Men are from Mars, Women are from Venus*. New York: HarperCollins.

Green, L. J. (2002) *African American English: A Linguistic Introduction*. New York: Cambridge University Press.

Grenoble, L. A. and Whaley, L. J. (eds) (1998) *Endangered Languages*. Cambridge: Cambridge University Press.

Grimshaw, A. D. (ed.) (1990) *Conflict Talk: Sociolinguistic Investigations of Arguments in Conversations*. Cambridge: Cambridge University Press.

Grin, F. (1996) The economics of language: Survey, assessment, and prospects. *International Journal of the Sociology of Language* 121: 17–44.

Grosjean, F. (1982) *Life with Two Languages: An Introduction to Bilingualism*. Cambridge, MA: Harvard University Press.

Grosjean, F. (2001) The bilingual's language modes. In J. L. Nicol (ed.), *One Mind, Two Languages: Bilingual Language Processing* (pp. 1–22). Oxford: Blackwell.

Grunwell, P. (1981) *The Nature of Phonological Disability in Children*. London: Academic Press.

Gudykunst, W. B. (1993) Toward a theory of effective interpersonal and intergroup communication: An anxiety/uncertainty management (AUM) perspective. In R. L. Wiseman and J. Koester (eds), *Intercultural Communication Competence* (pp. 33–71). Newbury Park, CA: Sage.

Gudykunst, W. B. (1995) Anxiety/uncertainty management (AUM) theory: Current status. In R. L. Wiseman (ed.), *Intercultural Communication Theory* (pp. 8–58). Thousand Oaks, CA: Sage.

Guendouzi, J. (1998) Negotiating socialized gender identity in women's time-out talk. Unpublished thesis, University of Wales.

Guendouzi, J. (2001) You'll think we're always bitching: The functions of cooperativity and competition in women's gossip. *Discourse Studies* 3: 55–77.

Gumperz, J. (1977) Sociocultural knowledge in conversational inference. In M. Saville-Troike (ed.), *Linguistics and Anthropology* (pp. 191–212). Washington, DC: Georgetown University Press.

Gumperz, J. (1982) *Discourse Strategies*. Cambridge: Cambridge University Press.

Gutierrez-Clellen, V. (1996) Language diversity: Implications for assessment. In K. Cole, P. Dale and D. Thal (eds), *Assessment of Communication and Language* (pp. 29–56). Baltimore, MD: Brookes.

Gutierrez-Clellen, V. and Peña, E. (2001) Dynamic assessment of diverse children: A tutorial. *Language, Speech and Hearing Services in Schools* 32: 212–24.

Guy, G. (1980) Variation in the group and in the individual: The case of final stop deletion. In W. Labov (ed.), *Locating Language in Time and Space* (pp. 1–36). New York: Academic Press.

Haarmann, H. (1990) Language planning in the light of a general theory of language. *International Journal of the Sociology of Language* 86: 103–26.

Habermas, J. (1984) *The Theory of Communicative Action*, vol. I: *Reason and the Rationalization of Society*. Boston: Beacon Press.

Hagège, C. (2000) *Halte à la mort des langues*. Paris: Odile Jacob.

Hagood, M. C. (2002) Critical literacy for whom? *Reading Research and Instruction* 41: 247–66.

Halliday, M. A. K. (1973) *Explorations in the Function of Language*. London: Edward Arnold.

Halliday, M. A. K. (1978) *Language as a Social Semiotic*. London: Edward Arnold.

Halliday, M. A. K., McIntosh, A. and Strevens, P. (1964) *The Linguistic Sciences and Language Teaching*. London: Longmans.

Harding, E. and Riley, P. (1986) *The Bilingual Family*. Cambridge: Cambridge University Press.

Harrington, J., Palethorpe, S. and Watson, C. I. (2000) Does the Queen still speak the Queen's English? *Nature* 407: 927–8.

Hart, B. and Risley, J. (1995) *Meaningful Differences in the Everyday Experience of Young American Children*. Baltimore, MD: Paul Brookes.

Hartley, L. and Preston, D. R. (1999) The names of US English: Valley girl, cowboy, Yankee, normal, nasal, and ignorant. In T. Bex and R. J. Watts (eds), *Standard English* (pp. 207–38). London: Routledge.

Haugen, E. (1953) *The Norwegian Language in America*. Philadelphia, PA: University of Pennsylvania Press.

Haugen, E. (1959) Planning for a standard language in modern Norway. *Anthropological Linguistics* 1: 8–21.

Haugen, E. (1972) *The Ecology of Language: Essays Edited by A. S. Dil*. Stanford, CA: Stanford University Press.

Haugen, E. (1983) The implementation of corpus planning: Theory and practice. In J. Cobarrubias and J. A. Fishman (eds), *Progress in Language Planning* (pp. 269–89). Berlin: Mouton.

Haviland, J. B. (1977) Gossip as competition in Zinacanton. *Journal of Communication* 27: 186–91.

Haviland, J. B. (1993) Anchoring, iconicity, and orientation in Guugu Yimithirr pointing gestures. *Journal of Linguistic Anthropology* 3(1): 3–45.

Heath, S. B. (1983) *Ways with Words: Language, Life, and Work in Communities and Classrooms*. Cambridge: Cambridge University Press.

Hechter, M. (1975) *Internal Colonialism*. Berkeley, CA: University of California Press.

Herman, R. and Pisoni, D. B. (2002) Perception of "elliptical speech" following cochlear implantation: Use of broad phonetic categories in speech perception. *Volta Review* 102: 321–47.

Hickey, R. (ed.) (2003) *Motives for Language Change*. Cambridge: Cambridge University Press.

Hillenbrand, J. (2003) American English: Southern Michigan. *Journal of the International Phonetic Association* 33(1): 121–6.

Hinchey, P. H. (1998) *Finding Freedom in the Classroom: A Practical Introduction to Critical Theory*. New York: Peter Lang.

Hock, H.-H. (1986) *Principles of Historical Linguistics*. Berlin: Mouton de Gruyter.

Hoffmann, C. (1985) Language acquisition in two trilingual children. *Journal of Multilingual and Multicultural Development* 6: 782–96.

Holdaway, D. (1979) *The Foundations of Literacy*. Sydney: Aston.

Holmes, J. (1995) *Women, Men and Politeness*. London: Longman.

Hoosain, R. (1991) *Psycholinguistic Implications for Linguistic Relativity: A Case Study of Chinese*. Hillsdale, NJ: Lawrence Erlbaum.

Hornberger, J., Itakura, H. and Wilson, S. R. (1997) Bridging language and cultural barriers between physicians and patients. *Public Health Reports* 112(5): 410–17.

Horvath, B. (1985) *Variation in Australian English: The Sociolects of Sydney*. Cambridge: Cambridge University Press.

Houston, D. M. (1999) The role of effects of talker variability in infant word representations. Doctoral dissertation, Johns Hopkins University, Baltimore, MD.

Houston, D. M. and Jusczyk, P. W. (2000) The role of talker-specific information in word segmentation by infants. *Journal of Experimental Psychology: Human Perception and Performance* 26: 1570–82.

Howard, S. and Heselwood, B. (2002) The contribution of phonetics to the study of vowel development and disorders. In M. J. Ball and F. Gibbon (eds), *Vowel Disorders* (pp. 37–82). Woburn, MA: Butterworth/Heinemann.

Howell, W. S. (1956) *Logic and Rhetoric in England*. Princeton, NJ: Princeton University Press.

Hudson, R. A. (1996) *Sociolinguistics*, 2nd edn. Cambridge: Cambridge University Press.

Hymes, D. (1967) Models of the interaction of language and social setting. *Journal of Social Issues* 23(2): 8–28.

Hymes, D. (1972) Models of the interaction of language and social life. In J. Gumperz and D. Hymes (eds), *Directions in Sociolinguistics: The Ethnography of Communication* (pp. 35–71). New York: Holt, Rinehart and Winston.

Hymes, D. (1974) *Foundations in Sociolinguistics: An Ethnographic Approach*. Philadelphia, PA: University of Pennsylvania Press.

Ijalba, E., Obler, L. K. and Chengappa, S. (2004) Bilingual aphasia. In T. K. Bhatia and W. C. Ritchie (eds), *The Handbook of Bilingualism* (pp. 71–89). Oxford: Blackwell.

Irvine, J. T. (1996) Shadow conversations: The indeterminacy of participant roles. In M. Silverstein and G. Urban (eds), *Natural Histories of Discourse* (pp. 131–59). Chicago: University of Chicago Press.

Irvine, J. T. (2001) "Style" as distinctiveness: The culture and ideology of linguistic differentiation. In P. Eckert and J. Rickford (eds), *Style and Sociolinguistic Variation* (pp. 21–43). Cambridge: Cambridge University Press.

Isaac, K. M. (2001) What about linguistic diversity? A different look at multicultural health care. *Communication Disorders Quarterly* 22(2): 110–13.

Isaac, K. M. (2002a) Breaking barriers, building bridges: clinician–interpreter interaction in speech pathology practice. Unpublished doctoral dissertation, University of Newcastle, New South Wales, Australia.

Isaac, K. M. (2002b) *Speech Pathology in Cultural and Linguistic Diversity*. London: Whurr.

Jackson, S. and Roberts, J. (2001) Complex syntax production of African American preschoolers. *Journal of Speech, Language, and Hearing Research* 44: 1083–96.

Jacoby, S. and Ochs, E. (1995) Co-construction: An introduction. *Research on Language and Social Interaction* 28(3): 171–83.

James, D. and Clark, S. (1993) Women men and interruptions: A critical review. In D. Tannen (ed.), *Gender and Conversational Interaction* (pp. 231–80). Oxford: Oxford University Press.

Janton, P. (1993) *Esperanto: Language, Literature and Community*, ed. Humphrey Tonkin. Albany: State University of New York Press.

Jerger, S., Martin, R., Pearson, D. A. and Dinh, T. (1995) Childhood hearing impairment: Auditory and linguistic interactions during multidimensional speech processing. *Journal of Speech and Hearing Research* 38: 930–48.

Jerger, S., Pirozzolo, F., Jerger, J., Elizondo, R., Desai, S., Wright, E. and Reynosa, R. (1993) Developmental trends in the interaction between auditory and linguistic processing. *Perception and Psychophysics* 54: 310–20.

Jespersen, O. (1922) *Language: Its Nature, Development and Origins*. London: Allen and Unwin.

Johnson, R., Liddell, S., and Erting, C. (1989) Unlocking the curriculum: Principles for achieving access in deaf education. *Gallaudet Research Institute Working Paper* 89-3. Washington, DC: Gallaudet University.

Johnson, S. and Meinhof, U. H. (1997) *Language and Masculinity*. Oxford: Blackwell.

Johnson, V. (2001) Fast mapping verb meaning from argument structure. Unpublished doctoral dissertation, University of Massachusetts, Amherst.

Jordan, D. K. (2002) Languages left behind: Keeping Taiwanese off the World Wide Web. *Language Problems and Language Planning* 26: 111–27.

Junker, D. and Stockman, I. (2002) Expressive vocabulary of German–English bilingual toddlers. *American Journal of Speech-language Pathology* 11: 381–94.

Junque, C., Vendrell, P., Vendrell-Brucet, J. M. and Tobena, A. (1989) Differential recovery in naming in bilingual aphasics. *Brain and Language* 36: 16–22.

Kalcik, S. (1975) "Like Ann's gynaecologist or the time I was almost raped:" Personal narratives in women's rap groups. *Journal of Personality* 48: 190–205.

Kamberelis, G. and Scott, K. D. (1993) Other people's voices: The coarticulation of texts and subjectivities. *Linguistics and Education* 4: 359–403.

Kamwangamalu, N. M. (1992) Mixers and mixing: English across cultures. *World Englishes* 11: 173–81.

Kannapell, B. (1991) *Language Choice: Identity Choice*. Burtonsville, MD: Linstok Press.

Kaplan, R. B. and Baldauf, R. B., Jr. (1997) *Language Planning: From Practice to Theory*. Clevedon: Multilingual Matters.

Kaye, A. (1970) Modern Standard Arabic and the colloquials. *Lingua* 24: 374–91.

Kaye, A. (1987) Arabic. In B. Comrie (ed.), *The Major Languages of the World* (pp. 664–85). Beckenham: Croom Helm.

Kayser, H. (1995) *Bilingual Speech-language Pathology: An Hispanic Focus*. San Diego, CA: Singular.

Kedar, L. (ed.) (1987) *Power through Discourse*. Norwood, NJ: Ablex.

Kelly, A. B. (1998) A brief history of Deaf Studies. *Disability Studies Quarterly* 18: 118–21.

Kelly, A. B. (2001) How deaf women construct teaching, language and culture, and gender: An ethnographic study of ASL teachers. Doctoral dissertation, University of Maryland.

Kendon, A. (1980) Gesticulation and speech: Two aspects of the process of utterance. In M. R. Key (ed.), *The Relationship of Verbal and Nonverbal Communication* (pp. 207–27). The Hague: Mouton.

Kendon, A. (1986) Some reasons for studying gesture. *Semiotica* 62(1/2): 3–28.

Kendon, A. (1997) Gesture. *Annual Review of Anthropology* 26: 109–28.

Kerswill, P. (1993) Rural dialect speakers in an urban speech community: The role of dialect contact in defining a sociolinguistic concept. *International Journal of Applied Linguistics* 3: 33–56.

Kerswill, P. and Williams, A. (2000) Creating a new town koine: Children and language change in Milton Keynes. *Language in Society* 29: 65–115.

Kessler, C. (1984) Language acquisition in bilingual children. In N. Miller (ed.), *Bilingualism and Language Disability* (pp. 26–54). London: Croom Helm.

Khattab, G. (2002) Sociolinguistic competence and the bilingual's adoption of phonetic variants: auditory and instrumental data from English–Arabic bilinguals. Unpublished PhD thesis, University of Leeds.

Kibbee, D. A. (ed.) (1998) *Language Legislation and Linguistic Rights*. Amsterdam: Benjamins.

Kirk, K. I., Houston, D. M., Pisoni, D. B., Sprunger, A. B. and Kim-Lee, Y. (2002) Talker discrimination and spoken word recognition by adults with cochlear implants. Poster presented at the 25th Midwinter Meeting of the Association for Research in Otolaryngology, St Petersburg, FL.

Kirk, K. I., Pisoni, D. B. and Miyamoto, R. C. (1997) Effects of stimulus variability on speech perception in listeners with hearing impairment. *Journal of Speech, Language, and Hearing Research* 40: 1395–405.

Klatt, D. H. (1989) Review of selected models of speech perception. In W. Marslen-Wilson (ed.), *Lexical Representation and Process* (pp. 169–226). Cambridge, MA: MIT Press.

Knowlson, J. (1975) *Universal Language Schemes in England and France, 1600–1800*. Toronto: University of Toronto Press.

Kochman, T. (1981) Classroom modalities: Black and White communicative styles in the classroom. In N. Mercer (ed.), *Language in School and Community* (pp. 96–114). London: Arnold.

Kohn, A. (2000) *The Case against Standardized Testing: Raising the Scores, Ruining the Schools*. Portsmouth, NH: Heinemann.

Kontra, M., Phillipson, R., Skutnabb-Kangas, T. and Várady, T. (eds) (1999) *Language: A Right and a Resource*. Budapest: Central European University Press.

Koppe, R. and Meisel, J. (1995) Code-switching in bilingual first language acquisition. In L. Milroy and P. Muysken (eds), *One Speaker Two Languages* (pp. 276–301). Cambridge: Cambridge University Press.

Kovarsky, D. (1990) Discourse markers in adult-controlled therapy: Implications for child centered intervention. *Journal of Childhood Communication Disorders* 13: 29–41.

Kovarsky, D. and Duchan, J. F. (1997) The interactional dimensions of language therapy. *Language, Speech, and Hearing Services in Schools* 28: 297–307.

Kurath, H. (1949) *A Word Geography of the Eastern United States*. Ann Arbor, MI: University of Michigan Press.

Labov, T. (1992) Social and language boundaries among adolescents. *American Speech* 67: 339–66.

Labov, W. (1963) The social motivation of a sound change. *Word* 19: 273–309. (Revised as Chap. 1, pp. 1–42 in *Sociolinguistic Patterns*, Philadelphia: University of Pennsylvania Press, 1972.)

Labov, W. (1966) *The Social Stratification of English in New York City*. Washington, DC: Center for Applied Linguistics.

Labov, W. (1968) The reflections of social processes in linguistic structures. In J. Fishman (ed.), *Readings in the Sociology of Language* (pp. 240–51). The Hague: Mouton.

Labov, W. (1972a) *Language in the Inner City: Studies in the Black English Vernacular*. Philadelphia, PA: University of Pennsylvania Press.

Labov, W. (1972b) *Sociolinguistic Patterns*. Philadelphia, PA: University of Pennsylvania Press and Oxford: Blackwell.

Labov, W. (1972c) Some principles of linguistic methodology. *Language in Society* 1: 97–120.

Labov, W. (1989) The exact description of a speech community: Short a in Philadelphia. In R. W. Fasold and D. Schiffrin (eds), *Language Change and Variation* (pp. 1–57). Washington, DC: Georgetown University Press.

Labov, W. (1994) *Principles of Linguistic Change*, vol. 1: *Internal Factors*. Oxford: Blackwell.

Labov, W. (1998) Coexistent systems in African-American vernacular English. In S. Mufwene, J. R. Rickford, G. Bailey and J. Baugh (eds), *African American English: Structure, History, and Use* (pp. 110–53). London: Routledge.

Labov, W. (2001) *Principles of Linguistic Change: Social Factors*. Oxford: Blackwell.

Labov, W. and Fanshel, D. (1977) *Therapeutic Discourse*. New York: Academic Press.

Ladson-Billings, G. (1995) Toward a theory of culturally relevant pedagogy. *American Education Research Journal* 32: 465–91.

Lahey, M. (1988) *Language Development and Language Disorders*. New York: Wiley.

Lahey, M. (2004) Therapy talk: Analyzing therapeutic discourse. *Language, Speech, and Hearing Services in Schools* 35: 70–81.

Lahey, M., Liebergott, J., Chesnick, M., Menyuk, P. and Adams, J. (1992) Variability in children's use of grammatical morphemes. *Applied Psycholinguistics* 13: 373–98.

Laitin, D. D. (1992) *Language Repertoires and State Construction in Africa*. Cambridge: Cambridge University Press.

Lakoff, R. (1975) *Language and Woman's Place*. New York: Harper and Row.

Lambert, W. E. (1967) A social psychology of bilingualism. *Journal of Social Issues* 23: 91–109.

Lambert, W. E., Hodgson, R., Gardner, R. and Fillenbaum, S. (1960) Evaluational reactions to spoken language. *Journal of Abnormal and Social Psychology* 60: 44–51.

Lane, H., Pillard, R. C. and French, M. (2000) Origins of the American DEAF-WORLD: Assimilating and differentiating societies and their relations to genetic patterning. *Sign Language Studies* 1(1): 17–44.

Langdon, H. (2002) Language interpreters and translators. *ASHA Leader* 7(6): 14–15.

Langdon, H. with Cheng, L.-R. (1992) *Hispanic Children and Adults with Communication Disorders*. Gathersburg, MD: Aspen.

Lanza, E. (1997) *Language Mixing in Infant Bilingualism*. Oxford: Oxford University Press.

Large, A. (1985) *The Artificial Language Movement*. Oxford: Blackwell.

Lass, N. J., Hughes, K. R., Bowyer, M. D., Waters, L. T. and Bourne, V. T. (1976) Speaker sex identification from voiced, whispered, and filtered isolated vowels. *Journal of the Acoustical Society of America* 59: 675–8.

Lass, R. (1997) *Historical Linguistics and Language Change*. Cambridge: Cambridge University Press.

Launer, J. (1978) Taking medical histories through interpreters: Practice in a Nigerian outpatient department. *British Medical Journal* 2: 934–5.

Lavandera, B. (1978) Where does the sociolinguistic variable stop? *Language in Society* 7(2): 1971–82.

Leadholm, B. and Miler, J. (1992) *Language Sample Analysis: The Wisconsin Guide*. Milwaukee: Wisconsin Department of Public Instruction.

Lee, A., Hewlett, N. and Nairn, M. (1995) Voice and gender in children. In S. Mills (ed.), *Language and Gender* (pp. 194–204). London: Longman.

Lee, D. M. (1982) Are there really signs of diglossia? Reexamining the situation. *Sign Language Studies* 35: 127–52.

Lee, L. (1974) *Developmental Sentence Analysis*. Evanston, IL: Northwestern University Press.

Leet-Pellegrini, H. M. (1980) Conversational dominance as a function of gender and expertise. In H. Giles, W. P. Robinson and P. M. Smith (eds), *Language: Social Psychological Perspectives* (pp. 97–104). New York: Pergamon.

Lemann, N. (1997) The reading wars. *Atlantic Monthly* November: 128–34.

Leonard, L. (1998) *Children with Specific Language Impairment*. Cambridge, MA: MIT Press.

Leopold, W. F. (1939–49) *Speech Development of a Bilingual Child* (4 vols). Evanston, IL: Northwestern University Press.

Le Page, R. B. (1964) *The National Language Question: Linguistic Problems of Newly Independent States*. London: Oxford University Press.

Le Page, R. B. and Tabouret-Keller, A. (1985) *Acts of Identity: Creole-based Approaches to Language and Identity*. Cambridge: Cambridge University Press.

Lepore, J. (2002) *A is for American: Letters and Other Characters in the Newly United States*. New York: Knopf.

Lippi-Green, R. (1997) *English with an Accent: Language, Ideology, and Discrimination in the United States*. London: Routledge.

Li Wei (1994) *Three Generations, Two Languages, One Family*. Clevedon: Multilingual Matters.

Lucas, C. (1995) Sociolinguistic variation in ASL: The case of DEAF. In C. Lucas (ed.), *Sociolinguistics in Deaf Communities*, vol. 1 (pp. 3–25). Washington, DC: Gallaudet University Press.

Lucas, C. (ed.) (2001) *The Sociolinguistics of Sign Languages*. Cambridge: Cambridge University Press.

Lucas, C., Bayley, R. and Valli, C. (2001) *Sociolinguistics in Deaf Communities*, vol. 7: *Sociolinguistic Variation in American Sign Language*. Washington, DC: Gallaudet University Press.

Lucas, C. and Valli, C. (1992) *Language Contact in the American Deaf Community*. San Diego, CA: Academic Press.

Luke, A. (1988) The non-neutrality of literacy instruction: A critical introduction. *Australian Journal of Reading* 11 (June): 79–83.

Lynch, E. W. (1992) Developing cross-cultural competence. In E. W. Lynch and M. J. Hanson (eds), *Developing Cross-cultural Competence: A Guide for Working with Young Children and Their Families* (pp. 35–62). Baltimore, MD: P. H. Brookes.

Lyon, G. R. (1999) In celebration of science in the study of reading development, reading difficulties, and reading instruction: The NICHD perspective. *Issues in Education: Contributions from Educational Psychology* 5: 85–115.

Mac Donnacha, J. (2000) An integrated language planning model. *Language Problems and Language Planning* 24: 11–35.

Mackey, W. (1989) La genèse d'une typologie de la diglossie. *Revue québécoise de linguistique théorique et appliquée* 8: 11–28.

Mallinson, C. and Wolfram, W. (2002) Dialect accommodation in a bi-ethnic mountain enclave community: More evidence on the development of African American Vernacular English. *Language in Society* 31: 743–75.

Maltz, D. N. and Borker, R. A. (1982) A cultural approach to male–female miscommunication. In J. Gumperz (ed.), *Language and Social Identity* (pp. 196–216). Cambridge: Cambridge University Press.

Mann, V. A., Diamond, R. and Carey, S. (1979) Development of voice recognition: Parallels with face recognition. *Journal of Experimental Child Psychology* 27: 153–65.

Marchman, V. and Martinez-Sussmann, C. (2002) Concurrent validity of caregiver/parent report measures of language for children who are learning both English and Spanish. *Journal of Speech, Language, and Hearing Research* 45: 983–97.

Martin-Jones, M. and Romaine, S. (1985) Semilingualism: A half-baked theory of communicative competence. *Applied Linguistics* 6: 105–17.

Mattes, L. and Omark, D. (1991) *Speech and Language Assessment for the Bilingual Handicapped*, 2nd edn. Oceanside, CA: Academic Communication.

May, S. (2001) *Language and Minority Rights*. Harlow: Longman/Pearson.

Mazrui, A. and Mazrui, A. (1998) *The Power of Babel*. Oxford: Currey.

McCabe, A. and Bliss, L. (2003) *Patterns of Narrative Discourse*. Boston: Allyn and Bacon.

McCauley, R. (1996) Familiar strangers: Criterion-referenced measures in communication disorders. *Language, Speech, Hearing in the Schools* 27: 122–31.

McDavid, R. I. and McDavid, V. G. (1951) The relationship of the speech of American Negroes to the speech of whites. *American Speech* 26: 3–17.

McDermott, R. P. and Gospodinoff, K. (1979) Social contexts for ethnic borders and school failure. In A. Wolfgang (ed.), *Nonverbal Behavior: Applications and Cultural Implications* (pp. 175–96). New York: Academic Press.

McDermott, R. P. and Tylbor, H. (1987) On the necessity of collusion in conversation. In L. Kedar (ed.), *Power through Discourse* (pp. 153–70). Norwood, NJ: Ablex.

McDonald, C. J., Kirk, K. I., Krueger, T. and Houston, D. (2003) Talker discrimination and spoken word recognition by adults with cochlear implants. Poster presented at the 26th Midwinter Meeting of the Association for Research in Otolaryngology, Daytona Beach, FL.

McLaughlin, B. (1978) *Second Language Acquisition in Childhood*. Hillsdale, NJ: Lawrence Erlbaum.

McLaughlin, B. (1984) Early bilingualism. In M. Paradis and Y. Lebrun (eds), *Early Bilingualism and Child Development* (pp. 19–45). Lisse: Swets and Zeitlinger.

McMahon, A. (1994) *Understanding Language Change*. Cambridge: Cambridge University Press.

McNeill, D. (1992) *Hand and Mind: What Gestures Reveal about Thought*. Chicago: University of Chicago Press.

McNeill, D., Cassell, J. and Levy, E. (1993) Abstract deixis. *Semiotica* 95(1/2): 5–19.

McTear, M. F. and King, F. (1990) Miscommunication in clinical contexts: The speech therapy interview. In N. Coupland, H. Giles and J. M. Weimann (eds), *Miscommunication and Problematic Talk* (pp. 195–214). London: Sage.

McWhorter, J. (1998) *The Word on the Street*. New York: Plenum.

Mead, G. H. (1934) *Mind, Self, and Society*. Chicago: University of Chicago Press.

Mehan, H. (1979) *Learning Lessons*. Cambridge, MA: Harvard University Press.

Mehl, M. R. and Pennebaker, J. W. (2002) Mapping students' natural language use in everyday conversations. Paper presented at the 3rd annual meeting of the Society for Personality and Social Psychology, Savannah, GA.

Meisel, J. (1989) Early differentiation of languages in bilingual children. In K. Hyltenstam and L. K. Obler (eds), *Bilingualism across the Lifespan* (pp. 13–40). Cambridge: Cambridge University Press.

Meisel, J. (1990) Grammatical development in the simultaneous acquisition of two first languages. In J. Meisel (ed.), *Two First Languages* (pp. 5–22). Dordrecht: Foris.

Meisel, J. (1994) Getting FAT: Finiteness, agreement and tense in early grammars. In J. Meisel (ed.), *Bilingual First Language Acquisition* (pp. 89–129). Amsterdam: Benjamins.

Mendelsohn, S. (1988) Language lateralization in bilinguals: Facts and fantasy. *Journal of Neurolinguistics* 3: 261–91.

Mendoza-Denton, N. (1997) Chicana/Mexicana identity and linguistic variation: An ethnographic and sociolinguistic study of gang affiliation in an urban high school. Unpublished PhD dissertation, Stanford University, CA.

Mendoza-Denton, N. (1999) Turn-initial "No:" Collaborative opposition among Latina adolescents. In M. Bucholtz, A. C. Liang and L. Sutton (eds), *Reinventing Identities: From Category to Practice in Language and Gender* (pp. 273–92). Oxford: Oxford University Press.

Mendoza-Denton, N. (forthcoming) *Homegirls: Symbolic Practices in the Making of Latina Youth Styles*. Oxford: Blackwell.

Merrifield, J., Bingman, M. B., Hemphill, D. and Bennett de Marrais, K. P. (1997) *Life at the Margins: Literacy, Language, and Technology in Everyday Life*. New York: Teachers College Press.

Metoyer-Duran, C. (1993) *Gatekeepers in Ethnolinguistic Communities*. Norwood, NJ: Ablex.

Meyerhoff, M. (2002) Communities of practice. In J. K. Chambers, P. Trudgill and N. Schilling-Estes (eds), *The Handbook of Language Variation and Change* (pp. 526–48). Oxford: Blackwell.

Miller, G. A. (1946) Articulation testing methods. In G. A. Miller, F. M. Weiner and S. S. Stevens (eds), *Transmission and Reception of Sounds under Combat Conditions* (pp. 69–80). Washington, DC: Division 17, NDRC.

Mills, C. W. (1956) *The Power Elite*. Oxford: Oxford University Press.

Milroy, J. (1992) *Linguistic Variation and Change*. Oxford: Blackwell.

Milroy, J. and Milroy, L. (1985) Linguistic change, social network and speaker innovation. *Journal of Linguistics* 21: 339–84.

Milroy, L. (1980) *Language and Social Networks*. Oxford: Blackwell.

Milroy, L. (1987) *Observing and Analysing Natural Language*. Oxford: Blackwell.

Milroy, L. (1992) *Language and Social Networks*, 2nd edn. Oxford: Blackwell.

Milroy, L. (2002) Social networks. In J. K. Chambers, P. Trudgill and N. Schilling-Estes (eds), *The Handbook of Language Variation and Change* (pp. 549–72). Oxford: Blackwell.

Milroy, L. and Gordon, M. (2003) *Sociolinguistics: Method and Interpretation*. Oxford: Blackwell.

Milroy, L. and McClenaghan, P. (1977) Stereotyped reactions to four educated accents in Ulster. *Belfast Working Papers in Language and Linguistics* 2: 1–11.

Milroy, L. and Muysken, P. (eds) (1995) *One Speaker, Two Languages: Cross-disciplinary Perspectives on Code-switching*. Cambridge: Cambridge University Press.

Moats, L. C. (1990) *Teaching Reading IS Rocket Science: What Expert Teachers of Reading Should Know and Be Able to Do*. Washington, DC: American Federation of Teachers.

Monaghan, E. (1980) A history of the syndrome of dyslexia with implications for its treatment. In C. McCullough (ed.), *Inchworm, Inchworm: Persistent Problems in Reading Education* (pp. 87–101). Newark, DE: International Reading Association.

Moore, E. F. (2003) Learning style and identity: a sociolinguistic analysis of a Bolton high school. Unpublished PhD dissertation, University of Manchester.

Morgan, W. (1997) *Critical Literacy in the Classroom: The Art of the Possible*. New York: Routledge.

Morris, G. and Chenail, R. (1995) *The Talk of the Clinic: Exploration in the Analysis of Medical and Therapeutic Discourse*. Hillsdale, NJ: Erlbaum.

Mufwene, S. S. (1996) The development of American Englishes: Some questions from a creole genesis perspective. In E. G. Schneider (ed.), *Focus on American English* (pp. 231–64). Philadelphia, PA: Benjamins.

Mufwene, S. S. (2001) *The Ecology of Language Evolution*. Cambridge: Cambridge University Press.

Mullennix, J. W. and Pisoni, D. B. (1990) Stimulus variability and processing dependencies in speech perception. *Perception and Psychophysics* 47: 379–90.

Mullennix, J. W., Pisoni, D. B. and Martin, C. S. (1989) Some effects of talker variability on spoken word recognition. *Journal of the Acoustical Society of America* 85: 365–78.

Muller, N. (1990) Developing two gender assignment systems simultaneously. In J. Meisel (ed.), *Two First Languages* (pp. 193–236). Dordrecht: Foris.

Müller, N. (1999) Kodewechsel in der irischen Übersetzungsliteratur: Exempla et desiderata. In E. Poppe and H. L. C. Tristram (eds), *Übersetzung, Adaptation und Akkulturation im Insularen Mittelalter* (pp. 73–86). Münster: Nodus Publikationen.

Müller, N. and Guendouzi, J. (2003) Order and disorder in conversations: Encounters with Alzheimer's disease. Presentation at IPrA Conference, Toronto.

Muysken, P. (2000) *Bilingual Speech*. Cambridge: Cambridge University Press.

Myers-Scotton, C. (1993a) *Duelling Languages: Grammatical Structure in Code-switching*. Oxford: Clarendon Press.

Myers-Scotton, C. (1993b) Elite closure as a powerful language strategy: The African case. *International Journal of the Sociology of Language* 103: 149–63.

Myers-Scotton, C. (1995) A lexically based model of code-switching. In L. Milroy and P. Muysken (eds), *One Speaker, Two Languages: Cross-disciplinary Perspectives on Code-switching* (pp. 233–56). Cambridge: Cambridge University Press.

Nahir, M. (1984) Language planning goals: A classification. *Language Problems and Language Planning* 8: 294–327.

Nahir, M. (2002) Corpus planning and codification in the Hebrew revival. *Language Problems and Language Planning* 26: 271–98.

Nathan, L. and Wells, B. (2001) Can children with speech difficulties process an unfamiliar accent? *Applied Psycholinguistics* 22: 343–61.

Nathan, L., Wells, B. and Donlan, C. (1998) Children's comprehension of unfamiliar regional accents: A preliminary investigation. *Journal of Child Language* 25: 343–65.

National Reading Panel (2000) *Teaching Children to Read: An Evidence-based Assessment of the Scientific Research Literature on Reading and Its Implications for Reading Instruction*. Washington, DC: National Institute of Child Health and Human Development.

Nelson, D. and Stojanovik, V. (2002) Prelinguistic primitives and the evolution of argument structure: Evidence from Specific Language Impairment. *Leeds Working Papers in Linguistics and Phonetics* 9: 131–40.

Nelson, N. (1991) Black English sentence scoring. Unpublished manuscript, Western Michigan University.

Nettle, D. and Romaine, S. (2000) *Vanishing Voices*. New York: Oxford University Press.

Newcomer, P. and Hammill, D. (1988, 1991) *Test of Language Development: Primary*. Austin, TX: ProEd.

Newman, A. P. and Beverstock, C. (1990) *Adult Literacy: Contexts and Challenges*. Newark, DE: International Reading Association.

Niedzielski, N. (1999) The effect of social information on the perception of sociolinguistic variables. *Journal of Language and Social Psychology* 18: 62–85.

Niedzielski, N. (2002) Sociolinguistics and speech sciences. Paper presented at the International Symposium of Linguistics and Speech/Hearing Sciences, Kuala Lumpur, July.

Niedzielski, N. and Preston, D. R. (1999) *Folk Linguistics*. Berlin: Mouton de Gruyter.

Nover, S. (1995) Politics and language: American Sign Language and English in Deaf education. In C. Lucas (ed.), *Sociolinguistics in Deaf Communities*, vol. 1 (pp. 109–63). Washington, DC: Gallaudet University Press.

Nuessel, F. (2000) *The Esperanto Language*. New York: Legas.

Nygaard, L. C., Sommers, M. S. and Pisoni, D. B. (1994) Speech perception as a talker-contingent process. *Psychological Science* 5: 42–6.

O'Barr, W. and Atkins, B. A. (1980) "Women's language" or "powerless language"? In S. McConnell-Ginet, R. Borker and N. Furman (eds), *Women and Language in Literature and Society* (pp. 93–110). New York: Praeger.

Ochs, E. (1992) Indexing gender. In A. Duranti and C. Goodwin (eds), *Rethinking Context: Language as an Interactive Phenomenon* (pp. 325–58). Cambridge: Cambridge University Press.

Ochs, E., Gonzales, P. and Jacoby, S. (1996) "When I come down I'm in the domain state": Grammar and graphic representation in the interpretive activity of physicists. In E. Ochs, E. Schegloff and S. Thompson (eds), *Interaction and Grammar* (pp. 328–69). New York: Cambridge University Press.

Ochs, E. and Schieffelin, B. B. (1984) Language acquisition and socialization: Three developmental stories and their implications. In R. Shweder and R. Levine (eds), *Culture Theory: Essays in Mind, Self and Emotion* (pp. 276–320). New York: Cambridge University Press.

O'Donnell, K. (1990) Difference and dominance: How labor and management talk conflict. In A. D. Grimshaw (ed.), *Conflict Talk: Sociolinguistic Investigations of Arguments in Conversation* (pp. 210–40). Cambridge: Cambridge University Press.

Oetting, J. (1999) Children with SLI use argument structure cues to learn verbs. *Journal of Speech, Language, and Hearing Research* 42: 1261–74.

Oetting, J., Cantrell, J. and Horohov, J. (1999) A study of specific language impairment (SLI) in the context of non-standard dialect. *Clinical Linguistics and Phonetics* 13: 25–44.

Oetting, J. and McDonald, J. (2001) Nonmainstream dialect use and specific language impairment. *Journal of Speech, Language, and Hearing Research* 44: 207–23.

Oetting, J. and McDonald, J. (2002) Methods for characterizing participants' nonmainstream dialect use within studies of child language. *Journal of Speech Language Hearing Research* 45: 505–18.

Ojemann, G. A. and Whitaker, H. A. (1978) The bilingual brain. *Archives of Neurology* 35: 409–12.

Oldfather, P. and Dahl, K. (1994) Toward a social constructivist reconceptualization of intrinsic motivation for literacy learning. *Journal of Reading Behavior* 26: 139–58.

Oller, D. K. and Eiler, R. (eds) (2002) *Language and Literacy in Bilingual Children*. Clevedon: Multilingual Matters.

Olson, D. (1994) *The World on Paper: The Conceptual and Cognitive Implications of Writing and Reading*. Cambridge: Cambridge University Press.

Ordoñez, C., Snow, C. and McLaughlin, B. (2002) Depth and breadth of vocabulary in two languages: Which vocabulary skills transfer? *Journal of Educational Psychology* 94: 719–28.

Osberger, M. J., Miyamoto, R. T., Zimmerman-Phillips, S., Kemink, J. L., Stroer, B. S., Firszt, J. B. and Novak, M. A. (1991) Independent evaluation of the speech perception abilities of children with the Nucleus 22-channel cochlear implant system. *Ear and Hearing* 12(Supplement): 66S–80S.

Osgood, C. H., Suci, G. J. and Tannenbaum, P. (1957) *The Measurement of Meaning*. Urbana, IL: University of Illinois Press.

O'Sullivan, K. (1994) *Understanding Ways: Communicating between Cultures*. Sydney: Hale and Iremonger.

Ozolins, U. (1998) *Interpreting and Translating in Australia: Current Issues and International Comparisons*. Melbourne: Language Australia.

Panagos, J. M. (1996) Speech therapy discourse: The input to learning. In M. Smith and J. S. Damico (eds), *Childhood Language Disorders* (pp. 41–63). New York: Thieme Medical Publishers.

Panagos, J. M., Bobkoff, K. and Scott, C. M. (1986) Discourse analysis of language intervention. *Child Language Teaching and Therapy* 2: 211–29.

Paradis, J. and Gensee, F. (1996) Syntactic acquisition in bilingual children. *Studies in Second Language Acquisition* 18: 1–25.

Paradis, M. (1977) Bilingualism and aphasia. In H. Whitaker and H. A. Whitaker (eds), *Studies in Neurolinguistics*, vol. 3 (pp. 65–121). New York: Academic Press.

Paradis, M. (1987) *The Assessment of Bilingual Aphasia*. Hillsdale, NJ: Lawrence Erlbaum.

Paradis, M. (1998) Aphasia in bilinguals: How atypical is it? In P. Coppens, Y. Lebrun and A. Basso (eds), *Aphasia in Aytpical Populations* (pp. 35–66). Mahwah, NJ: Lawrence Erlbaum.

Paterson, S. (2002) Fears over "Rab C" accents fuel speech therapy surge. *Scotland on Sunday* October 6.

Patrick, P. (2002) The speech community. In J. K. Chambers, P. Trudgill, and N. Schilling-Estes (eds), *The Handbook of Language Variation and Change* (pp. 573–97). Oxford: Blackwell.

Paulston, C. B. and Tucker, G. R. (eds) (1997) *The Early Days of Sociolinguistics*. Dallas, TX: Summer Institute of Linguistics.

Pauwels, A. (1995) *Cross-cultural Communication in the Health Sciences: Communicating with Migrant Patients*. South Melbourne: Macmillan Education Australia.

Payne, A. (1980) Factors controlling the acquisition of the Philadelphia dialect by out-of-state children. In W. Labov (ed.), *Locating Language in Time and Space* (pp. 143–78). New York: Academic Press.

Pearson, B. Z., Fernández, S., Lewedeg, V. and Oller, D. K. (1997) The relation of input factors to lexical learning by bilingual infants. *Applied Psycholinguistics* 18: 41–58.

Pearson, B. Z., Fernández, S. and Oller, D. K. (1993) Lexical development in bilingual infants and toddlers: Comparison to monolingual norms. *Language Learning* 43: 93–120.

Pearson, B. Z., Fernández, S. and Oller, D. K. (1995) Cross-language synonyms in the lexicons of bilingual infants: One language or two? *Journal of Child Language* 22: 345–68.

Peña, E., Bedore, L. and Zlatic-Giunta, R. (2002) Category-generation performance of bilingual children: The influence of condition, category, and language. *Journal of Speech, Language, and Hearing Research* 45: 938–47.

Peña, E., Iglesias, A. and Lidz, C. (2001) Reducing test bias through dynamic assessment of children's word learning ability. *American Journal of Speech-language Pathology* 10: 128–54.

Peñalosa, F. (1981) *Introduction to the Sociology of Language*. Rowley, MA: Newbury House.

Pennycook, A. (1994) *The Cultural Politics of English as an International Language*. New York: Longman.

Pennycook, A. (1998) *English and the Discourses of Colonialism*. London: Routledge.

Petyt, K. (1985) *Dialect and Accent in Industrial West Yorkshire*. Amsterdam: Benjamins.

Pfaff, C. and Savas, T. (1988) Language development in a bilingual setting. Manuscript of paper presented at the 4th Turkish Linguistics Conference, Ankara.

Philips, S. (1976) Some sources of cultural variability in the regulation of talk. *Language in Society* 5: 81–95.

Phillipson, R. (1992) *Linguistic Imperialism*. Oxford: Oxford University Press.

Phillipson, R. (2003) *English-only Europe?* London: Routledge.

Pisoni, D. B. (1997) Some thoughts on "normalization" in speech perception. In K. Johnson and J. W. Mullennix (eds), *Talker Variability in Speech Processing* (pp. 9–32). San Diego, CA: Academic Press.

Platt, J. (1977) A model for polyglossia and multilingualism (with special reference to Singapore and Malaysia). *Language in Society* 6: 361–78.

Poizner, H., Klima, E. S. and Bellugi, U. (1987) *What the Hands Reveal about the Brain*. Cambridge, MA: MIT Press.

Pollack, I., Pickett, J. M. and Sumby, W. H. (1954) On the identification of speakers by voice. *Journal of the Acoustical Society of America* 26: 403–6.

Pool, J. and Fettes, M. (1998) The challenge of interlingualism: A research invitation. *Esperantic Studies* 10: 1–2.

Poplack, S. (1980) Sometimes I'll start a sentence in English Y TERMINÓ EN ESPAÑOL. *Linguistics* 18: 581–618.

Poplack. S. (ed.) (1999) *The English History of African American English*. Malden, MA: Blackwell.

Poplack, S. and Tagliamonte, S. (1991) African–American English in the diaspora: Evidence from old-line Nova Scotians. *Language Variation and Change* 3: 301–39.

Poplack, S. and Tagliamonte, S. (2001) *African American English in the Diaspora*. Malden, MA: Blackwell.

Porac, C. and Coren, S. (1981) *Lateral Preferences and Human Behavior*. New York: Springer-Verlag.

Poss, J. E. and Rangel, R. (1995) Working effectively with interpreters in the primary care setting. *Nurse Practitioner* 20(12): 43–7.

Preston, D. R. (1989) *Perceptual Dialectology*. Dordrecht: Foris.

Preston, D. R. (1991) Sorting out the variables in sociolinguistic theory. *American Speech* 66: 33–55.

Preston, D. R. (1993) Folk dialectology. In D. R. Preston (ed.), *American Dialect Research* (pp. 333–77). Amsterdam: Benjamins.

Preston, D. R. (1994) Content-oriented discourse analysis and folk linguistics. *Language Sciences* 16(2): 285–331.

Preston, D. R. (1996a) Whaddayaknow: The modes of folk linguistic awareness. *Language Awareness* 5(1): 40–74.

Preston, D. R. (1996b) Where the worst English is spoken. In E. Schneider (ed.), *Focus on the USA* (pp. 297–360). Amsterdam: Benjamins.

Preston, D. R. and Howe, G. M. (1987) Computerized generalizations of mental dialect maps. In K. M. Denning, S. Inkelas, F. C. McNair-Knox and J. R. Rickford (eds), *Variation in Language: NWAV-XV at Stanford* (pp. 361–78). Stanford, CA: Department of Linguistics, Stanford University.

Prutting, C. A., Bagshaw, N., Goldstein, H., Juskowitz, S. and Umen, I. (1978) Clinician–child discourse: Some preliminary questions. *Journal of Speech and Hearing Disorders* 43: 123–39.

Pullum, G. (2003) It's like, so unfair. *Language Log* Nov. 22, 2003. Accessed at: http://itre.cis.upenn.edu/~myl/languagelog/archives/000138.html.

Purnell, T., Idsardi, W. and Baugh, J. (1999) Perceptual and phonetic experiments on American English dialect identification. *Journal of Language and Social Psychology* 18: 10–30.

Putsch, R. W. (1985) Cross-cultural communication: The special case of interpreters in health care. *Journal of the American Medical Association* 254(23): 3344–8.

Pütz, M. (ed.) (1997) *Language Choices*. Amsterdam: Benjamins.

Quay, S. (1995) The bilingual lexicon: Implications for studies of language choice. *Journal of Child Language* 22: 369–87.

Quinto-Pozos, D. (2002) Contact between Mexican sign language and American sign language in two Texas border areas. PhD dissertation, University of Texas at Austin.

Ramsey, C. L. (1989) Language planning in Deaf education. In C. Lucas (ed.), *The Sociolinguistics of the Deaf Community* (pp. 123–46). San Diego, CA: Academic Press.

Ratey, J. (2002) *A Users Guide to the Brain*. New York: Vintage.

Reagan, T. G. (2002) *Language, Education, and Ideology*. Westport, CT: Praeger.

Reagan, T. G. and Osborn, T. A. (2002) *The Foreign Language Educator in Society*. Mahwah, NJ: Erlbaum.

Reid, E. (1978) Social and stylistic variation in the speech of children. In P. Trudgill (ed.), *Sociolinguistic Patterns in British English* (pp. 158–71). London: Edward Arnold.

Reilly, J. and McIntire, M. (1980) American Sign Language and Pidgin Sign English: What's the difference? *Sign Language Studies* 27: 151–92.

Reisman, K. (1974) Contrapuntal conversations in an Antiguan village. In R. Bauman and J. Sherzer (eds), *Explorations in the Ethnography of Speaking* (pp. 110–24). Cambridge: Cambridge University Press.

Remez, R. E., Fellowes, J. M. and Rubin, P. E. (1997) Talker identification based on phonetic information. *Journal of Experimental Psychology: Human Perception and Performance* 23: 651–66.

Restak, R. M. (1988) *The Mind.* New York: Bantam Books.

Restrepo, M. A. (1998) Identifiers of predominantly Spanish-speaking children with language impairment. *Journal of Speech, Language, and Hearing Research* 41: 1398–411.

Reynolds, J. (1990) Abnormal vowel patterns in phonological disorder: Some data and a hypothesis. *British Journal of Disorders of Communication* 25: 115–48.

Reynolds, J. (2002) Recurring patterns and idiosyncratic systems in some English children with vowel disorders. In M. J. Ball and F. Gibbon (eds), *Vowel Disorders* (pp. 115–43). Woburn, MA: Butterworth/Heinemann.

Rice, M., Cleave, P. and Oetting, J. (2000) Use of syntactic cues in lexical acquisition by children with SLI. *Journal of Speech, Language, and Hearing Research* 43: 582–95.

Rice, M., Sell, M. and Hadley, P. (1990) The Social-interactive Coding System (SICS): An on-line, clinically relevant descriptive tool *Language, Speech and Hearing Services in the Schools* 21: 2–14.

Rickford, J. R. (1999) *African American Vernacular English: Features, Evolution, Educational Implications.* Malden, MA: Blackwell.

Rickford, J. R. and Théberge, R. C. (1996) Preterit *had* + V-ed in narratives of African-American preadolescents. *American Speech* 71: 227–54.

Roberts, C. and Street, B. (1997) Spoken and written language. In F. Coulmas (ed.), *The Handbook of Sociolinguistics* (pp. 168–86). Oxford: Blackwell.

Roberts, J. (1997a) Acquisition of variable rules: A study of (-t, d) deletion. *Journal of Child Language* 24: 351–72.

Roberts, J. (1997b) Hitting a moving target: Acquisition of sound change in progress in Philadelphia children. *Language Variation and Change* 9: 249–66.

Roberts, J. (2002) Child language variation. In J. K. Chambers, P. Trudgill and N. Schilling-Estes (eds), *The Handbook of Language Variation and Change* (pp. 333–48). Oxford: Blackwell.

Roberts, J. and Labov, W. (1995) Learning to talk Philadelphian. *Language Variation and Change* 7: 101–22.

Rockhill, K. (1993) Gender, language, and the politics of literacy. In B. Street (ed.), *Cross-cultural Approaches to Literacy* (pp. 156–75). Cambridge: Cambridge University Press.

Rodekohr, R. and Haynes, W. (2001) Differentiating dialect from disorder: A comparison of two processing tasks and a standardized language test. *Journal of Communication Disorders* 34: 1–18.

Roger, P., Code, C. and Sheard, C. (2000) Assessment and management of aphasia in a linguistically diverse society. *Asia Pacific Journal of Speech, Language and Hearing* 5(1): 21–34.

Romaine, S. (1975) Linguistic variability in the speech of some Edinburgh school children. Unpublished M Litt thesis, University of Edinburgh.

Romaine, S. (1995) *Bilingualism*, 2nd edn. Oxford: Blackwell.

Roseberry-McKibben, C. (1995) *Multicultural Students with Special Language Needs.* Oceanside, CA: Academic Communication Associates.

Ross, A. S. C. and Mitford, N. (1989) *Noblesse Oblige*. Oxford: Oxford University Press. (Originally published London: H. Hamilton, 1956.)

Ross, E. D. (1981) The aprosodias. *Archives of Neurology* 38: 561–9.

Rossi, P. (2000) *Logic and the Art of Memory*, trans. S. Clucas. Chicago: University of Chicago Press.

Routman, R. (1988) *Transitions: From Literature to Literacy*. Portsmouth, NH: Heinemann.

Rubin, J. and Jernudd, B. H. (1971) *Can Language Be Planned?* Honolulu: East West Center and University of Hawaii Press.

Ruiz, I. (1996) Recommendations for working with interpreters. *Work* 6: 41–6.

Ryalls, B. O. and Pisoni, D. B. (1997) The effect of talker variability on word recognition in preschool children. *Developmental Psychology* 33: 441–52.

Rysman, A. R. (1977) Gossip and occupational ideology. *Journal of Communication* 26: 64–8.

Sacks, H., Schegloff, E. A. and Jefferson, G. (1974) A simplest systematics for the organization of turn-taking for conversation. *Language* 50: 696–735.

Sadker, M. and Sadker, D. (1985) Sexism in the classroom of the 80s. *Psychology Today* March: 54–7.

Sankoff, D. and Poplack, S. (1981) A formal grammar for code-switching. *Papers in Linguistics* 14: 3–46.

Sapir, E. (1949) The unconscious patterning of behavior in society. In D. G. Mandelbaum (ed.), *Selected Writings of Edward Sapir in Language, Culture and Personality* (pp. 544–59). Berkeley, CA: University of California Press.

Sasanuma, S. and Park, H. S. (1995) Patterns of language deficits in two Korean–Japanese bilingual aphasic patients: A clinical report. In M. Paradis (ed.), *Aspects of Bilingual Aphasia* (pp. 111–22). Oxford: Pergamon.

Sattel, J. (1983) Men, inexpressiveness, and power. In B. Thorne, C. Kramerae and N. Henley (eds), *Language Gender and Society* (pp. 119–24). Rowley, MA: Newbury House.

Saville-Troike, M. (1989) *The Ethnography of Communication*, 2nd edn. Oxford: Blackwell.

Saville-Troike, M. (2003) *The Ethnography of Communication*, 3rd edn. Oxford: Blackwell.

Scarborough, H. (1991) Index of productive syntax. *Applied Psycholinguistics* 11: 1–22.

Scheflen, A. E. (1973) *Communicational Structure: Analysis of a Psychotherapy Trans-action*. Bloomington, IN: Indiana University Press.

Schiffman, H. F. (1996) *Linguistic Culture and Language Policy*. London: Routledge.

Schiffrin, D. (1987) *Discourse Markers*. London: Cambridge University Press.

Schiffrin, D. (1994) *Approaches to Discourse*. Oxford: Oxford University Press.

Scribner, S. and Cole, M. (1981) *The Psychology of Literacy*. Cambridge, MA: Harvard University Press.

Searle, J. (1969) *Speech Acts: An Essay in the Philosophy of Language*. New York: Oxford University Press.

Seldin, N. (1998) Characteristics of young learning disabled students. Learning Disabilities. Online: http://www.ldonline.org

Selten, R. and Pool, J. (1991) The distribution of foreign language skills as a game equilibrium. In R. Selten (ed.), *Game Equilibrium Models* (pp. 64–87). Berlin: Springer.

Semel, E. K., Wiig, E. and Secord, W. (1995) *Clinical Evaluation of Language Fundamentals-3 (CELF-3)*. San Antonio, TX: Psychological Corporation.

Seymour, H., Roeper, T. and de Villiers, J. (2003) *Diagnostic Evaluation of Language Variation*. San Antonio, TX: Psychological Corporation.

Sheffert, S. M., Fellowes, J. M., Pisoni, D. B. and Remez, R. E. (2002) Learning to recognize talkers from natural, sinewave, and reversed speech samples. *Journal of Experimental Psychology: Human Perception and Performance* 28: 1447–69.

Sheldon, A. (1990) Pickle fights: Gendered talking preschool disputes. *Discourse Processes* 13: 5–32.

Shockey, L. and Coates, J. (2003) *Men's Stories*. Oxford: Blackwell.

Shor, I. (1992) *Empowering Education: Critical Teaching for Social Change*. Chicago: University of Chicago Press.

Shor, I. and Freire, P. (1987) *A Pedagogy of Liberation: Dialogues on Transforming Education*. South Hadley, MA: Bergin and Garvey.

Shuy, R. (1987) Conversational power in FBI covert tape recordings. In L. Kedah (ed.), *Power through Discourse* (pp. 43–56). Norwood, NJ: Ablex.

Sies, L. F., Gitterman, M. R. and Foo, S. (1989) The investigation of non-biological influences on the organization of language in the brain: An interdisciplinary approach. *Journal of Neurolinguistics* 4: 497–507.

Simmons-Mackie, N. N. and Damico, J. S. (1999) Social role negotiation in aphasia therapy: Competence, incompetence, and conflict. In D. Kovarsky, J. Duchan and M. Maxwell (eds), *Constructing (In)Competence: Disabling Evaluations in Clinical and Social Interaction* (pp. 313–42). Mahwah, NJ: Lawrence Erlbaum.

Simmons-Mackie, N. N., Damico, J. S. and Damico, H. L. (1999) A qualitative study of feedback in aphasia treatment. *American Journal of Speech-language Pathology* 8: 218–30.

Simon, C. (1987) Out of the broom closet and into the classroom: The emerging SLP. *Journal of Childhood Communication Disorders* 11: 41–66.

Skutnabb-Kangas, T. (2000) *Linguistic Genocide in Education – or Worldwide Diversity and Human Rights?* Mahwah, NJ: Erlbaum.

Skutnabb-Kangas, T. and Phillipson, R. (eds) (1995) *Linguistic Human Rights.* Berlin: Mouton de Gruyter.

Slaughter, M. M. (1982) *Universal Languages and Scientific Taxonomy in the Seventeenth Century.* Cambridge: Cambridge University Press.

Smith, F. (1998) *The Book of Learning and Forgetting.* New York: Teachers College Press.

Smith, F. (2003) *Unspeakable acts, Unnatural Practices: Flaws and Fallacies in Scientific Reading Instruction.* Portsmouth, NH: Heinemann.

Smith, J. (2000) "You Ø na hear o' that kind o' things": Negative *do* in Buckie Scots. *English World-Wide* 21(2): 231–59.

Smith, J. and Steele, H. (2003) Variation at the source: Caregiver and child in the acquisition of variable dialect features. Paper presented at the 4th UK Language Variation and Change Conference, Sheffield, September.

Smith, T., Lee, E. and McDade, H. (2001) An investigation of T-units in African American English-speaking and Standard American English-speaking fourth-grade children. *Communication Disorders Quarterly* 22: 148–57.

Smitherman, G. (1994) *Black Talk: Words and Phrases from the Hood to the Amen Corner.* Boston: Houghton Mifflin.

Sommers, M. S., Kirk, K. I. and Pisoni, D. B. (1997) Some considerations in evaluating spoken word recognition by normal-hearing, noise-masked normal-hearing, and cochlear implant listeners I: The effects of response format. *Ear and Hearing* 18: 89–99.

Spears, A. K. (1982) The Black English semi-auxiliary *come. Language* 58: 850–72.

Spence, M. J., Rollins, P. R. and Jerger, S. (2002) Children's recognition of cartoon voices. *Journal of Speech, Language, and Hearing Research* 45: 214–22.

Spender, D. (1980) *Man Made Language.* London: Routledge and Kegan Paul.

Spender, D. (1982) *Invisible Women: The Schooling Scandal.* London: Writers and Readers Publishing Cooperative.

Sperber, D. and Wilson, D. (1995) *Relevance: Communication and Cognition.* Oxford: Blackwell.

Staller, S. J., Dowell, R. C., Beiter, A. L. and Brimacombe, J. A. (1991) Perceptual abilities of children with the Nucleus 22-channel cochlear implant. *Ear and Hearing* 12(Supplement): 34S–47S.

Stenström, A.-B. and Andersen, G. (1996) More trends in teenage talk: A corpus-based investigation of the discourse items *cos* and *innit.* In C. Percy, C. Meyer and I. Lancashire (eds), *Synchronic Corpus Linguistics* (pp. 189–203). Amsterdam: Rodopi.

Stewart, W. (1963) Functional distribution of Creole and French in Haiti. In E. Woodworth and R. DiPietro (eds), *Georgetown University Roundtable on Languages and Linguistics 1962* (pp. 15–25). Washington, DC: Georgetown University Press.

Stewart, W. A. (1967) Sociolinguistic factors in the history of American Negro dialects. *Florida FL Reporter* 5(2): 11, 22, 24, 26.

Stewart, W. A. (1968a) Continuity and change in American Negro dialects. *Florida FL Reporter* 6(2): 14–16, 18, 304.

Stewart, W. (1968b) A sociolinguistic typology for describing national multilingualism. In J. Fishman (ed.), *Readings in the Sociology of Language* (pp. 531–45). The Hague: Mouton.

Stillman, R. E. (1995) *Universal Languages and the Natural Philosophy in Seventeenth-century England*. Lewisburg, VA: Associated University Presses.

Stockman, I. J. (1996) The promises and pitfalls of language sample analysis as an assessment tool for linguistic minority children. *Language, Speech, and Hearing Services in the Schools* 27: 355–66.

Stockman, I. J. and Vaughn-Cooke, A. F. (1986) Implications of semantic category research for the language assessment of nonstandard speakers. *Topics in Language and Language Disorders* 6: 15–25.

Stokoe, W. (1960) Sign language structure: An outline of visual communication systems of the American deaf. *Studies in Linguistics* Occasional Paper No. 8. Buffalo, NY: University of Buffalo.

Stokoe, W. (1969) Sign language diglossia. *Studies in Linguistics* 21: 27–41.

Stokoe, W., Casterline, D. C. and Croneberg, C. G. (1965) *A Dictionary of American Sign Language on Linguistic Principles*. Silver Spring, MD: Linstok Press.

Streeck, J. (1994) Gesture as communication II: The audience as co-author. *Research on Language and Social Interaction* 27: 239–67.

Street, B. (1993) Introduction: The new literacy studies. In B. Street (ed.), *Cross-cultural Approaches to Literacy* (pp. 1–21). Cambridge: Cambridge University Press.

Street, B. (1995) *Social Literacies: Critical Approaches to Literacy in Development, Ethnography, and Education*. London: Longman.

Strum, J. M. and Nelson, N. W. (1997) Formal classroom lessons: New perspectives on a familiar discourse event. *Language, Speech, and Hearing Services in Schools* 28: 255–73.

Supple, M. (1993) Sociolinguistics: The clinical perspective. In M. Leahy and J. L. Kallen (eds), *International Perspectives in Speech and Language Pathology* (pp. 24–9). Dublin: Trinity College.

Swain, M. (1972) Bilingualism as first language. PhD thesis, University of California, Irvine.

Swann, J. (1996) Style shifting, code-switching. In D. Graddol, D. Leith and J. Swann (eds), *English: History, Diversity and Change* (pp. 301–37). London: Routledge.

Swann, J. and Graddol, D. (1988) Gender inequalities in classroom talk. *English in Education* 22(1): 48–65.

Swann, J. and Graddol, D. (1995) Feminising classroom talk. In S. Mills (ed.), *Language and Gender: Interdisciplinary Perspectives* (pp. 135–48). London: Longman.

Sweeney, M. (1997) No easy road to freedom: Critical literacy in a fourth-grade classroom. *Reading and Writing Quarterly* 13: 279–92.

Tabors, P. (1997) *One Child, Two Languages: A Guide for Preschool Educators of Children Learning English as a Second Language*. Baltimore, MD: Brookes.

Taeschner, T. (1983) *The Sun Is Feminine: A Study on Language Acquisition in Bilingual Children*. Berlin: Springer.

Tagliamonte, S. and Hudson, R. (1999) *Be like* et al. beyond America: The quotative system in British and Canadian youth. *Journal of Sociolinguistics* 3: 147–72.

Tagliamonte, S. and Smith, J. (forthcoming) No momentary fancy: the zero complementizer in English dialects. *English Language and Linguistics*.

Tagliamonte, S., Smith, J. and Lawrence, H. (2004) You've *got to* speak properly; you *have to* keep up with the Jones's: The changing modals in British dialects. Paper presented at Sociolinguistics Symposium 15, Newcastle upon Tyne, April.

Tallal, P., Ross, R. and Curtiss, S. (1989) Familial aggregation in specific language impairment. *Journal of Speech and Hearing Disorders* 54: 167–73.

Tannen, D. (1984) *Conversational Style: Analyzing Talk among Friends*. Norwood, NJ: Ablex.

Tannen, D. (1985) Silence: Anything but. In D. Tannen and M. Saville-Troike (eds), *Perspectives on Silence* (pp. 93–111). Norwood, NJ: Ablex.

Tannen, D. (1987) Remarks on discourse and power. In L. Kedar (ed.), *Power through Discourse* (pp. 3–10). Norwood, NJ: Ablex.

Tannen, D. (1991) *You Just Don't Understand*. London: Virago.

Tannen, D. (1993) *Gender and Conversational Interaction*. Oxford: Oxford University Press.

Tannen, D. (1994) *Gender and Discourse*. Oxford: Oxford University Press.

Taylor, N. (2002) Agentive "boobs" and "outta control" stomachs: The performance of gesture and reported speech by college undergraduates. Presented at Gesture: The Living Medium, University of Texas at Austin, June.

Taylor, O. L., Payne, K. and Anderson, N. (1987) Distinguishing between communication disorders and communication differences. *Seminars in Speech and Language* 8(4): 415–28.

Teale, W. H. and Sulzby, E. (eds) (1986) *Emergent Literacy: Writing and Reading*. Norwood, NJ: Ablex.

Thomas, B. (1989) Differences of sex and sects: Linguistic variation and social networks in a Welsh mining village. In J. Coates and D. Cameron (eds), *Women in Their Speech Communities* (pp. 51–60). London: Longman.

Thomas, E. R. and Jeffrey Reaser, J. L. (2004) Delimiting perceptual cues used for the ethnic labeling of African American and European American voices. *Journal of Sociolinguistics* 8: 54–87.

Thorndike, R., Hagen, E. and Sattler, J. (1986) *Stanford–Binet Intelligence Scale*, 4th edn. Chicago: Riverside.

Tollefson, J. W. (1991) *Planning Language, Planning Inequality*. London: Longman.

Tonkin, H. (1996) Language hierarchy at the United Nations. In S. Léger (ed.), *Towards a Language Agenda: Futurist Outlook on the United Nations* (pp. 3–28). Ottawa: Canadian Center for Linguistic Rights, University of Ottawa.

Tonkin, H. and Reagan, T. (eds) (2003) *Language in the Twenty-first Century.* Amsterdam: Benjamins.

Trager, G. L. (1940) One phonemic entity becomes two: The case of "short a." *American Speech* 17: 30–41.

Trudgill, P. (1972) Sex, covert prestige and linguistic change in the urban British English of Norwich. *Language in Society* 1(2): 179–95.

Trudgill, P. (1974) *The Social Differentiation of English in Norwich.* Cambridge: Cambridge University Press.

Trudgill, P. (2000) *Sociolinguistics: An Introduction to Language and Society.* Harmondsworth: Penguin.

Turi, J.-G. (1995) Typology of language legislation. In T. Skutnabb-Kangas and R. Phillipson (eds), *Linguistic Human Rights* (pp. 111–19). Berlin: Mouton de Gruyter.

Ukrainetz, T., Harpell, S., Walsh, C. and Coyle, C. (2000) A preliminary investigation of dynamic assessment with Native American kindergartners. *Language, Speech, Hearing Services in Schools* 31: 142–54.

Ulichny, P. and Watson-Gegeo, K. A. (1989) Interactions and authority: The dominant interpretive framework in writing conferences. *Discourse Processes* 12: 309–28.

Ullman, M. and Gopnik, M. (1999) Inflectional morphology in a family with inherited Specific Language Impairment. *Applied Psycholinguistics* 20: 51–117.

Upton, C. and Widdowson, J. D. A. (1996) *An Atlas of English Dialects.* Oxford: Oxford University Press.

Vaillancourt, F. (1983) The economics of language and language planning. *Language Problems and Language Planning* 7: 162–78.

Van Bezooijen, R. and Gooskens, C. (1999) Identification of language varieties: The contribution of different linguistic levels. *Journal of Language and Social Psychology* 18: 31–48.

Van Bezooijen, R. and Ytsma, J. (1999) Accents of Dutch: Personality impression, divergence, and identifiability. *Belgian Journal of Linguistics* 13: 105–28.

Van Cleve, J. V. and Crouch, B. A. (1989) *A Place of Their Own: Creating the Deaf Community in America.* Washington, DC: Gallaudet University Press.

van der Lely, H., Rosen. S. and McClelland, A. (1998) Evidence for a grammar-specific deficit in children. *Current Biology* 8: 1253–8.

Van Lancker, D. R., Kreiman, J. and Cummings, J. (1989) Voice perception deficits: Neuroanatomical correlates of phonagnosia. *Journal of Clinical and Experimental Neuropsychology* 11: 665–74.

Vaughn-Cooke, A. F. (1980) Evaluating the language of Black English speakers: Implications of the Ann Arbor decision. In M. F. Whiteman (ed.), *Reactions to Ann Arbor: Vernacular Black English and Education* (pp. 24–55). Washington, DC: Center for Applied Linguistics.

Vaughn-Cooke, A. F. (1983) Improving language assessment in minority children. *Asha* 25(6): 29–34.

Vaughn-Cooke, F. (1986) The challenge of assessing the language of nonmainstream speakers. In O. Taylor (ed.), *Treatment of Communication Disorders in Culturally and Linguistically Diverse Populations* (pp. 23–48). San Diego, CA: College-Hill Press.

Verdoodt, A. (1972) The differential impact of immigrant French speakers on indigenous German speakers: A case study in the light of two theories. In J. Fishman (ed.), *Advances in the Sociology of Language*, vol. 2 (pp. 377–85). The Hague: Mouton.

Vihman, M. M. (1985) Language differentiation by the bilingual infant. *Journal of Child Language* 12: 297–324.

Vihman, M. M. (1996) *Phonological Development: The Origins of Language in the Child*. Oxford: Blackwell.

Volterra, V. and Taeschner, T. (1978) The acquisition and development of language by bilingual children. *Journal of Child Language* 5: 311–26.

Wadensjö, C. (1998) *Interpreting as Interaction*. London: Longman.

Walker, A. G. (1987) Linguistic manipulation, power, and the legal setting. In L. Kedah (ed.) *Power through Discourse* (pp. 57–80). Norwood, NJ: Ablex.

Ward, M. (1971) *Them Children: A Study in Language Learning*. New York: Holt, Reinhart, and Winston.

Wardhaugh, R. (1999) *Proper English: Myths and Misunderstandings about Language*. Oxford: Blackwell.

Warner, A. (1982) *Complementation in Middle English and the Methodology of Historical Syntax: A Study of the Wycliffe Sermons*. London: Croom Helm.

Washington, J. and Craig, H. (1994) Dialectal forms during discourse of poor, urban African American preschoolers. *Journal of Speech and Hearing Research* 37: 816–23.

Watt, D. and Allen, W. (2003) Tyneside English. *Journal of the International Phonetic Association* 33(2): 267–71.

Watt, D. and Tillotson, J. (2001) A spectrographic analysis of vowel fronting in Bradford English. *English World-Wide* 22(2): 269–302.

Weaver, C. (1998) Reconceptualizing reading and dyslexia. In C. Weaver (ed.), *Practicing What We Know: Informed Reading Instruction* (pp. 292–324). Urbana, IL: National Council of Teachers of English.

Weber, M. (1947) *Theory of Social and Economic Organization*. London: William Hodge.

Weinreich, U. (1953) *Languages in Contact*. The Hague: Mouton.

Weinstein, B. (1990) *Language Policy and Political Development*. Norwood, NJ: Ablex.

Wellborn, J. (1997) *Accent Reduction Made Easy*. Carlsbad, CA: Penton Overseas.

Wells, G. (1986) *The Meaning Makers: Children Learning Language and Using Language to Learn*. Portsmouth, NH: Heinemann Educational.

Wells, G. (1990) Talk about text: Where literacy is learned and taught. *Curriculum Inquiry* 20: 369–405.

Wells, G. (1994) The complementary contributions of Halliday and Vygotsky to a "language-based theory of learning." *Linguistics and Education* 6: 41–90.

Wells, J. C. (1982) *Accents of English* (3 vols). Cambridge: Cambridge University Press.

Werker, J. F. and Tees, R. C. (1984) Cross-language speech perception: Evidence for perceptual reorganization during the first year of life. *Infant Behavior and Development* 7: 49–64.

Westby, C. (1990) Ethnographic interviewing: Asking the right questions to the right people in the right ways. *Journal of Childhood Communication Disorders* 13: 101–11.

Westby, C. (1997) There's more to passing than knowing the answers. *Language, Speech, and Hearing Services in Schools* 28: 274–87.

Whiteley, W. H. (1984) Sociolinguistic surveys at the national level. In C. Kennedy (ed.), *Language Planning and Language Education* (pp. 68–79). London: Allen and Unwin.

Whorf, B. L. (1956) The relation of habitual thought and behavior to language. In J. B. Carroll (ed.), *Language, Thought, and Reality: Selected Writings of Benjamin Lee Whorf* (pp. 134–59). Cambridge, MA: MIT Press.

Wiener, D., Obler, L. K. and Taylor Sarno, M. (1995) Speech/language management of the bilingual aphasic in a US urban rehabilitation hospital. In M. Paradis (ed.), *Aspects of Bilingual Aphasia* (pp. 37–56). Oxford: Pergamon.

Williams, A., Garrett, P. and Coupland, N. (1999) Dialect recognition. In D. R. Preston (ed.), *Handbook of Perceptual Dialectology* (pp. 345–58). Amsterdam: Benjamins.

Wolfram, W. (1989) Structural variability in phonological development: Final nasals in Vernacular Black English. In R. W. Fasold and D. Schiffrin (eds), *Language Change and Variation* (pp. 301–32). Amsterdam: Benjamins.

Wolfram, W. (1993) Research to practice: A proactive role for speech-language pathologists in sociolinguistic education. *Language, Speech, and Hearing Services in Schools* 24: 181–6.

Wolfram, W. (1994) The phonology of a socio-cultural variety: The case of African American Vernacular English. In J. E. Bernthal and N. W. Bankson (eds), *Child Phonology: Characteristics, Assessment, and Intervention with Special Populations* (pp. 227–44). New York: Thieme Medical Publishers.

Wolfram, W. (1997) Dialect in society. In F. Coulmas (ed.), *The Handbook of Sociolinguistics* (pp. 107–26). Oxford: Blackwell.

Wolfram, W. and Schilling-Estes, N. (1998) *American English.* Malden, MA: Blackwell.

Wolfram, W. and Thomas, E. R. (2002) *The Development of African American English.* Malden, MA: Blackwell.

Wolfram, W., Thomas, E. R. and Green, E. W. (2000) The regional context of Earlier African American Speech: Reconstructing the development of African American Vernacular English. *Language in Society* 29: 315–55.

Woods, N. (1989) Talking shop: Sex and status as determinants of floor appointments in a work setting. In J. Coates and D. Cameron (eds), *Women in Their Speech Communities* (pp. 141–57). London: Longman.

Woodward, J. C. (1973) Some characteristics of Pidgin Sign English. *Sign Language Studies* 3: 39–46.

Woodward, J. C. (1996) Modern standard Thai Sign Language, influence from ASL, and its relationship to original Thai sign varieties. *Sign Language Studies* 92: 227–52.

Woodward, J. C. and DeSantis, S. (1977a) Negative incorporation in French and American Sign Language. *Language in Society* 6(3): 379–88.

Woodward, J. C. and DeSantis, S. (1977b) Two to one it happens: Dynamic phonology in two sign languages. *Sign Language Studies* 17: 329–46.

Yerkovich, S. (1977) Gossiping as a way of speaking. *Journal of Communication* 27: 192–6.

Yukawa, E. (1997) L1 Japanese attrition and regaining. PhD thesis, University of Stockholm.

Zhu Hua and Dodd, B. (eds) (2005) *Phonological Development and Disorder: A Cross-linguistic Perspective*. Clevedon: Multilingual Matters.

Zimmerman, D. and West, C. (1975) Sex roles, interruptions and silences in conversation. In B. Thorne and N. Henley (eds), *Language and Sex: Difference and Dominance* (pp. 105–29). Rowley, MA: Newbury House.

Name Index

Subject Index